iOS 5 By Tutorials

Volume 1

Second Edition

By the raywenderlich.com Tutorial Team

Steve Baranski, Adam Burkepile, Jacob Gundersen, Matthijs Hollemans, Felipe Laso Marsetti, Cesare Rocchi, Marin Todorov, and Ray Wenderlich

Copyright © 2011, 2012 Razeware LLC.

W9-CNA-477

Table of Contents

Dedications

To Kristine, Emily, and Sam.

Steve Baranski

My parents, James and Donna, for putting up with me and stuff.

- Adam Burkepile

To my boys, John and Eli, may I be as cool as you two.

- Jacob Gundersen

To all the coders out there who are making the world a better place through their software.

- Matthijs Hollemans

To my amazing mother Patricia, and my beautiful nephew Leonardo, I love you guys with all my heart. I'd also like to thank Ray for making me a part of his team and helping boost my career to the next level. Finally I'd like to dedicate this to Steve Jobs. God bless you and rest in your peaceful iCloud!

- Felipe Laso Marsetti

To my parents, my friends around the globe, and my inspirers. Also thanks to Ray for inviting me in.

-Marin Todorov

To the iOS Tutorial Team - together we have made something truly amazing!

-Cesare Rocchi and Ray Wenderlich

Chapter 1: Introduction

When the raywenderlich.com Tutorial Team first started looking into iOS 5, we were amazed by the wealth of new libraries, new libraries, and new features available. iOS 5 was one of the biggest upgrades to iOS yet, containing tons of cool new stuff you can start using in your apps – even in iOS 6 and beyond.

But as we were researching iOS 5, we realized there wasn't a lot of high quality sample code, tutorials, and documentation to help developers (such as ourselves) get up to speed quickly on all of these new features.

So we decided to team up and solve that problem by writing this book. Our goal was to create the definitive guide to help intermediate and advanced iOS developers learn the new iOS 5 APIs in the quickest and easiest way – via tutorials!

The Tutorial Team takes pride in making sure each tutorial we write holds to the highest standards of quality. We want our tutorials to be well written, easy to follow, and fun. And we don't want to just skim the surface of a subject – we want to really dig into it, so you can truly understand how it works and apply the knowledge directly in your own apps.

If you've enjoyed the tutorials we've written in the past at raywenderlich.com, you're in for a treat. The tutorials in this book are some of our best yet – and this book contains detailed technical knowledge you simply won't be able to find anywhere else.

So if you're eager to learn what iOS 5 introduced for you, you're in the right place. Sit back, relax, and prepare for some fun and informative tutorials.

Introducing the second edition

It's been a year since we originally wrote *iOS 5 by Tutorials*, and we are happy to announce that you are holding a brand new second edition of the book, fully revised for iOS 6.

We went through each and every chapter of this book and updated the code so that everything works on iOS 6, uses the latest and greatest technologies and API calls where necessary, and uses Modern Objective-C syntax like auto-synthesis and literals. We also made a ton of other improvements and updates along the way.

This book has been designed to act as a good companion to its sister book, *iOS 6 by Tutorials*. This book focuses on all of the new APIs that came out in iOS 5 such as ARC, Storyboards, and iCloud. Similarly, *iOS 6 by Tutorials* focuses on all of the new APIs that came out in iOS 6 such as Auto Layout, Collection Views, and Passbook. If you have them both, you have it all – over 2,300 pages of up-to-date high quality tutorials.

Wondering what's changed in the second edition? Here's the full list.

- Updated all chapters to be compatible with iOS 6, including using new APIs where possible and adding notes about relevant updates for iOS 6.

- Updated all chapters to be compatible with the latest version of Xcode (4.5 at the time of this update).

- Updated all chapters to use Modern Objective-C syntax (auto-synthesis, literal syntax, etc).

- Updated many chapters to use Storyboards instead of XIBs.

- Updated chapters to use most recent version of imported libraries, such as Cocos2D.

- Added additional clarifications and useful notes to many chapters.

- Streamlined many chapters by removing instructions that were not relevant to the main topic at hand (such as creating user interfaces), instead moving that to a starter project. The chapters should now be more focused on the main topic.

> Note: This book requires the latest version of Xcode, which is 4.5 at the time of writing this book. If you are running an older version of Xcode, you should either update your version of Xcode (our suggestion), or use an older version of *iOS 5 by Tutorials* (links available on the private PDF forums).

Also, as mentioned above all chapters in this book have been updated to use Modern Objective-C syntax. If some of this looks unfamiliar to you and you are still "stuck in the old days", you should check out Chapter 2 in *iOS 6 by Tutorials*, "Modern Objective-C Syntax".

Who this book is for

This book is for intermediate or advanced iOS developers, who already know the basics of iOS development but want to firm up their knowledge about technologies introduced in iOS 5.

If you're a complete beginner, you can follow along with this book as well, because the tutorials are always in a step-by-step process, but there may be some missing gaps in your knowledge. You might want to go through the *iOS Apprentice* series available on the raywenderlich.com store before you go through this book.

iOS 6 by Tutorials

This book was such as success that we have released a sequel to this book as well – *iOS 6 by Tutorials*.

Note that *iOS 5 by Tutorials* and *iOS 6 by Tutorials* are completely different books, with completely different content.

iOS 5 by Tutorials covers the new APIs introduced in iOS 5, and similarly *iOS 6 by Tutorials* covers the new APIs introduced in iOS 6. There are so many new APIs introduced with each version of iOS, that each release warrants an entirely new book with unique chapters.

After you finish reviewing this book, reading *iOS 6 by Tutorials* is a natural next step. IT will introduce you to the new APIs introduced in iOS 6 (like Auto Layout, Collection Views, or Passbook). If you read both books, you will be an iOS master!

How to use this book

This book is huge! We wanted to provide you guys with detailed top quality content so you could really understand each topic, so included a ton of material for you.

In fact, *iOS 5 by Tutorials* is so huge that we had to split it into two volumes. You are holding Volume 1, which contains the most important/critical APIs in iOS 5 such as ARC, Storyboards, and iCloud. Volume 2 rounds you off with some other lesser known but quite useful APIs such as Newsstand, Core Image, Turn-Based Gaming, and more. The tutorials in each volume are independent of each other.

You're welcome to read through this book chapter by chapter of course (the chapters have been arranged to have a good reading order), but we realize that as a developer your time is limited so you might not have time to go through the entire book.

If that is the case, we recommend you just pick and choose the subjects you are interested in or need for your projects, and jump directly to those chapters. Most tutorials are self-contained so there will not be a problem if you go through them in a different order.

Not sure which ones are the most important? Here's our recommended "core reading list": Beginning ARC, Beginning Storyboards, Beginning iCloud, and Beginning UIKit Customization. That covers the "big 4" topics of iOS 5, and from there you can dig into other topics that are particularly interesting to you.

Volume 1 overview

iOS 5 introduced a ton of killer new APIs that you'll want to start using in your apps right away. Here's what you'll be learning about in Volume 1:

Beginning and Intermediate ARC

ARC stands for Automatic Reference Counting, and is a fancy way of saying, "remember all that memory management code you used to have to write? Well, you don't need that anymore!"

This is a huge new feature, and will save you a lot of memory management headaches and make your code easier to write and read. In this book, not only will you learn about how to use ARC, but also how it works under the hood, how to port your old projects to ARC, how to use third party libraries that haven't been converted to ARC, how to handle subtle problems and issues with ARC, and much more.

Beginning and Intermediate Storyboards

In the old days, you would generally have one XIB per view controller. This worked well, except it wasn't very easy to visualize the flow of your app without resorting to third party diagramming tools.

iOS 5 introduced a new way to design view controllers – the Storyboard editor. You can now design the visual look of multiple view controllers in one place, and easily visualize the transitions between view controllers.

What's more, Storyboards can save you a ton of time, because they introduce cool new features such as creating table view cells directly within the editor. In this book, you'll dive deep into Storyboards and learn how you can use all the major new features in your apps.

Beginning and Intermediate iCloud

Before iOS 5, if you wanted to share data between devices, you would have to write your own web service, or integrate with a third party API like Dropbox. This was usually quite error prone and a lot of work.

Now with iCloud, there's built-in functionality provided by Apple that lets you save your app's data in the cloud, and easily synchronize it between your apps on different devices. Customers are going to start expecting your apps to have this feature, so in this book you'll get to dive in and get some hands-on experience working with this cool new technology,

Beginning and Intermediate OpenGL ES 2.0 with GLKit

If you've been wanting to get into OpenGL ES 2.0 programming but have been a bit scared by the complexity, the new GLKit framework has made things a lot easier for you to get started. Experienced OpenGL developers will love GLKit too, because you can use it to remove a ton of boilerplate code from your apps and make transitioning from OpenGL ES 1.0 to OpenGL ES 2.0 much easier.

In this book, you'll dive into the new `GLKView`, `GLKViewController`, `GLKBaseEffect`, `GLKTextureLoader`, and `GLKMath` APIs – in a manner easy to follow, whether you are a complete beginner or an advanced developer.

Beginning and Intermediate UIKit Customization

To have a successful app on the App Store these days, your app has to look good. Almost everyone wants to customize the default look of the UIKit controls, but in the old days you had to resort to some strange workarounds to make this work.

With iOS 5, this has become a lot easier, so in this book you're going to dig into some practical examples of customizing just about every control you might want in UIKit.

Want more?

This is just the beginning – pick up Volume 2 for tons of additional iOS 5 tutorials!

Book source code and forums

You can get the source code for the book here:

- http://www.raywenderlich.com/store/ios-5-by-tutorials/source-code

We've also set up an official forum for the book at raywenderlich.com/forums. This is a great place to ask any questions you have about the book or about iOS 5 in general, or to submit any errata you may find.

We hope to see you on the forums! ☺

PDF Version

We also have a PDF version of this book available, which can be handy if you ever want to copy/paste code or search for a specific term through the book as you're developing.

And speaking of the PDF version, we have some good news!

Since you purchased the physical copy of this book, you are eligible to buy the PDF version at a significant discount if you would like (if you don't have it already). For more details, see this page:

- http://www.raywenderlich.com/store/ios-5-by-tutorials/upgrade

Acknowledgements

We would like to thank several people for their assistance making this book possible:

- **Our families:** For bearing with us in this crazy time as we worked all hours of the night to get this book ready for publication.

- **Everyone at Apple:** For developing an amazing set of APIs, constantly inspiring us to improve our apps and skills, and making it possible for many developers to have their dream jobs as app developers.

- **Andrea Coulter**: For doing all the painstaking formatting and layout of the first version of this book.

- **Vicki Wenderlich**: For designing the book cover, formatting and layout of the second edition of this book, and for much of the lovely artwork and illustrations in the book.

- **Mike Daley**: For helping out in our investigations of GLKit.

- **Adam Burkepile, Richard Casey, Adam Eberbach, Brandon Lassiter, Marcio Valenzuela, and Nick Waynik**: For being excellent forum moderators and generously donating their time and experience to the iOS community.

- **Steve Jobs**: You were an inspiration to all of us, and without you this book (or our careers) wouldn't be possible. We are immensely grateful.

- And most importantly, the **readers of raywenderlich.com and you**! Thank you so much for reading our site and purchasing this book. Your continued readership and support is what makes this all possible.

About the authors

Harken all genders! You may or may not have noticed that all of this book's authors are men. This is unfortunate, and not by design. If you are a woman developing for iOS and are interested in joining the Tutorial Team, we'd love to hear from you.

Steve Baranski is the founder of Komorka Technology, a creator of original and commissioned mobile apps based in Oklahoma City. When not making apps or spending time with his family, he can usually be found on a bicycle of some sort.

Adam Burkepile is a software developer with experience on many platforms and languages. He regularly writes tutorials for raywenderlich.com and moderates the forums. He also maintains a few projects at github. When he's not on the computer, he enjoys drinking tea or doing Krav Maga.

Jake Gundersen is a gamer, maker, and programmer. He is Co-Founder of the educational game company, Third Rail Games. He has a particular interest in gaming, image processing, and computer graphics. You can find his musings and codings at http://indieambitions.com.

Matthijs Hollemans is an independent designer and developer who loves to create awesome software for the iPad and iPhone. He also enjoys teaching others to do the same, which is why he wrote The iOS Apprentice series of eBooks. In his spare time, Matthijs is learning to play jazz piano (it's hard!) and likes to go barefoot running when the sun is out. Check out his blog at http://www.hollance.com.

Felipe Laso Marsetti is an iOS programmer working at Lextech Global Services. He loves everything related to Apple, video games, cooking and playing the violin, piano or guitar. In his spare time, Felipe loves to read and learn new programming languages or technologies. You can find him on Twitter as @Airjordan12345 or on his blog at http://iFe.li.

Cesare Rocchi is a UX designer and developer. He runs Studio Magnolia (http://www.studiomagnolia.com), an interactive studio that creates compelling web and mobile applications. You can find him on Twitter as @_funkyboy and LinkedIn as cesarerocchi. When off duty he enjoys snowboarding and beach tennis.

Marin Todorov is an independent iOS developer and publisher, with background in various platforms and languages. He has published several books, written about iOS development on his blog, and authored an online game programming course. He loves to read, listen and produce music, and travel. Visit his web site: http://www.touch-code-magazine.com

Ray Wenderlich is an iPhone developer and gamer, and the founder of Razeware LLC. Ray is passionate about both making apps and teaching others the techniques to make them. He and the Tutorial Team have written a bunch of tutorials about iOS development available at http://www.raywenderlich.com.

About the artist

Vicki Wenderlich is a ceramic sculptor who was convinced two years ago to make art for her husband's iPhone apps. She discovered a love of digital art, and has been making app art and digital illustrations ever since. She is passionate about helping people pursue their dreams, and makes free app art for developers available on her website, http://www.vickiwenderlich.com.

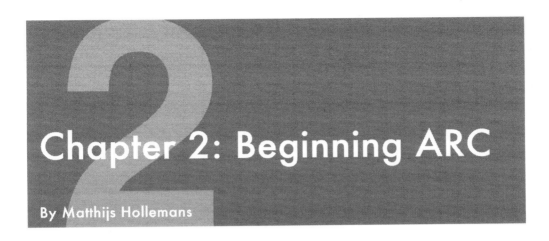

Chapter 2: Beginning ARC

By Matthijs Hollemans

The most disruptive change in iOS 5 is the addition of Automatic Reference Counting, or ARC for short. ARC is a feature of the new LLVM 3.0 compiler and it completely does away with the manual memory management that all iOS developers love to hate.

Using ARC in your own projects is extremely simple. You keep programming as usual, except that you no longer call `retain`, `release` and `autorelease`. That's basically all there is to it.

With Automatic Reference Counting enabled, the compiler will automatically insert `retain`, `release` and `autorelease` in the correct places in your program. You no longer have to worry about any of this, because the compiler does it for you. I call that freaking awesome. In fact, using ARC is so simple that you can stop reading this tutorial now. ;-)

But if you're still skeptical about ARC – maybe you don't trust that it will always do the right thing, or you think that it somehow will be slower than doing memory management by yourself – then read on. The rest of this chapter will dispel those myths and show you how to deal with some of the less intuitive consequences of enabling ARC in your projects.

In addition, you'll get hands-on experience with converting an app that doesn't use ARC at all to using ARC. You can use these same techniques to move your existing iOS projects over to ARC, saving yourself tons of memory headaches!

Memory Management is... Yuck

You're probably already familiar with manual memory management, which basically works like this:

- If you want to keep an object around you need to retain it, unless it already was retained for you.

- If you want to stop using an object you need to release it, unless it was already released for you (with autorelease).

As a beginner you may have had a hard time wrapping your head around the concept but after a while it became second nature and now you'll always properly balance your retains with your releases. Except when you forget.

The principles of manual memory management aren't hard but it's very easy to make a mistake. And these small mistakes can have dire consequences. Either your app will crash at some point because you've released an object too often and your variables are pointing at data that is no longer valid, or you'll run out of memory because you don't release objects enough and they stick around forever.

The static analyzer from Xcode is a great help in finding these kinds of problems but ARC goes a step further. It avoids memory management problems completely by automatically inserting the proper retains and releases for you!

It is important to realize that ARC is a feature of the Objective-C compiler and therefore all the ARC stuff happens when you build your app. ARC is not a runtime feature (except for one small part, the weak pointer system), nor is it *garbage collection* that you may know from other languages.

All that ARC does is insert retains and releases into your code when it compiles it, exactly where you would have – or at least should have – put them yourself. That makes ARC just as fast as manually managed code, and sometimes even a bit faster because it can perform certain optimizations under the hood.

Pointers Keep Objects Alive

The new rules you have to learn for ARC are quite simple. With manual memory management you needed to retain an object to keep it alive. That is no longer necessary; all you have to do is make a pointer to the object. As long as there is a variable pointing to an object, that object stays in memory. When the pointer gets a new value or ceases to exist, the associated object is released. This is true for all variables: instance variables, synthesized properties, and even local variables.

It makes sense to think of this in terms of ownership. When you do the following,

```
NSString *firstName = self.textField.text;
```

the `firstName` variable becomes a pointer to the `NSString` object that holds the contents of text field. That `firstName` variable is now the owner of that string object.

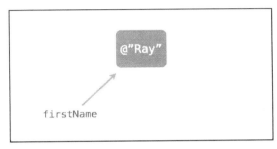

An object can have more than one owner. Until the user changes the contents of the `UITextField`, its `text` property is also an owner of the string object. There are two pointers keeping that same string object alive:

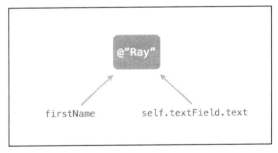

Moments later the user will type something new into the text field and its `text` property now points at a new string object. But the original string object still has an owner – the `firstName` variable – and therefore stays in memory.

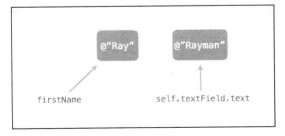

Only when `firstName` gets a new value too, or goes out of scope – because it's a local variable and the method ends, or because it's an instance variable and the object it belongs to is deallocated – does the ownership expire. The string object no longer has any owners, its retain count drops to 0, and the object is deallocated.

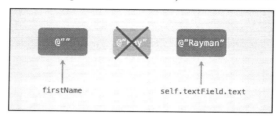

We call pointers such as `firstName` and `textField.text` "strong" because they keep objects alive. By default all instance variables and local variables are strong pointers.

There is also a "weak" pointer. Variables that are weak can still point to objects but they do not become owners:

```
__weak NSString *weakName = self.textField.text;
```

Note that the __weak symbol is spelled with two leading underscore characters.

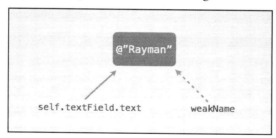

The `weakName` variable points at the same string object that the `textField.text` property points to, but it is not an owner. If the text field contents change, then the string object no longer has any owners and is deallocated:

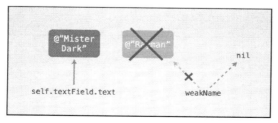

When this happens, the value of `weakName` automatically becomes `nil`. It is said to be a "zeroing" weak pointer.

Note that this is extremely convenient because it prevents weak pointers from pointing to deallocated memory. This sort of thing used to cause a lot of bugs – you may have heard of the term "dangling pointers" or "zombies" – but thanks to these zeroing weak pointers, that is no longer an issue. The variable either points to a valid object, or is nil, but it never references memory that has been freed.

You probably won't use weak pointers very much. They are mostly useful when two objects have a parent-child relationship. The parent will have a strong pointer to the child – and therefore "owns" the child – but in order to prevent ownership cycles, the child only has a weak pointer back to the parent.

A typical example of this is the delegate pattern. Your view controller may own a UITableView through a strong pointer. The table view's data source and delegate pointers point back at the view controller, but are weak. You'll read more about this later in the chapter.

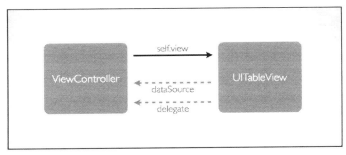

Note that the following isn't very useful:

```
__weak NSString *str = [[NSString alloc] initWithFormat:. . .];
NSLog(@"%@", str);  // will output "(null)"
```

There is no owner for the NSString object (because str is weak) and the object will be deallocated immediately after it is created. Xcode gives a warning when you attempt to do this because it's probably not what you intended to happen ("Warning: assigning retained object to weak variable; object will be released after assignment").

You can use the __strong keyword to signify that a variable is a strong pointer:

```
__strong NSString *firstName = self.textField.text;
```

But because variables are strong by default this is a bit superfluous.

Properties can also be strong and weak. The notation for properties is:

```
@property (nonatomic, strong) NSString *firstName;
@property (nonatomic, weak) id <MyDelegate> delegate;
```

ARC is great and will really remove a lot of clutter from your code. You no longer have to think about when to retain and when to release, just about how your objects relate to each other. The question that you'll be asking yourself is: who owns what?

For example, it was impossible to write code like this before:

```
id obj = [array objectAtIndex:0];
[array removeObjectAtIndex:0];
NSLog(@"%@", obj);
```

Under manual memory management, removing the object from the array would invalidate the contents of the obj variable. The object got deallocated as soon as it no longer was part of the array. Printing the object with NSLog() would likely crash your app. To work around this, you first had to do [obj retain] before removing the object from the array, and not forget to release it again later.

On ARC the above code works as intended. Because you put the object into the obj variable, which is a strong pointer, the array is no longer the only owner of the object. Even after you remove the object from the array, the object is still alive because obj keeps pointing at it.

I have seen the future and it is ARC

Automatic Reference Counting also has a few limitations. For starters, ARC only works on Objective-C objects. If your app uses Core Foundation or malloc() and free(), then you're still responsible for doing the memory management there. You'll see examples of this later in the tutorial. In addition, certain language rules have been made stricter in order to make sure ARC can always do its job properly. These are only small sacrifices; you gain a lot more than you give up!

Just because ARC takes care of doing retain and release for you in the proper places doesn't mean you can forget about memory management altogether. Because strong pointers keep objects alive, there are still situations where you will need to set these pointers to nil by hand, or your app might run out of available memory. If you keep holding on to all the objects you've ever created, then ARC will never be able to release them. Therefore, whenever you create a new object, you still need to think about who owns it and how long the object should stay in existence.

There is no doubt about it: ARC is the future of Objective-C. Apple encourages developers to turn their backs on manual memory management and to start writing their new apps using ARC. It makes for simpler source code and more robust apps. With ARC, memory-related crashes are a thing of the past. Believe it or not, ARC even combines well with C++. With a few restrictions you can also use ARC on iOS 4, which should only help to speed up the adoption.

As the developer community is entering a transitioning period from manual to automatic memory management you'll often come across code that isn't compatible with ARC yet, whether it's your own code or third-party libraries. Fortunately you can combine ARC with non-ARC code in the same project and this chapter will show you several ways how.

A smart developer tries to automate as much of his job as possible, and that's exactly what ARC offers: automation of menial programming work that you had to do by hand previously. To me, switching is a no-brainer.

The Artists App

To illustrate how to use Automatic Reference Counting in practice, you are going to convert a simple app from manual memory management to ARC. The app, *Artists*, consists of a single screen with a table view and a search bar. When you type something into the search bar, the app employs the MusicBrainz API to search for musicians with matching names.

The app looks like this on the iPhone 5 simulator:

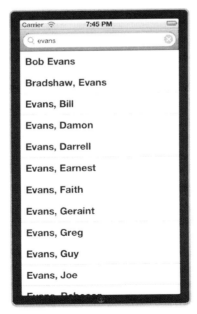

In their own words, MusicBrainz is "an open music encyclopedia that collects, and makes available to the public, music metadata". They have a free XML web service that you can use from your own apps. To learn more about MusicBrainz, check out their website at http://musicbrainz.org.

You can find the starter code for the Artists app in this chapter's folder. The Xcode project contains the following source files:

- **AppDelegate.h/.m**: The application delegate. Nothing special here, every app has one. It loads the view controller and puts it into the window.

- **MainViewController.h/.m/.xib**: The view controller for the app. It has a table view and a search bar, and does most of the work.

- **SoundEffect.h/.m**: A simple class for playing sound effects. The app will make a little beep when the MusicBrainz search is completed.

- **main.m**: The entry point for the app.

In addition, the app makes use of two third-party libraries. Your apps probably use a few external components of their own and it's good to learn how to make these libraries play nice with ARC.

- **AFHTTPRequestOperation.h/.m**: Part of the AFNetworking library that makes it easy to perform requests to web services. The Artists project does not include the full library because you only need this one class. You can find the complete package at: https://github.com/AFNetworking/AFNetworking/

- **SVProgresHUD.h/.m/.bundle**: A progress indicator or "HUD" that will pop up on the screen while the search is taking place. You may not have seen ".bundle" files before. This is a special type of folder that contains the image files that are used by SVProgressHUD. To view these images, right-click the .bundle file in Finder and choose the Show Package Contents menu option. For more info about this component, see: https://github.com/samvermette/SVProgressHUD

> **Note:** Since the first edition of this book was published, both AFNetworking and SVProgressHUD were converted to use ARC, so if you insert the latest versions of these components into your ARC-enabled apps they should work without problems. However, for the purposes of this chapter you are intentionally using an older version so that you can learn how to convert other people's code to ARC by yourself. Over time, this will become less of a necessity as more and more libraries are switched to ARC by their maintainers.

A quick tour of the app

Let's quickly go through the code for the view controller so you have a decent idea of how the app works. `MainViewController` is a subclass of `UIViewController`. Its nib file contains a `UITableView` object and a `UISearchBar` object:

The table view displays the contents of the `searchResults` array. Initially this pointer is `nil`. When the user performs a search, the code fills up the array with the response from the MusicBrainz server. If there were no search results, the array is empty (but not `nil`) and the table says: "(Nothing found)". This all takes place in the usual `UITableView-DataSource` methods: `numberOfRowsInSection` and `cellForRowAtIndexPath`.

The actual search is initiated from the `searchBarSearchButtonClicked` method, which is part of the `UISearchBarDelegate` protocol.

```
- (void)searchBarSearchButtonClicked:(UISearchBar *)theSearchBar
{
    [SVProgressHUD showInView:self.view status:nil
        networkIndicator:YES posY:-1
        maskType:SVProgressHUDMaskTypeGradient];
```

First, this method creates a new HUD and shows it on top of the table view and search bar, blocking any user input until the network request is done:

Then it creates the URL for the HTTP request, using the MusicBrainz API to search for artists:

```
NSString *urlString = [NSString stringWithFormat:
  @"http://musicbrainz.org/ws/2/artist?query=artist:%@&limit=20"
  , [self escape:self.searchBar.text]];

NSMutableURLRequest *request = [NSMutableURLRequest
  requestWithURL:[NSURL URLWithString:urlString]];
```

Note that the search text is URL-encoded using the escape: method to ensure that you're making a valid URL. Spaces and other special characters are turned into escape sequences such as %20.

```
NSDictionary *headers = [NSDictionary dictionaryWithObject:
                          [self userAgent] forKey:@"User-Agent"];

[request setAllHTTPHeaderFields:headers];
```

This adds a custom User-Agent header to the HTTP request. The MusicBrainz API requires this. All requests should "have a proper User-Agent header that identifies the application and the version of the application making the request." It's always a good idea to play nice with the APIs you're using, so you construct a User-Agent header that looks like:

```
com.yourcompany.Artists/1.0 (unknown, iPhone OS 5.0, iPhone
Simulator, Scale/1.000000)
```

This formula was taken from another part of the AFNetworking library and placed into the userAgent method in the view controller.

> Note: The MusicBrainz API has a few other restrictions too. Client applications must not make more than one web service call per second or they risk getting their IP address blocked. That won't be too big of an issue for this app – it's unlikely that a user will be doing that many searches – so the code does not take any particular precautions for this.

Given the newly constructed NSMutableURLRequest object, AFHTTPRequest-Operation can perform the request:

```
AFHTTPRequestOperation *operation = [AFHTTPRequestOperation
    operationWithRequest:request
    completion:^(NSURLRequest *request,
             NSHTTPURLResponse *response,
             NSData *data, NSError *error)
    {
        ...
    }];

    [_queue addOperation:operation];
```

AFHTTPRequestOperation is a subclass of NSOperation, which means you can add it to an NSOperationQueue (in the _queue instance variable) and it will be handled asynchronously. Because the HUD blocks the screen, the app ignores any user input while the request is taking place.

You give AFHTTPRequestOperation a block that it invokes when the request completes. Inside the block the code first checks whether the request was successful (HTTP status code 200) or not. For this app we're not particularly interested in why a request failed; if it does we simply tell the HUD to dismiss with a special "error" animation.

Note that the completion block is not necessarily executed on the main thread and therefore you need to wrap the call to SVProgressHUD in dispatch_async().

```
if (response.statusCode == 200 && data != nil)
{
    . . .
}
else  // something went wrong
{
    dispatch_async(dispatch_get_main_queue(), ^
    {
        [SVProgressHUD dismissWithError:@"Error"];
    });
}
```

Now for the interesting part. If the request succeeds, we allocate the searchResults array and parse the response. The response is XML so the app uses NSXMLParser to do the job.

```
self.searchResults = [NSMutableArray arrayWithCapacity:10];

NSXMLParser *parser = [[NSXMLParser alloc]
                                initWithData:data];
[parser setDelegate:self];
[parser parse];
[parser release];

[self.searchResults sortUsingSelector:
            @selector(localizedStandardCompare:)];
```

You can look up the logic for the XML parsing in the NSXMLParserDelegate methods, but essentially it just looks for elements named "sort-name". These contain the names of the artists. Those names are added as NSString objects to the searchResults array.

When the XML parser is done, we sort the results alphabetically, and then update the screen on the main thread:

```
dispatch_async(dispatch_get_main_queue(), ^
{
    [self.soundEffect play];
    [self.tableView reloadData];
    [SVProgressHUD dismiss];
});
```

That's it for how the app works. It's written using manual memory management and doesn't use any iOS 5 specific features. Now let's convert it to ARC.

Automatic Conversion

You are going to convert the Artists app to ARC. Basically this means you'll just get rid of all the calls to `retain`, `release`, and `autorelease`, but you'll also run into a few situations that require special attention.

There are three things you can do to make your app ARC-compatible:

1. Xcode has an automatic conversion tool that can migrate your source files.

2. You can convert the files by hand.

3. You can disable ARC for source files that you do not want to convert. This is useful for third-party libraries that you don't feel like messing with.

You will use all of these options on the Artists app, just to get an idea of how it all works.

In this section, you are going to convert the source files with Xcode's automated conversion tool, except for `MainViewController` and `AFHTTPRequestOperation`.

> **Note:** Before you continue, you should make a copy of the project, as the ARC conversion tool will overwrite the original files. Xcode does offer to make a snapshot of the source files but just as a precaution it is wise to make a backup anyway.

ARC is a feature of the new LLVM 3.0 and 4.0 compilers. Your existing projects most likely use the older GCC 4.2 or LLVM-GCC compilers, so it's a good idea to switch the project to the new compiler first and see if it compiles cleanly in non-ARC mode.

Go to the **Project Settings** screen, select the **Artists target** and under **Build Settings** type "compiler" into the search box. This will filter the list to bring up just the compiler options:

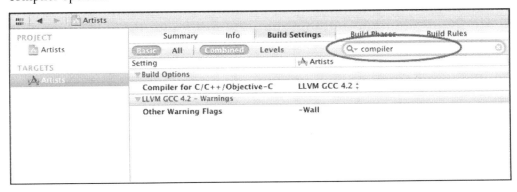

Make sure the **Compiler for C/C++/Objective-C** option says "Apple LLVM compiler" version 3.0 or higher.

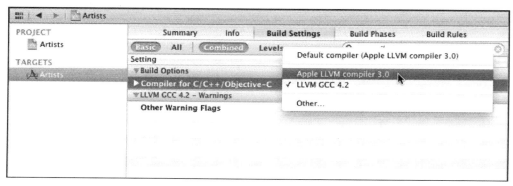

Under the **Warnings** header, also set the **Other Warning Flags** option to -**Wall**. The compiler will now check for all possible situations that can cause problems. By default many of these warnings are turned off but it is useful to always have all warnings on and to treat them as fatal errors. In other words, if the compiler gives a warning it is smart to fix the problem before continuing. Whether that is something you may want to do on your own projects is up to you, but during the conversion to ARC it is recommended that you take a good look at any issues the compiler may complain about.

For the same reason, also enable the **Run Static Analyzer** option under the **Build Options** header:

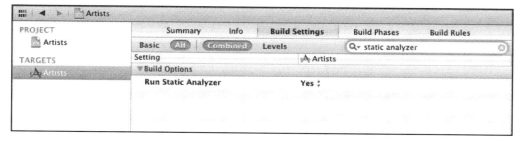

Xcode will now run the analyzer every time you build the app. That makes the builds a bit slower but for an app of this size, that's barely noticeable.

Let's build the app to see if it gives any problems with the new compiler. First do a clean using the **Product\Clean** menu option (or Shift-Cmd-K). Then press **Cmd-B** to build the app. Xcode should give no errors or warnings, so that's cool. If you're converting your own app to ARC and you get any warning messages at this point, then now is the time to fix them.

Trying out ARC

Just for the fun of it, let's switch the compiler to ARC mode and make it build the app again. You're going to get a ton of error messages but it's instructive to see what exactly these are.

Still in the Build Settings screen, switch to "All" to see all the available settings (instead of Basic, which only shows the most-often used settings). Search for "automatic" and set the Objective-C Automatic Reference Counting option to Yes. This is a project-wide flag that tells Xcode that you wish to compile all of the source files in your project using the ARC compiler.

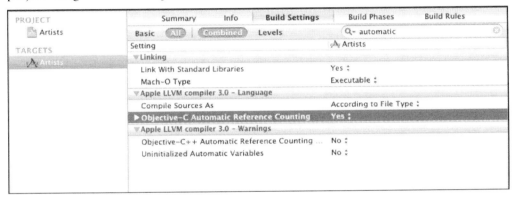

Build the app again. Whoops, you will get a ton of errors:

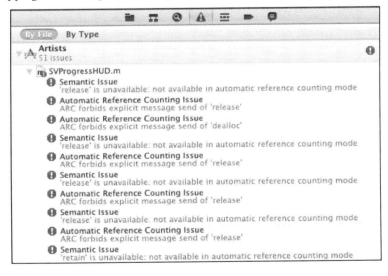

Clearly you have some migrating to do! Most of these errors are pretty obvious; they say you can no longer use `retain`, `release` and `autorelease`. You could fix all of these errors by hand but it's much easier to employ the automatic conversion tool.

The tool will compile the app in ARC mode and rewrites the source code for every error it encounters, until the whole thing compiles cleanly.

Putting the conversion tool into action

From Xcode's menu, choose Edit\Refactor\Convert to Objective-C ARC.

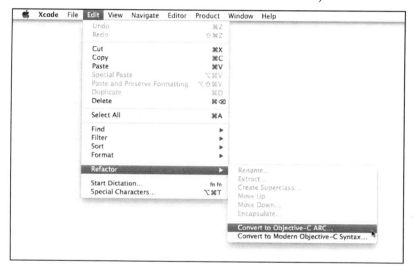

A new window appears that lets you select which parts of the app you want to convert:

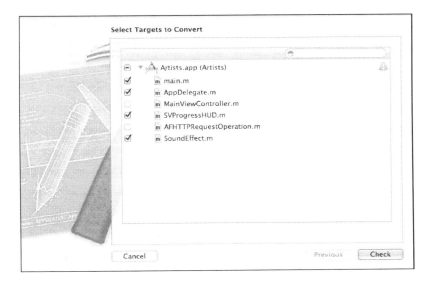

For the purposes of this tutorial, you don't want to do the whole app, so select only the following files:

- main.m

- AppDelegate.m

- SVProgressHUD.m

- SoundEffect.m

Note: The dialog shows a little warning icon indicating that the project already uses ARC. That's because earlier you've enabled the Objective-C Automatic Reference Counting option in the Build Settings and now the conversion tool thinks this is already an ARC project. You can ignore the warning; it won't interfere with the conversion.

Press the Check button to begin. The tool first checks whether your code is in a good enough state to be converted to ARC. You did manage to build the app successfully with the new LLVM compiler earlier, but apparently that left something to be desired. Xcode gives the following error message:

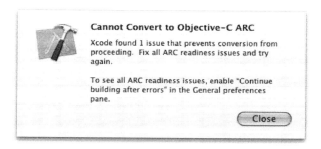

It complains about "ARC readiness issues" and that you should enable the "Continue building after errors" option. Open the Xcode Preferences window (from the menubar, under Xcode) and go to the General tab. Enable the option Continue building after errors:

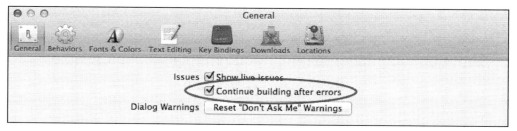

Let's try again. Choose Edit\Refactor\Convert to Objective-C ARC and check the source files except for MainViewController.m and AFHTTPRequestOperation.m. Press Check to begin.

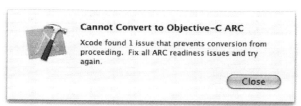

No luck, again you get an error message. The difference is that this time at least the compiler was able to identify all the issues that you need to fix before you can do the conversion. Fortunately, there is only one:

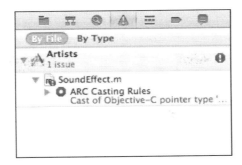

(You may have more errors in this list than are displayed here. Sometimes the conversion tool also complains about things that are not really "ARC readiness" issues.)

Get ready for ARC

The full description of the one ARC readiness issue that you found is:

Cast of Objective-C pointer type 'NSURL *' to C pointer type 'CFURLRef' (aka 'const struct __CFURL *') requires a bridged cast

This is what it looks like in the source editor:

```
17  #import "SoundEffect.h"
18
19  @implementation SoundEffect
20
21  - (id)initWithSoundNamed:(NSString *)filename
22  {
23      if ((self = [super init]))
24      {
25          NSURL *fileURL = [[NSBundle mainBundle] URLForResource:filename withExtension:nil];
26          if (fileURL != nil)
27          {
28              SystemSoundID theSoundID;
29              OSStatus error = AudioServicesCreateSystemSoundID((CFURLRef)fileURL, &theSoundID);
30              if (error == kAudioServicesNoError)   Cast of Objective-C pointer type 'NSURL *' to C pointer type 'CFURLRef' (aka 'const struct...
31                  _soundID = theSoundID;
32          }
33      }
34      return self;
35  }
36
```

We will go into more detail about this later, but the source code attempts to cast an NSURL object to a CFURLRef object. The AudioServicesCreateSystemSoundID() function takes a CFURLRef that describes where the sound file is located, but we are giving it an NSURL object instead. CFURLRef and NSURL are "toll-free bridged", which makes it possible to use an NSURL object in place of a CFURLRef and vice versa.

Often the C-based APIs from iOS use Core Foundation objects (that's what the CF stands for) while the Objective-C based APIs use "true" objects that extend the NSObject class. Sometimes you need to convert between the two and that is what the toll-free bridging technique allows for.

However, when you use ARC the compiler needs to know what it should do with those toll-free bridged objects. If you use an `NSURL` in place of a `CFURLRef`, then who is responsible for releasing that memory at the end of the day? To solve this conundrum, a set of new keywords was introduced for doing so-called "bridged casts": `__bridge`, `__bridge_transfer` and `__bridge_retained`. You'll learn about the differences between them later in the chapter.

For now, change the source code to the following:

```
OSStatus error = AudioServicesCreateSystemSoundID(
                        (__bridge CFURLRef) fileURL, &theSoundID);
```

You added the `__bridge` keyword inside the cast to `CFURLRef`. (Again, that is two underscores.)

The pre-check may have given you errors other than just this one. You can safely ignore those; the above change in SoundEffect.m is the only one you need to make. The conversion tool just seems a little uncertain in what it considers an "ARC readiness issue" from time to time.

Let's run the conversion tool once more - Edit\Refactor\Convert to Objective-C ARC. This time the pre-check runs without problems and you're presented with the following screen:

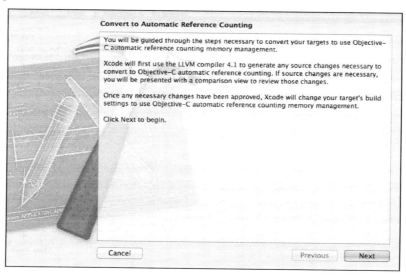

Click Next to continue. After a few seconds, Xcode will show a preview of all the files that it will change and which changes it will make inside each file. The left-hand pane shows the changed files while the right-hand pane shows the originals.

It's always a good idea to step through these files to make sure Xcode doesn't mess up anything. Let's go through the changes that the conversion tool is proposing to make.

AppDelegate.h

```
@property (strong, nonatomic) UIWindow *window;
@property (strong, nonatomic) MainViewController
                                    *viewController;
```

The app delegate has two properties, one for the window and one for the main view controller. This particular project does not use a MainWindow.xib file, so these two objects are created by the AppDelegate itself in application:didFinishLaunching-WithOptions: and stored into properties in order to simplify memory management.

These property declarations will change from this,

```
@property (retain, nonatomic)
```

to this:

```
@property (strong, nonatomic)
```

The strong keyword tells ARC that the synthesized instance variable that backs this property holds a strong reference to the object in question.

In other words, the window property contains a pointer to a UIWindow object and also acts as the owner of that UIWindow object. As long as the window property keeps its value, the UIWindow object stays alive. The same thing goes for the viewController property and the MainViewController object.

AppDelegate.m

In AppDelegate.m the lines that create the window and view controller objects have changed and the `dealloc` method is removed completely:

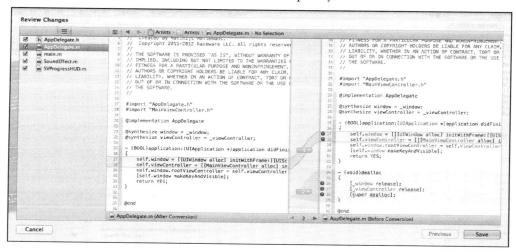

Spot the differences between this,

```
self.window = [[[UIWindow alloc] initWithFrame:
                       [[UIScreen mainScreen] bounds]] autorelease];
```

and this:

```
self.window = [[UIWindow alloc] initWithFrame:
                       [[UIScreen mainScreen] bounds]];
```

As you might have noticed, the call to `autorelease` is no longer needed. Likewise for the line that creates the view controller:

```
self.viewController = [[[MainViewController alloc]
                       initWithNibName:@"MainViewController"
                       bundle:nil] autorelease];
```

which now becomes:

```
self.viewController = [[MainViewController alloc]
                       initWithNibName:@"MainViewController"
                       bundle:nil];
```

Before ARC, if you wrote the following you created a memory leak if the property was declared "retain":

```
self.someProperty = [[SomeClass alloc] init];
```

The init method returns an object that is retained already, and placing it into the property would retain the object again. That's why you had to use `autorelease`, to balance the retain from the init method. But with ARC the above is just fine. The compiler is smart enough to figure out that it shouldn't do two retains here.

One of the things everyone loves about ARC is that in most cases it completely does away with the need to write `dealloc` methods. When an object is deallocated, its instance variables and synthesized properties are automatically released.

You no longer have to write:

```
- (void)dealloc
{
    [_window release];
    [_viewController release];
    [super dealloc];
}
```

because Objective-C automatically takes care of this now. In fact, it's not even possible to write the above anymore. Under ARC you are not allowed to call `release`, nor `[super dealloc]`. You can still implement `dealloc` – and you'll see an example of this later – but it's no longer necessary to release your instance variables by hand.

> Note: Something that the conversion tool doesn't do is make `AppDelegate` a subclass of `UIResponder` instead of `NSObject`. When you create a new app using one of Xcode's templates, as of iOS 5 the `AppDelegate` class is now a subclass of `UIResponder`. It doesn't seem to do any harm to leave it as `NSObject`, but you can make it a `UIResponder` if you want to:
>
> `@interface AppDelegate : UIResponder <UIApplicationDelegate>`

Main.m

In manually memory managed apps, the `[autorelease]` method works closely together with an "autorelease pool", which is represented by an `NSAutoreleasePool` object.

Every main.m has one and if you've ever worked with threads directly you've also had to make your own `NSAutoreleasePool` for each thread. Sometimes developers also put their own `NSAutoreleasePools` inside loops that do a lot of processing, just to make sure autoreleased objects created in that loop don't take up too much memory and get deleted from time to time.

Autorelease didn't go away with ARC, even though you never directly call the [autorelease] method on objects anymore. Any time you return an object from a method whose name doesn't start with alloc, init, copy, mutableCopy or new, the ARC compiler will autorelease it for you. These objects still end up in an autorelease pool that gets drained periodically. Should you care? Not really. It just works.

The big difference with before is that the NSAutoreleasePool has been retired in favor of a new language construct, @autoreleasepool.

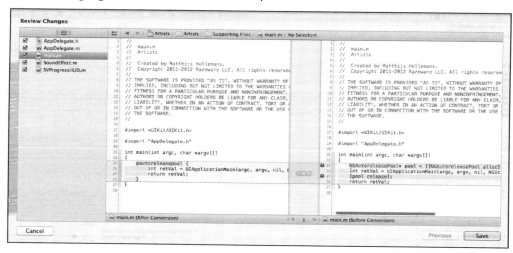

The conversion tool turned the main() function from this,

```
NSAutoreleasePool* pool = [[NSAutoreleasePool alloc] init];
int retVal = UIApplicationMain(argc, argv, nil,
                    NSStringFromClass([AppDelegate class]));
[pool release];
return retVal;
```

into this:

```
@autoreleasepool {
    int retVal = UIApplicationMain(argc, argv, nil,
                    NSStringFromClass([AppDelegate class]));
    return retVal;
}
```

Not only is it simpler to read for us programmers but under the hood a lot has changed as well, making these new autorelease pools much faster than before. You hardly ever need to worry about autorelease with ARC, except that if you used NSAutoreleasePool in your code before, you will need to replace it with an @autoreleasepool section. The conversion tool should do that automatically for you as it did here.

SoundEffect.m

Not much changed in this file. Only the call to [super dealloc] was removed. You are no longer allowed to call super in your dealloc methods.

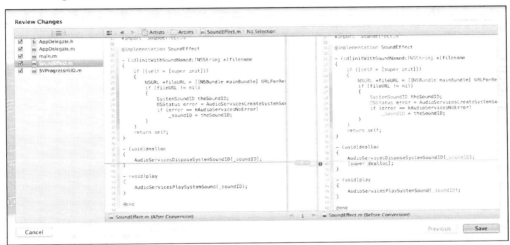

Notice that a dealloc method is still necessary here. In most of your classes you can simply forget about dealloc and let the compiler take care of things. Sometimes, however, you will need to release resources manually. That's the case with this class as well.

When the SoundEffect object is deallocated, a call to AudioServicesDispose-SystemSoundID() is still necessary to clean up the sound object and dealloc is the perfect place for that.

SVProgressHUD.m

This file has the most changes of them all but again they're quite trivial.

At the top of SVProgressHUD.m you will find a so-called "class extension" that has several property declarations.

Class extensions are like categories except they have special powers. The declaration of a class extension looks like that of a category but it has no name between the () parentheses. Class extensions can have properties and instance variables, something that categories can't, but you can only use them inside your .m file. (In other words, you can't create a class extension for someone else's class.)

The cool thing about class extensions is that they allow you to add private properties and method names to your classes. If you don't want to expose certain properties or methods in your public @interface, then you can put them in a class extension. That's exactly what the author of SVProgressHUD did:

```
@interface SVProgressHUD ()

. . .
@property (nonatomic, readwrite) SVProgressHUDMaskType maskType;
@property (nonatomic, strong) NSTimer *fadeOutTimer;
@property (nonatomic, strong) UILabel *stringLabel;
@property (nonatomic, strong) UIImageView *imageView;
@property (nonatomic, strong) UIActivityIndicatorView
                                             *spinnerView;

. . .

@end
```

As you've seen before, retain properties will become strong properties. If you scroll through the preview window you'll see that all the other changes are simply removal of retain and release statements.

Doing It For Real

When you're satisfied with the changes that the conversion tool will make, press the Save button to make it happen. Xcode first asks whether you want it to take a snapshot of the project before it changes the files:

You should press Enable here. If you ever need to go back to the original code, you can find the snapshot in the Organizer window under Projects.

After the ARC conversion tool finishes, press Cmd+B to build the app. The build should complete successfully but there will be several new warnings in **SVProgressHUD.m**:

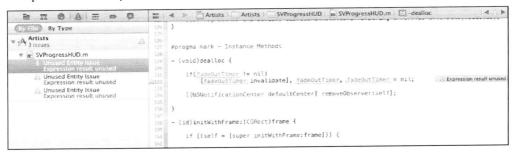

Notice again that the `dealloc` method is still used in this class, in this case to stop a timer and to unregister for notifications from **NSNotificationCenter**. These are not things ARC will do for you.

The code at the line with the warning used to look like this:

```
if(fadeOutTimer != nil)
    [fadeOutTimer invalidate], [fadeOutTimer release],
                                        fadeOutTimer = nil;
```

Now it says:

```
if(fadeOutTimer != nil)
    [fadeOutTimer invalidate], fadeOutTimer, fadeOutTimer = nil;
```

The tool did remove the call to [release], but it left the variable in place. A variable all by itself doesn't do anything useful, hence the Xcode warning. This appears to be a situation the automated conversion tool did not foresee.

> Note: If the commas confuse you, then know that it is valid in Objective-C to combine multiple expressions into a single statement using commas. The above trick is a common idiom for releasing objects and setting the corresponding instance variable to nil. Because everything happens in a single statement, the if doesn't need curly braces.

To silence the warning you can change this line, and the others like it, to:

```
if(fadeOutTimer != nil)
    [fadeOutTimer invalidate], fadeOutTimer = nil;
```

Technically speaking you don't need to set fadeOutTimer to nil in dealloc, because the object will automatically release any instance variables when it gets deleted.

In the other methods where the timer is invalidated, however, you definitely should set fadeOutTimer to nil. If you don't, the SVProgressHUD hangs on to the invalidated NSTimer object longer than it is supposed to. (Remember, as long as there is at least one strong pointer to an object, that object stays alive.)

Build the app again and now there should be no warnings. Conversion complete!

But wait a minute... you skipped two entire classes, MainViewController and AFHTTPRequestOperation, when you did the conversion. How come they suddenly compile without problems? When you tried building the project with ARC enabled earlier there were certainly plenty of errors in those files.

The answer is simple: the conversion tool has disabled ARC for these two source files. You can see that in the Build Phases tab on the Project Settings screen:

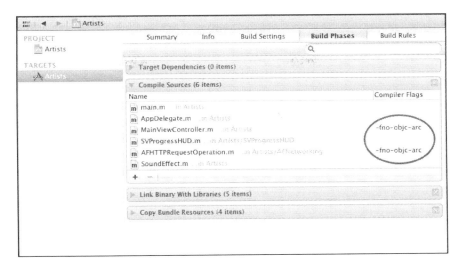

You enabled ARC on a project-wide basis earlier when you changed the Objective-C Automatic Reference Counting setting under Build Settings to Yes. But you can make exceptions to this by telling the compiler to ignore ARC for specific files, using the -fno-objc-arc flag. Xcode will compile these files with ARC disabled.

Because it's unreasonable to expect developers to switch their entire projects to ARC at once, the folks at Apple made it possible to combine ARC code with non-ARC code in the same project.

Tip: An easy way to move only a small portion of your project to ARC is to convert only the files that you want to migrate with the conversion tool, and let it automatically add the -fno-objc-arc flag to the rest. You can also add this flag by hand but that's incredibly annoying when you have many files that you don't want to ARCify.

Migration Woes

As far as conversions to ARC go, this one went fairly smooth. You only had to make a single change to SoundEffect.m (inserting a __bridge statement) and then the tool did the rest.

However, the LLVM compiler is a little less forgiving in ARC mode than previous compilers so it is possible that you run into additional problems during the pre-check. You may have to edit your own code more extensively before the tool can take over.

Here's a handy reference of some issues you might run into, and some tips for how to resolve them:

"Cast ... requires a bridged cast"

This is the one you've seen before. When the compiler can't figure out by itself how to do a toll-free bridged cast, it expects you to insert a __bridge modifier. There are two other bridge types, __bridge_transfer and __bridge_retained, and which one you're supposed to use depends on exactly what you're trying to do. More about these other bridge types in the section on Toll-Free Bridging.

"Receiver type 'X' for instance message is a forward declaration"

If you have a class, let's say MyView that is a subclass of UIView, and you call a method on it or use one of its properties, then you have to #import the definition for that class. That is usually a requirement for getting your code to compile in the first place, but not always, due to the dynamic nature of Objective-C.

For example, you added a forward declaration in your .h file to announce that MyView is class:

```
@class MyView;
```

Later in your .m file you do something like:

```
[myView setNeedsDisplay];
```

Previously this might have compiled and worked just fine, even without an #import statement. With ARC you always need to explicitly add an import:

```
#import "MyView.h"
```

"Switch case is in protected scope"

You get this error when your code does the following:

```
switch (X)
{
    case Y:
        NSString *s = ...;
        break;
```

```
    }
```

This is no longer allowed. If you declare new pointer variables inside a case statement you must enclose the whole thing in curlies:

```
switch (X)
{
    case Y:
    {
        NSString *s = ...;
        break;
    }
}
```

Now it is clear what the scope of the variable is, which ARC needs to know in order to release the object at the right moment.

"A name is referenced outside the NSAutoreleasePool scope that it was declared in"

You may have some code that creates its own autorelease pool:

```
NSAutoreleasePool* pool = [[NSAutoreleasePool alloc] init];

// . . . do calculations . . .

NSArray* sortedResults = [[filteredResults
    sortedArrayUsingSelector:@selector(compare:)] retain];

[pool release];
return [sortedResults autorelease];
```

The conversion tool needs to turn that into something like this:

```
@autoreleasepool
{
    // . . . do calculations . . .

    NSArray* sortedResults = [filteredResults
        sortedArrayUsingSelector:@selector(compare:)];
}
return sortedResults;
```

But that is no longer valid code. The sortedResults variable is declared inside the @autoreleasepool scope and is therefore not accessible outside of that scope. To fix the issue you will need to move the declaration of the variable above the creation of the NSAutoreleasePool before starting the conversion:

```
NSArray* sortedResults;
NSAutoreleasePool* pool = [[NSAutoreleasePool alloc] init];
. . .
```

Now the ARC conversion tool can properly rewrite your code.

"ARC forbids Objective-C objects in structs or unions"

One of the restrictions of ARC is that you can no longer put Objective-C objects inside C structs. The following code is not valid anymore:

```
typedef struct
{
    UIImage *selectedImage;
    UIImage *disabledImage;
}
ButtonImages;
```

You are recommended to replace such structs with true Objective-C classes instead. We'll talk more about this one later, and then I'll show you some other workarounds.

There may be other pre-check errors but these are the most common ones.

> Note: The automated ARC conversion tool can be a little flakey if you use it more than once. If you don't convert all the files but leave some unchecked the way we did, the conversion tool may not actually do anything when you try to convert the remaining files later. My suggestion is that you run the tool just once and don't convert your files in batches.

Converting By Hand

You've converted almost the entire project to ARC already, except for MainView-Controller and AFHTTPRequestOperation. In this section you will find out how to convert MainViewController by hand. Sometimes it's fun to do things yourself so you get a better feel for what truly happens.

If you look at MainViewController.h you'll see that the class declares two instance variables:

```
@interface MainViewController : UIViewController
    <UITableViewDataSource, UITableViewDelegate,
    UISearchBarDelegate, NSXMLParserDelegate>
```

```
{
    NSOperationQueue *_queue;
    NSMutableString *_currentStringValue;
}
```

When you think about it, the public interface of a class is a strange place to put instance variables. Usually, instance variables are a part of the internals of your class and not something you want to expose in its public interface.

To a user of your class it isn't important to know what the class's instance variables are. From the perspective of data hiding it is better if you move such implementation details into the @implementation section of the class. The new LLVM compiler version 3.0 and up make this now possible (whether you use ARC or not).

Remove the instance variable block from MainViewController.h and put it into MainViewController.m. The header file should now look like:

```
#import <UIKit/UIKit.h>

@interface MainViewController : UIViewController
    <UITableViewDataSource, UITableViewDelegate,
     UISearchBarDelegate, NSXMLParserDelegate>

@property (nonatomic, retain) IBOutlet UITableView *tableView;
@property (nonatomic, retain) IBOutlet UISearchBar *searchBar;

@end
```

And the top of MainViewController.m looks like:

```
@implementation MainViewController
{
    NSOperationQueue *_queue;
    NSMutableString *_currentStringValue;
}
```

Build the app and... it just works. This makes your .h files a lot cleaner and puts the instance variables where they really belong.

You can do the same for the SoundEffect class. Simply move the instance variable section into the .m file. Because you no longer reference the SystemSoundID symbol anywhere in SoundEffect.h, you can also move the #import for AudioServices.h into SoundEffect.m. The SoundEffect header no longer exposes any details of its implementation. Nice and clean.

Note: You can also put instance variables in class extensions. This is useful for big projects where the implementation of a single class is spread over multiple files. You can then put the extension in a shared, private header file, so that all these different implementation files have access to the same instance variables.

It's time to enable ARC on MainViewController.m. Go into the Build Phases settings and remove the −fno−objc−arc compiler flag from MainViewController.m. Then press Cmd+B to do a new build.

You may have some problems getting Xcode to recognize these changes. You should get a ton of compiler errors but if Xcode still says "Build Succeeded", then close the project and reopen it.

What's up with dealloc?

Let's go through these errors and fix them one by one, beginning with dealloc:

```
57      self.searchBar = nil;
58      self.soundEffect = nil;
59  }
60
61  - (void)dealloc
62  {
63      [_tableView release];          ❶ ARC forbids explicit message send of 'release'
64      [_searchBar release];          ❶ ARC forbids explicit message send of 'release'
65      [_queue release];              ❶ 'release' is unavailable: not available in automatic reference counting mode
66      [_searchResults release];      ❶ 'release' is unavailable: not available in automatic reference counting mode
67      [_soundEffect release];        ❶ ARC forbids explicit message send of 'release'
68      [super dealloc];               ❶ ARC forbids explicit message send of 'dealloc'
69  }
70
71  - (BOOL)shouldAutorotateToInterfaceOrientation:(UIInterfaceOrientation)interfaceOrientation
72  {
73      return (interfaceOrientation == UIInterfaceOrientationPortrait);
74  }
75
```

Every single line in dealloc gives an error. You're not supposed to call [release] anymore, nor [super dealloc]. Because this dealloc method isn't doing anything else, you can simply remove the entire method.

The only reason for keeping a dealloc method around is when you need to free certain resources that do not fall under ARC's umbrella. Examples of this are calling CFRelease() on Core Foundation objects, calling free() on memory that you allocated with malloc(), unregistering for notifications, invalidating a timer, and so on.

Note: Sometimes it is necessary to explicitly break a connection with an object if you are its delegate but usually this happens automatically. Most of the time delegates are weak references so when the object to be deallocated is someone else's delegate, the delegate pointer will be set to nil automatically when the object is destroyed. Weak pointers clean up after themselves.

By the way, in your dealloc method you can still use your instance variables because they haven't been released yet. That doesn't happen until after dealloc returns.

The SoundEffect getter

The soundEffect method calls release, so that's an easy fix:

```
65
66    - (SoundEffect *)soundEffect
67    {
68        if (_soundEffect == nil)  // lazy loading
69        {
70            SoundEffect *theSoundEffect = [[SoundEffect alloc] initWithSoundNamed:@"Sound.caf"];
71            self.soundEffect = theSoundEffect;
72            [theSoundEffect release];              ⓘ ARC forbids explicit message send of 'release'
73        }
74        return _soundEffect;
75    }
76
```

This method is actually the getter method for the soundEffect property. It employs a lazy loading technique to load the sound effect the first time it is used. The code here uses a common pattern for creating objects under manual memory management. First the new object is stored in a temporary local variable, then it is assigned to the actual property, and finally the value from the local variable is released.

This is how most Objective-C programmers used to write this sort of thing and you may have been doing it too:

```
SoundEffect *theSoundEffect = [[SoundEffect alloc]
                              initWithSoundNamed:@"Sound.caf"];
self.soundEffect = theSoundEffect;
[theSoundEffect release];
```

You could just remove the call to release and leave it at that, but now having a separate local variable isn't very useful anymore:

```
SoundEffect *theSoundEffect = [[SoundEffect alloc]
                              initWithSoundNamed:@"Sound.caf"];
self.soundEffect = theSoundEffect;
```

So instead, you can simplify it to just one line:

```
self.soundEffect = [[SoundEffect alloc]
                   initWithSoundNamed:@"Sound.caf"];
```

Under manual memory management this would cause a leak (there is one retain too many going on) but with ARC this sort of thing is just fine.

Please (auto)release me, let me go

Just like you can't call release anymore, you also cannot call autorelease:

```
86
87    - (UITableViewCell *)tableView:(UITableView *)theTableView cellForRowAtIndexPath:(NSIndexPath *)indexPath
88    {
89        static NSString *CellIdentifier = @"Cell";
90
91        UITableViewCell *cell = [theTableView dequeueReusableCellWithIdentifier:CellIdentifier];
92        if (cell == nil)
93            cell = [[UITableViewCell alloc] initWithStyle:UITableViewCellStyleDefault reuseIdentifier:CellIdentifier] autorelease];
                                                                        autorelease is unavailable: not available in automatic reference counting mode
94
95        if ([self.searchResults count] == 0)
96            cell.textLabel.text = @"(Nothing found)";
97        else
98            cell.textLabel.text = [self.searchResults objectAtIndex:indexPath.row];
99
100       return cell;
101   }
102
```

The fix is straightforward. Instead of doing,

```
cell = [[[UITableViewCell alloc]
        initWithStyle:UITableViewCellStyleDefault
        reuseIdentifier:CellIdentifier] autorelease];
```

this line becomes:

```
cell = [[UITableViewCell alloc]
        initWithStyle:UITableViewCellStyleDefault
        reuseIdentifier:CellIdentifier];
```

The next method that has errors is escape:, but we'll skip it just for a second. These issues are related to toll-free bridging, a topic that has a special section dedicated to it.

The remaining two errors are releases, in searchBarSearchButtonClicked: and in parser:didEndElement:. You can simply remove these two lines.

Do you really need all those properties?

If you look at the top of MainViewController.m, you'll see that it uses a class extension to declare two private properties, searchResults and soundEffect:

```
@interface MainViewController ()
@property (nonatomic, retain) NSMutableArray *searchResults;
@property (nonatomic, retain) SoundEffect *soundEffect;
@end
```

This is done primarily to make manual memory management easier and it's a common reason why developers use properties. When you do,

```
self.searchResults = [NSMutableArray arrayWithCapacity:10];
```

the setter will release the old value that is stored in the property (if any) and retrain the new value. Developers have been using properties as a way of having to think less about when they need to retain and when they need to release. But now with ARC they don't have to think about this at all!

In my opinion, using properties just for the purposes of simplifying memory management is no longer necessary. You can still do so if you want to but it's simpler to just use instance variables now, and only use properties when you need to make data accessible to other classes from your public interface.

Therefore, remove the class extension and the @synthesize statements for searchResults and soundEffect. Add new instance variables to replace them:

```
@implementation MainViewController
{
    NSOperationQueue *_queue;
    NSMutableString *_currentStringValue;
    NSMutableArray *_searchResults;
    SoundEffect *_soundEffect;
}
```

Note that these new instance variables have an underscore in front of their names. That's a common Objective-C convention to make it clear whether a symbol represents a local variable (no prefix), an instance variable (underscore prefix), or a property (using the "self." prefix).

Of course, replacing the properties with instance variables means you can no longer refer to them as self.searchResults and self.soundEffect. Change viewDidUnload to the following:

```
- (void)viewDidUnload
{
    [super viewDidUnload];
    self.tableView = nil;
    self.searchBar = nil;
    _soundEffect = nil;
}
```

The soundEffect method now becomes:

```
- (SoundEffect *)soundEffect
{
    if (_soundEffect == nil)  // lazy loading
    {
        _soundEffect = [[SoundEffect alloc]
```

```
                                       initWithSoundNamed:@"Sound.caf"];
    }
    return _soundEffect;
}
```

That's about as simple as you can make it. The `SoundEffect` object is allocated and assigned to the `_soundEffect` instance variable. This variable becomes its owner and the object will stay alive until `_soundEffect` is set to `nil` (in `viewDidUnload`), or until the `MainViewController` is deallocated (because that will also release all its instance variables).

In the rest of the file, replace anywhere where it says `self.searchResults` with just `_searchResults`. When you build the app again, the only errors it should give are on the `escape:` method.

Note that `searchBarSearchButtonClicked` still does:

```
[self.soundEffect play];
```

This will work even though you no longer have a property named `soundEffect`. The dot syntax isn't restricted to just properties, although that's what it is most commonly used for.

If using dot syntax here offends you, you can change this line to a regular method call:

```
[[self soundEffect] play];
```

Don't change it to this, though:

```
[_soundEffect play];
```

Because the code uses lazy loading to create the `SoundEffect` object, the `_soundEffect` instance variable will always be `nil` until you call the `soundEffect` method at least once. Therefore, to be certain you actually have a loaded `SoundEffect` object, you should always access it through `self`.

Note: If you feel that this usage pattern does morally require you to declare `soundEffect` as a `@property`, then go right ahead. Different strokes for different folks. :-)

If it's a property, always use self

As a best practice, if you define something as a property, then you should *always* use it as a property and not through its backing variable.

The only places where you can access the property's backing instance variable directly is in the `init` and `dealloc` methods for your class and when you provide a custom getter and setter. Anywhere else you should access the property through `self.propertyName`.

That is why `@synthesize` statements often rename the instance variable by putting an underscore in front:

```
@synthesize propertyName = _propertyName;
```

This construct will prevent you from accidentally using the backing instance variable by typing "`propertyName`" when you really meant to use "`self.propertyName`".

> Tip: With the latest versions of Xcode you're no longer required to synthesize your properties. You can completely leave out the `@synthesize` statement and the compiler will automatically create the backing instance variable for you. The name of this variable is the same as the property name, but again with an additional underscore in front.

This rule is especially important for `readonly` properties. ARC can get confused if you modify such properties by changing their instance variables, and strange bugs will result. The correct way is to redefine the property as `readwrite` in a class extension.

In the .h file, you declare the property as `readonly`:

```
@interface WeatherPredictor
@property (nonatomic, strong, readonly) NSNumber *temperature;
@end
```

And in the .m file you declare the property again but now as `readwrite`:

```
@interface WeatherPredictor ()
@property (nonatomic, strong, readwrite) NSNumber *temperature;
@end
```

Make it weak or leak

Speaking of properties, `MainViewController` still has two outlet properties in its .h file:

```
@property (nonatomic, retain) IBOutlet UITableView *tableView;
```

```
@property (nonatomic, retain) IBOutlet UISearchBar *searchBar;
```

The `retain` keyword for properties still works with ARC and is simply a synonym for `strong`. It is best to call your properties `strong` because that's the proper term from now on.

For these two particular properties, however, we have other plans. Instead of strong, you will declare them as `weak`:

```
@property (nonatomic, weak) IBOutlet UITableView *tableView;
@property (nonatomic, weak) IBOutlet UISearchBar *searchBar;
```

Weak is the recommended relationship for all *outlet* properties, in other words properties that point to views in your nib or storyboard. These view objects are already part of the view controller's view hierarchy and don't need to be retained elsewhere. Your view controller just wants to refer to them but not become their co-owner.

What is the benefit of declaring your outlets `weak` instead of `strong`? Peace of mind. When you make an outlet a strong pointer, you give the view controller partial responsibility for managing the lifetime of the view, but that really is UIKit's business, not yours.

By setting the outlet properties to be weak, you relieve the view controller of any ownership duties. Primarily that means you no longer have to worry about setting your outlet properties to `nil` when the view gets unloaded in a low-memory situation.

> **Note:** Exactly what happens when the iPhone receives a low-memory warning varies depending on the version of iOS you're using. On iOS 5 and below, UIKit will unload the view of any view controller that is not currently visible and calls the `viewDidUnload` method to let the view controller know that its view object is no longer alive.
>
> On iOS 6, however, views are no longer automatically unloaded and as a result, `viewDidUnload` is never called. If you're unaware of this difference, your code can have subtle bugs that only show up when the iPhone runs out of free memory space — and you don't want your apps to crash because of that!

The `viewDidUnload` method currently looks like this:

```
- (void)viewDidUnload
{
    [super viewDidUnload];
```

```
    self.tableView = nil;
    self.searchBar = nil;
    _soundEffect = nil;
}
```

When the iPhone receives a low-memory warning on iOS 5, the view controller's main view gets unloaded, which releases all of its subviews as well. At that point the UITableView and UISearchBar objects cease to exist and the zeroing weak pointer system automatically sets self.tableView and self.searchBar to nil.

Because they are now zeroing weak pointers, there is no more need to set the properties to nil by yourself in viewDidUnload. In fact, by the time viewDidUnload gets called these properties already are nil. Therefore, you can simplify this method to do just:

```
- (void)viewDidUnload
{
    [super viewDidUnload];
    _soundEffect = nil;
}
```

But remember, if your app is running on iOS 6 and a low-memory situation occurs, the view will not be unloaded and viewDidUnload method will *not* be called. So how do you handle this in a way that works on both iOS 5 and 6?

The recommendation is to no longer write viewDidUnload methods, even if you still want to support iOS 5, and to move any cleanup code into didReceiveMemoryWarning instead. Because the outlets are now weak, you no longer have to worry about them, but you're still responsible for cleaning up any other data that you do own. If you no longer want to hang on to objects, you need to set their pointers to nil explicitly.

Remove viewDidUnload and replace it with:

```
- (void)didReceiveMemoryWarning
{
    [super didReceiveMemoryWarning];
    _soundEffect = nil;
}
```

In the event of a low-memory warning, this method sets _soundEffect to nil to force the deallocation of the SoundEffect object. You should free as much memory as possible and the SoundEffect object is expendable at that point. It can be reloaded whenever you need it again.

Because instance variables create strong relationships by default, setting _soundEffect to nil will remove the owner from the SoundEffect object and it will be deallocated immediately.

Properties recap

To summarize, the new modifiers for properties are:

- strong. This is a synonym for the old "retain". A strong property becomes an owner of the object it points to.

- weak. This is a property that represents a weak pointer. It will automatically be set to nil when the pointed-to object is destroyed. Remember, use this for outlets.

- unsafe_unretained. This is a synonym for the old "assign". You use it only in exceptional situations and when you want to target iOS 4. More about this later.

- copy. This is still the same as before. It makes a copy of the object and creates a strong relationship.

- assign. You're no longer supposed to use this for objects, but you still use it for primitive values such as BOOL, int, and float.

> Note: Remember that strong and weak are only for objects. For primitive values such as int, float, NSInteger, and BOOL you keep using assign, just like you did before.
>
> ```
> Correct:   @property (nonatomic, assign) BOOL yesOrNo;
> WRONG:     @property (nonatomic, strong) BOOL yesOrNo;
> ```

Toll-Free Bridging

Let's fix that one last method so you can run the app again.

```
117
118   - (NSString *)escape:(NSString *)text
119   {
120       return [(NSString *)CFURLCreateStringByAddingPercentEscapes(
121           NULL,                          Cast of C pointer type 'CFStringRef' (aka 'const struct __CFString *') to Objective-C pointer type 'NSString *' requires a bridged cast
122           (CFStringRef)text,             'autorelease' is unavailable: not available in automatic reference counting mode
123           NULL,                          ARC forbids explicit message send of 'autorelease'
124           (CFStringRef)@"!*'();:@&=+$,/?%#[]",
125           CFStringConvertNSStringEncodingToEncoding(NSUTF8StringEncoding))
126           autorelease];
127   }
128
```

This method uses the CFURLCreateStringByAddingPercentEscapes() function to URL-encode a string. We use it to make sure any spaces or other characters in the search text that the user types get converted to something that is valid for use in an HTTP GET request.

The compiler gives several errors:

- ARC Casting Rules: Cast of C pointer type 'CFStringRef' (aka 'const struct __CFString *') to Objective-C pointer type 'NSString *' requires a bridged cast

- Semantic Issue: 'autorelease' is unavailable: not available in automatic reference counting mode

- ARC Restrictions: ARC forbids explicit message send of 'autorelease'

The last two errors are really the same and simply mean that you cannot call [autorelease]. Let's get rid of that statement first. What remains is this:

```
- (NSString *)escape:(NSString *)text
{
    return (NSString *)CFURLCreateStringByAddingPercentEscapes(
        NULL,
        (CFStringRef)text,
        NULL,
        (CFStringRef)@"!*'();:@&=+$,/?%#[]",
        CFStringConvertNSStringEncodingToEncoding(
                                    NSUTF8StringEncoding));
}
```

The remaining error has to do with a cast that apparently should be "bridged". There are three casts in this method:

- (NSString *)CFURLCreateStringByAddingPercentEscapes(...)

- (CFStringRef)text

- (CFStringRef)@"!*'();:@&=+$,/?%#[]"

The compiler only complains about the first one. Before you'll fix it, let's take a closer look at what "bridging" really means.

Bridged casts are necessary when you move an object between worlds. On the one hand there is the world of Objective-C, on the other there is Core Foundation.

For most apps these days there isn't a big need to use Core Foundation. You can do almost anything you want from comfortable Objective-C classes. However, some lower-levels APIs such as Core Graphics and Core Text are based on Core Foundation and it's unlikely there will ever be an Objective-C version of them. Fortunately, the designers of iOS made it really easy to move certain objects between these two different kingdoms. And you won't be charged a thing!

NSString is an Objective-C object that represents a list of characters – you've probably used it once or twice before – and CFStringRef is a Core Foundation object that does the same thing. For all intents and purposes, NSString and CFStringRef can be treated as the being same.

You can take an NSString object and use it as if it were a CFStringRef, and take a CFStringRef object and use it as if it were an NSString. That's the idea behind toll-free bridging.

Previously, in the days before ARC, that was as simple as doing:

```
CFStringRef s1 = [[NSString alloc] initWithFormat:
                                   @"Hello, %@!", name];
```

Of course, you also had to remember to release the object when you were done with it:

```
CFRelease(s1);
```

The other way around, from Core Foundation to Objective-C, was just as easy:

```
CFStringRef s2 = CFStringCreateWithCString(kCFAllocatorDefault,
                   bytes, kCFStringEncodingMacRoman);

NSString *s3 = (NSString *)s2;

// release the object when you're done
[s3 release];
```

Now that we have ARC, the compiler needs to know who is responsible for releasing such casted objects. If you treat an NSObject as a Core Foundation object, then it is no longer ARC's responsibility to release it. But you do need to tell ARC about your intentions; the compiler cannot infer this by itself.

Likewise, if you create a Core Foundation object but then cast it to an NSObject, you need to tell ARC to take ownership of it and delete that object when its time comes. That's what the bridging casts are for.

The CFURLCreateStringByAddingPercentEscapes() function takes a handful of parameters, two of which are CFStringRef objects. It also returns a new CFStringRef object. Because we're Objective-C programmers, we prefer to work with NSStrings instead. Previously you could just cast these NSString objects into a CFStringRef, and vice versa, but with ARC the compiler needs more information.

The cast,

```
(CFStringRef)@"!*'();:@&=+$,/?%#[]"
```

is a cast of a constant object and that doesn't require any special memory management. This is a string literal that will be baked into the application executable. Unlike "real" objects, it is never allocated nor freed. No problems here.

> **Note:** If you wanted to, you could also write this as:
>
> CFSTR("!*'();:@&=+$,/?%#[]")
>
> The CFSTR() macro creates a CFStringRef object from the specified string. The string literal here is a regular C string and therefore doesn't begin with the @ sign. Instead of making an NSString object and casting it to a CFStringRef, you now directly make a CFStringRef object. Which one you like better is largely a matter of taste, as they both deliver the exact same results.

The cast,

```
(CFStringRef)text
```

converts the contents of the text parameter, which again is an NSString object, into a CFStringRef. Like local variables, method parameters are strong pointers; their objects are retained upon entry to the method. The value from the text variable will continue to exist until the pointer is destroyed. Because it is a local variable, that happens when the escape: method ends.

We want ARC to stay the owner of this variable but we also want to temporarily treat it as a CFStringRef. For this type of situation, the __bridge specifier is used. It tells ARC that no change in ownership is taking place and that it should release the object using the normal rules.

You've already used __bridge before in SoundEffect.m:

```
OSStatus error = AudioServicesCreateSystemSoundID(
                   (__bridge CFURLRef) fileURL, &theSoundID);
```

The exact same situation applies there. The fileURL variable contains an NSURL object and is managed by ARC. The AudioServicesCreateSystemSoundID() function, however, expects a CFURLRef object. Fortunately, NSURL and CFURLRef are toll-free bridged so you can cast the one into the other. Because you still want ARC to release the object when you're done with it, you use the __bridge keyword to indicate that ARC remains in charge.

Change the escape: method to the following:

```
- (NSString *)escape:(NSString *)text
{
    return (NSString *)CFURLCreateStringByAddingPercentEscapes(
        NULL,
        (__bridge CFStringRef)text,
        NULL,
        (CFStringRef)@"!*'();:@&=+$,/?%#[]",
        CFStringConvertNSStringEncodingToEncoding(
                                    NSUTF8StringEncoding));
}
```

Now the value from the text parameter is properly bridged. It lets the compiler know that the ownership of this object did not change and that ARC is still responsible for cleaning up afterwards.

> Note: With the latest version of the LLVM compiler, the __bridge specifier isn't really required anymore for simple cases such as this. The compiler is smart enough to figure out that you intended a bridge cast here.

Most of the time when you cast an Objective-C object to a Core Foundation object or vice versa, you'll want to use __bridge. However, there are times when you do want to give ARC ownership of a Core Foundation object, or relieve ARC of its ownership. In that case there are two other bridging casts that you can use:

• __bridge_transfer: Give ARC ownership

• __bridge_retained: Relieve ARC of its ownership

Instead of __bridge_transfer, the helper function CFBridgingRelease() is often used, as that makes it a bit clearer what the purpose of the cast is. You use it where you would normally have used a CFRelease(). In a similar vein, the helper function for __bridge_retained is CFBridgingRetain() and it is used in the place of the regular CFRetain().

There is one error remaining in the source file, on the line:

```
return (NSString *)CFURLCreateStringByAddingPercentEscapes(
```

Click on the error message and the following Fix-it will pop up:

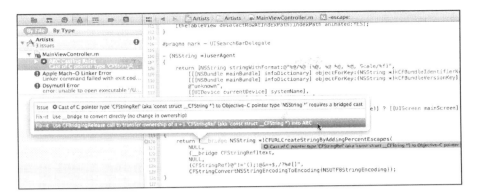

It gives two possible solutions: __bridge and CFBridgingRelease(). The correct choice here is CFBridgingRelease(), which is the same as the __bridge_transfer cast.

The CFURLCreateStringByAddingPercentEscapes() function creates and returns a new CFStringRef object. Of course, you'd rather use NSString so you need to do a bridging cast. What you're really attempting to do in this method is this:

```
CFStringRef result = CFURLCreateStringByAddingPercentEscapes();
NSString *s = (NSString *)result;
return s;
```

Because the function has the word "Create" in its name, it returns a retained object (according to the Core Foundation memory management rules). Someone is responsible for releasing that retained object at some point. If the escape: method wasn't returning this object as an NSString, then the code may have looked something like this:

```
- (void)someMethod
{
    CFStringRef s = CFURLCreateStringByAddingPercentEscapes();

    // do something with the string
    // . . .

    CFRelease(s);
}
```

Remember that ARC only works for Objective-C objects, not for objects that are created by Core Foundation. You still need to call CFRelease() on such objects yourself!

What you want to do in escape: is convert that new CFStringRef object to an NSString object, and then ARC should automatically release that string whenever you're no longer using it. But ARC needs to be told about this.

Therefore, you use the CFBridgingRelease() function (or the __bridge_transfer cast) to say: "Hey ARC, this CFStringRef object is now an NSString object and I want you to dispose of it, so that I don't have to call CFRelease() on it myself."

The final version of the escape: method becomes:

```
- (NSString *)escape:(NSString *)text
{
    return (NSString *)CFBridgingRelease(
        CFURLCreateStringByAddingPercentEscapes(
            NULL,
            (__bridge CFStringRef)text,
            NULL,
            (CFStringRef)@"!*'();:@&=+$,/?%#[]",
            CFStringConvertNSStringEncodingToEncoding(
                                  NSUTF8StringEncoding)));
}
```

If you were to just use __bridge instead, then your app would have a memory leak. ARC doesn't know that it should release the object when you're done with it and no one calls CFRelease(). As a result, the object will stay in memory forever. It's important that you pick the proper bridge specifier!

Another common framework that requires these bridging casts is the AddressBook framework. For example:

```
- (NSString *)firstName
{
    return CFBridgingRelease(ABRecordCopyCompositeName(...));
}
```

Remember, anywhere you call a Core Foundation function named Create, Copy, or Retain you must do CFBridgingRelease() to safely transfer the value to ARC.

What about the other one, CFBridgingRetain() or __bridge_retained? You would use that going the other way around. Suppose you have an NSString and you need to give that to some Core Foundation API that wants to take ownership of your string object. You don't want ARC to also release that object, because then it would be released one time too many and apps have a tendency to crash when that happens.

In other words, you use CFBridgingRetain() to give the object to Core Foundation so that ARC is no longer responsible for releasing it. An example:

```
NSString *s1 = [[NSString alloc] initWithFormat:
                                    @"Hello, %@!", name];

CFStringRef s2 = CFBridgingRetain(s1);
```

```
// do something with s2
// . . .

CFRelease(s2);
```

As soon as the `CFBridgingRetain()` cast happens, ARC considers itself no longer duty-bound to release the string object. The call to `CFRelease()` is properly balanced by `CFBridgingRetain()`. If you had used `__bridge` in this example, then the app would likely crash. ARC might deallocate the string object before the Core Foundation code is done with it.

I doubt you'll need to use this particular bridge type often. Off the top of my head, I can't think of a single API that is commonly used that requires this.

It is unlikely that you have a lot of Core Foundation code in your apps anyway. Most frameworks that you'll use are Objective-C, with the exception of Core Graphics (which doesn't have any toll-free bridged types), the Address Book, and the occasional low-level function. But if you do, rest assured that the compiler would point out to you when you need to use a bridging cast.

> **Note:** Not all Objective-C and Core Foundation objects that sound alike are toll-free bridged. For example, `CGImage` and `UIImage` cannot be cast to each another, and neither can `CGColor` and `UIColor`. The following page lists the types that can be used interchangeably: http://bit.ly/j65Ceo

The bridging casts are not limited to interactions with Core Foundation. Some APIs take `void *` pointers that let you store a reference to anything you want, whether that's an Objective-C object, a Core Foundation object, a `malloc()`'d memory buffer, and so on. The notation `void *` means: this is a pointer but the actual datatype of what it points to could be anything.

To convert from an Objective-C object to `void *`, or the other way around, you will need to do a `__bridge` cast. For example:

```
MyClass *myObject = [[MyClass alloc] init];
[UIView beginAnimations:nil context:(__bridge void *)myObject];
```

In the animation delegate method, you do the conversion in reverse to get your object back:

```
- (void)animationDidStart:(NSString *)animationID
                  context:(void *)context
```

```
{
    MyClass *myObject = (__bridge MyClass *)context;
    . . .
}
```

You'll see another example of this in the next chapter, where we cover using ARC with Cocos2D.

To summarize:

- When changing ownership from Core Foundation to Objective-C you use `CFBridgingRelease()` or `__bridge_transfer`.

- When changing ownership from Objective-C to Core Foundation you use `CFBridgingRetain()` or `__bridge_retained`.

- When you want to use one type temporarily as if it were another without ownership change, you use `__bridge`.

That's it as far as `MainViewController` is concerned. All the errors should be gone now and you can build and run the app.

The conversion of the Artists app to ARC is complete!

(We won't convert `AFHTTPRequestOperation` to ARC in this tutorial. Compiling it with the flag `–fno-objc-arc` is sufficient to make it work.)

> **Note:** For the near future you may find that many of your favorite third-party libraries do not come in an ARC flavor yet. It's no fun to maintain two versions of a library, one without ARC and one with, so expect many library maintainers to pick just one.
>
> New libraries might be written for ARC only but older ones may prove too hard to convert. Therefore it's likely that a portion of your code will remain with ARC disabled (the `–fno-objc-arc` compiler flag).
>
> Fortunately, ARC works on a per-file basis so it's no problem at all to combine these libraries with your own ARCified projects. Because it's sometimes a bit of a hassle to disable ARC for a large selection of files, we'll talk about smarter ways to put non-ARC third-party libraries into your projects in the next chapter.

Delegates and Weak Properties

The app you've seen so far is very simple and demonstrates only a few facets of ARC. To show you the rest, you'll first have to add a new screen to the app.

Using Xcode's File\New File menu, add a new UIViewController subclass to the project, with XIB for user interface, and name it DetailViewController.

Add two action methods to DetailViewController.h:

```objc
@interface DetailViewController : UIViewController

- (IBAction)coolAction;
- (IBAction)mehAction;

@end
```

You will connect these actions to two buttons in the nib.

Open DetailViewController.xib and add a navigation bar and two buttons:

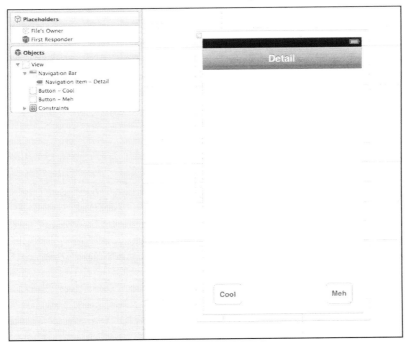

Note: By default, Xcode enables Auto Layout for all new nib files you create. This technology was added to make user interfaces easily resizable to fit different screen sizes – particularly the new dimensions of the iPhone 5 – and works on iOS 6 only. To make sure the Artists app still runs on iOS 5 as well, you should uncheck the Use Autolayout box in the nib's File Inspector.

Control-drag from each button to File's Owner and connect their Touch Up Inside events to their respective actions.

In DetailViewController.m, add the implementation of the two action methods to the bottom. For now leave these methods empty:

```
- (IBAction)coolAction
{
}

- (IBAction)mehAction
{
}
```

You will make some changes to the main view controller so that it invokes this Detail screen when you tap on a search result.

First, add an import to MainViewController.h (and not in the .m, for reasons that will become clear soon):

```
#import "DetailViewController.h"
```

Then in MainViewController.m, change the didSelectRowAtIndexPath to:

```
- (void)tableView:(UITableView *)theTableView
        didSelectRowAtIndexPath:(NSIndexPath *)indexPath
{
    [theTableView deselectRowAtIndexPath:indexPath animated:YES];

    DetailViewController *controller =
        [[DetailViewController alloc]
            initWithNibName:@"DetailViewController" bundle:nil];

    [self presentViewController:controller animated:YES
                    completion:nil];
}
```

This instantiates the DetailViewController and presents it on top of the current one.

Add the following method:

```objc
- (NSIndexPath *)tableView:(UITableView *)tableView
  willSelectRowAtIndexPath:(NSIndexPath *)indexPath
{
    if ([_searchResults count] == 0)
        return nil;
    else
        return indexPath;
}
```

If there are no search results the app puts a single row into the table that says "(Nothing found)". You don't want to open the Detail screen when the user taps that row.

If you run the app now, tapping on a row brings up the Detail screen, but you cannot close it yet. The actions that are wired to the "Cool" and "Meh" buttons are still empty and pressing the buttons has no effect.

To fix this, you will give the Detail screen a delegate. That's how you commonly make this type of arrangement work. If screen A invokes screen B, and screen B needs to tell A something – for example, that it needs to close – you make A the delegate of B. Certainly you've seen this pattern before as it's used throughout the iOS API.

Change DetailViewController.h to the following:

```objc
#import <UIKit/UIKit.h>

@class DetailViewController;
```

```
@protocol DetailViewControllerDelegate <NSObject>

- (void)detailViewController:(DetailViewController *)controller
      didPickButtonWithIndex:(NSInteger)buttonIndex;

@end

@interface DetailViewController : UIViewController

@property (nonatomic, weak) id <DetailViewControllerDelegate>
                                                       delegate;

- (IBAction)coolAction;
- (IBAction)mehAction;

@end
```

You've added a delegate protocol with a single method, as well as a property for that delegate. Notice that the property is declared "weak". Making the delegate pointer weak is necessary to prevent ownership cycles.

You may be familiar with the concept of a retain cycle, where two objects retain each other so neither will ever be deallocated. That's a common form of memory leak. In systems that employ garbage collection (GC) to handle their memory management, the garbage collector can recognize such cycles and release them anyway. But ARC is not garbage collection and for dealing with ownership cycles you're still on your own. The weak pointer is an important tool for breaking such cycles.

The MainViewController creates the DetailViewController and presents it on the screen. That gives it a strong reference to this object. The DetailViewController in turn has a reference to a delegate. It doesn't really care which object is its delegate but most of the time that will be the view controller that presented it, in other words MainViewController. So here is a situation where two objects point at each other:

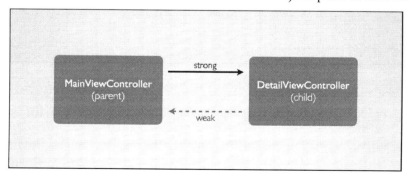

If both of these pointers were strong, then you would have an ownership cycle. It is best to prevent such cycles. The parent (MainViewController) owns the child (DetailViewController) through a strong pointer. If the child needs a reference back to the parent, through a delegate or otherwise, it should use a weak pointer.

Therefore, the rule is that delegates should be declared weak. Most of the time your properties and instance variables will be strong, but this is an exception.

In DetailViewController.m, change the action methods to:

```
- (IBAction)coolAction
{
    [self.delegate detailViewController:self
              didPickButtonWithIndex:0];
}

- (IBAction)mehAction
{
    [self.delegate detailViewController:self
              didPickButtonWithIndex:1];
}
```

In MainViewController.h, add DetailViewControllerDelegate to the @interface line:

```
@interface MainViewController : UIViewController
    <UITableViewDataSource, UITableViewDelegate,
     UISearchBarDelegate, NSXMLParserDelegate,
     DetailViewControllerDelegate>
```

(This is why you added the #import statement to the .h file earlier, instead of to the .m file, so that it knows about the DetailViewControllerDelegate protocol.)

In MainViewController.m, change didSelectRowAtIndexPath to set the delegate property:

```
- (void)tableView:(UITableView *)theTableView
      didSelectRowAtIndexPath:(NSIndexPath *)indexPath
{
    [theTableView deselectRowAtIndexPath:indexPath animated:YES];

    DetailViewController *controller =
        [[DetailViewController alloc]
          initWithNibName:@"DetailViewController" bundle:nil];

    controller.delegate = self;

    [self presentViewController:controller animated:YES
                    completion:nil];
```

```
}
```

And finally, add the following to the bottom:

```
#pragma mark - DetailViewControllerDelegate

- (void)detailViewController:(DetailViewController *)controller
    didPickButtonWithIndex:(NSInteger)buttonIndex
{
    NSLog(@"Picked button %d", buttonIndex);
    [self dismissViewControllerAnimated:YES completion:nil];
}
```

Here you simply dismiss the view controller. Run the app and try it out. Now you can press the Cool or Meh buttons to close the Detail screen.

Just to verify that `DetailViewController` gets released, give it a `dealloc` method that prints something to the Xcode debug pane:

```
- (void)dealloc
{
    NSLog(@"dealloc DetailViewController");
}
```

In this case you could actually get away with making the delegate property strong (try it out if you don't believe me). As soon as the `MainViewController` calls `dismiss-ViewControllerAnimated`, it loses the strong reference to `DetailViewController`. At that point there are no more pointers to that object and it will go away.

Still, it's a good idea to stick to the recommended pattern:

• parent pointing to a child: strong

• child pointing to a parent: weak

The child should not be helping to keep the parent alive. You'll see examples of ownership cycles that do cause problems when we talk about blocks in the Intermediate ARC chapter.

The devil is in the details

The Detail screen isn't very exciting yet but you can make it a little more interesting by putting the name of the selected artist in the navigation bar.

Add the following to DetailViewController.h:

```
@property (nonatomic, strong) NSString *artistName;
@property (nonatomic, weak) IBOutlet UINavigationBar
```

```
                                        *navigationBar;
```

The `artistName` property will contain the name of the selected artist. Previously you would have made this a `retain` property (or perhaps `copy`), so now it becomes `strong`.

The `navigationBar` property is an outlet. As before, outlets that are not top-level objects in the nib should be made weak so they are automatically released in low-memory situations on iOS 5 (but not on iOS 6).

There is no need to synthesize these properties as the LLVM compiler that comes with Xcode 4.5 automatically does that for you. Thank goodness for small favors. ☺

In DetailViewController.m, change `viewDidLoad` to:

```
- (void)viewDidLoad
{
    [super viewDidLoad];
    self.navigationBar.topItem.title = self.artistName;
}
```

Don't forget to connect the navigation bar from the nib file to the outlet! (Hint: ctrl-drag from File's Owner to the navigation bar.)

In MainViewController.m, change `didSelectRowAtIndexPath` to:

```
- (void)tableView:(UITableView *)theTableView
        didSelectRowAtIndexPath:(NSIndexPath *)indexPath
{
    [theTableView deselectRowAtIndexPath:indexPath animated:YES];

    NSString *artistName = _searchResults[indexPath.row];

    DetailViewController *controller =
        [[DetailViewController alloc]
            initWithNibName:@"DetailViewController" bundle:nil];

    controller.delegate = self;
    controller.artistName = artistName;

    [self presentViewController:controller animated:YES
                    completion:nil];
}
```

Run the app and you'll see the name of the artist in the navigation bar:

> **Note:** To read the artist name from the search results array, the code does:
>
> ```
> NSString *artistName = _searchResults[indexPath.row];
> ```
>
> This is a sweet new feature in Objective-C. You are probably used to calling the `[array objectAtIndex:]` method to index an `NSArray`, but with the latest LLVM compiler you can use the simpler `[ ]` notation instead.

Often developers use "`copy`" properties for objects of classes such as `NSString` and `NSArray`. This is done to make sure no one can change that object after you have put it into the property. Even though an `NSString` object is immutable once created, the actual object given to the property could be an `NSMutableString` that can be modified afterward.

Using the `copy` modifier is still possible with ARC. If you're slightly paranoid about your properties being truly immutable, then change the declaration of the `artistName` property to:

```
@property (nonatomic, copy) NSString *artistName;
```

By adding the `copy` modifier, it makes it so that when we assign to the property like this,

```
controller.artistName = artistName;
```

the app first makes a copy of the string object from the local variable and then stores that copy into the property. Other than that, this property works exactly the same way as a strong reference.

Let's see what happens when you log the values of `artistName` and `navigationBar` in the `dealloc` method in DetailViewController.m:

```
- (void)dealloc
{
    NSLog(@"dealloc DetailViewController");
    NSLog(@"artistName '%@'", self.artistName);
    NSLog(@"navigationBar %@", self.navigationBar);
}
```

Run the app and close the Detail screen, and you will see that both properties still have their values:

```
Artists[6989:c07] dealloc DetailViewController
Artists[6989:c07] artistName 'Evans, Bill'
Artists[6989:c07] navigationBar <UINavigationBar: 0x8142700;
frame = (0 0; 320 44); autoresize = W+BM; gestureRecognizers =
<NSArray: 0x8144370>; layer = <CALayer: 0x8141800>>
```

However, as soon as `dealloc` is over, these objects will be released and deallocated (since no one else is holding on to them). That is to say, the string object from `artistName` will be released and the `UINavigationBar` object is freed as part of the view hierarchy. The `navigationBar` property itself is weak and is therefore excluded from memory management.

Now that we have this second screen in the app, you can test what happens with the `MainViewController`'s view in low-memory situations. To do this, add some `NSLog()` statements to the `didReceiveMemoryWarning` method in MainViewController.m:

```
- (void)didReceiveMemoryWarning
{
    [super didReceiveMemoryWarning];
    _soundEffect = nil;

    NSLog(@"tableView %@", self.tableView);
    NSLog(@"searchBar %@", self.searchBar);
}
```

Run the app and open the Detail screen. Then from the Simulator's Hardware menu, choose **Simulate Memory Warning**. What you will see next in the Xcode debug pane depends on which version of iOS you're running the app.

On iOS 6, you will get the following output:

```
Artists[7049:c07] Received memory warning.
Artists[7049:c07] tableView <UITableView: 0x8a01000; ...>
Artists[7049:c07] searchBar <UISearchBar: 0x81abfd0; ...>
```

Because iOS 6 no longer unloads the views of any view controllers that are not visible, the UITableView and UISearchBar objects stay in memory. Simulate another memory warning and you should see the same pointer values in the debug output.

On iOS 5, however, the output looks like this:

```
Artists[7123:c07] Received memory warning.
Artists[7123:c07] tableView (null)
Artists[7123:c07] searchBar (null)
```

Because tableView and searchBar are weak properties, the UITableView and UISearchBar objects are only owned by the view hierarchy. As soon as the main view gets unloaded, it releases all its subviews. The view controller doesn't hold on to these views with strong pointers, so they get deleted before didReceiveMemoryWarning is invoked.

Note: This means there is a subtle difference between how iOS 5 and 6 handle these sorts of situations. On iOS 5 it is possible that your viewDidLoad method gets invoked for a second time when a previously unloaded view controller becomes visible again. If you want your app to behave the same way on iOS 6, then change the didReceiveMemoryWarning method to:

```
- (void)didReceiveMemoryWarning
{
    [super didReceiveMemoryWarning];
    _soundEffect = nil;

    if ([self isViewLoaded] && self.view.window == nil)
    {
        NSLog(@"forcing my view to unload");
        self.view = nil;
    }
}
```

Unsafe_unretained

We're almost done covering the basics of ARC – I just wanted to mention one more thing you should know.

Besides `strong` and `weak` there is another new modifier, `unsafe_unretained`. You typically don't want to use that. The compiler will add no automated retains or releases for variables or properties that are declared as `unsafe_unretained`.

The reason this new modifier has the word "unsafe" in its name is that it can point to an object that no longer exists. If you try to use such a pointer it's very likely your app will crash. This is the sort of thing you used the NSZombieEnabled debugging tool to find.

Technically speaking, if you don't use any `unsafe_unretained` properties or variables, you can never send messages to deallocated objects anymore.

Most of the time you want to use `strong`, sometimes `weak`, and almost never `unsafe_unretained`. The reason `unsafe_unretained` still exists is for compatibility with iOS 4, where the weak pointer system is not available, and for a few other tricks.

Let's see how this works. Change the properties in **MainViewController.h**:

```
@property (nonatomic, unsafe_unretained) IBOutlet UITableView
                                             *tableView;
@property (nonatomic, unsafe_unretained) IBOutlet UISearchBar
                                             *searchBar;
```

Make sure the `didReceiveMemoryWarning` method still has an `NSLog()` at the bottom:

```
- (void)didReceiveMemoryWarning
{
    . . .

    NSLog(@"tableView %@", self.tableView);
    NSLog(@"searchBar %@", self.searchBar);
}
```

Run the app and simulate the low-memory warning. You should try this on the iOS 5.x simulator for maximum effect:

```
Artists[982:207] Received memory warning.
Artists[982:207] *** -[UITableView retain]: message sent to
deallocated instance 0x7033200
```

Whoops, the app crashes. An `unsafe_unretained` pointer does not have ownership over the object it points to. That means the `UITableView` was not kept alive by this pointer and it got deallocated before `didReceiveMemoryWarning` was called (its only owner was the main view). If this were a true weak pointer, then its value would have been set to nil. Remember, that was the cool feature of "zeroing" weak pointers. You saw that earlier when the NSLog() said "(null)".

However, unlike a true weak pointer, an unsafe_unretained pointer is not reset to nil when the associated object dies. It keeps its old value. When you try to send a message to the object – which is what happens when you NSLog() it – you're sending the message to an object that no longer exists.

Sometimes this may accidentally work, if the memory for that object hasn't been overwritten yet by another object, but often it will crash your app... which is exactly what you saw happening here. That should illustrate why these things are called "unsafe".

> Note: This bug got caught because the active scheme for this project has enabled the Zombie Objects debug tool in the Diagnostics tab. To see this settings panel, choose **Product\Edit Scheme...** from the menu bar.

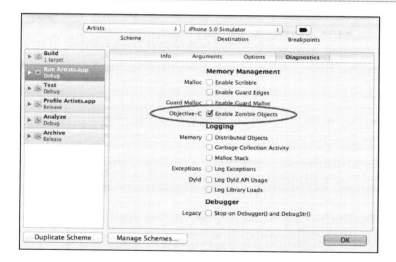

Without this setting, the app may not have crashed at all, or it may have crashed at some later point. Good luck trying to figure that one out! Those are tricky bugs to fix.

By the way, this is probably a good point to return the properties to weak:

```
@property (nonatomic, weak) IBOutlet UITableView *tableView;
@property (nonatomic, weak) IBOutlet UISearchBar *searchBar;
```

For ARC-enabled apps the Enable Zombie Objects setting (also known as NSZombieEnabled) isn't terribly useful anymore, so you can disable it... except when you're using unsafe_unretained pointers!

If it is so harmful then why use unsafe_unretained in the first place? A big reason is compatibility with iOS 4.

Using ARC on iOS 4

Because ARC is largely a new feature of the LLVM compiler and not specifically of iOS 5, you can also use it on iOS 4.0 and up. The only part of ARC that does require iOS 5 is the weak pointer system. That means if you wish to deploy your ARC app on iOS 4, you cannot use weak properties or __weak variables.

You don't need to do anything special to make your ARC project work on iOS 4. If you choose a version of iOS 4 as your Deployment Target, then the compiler will automatically insert a compatibility library ("ARCLite") into your project that makes the ARC functionality available on iOS 4. That's it, just pick iOS 4.x as the Deployment Target and you're done.

If you use weak references anywhere in your code, the compiler will give the following error:

```
"Error: the current deployment target does not support automated
 __weak references"
```

You cannot use weak or __weak on iOS 4, so replace weak properties with unsafe_unretained and __weak variables with __unsafe_unretained. Remember that these variables aren't set to nil when the referenced object is deallocated, so if you're not careful your variables may be pointing at objects that no longer exist. Be sure to test your app with NSZombieEnabled!

> **Tip:** The open source PLWeakCompatibility library is a cool hack that you can use to have your cake and eat it too! This library adds __weak support to iOS 4. Check it out at https://github.com/plausiblelabs/PLWeakCompatibility

Where To Go From Here?

Congratulations, you've covered the basics of ARC and are ready to start using it in your own new apps – and you know how to port your old ones!

If you want to learn more about ARC, stay tuned for the next chapter, where we'll cover:

- **Using blocks with ARC.** The rules for using blocks have changed a little. You need to take special care to avoid ownership cycles, the only memory problem that even ARC cannot take care of automatically.

- **How to make singletons with ARC.** You can no longer override `retain` and `release` to ensure your singleton classes can have only one instance, so how do you make singletons work with ARC?

- **More about autorelease.** All about `autorelease` and the autorelease pool.

- **Making games with ARC and Cocos2D.** Also explains how ARC fits in with Objective-C++, which you need to know if your game uses the Box2D physics engine.

- **Static libraries.** How to make your own static library to keep the ARC and non-ARC parts of your project separate.

Chapter 3: Intermediate ARC

By Matthijs Hollemans

At this point, you are pretty familiar with ARC and how to use it in new and existing projects.

However, ARC is such an important new aspect of iOS 5 development that there are several more aspects of ARC development that I thought you should know about.

So in this chapter, you're going to continue your investigations of ARC. We'll start by discussing how ARC and Blocks work together, continue with a discussion of autorelease and singletons, cover how to use ARC with the ever-popular Cocos2D and Box2D game frameworks, and end with a section on making your own static libraries.

This chapter continues where we left it off in the Beginning ARC chapter – you'll still be working with the Artists project. So open it in Xcode if you haven't already, and let's get started.

Blocks

Blocks and ARC go well together. In fact, ARC makes using blocks even easier than before. As you may know, blocks are initially created on the stack. If you wanted to keep a block alive beyond the current scope you had to copy it to the heap with [copy] or Block_copy() functions. ARC now takes care of that automatically.

However, a few things are different with blocks with ARC so we will go over those differences in this section.

You're going to add a new view to the Detail screen called AnimatedView. This is a UIView subclass that redraws itself several times per second. The drawing instructions are provided by a block and can be whatever you want. This makes it easy to create new animations without having to subclass the AnimatedView object.

Add a new Objective-C class file to the project named AnimatedView, subclass of UIView. Then replace the contents of AnimatedView.h with the following:

```
#import <UIKit/UIKit.h>

typedef void (^AnimatedViewBlock)(CGContextRef context, CGRect
    rect, CFTimeInterval totalTime, CFTimeInterval deltaTime);

@interface AnimatedView : UIView

@property (nonatomic, copy) AnimatedViewBlock block;

@end
```

The class has a single property, block. This is an Objective-C block that takes four parameters: context, rect, totalTime and deltaTime. The context and rect are for drawing, while the two time parameters can be used to determine by how big a step the animation should proceed.

Replace the contents of AnimatedView.m with the following:

```
#import "AnimatedView.h"

@implementation AnimatedView

- (void)dealloc
{
    NSLog(@"dealloc AnimatedView");
}

@end
```

The implementation doesn't do much yet. First you will hook up this class to the nib.

Open DetailViewController.xib and drag a new View object (a plain white view) into the view controller. Change the background color of the new view to Light Gray Color so you can actually see what you're doing, and set its dimensions to 280 by 280 points. The new layout should look something like this:

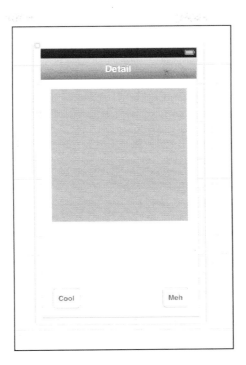

Select the new view and in the Identity inspector set its Class to AnimatedView. Now the DetailViewController will instantiate your view subclass for this view.

Add an outlet property for the view in DetailViewController.h. This should be a weak property because it is an outlet for a subview. Also add a forward declaration so the compiler knows that AnimatedView is an object:

```
@class AnimatedView;

. . .

@property (nonatomic, weak) IBOutlet AnimatedView *animatedView;
```

In DetailViewController.m, import the header:

```
#import "AnimatedView.h"
```

The final step is to go into Interface Builder and connect the view from the nib to this new outlet property. After you've done that, build and run the app to make sure everything still works.

When you close the Detail screen, the Xcode Debug pane should also say:

```
Artists[1389:207] dealloc AnimatedView
```

The NSLog() in dealloc is there to verify that the AnimatedView is truly deallocated when you're done with it. Even though ARC makes it nearly impossible for your apps to crash because you forgot a retain or over-released an object, you still need to be careful about memory leaks. Objects stay alive as long as they are being pointed to, and as you will soon see, sometimes those strong pointers aren't immediately obvious.

Let's make the view actually do something. AnimatedView will get a timer. Every time the timer fires it asks the view to redraw itself and inside the drawRect: method the view invokes the block to do the actual drawing.

These are the changes to AnimatedView.m:

```objc
#import <QuartzCore/QuartzCore.h>
#import "AnimatedView.h"

@implementation AnimatedView
{
    NSTimer *_timer;
    CFTimeInterval _startTime;
    CFTimeInterval _lastTime;
}

- (id)initWithCoder:(NSCoder *)aDecoder
{
    if ((self = [super initWithCoder:aDecoder]))
    {
        _timer = [NSTimer scheduledTimerWithTimeInterval:0.1
                        target:self
                     selector:@selector(handleTimer:)
                     userInfo:nil
                      repeats:YES];

        _startTime = _lastTime = CACurrentMediaTime();
    }
    return self;
}

- (void)dealloc
{
    NSLog(@"dealloc AnimatedView");
    [_timer invalidate];
}

- (void)handleTimer:(NSTimer*)timer
{
    [self setNeedsDisplay];
}

- (void)drawRect:(CGRect)rect
```

```
{
    CFTimeInterval now = CACurrentMediaTime();
    CFTimeInterval totalTime = now - _startTime;
    CFTimeInterval deltaTime = now - _lastTime;
    _lastTime = now;

    if (self.block != nil)
        self.block(UIGraphicsGetCurrentContext(), rect,
                   totalTime, deltaTime);
}

@end
```

The various "time" instance variables simply keep track of how much time has passed since the view was created and since the previous call to handleTimer. It's handy to know both how long the animation has been running and how much time has elapsed since the previous frame.

This implementation seems to make sense – you create the timer in initWithCoder: and stop the timer in dealloc – but already you're dealing with an ownership cycle. Run the app and close the Detail screen. Notice that the dealloc method from AnimatedView isn't called anymore. There is no NSLog() message in the output pane.

NSTimer apparently holds a strong reference to its target, which happens to be the AnimatedView object itself. So AnimatedView has a strong reference to NSTimer and NSTimer has a strong reference back to AnimatedView. Unless you explicitly release one of these objects, they will keep each other alive indefinitely.

You can break this particular retain cycle by adding a stopAnimation method. Change dealloc to the following and add stopAnimation:

```
- (void)stopAnimation
{
    [_timer invalidate], _timer = nil;
}

- (void)dealloc
{
    NSLog(@"dealloc AnimatedView");
}
```

Also add the method signature for the new method to the AnimatedView.h header:

```
- (void)stopAnimation;
```

Before the `AnimatedView` object gets released, the user of this class should call `stop-Animation`. In this app that becomes the responsibility of `DetailViewController`. Change the `dealloc` method from DetailViewController.m to the following:

```
- (void)dealloc
{
    NSLog(@"dealloc DetailViewController");
    [self.animatedView stopAnimation];
}
```

If you now run the app again, you'll see the `AnimatedView` does properly get deallocated when the Detail screen closes.

No doubt there are other ways to solve this ownership cycle. However, simply making the `_timer` instance variable weak doesn't work:

```
@implementation AnimatedView
{
    __weak NSTimer *_timer;
    CFTimeInterval _startTime;
    CFTimeInterval _lastTime;
}
```

This causes `AnimatedView` no longer to be the owner of the `NSTimer` object. But that won't do you any good. The `NSTimer` is still owned by another object, the run loop, and because the timer has a strong reference back to `AnimatedView`, it will keep `Animated-View` existing forever. The timer does not release its target until you invalidate it.

Let's make the view do some drawing. You're not going to make it animate just yet. It will simply draw the same thing – the name of the selected artist – over and over. In DetailViewController.m, change `viewDidLoad` to create the block with the drawing code and assign it to the `AnimatedView`:

```
- (void)viewDidLoad
{
    [super viewDidLoad];
    self.navigationBar.topItem.title = self.artistName;

    UIFont *font = [UIFont boldSystemFontOfSize:24.0f];
    CGSize textSize = [self.artistName sizeWithFont:font];

    self.animatedView.block = ^(CGContextRef context, CGRect
        rect, CFTimeInterval totalTime, CFTimeInterval deltaTime)
    {
        NSLog(@"totalTime %f, deltaTime %f", totalTime,
                                             deltaTime);
```

```
        CGPoint textPoint = CGPointMake(
            (rect.size.width - textSize.width)/2,
            (rect.size.height - textSize.height)/2);

        [self.artistName drawAtPoint:textPoint withFont:font];
    };
}
```

Outside the block you create a UIFont object and calculate how big the text will be when drawn. Inside the block you use the value from that textSize variable to center the text in the rectangle and then draw it. The NSLog() is there just to show you that this block is called every couple of milliseconds.

This looks innocuous enough but when you run the app you'll notice something is missing from the Debug output: not only will AnimatedView no longer be deallocated, neither will DetailViewController.

If you've used blocks before then you know the block captures the value of every variable that you use inside the block. If those variables are pointers, the block retains the objects they point to. That means the block retains self, i.e. the DetailViewController, because self.artistName is accessed inside the block.

As a result, DetailViewController will never be deallocated even after it gets closed because the block keeps holding on to it. The timer also keeps running because the app never got around to calling stopAnimation, although you don't see that in the Debug pane (because the view doesn't redraw anymore).

There are a few possible solutions to this problem. One is to not use self inside the block. That means you cannot access any properties, instance variables, or methods from the block. Local variables are fine. The reason you cannot use instance variables is that this does self->variable behind the scenes and therefore still refers to self.

For example, you could capture the artist name into a local variable and use that inside the block instead:

```
    NSString *text = self.artistName;

    self.animatedView.block = ^(CGContextRef context, CGRect
        rect, CFTimeInterval totalTime, CFTimeInterval deltaTime)
    {
        CGPoint textPoint = CGPointMake(
            (rect.size.width - textSize.width)/2,
            (rect.size.height - textSize.height)/2);

        [text drawAtPoint:textPoint withFont:font];
    };
```

This will work. All the values captured by the block are now local variables. Nothing refers to self and therefore the block will not capture a pointer to the DetailView-Controller. Run the app and notice that everything gets dealloc'd just fine.

Sometimes you can't avoid referring to self in the block. Before ARC, you could use the following trick:

```
__block DetailViewController *blockSelf = self;

self.animatedView.block = ^(CGContextRef context, CGRect
    rect, CFTimeInterval totalTime, CFTimeInterval deltaTime)
{
    . . .

    [blockSelf.artistName drawAtPoint:textPoint
                            withFont:font];
};
```

The block did not retain any variables prefixed with the __block keyword. Therefore, blockSelf.artistName could be used to access the artistName property without the block capturing the true self object.

Alas, this no longer works with ARC. Variables are strong by default, even if they are marked as __block variables. The only function of __block is to allow you to change captured variables (without __block, they are read-only).

The solution is to use a __weak variable instead:

```
__weak DetailViewController *weakSelf = self;

self.animatedView.block = ^(CGContextRef context, CGRect
    rect, CFTimeInterval totalTime, CFTimeInterval deltaTime)
{
    DetailViewController *strongSelf = weakSelf;
    if (strongSelf != nil)
    {
        NSLog(@"totalTime %f, deltaTime %f", totalTime,
                                            deltaTime);
        CGPoint textPoint = CGPointMake(
            (rect.size.width - textSize.width)/2,
            (rect.size.height - textSize.height)/2);

        [strongSelf.artistName drawAtPoint:textPoint
                                withFont:font];
    }
};
```

The weakSelf variable refers to self but does not retain it. You let the block capture weakSelf instead of self, so there is no ownership cycle. However, you shouldn't actually use weakSelf inside the block. Because this is a weak pointer, it will become nil when DetailViewController is deallocated.

While you are allowed to send messages to nil in Objective-C, it's still a good idea to check inside the block whether the object is still alive. Even better, by assigning the weak pointer to a new variable, strongSelf, you temporarily turn it into a strong reference so that the object cannot be destroyed out from under you while you're using it.

For the Artists app this is probably a bit of overkill. You could have simply used weakSelf and everything would have worked fine. After all, it is impossible for the DetailViewController to be deallocated before the AnimatedView, because AnimatedView is part of the controller's view hierarchy.

However, this may not be true in other situations. For example, if the block is used asynchronously then creating a strong reference to keep the object in question alive is a good idea. Additionally, if you were using the _artistName instance variable directly, you might have written something like this:

```
__weak DetailViewController *weakSelf = self;

self.animatedView.block = ^(CGContextRef context, CGRect
    rect, CFTimeInterval totalTime, CFTimeInterval deltaTime)
{
    . . .
    [weakSelf->_artistName drawAtPoint:textPoint
                             withFont:font];
}
```

This works fine until the DetailViewController is deallocated and weakSelf becomes nil. Sending messages to nil works fine, including accessing nil properties, but doing nil->artistName will definitely crash your app!

Therefore, if you're using blocks with ARC and you want to avoid capturing self, the following pattern is recommended:

```
__weak id weakSelf = self;
block = ^()
{
    id strongSelf = weakSelf;
    if (strongSelf != nil)
    {
        // do stuff with strongSelf
    }
};
```

If you're targeting iOS 4, you cannot use __weak. Instead do:

```
__block __unsafe_unretained id unsafeSelf = self;
```

Note that in this case you will never know if `unsafeSelf` still points to a valid object because unlike __weak pointers, __unsafe_unretained pointers do not automatically get set to nil (that's why they are "unsafe"). You will need to take additional steps to make sure the pointer is still valid before you dereference it. If you don't, get ready to face the zombies!

> Note: Even though ARC takes care to copy blocks to the heap when you assign them to instance variables or return them, there are still a few situations where you need to copy blocks manually. In the @property declaration for the block you specified the ownership qualifier copy instead of strong. If you try it with strong, the app might crash when you open the Detail screen. You may run into other situations in your apps where just passing a block crashes the whole thing. In that case, see if [block copy] makes any difference.

On the whole, writing ARC code is exactly the same as what you did before except now you don't call `retain` and `release`. But this can also introduce subtle bugs that were not there before, because removing the call to `retain`, `release` or `autorelease` can mean the block no longer captures an object and therefore the object may not stay alive for as long as you think it does.

Take an imaginary class, `DelayedOperation`. It waits for "delay" number of seconds and then executes the block. Inside the block you could previously call `autorelease` to free the `DelayedOperation` instance. Because the block captures the `operation` instance and thereby keeps it alive, this pattern worked without problems before ARC.

```
DelayedOperation *operation = [[DelayedOperation alloc]
      initWithDelay:5 block:^
{
    NSLog(@"Performing operation");

    // do stuff

    [operation autorelease];
}];
```

However, with ARC you can no longer call `autorelease` and the code becomes:

```
DelayedOperation *operation = [[DelayedOperation alloc]
      initWithDelay:5 block:^
  {
```

```
    NSLog(@"Performing operation");

    // do stuff
}];
```

Guess what, the block will never execute. The `DelayedOperation` instance is destroyed as soon as it is created because there is nothing holding on to it. Converting this to ARC has actually introduced a bug! Very sneaky...

One way to fix this is to capture the `operation` instance and set it to nil when you're done:

```
__block DelayedOperation *operation = [[DelayedOperation alloc]
    initWithDelay:5 block:^
{
    NSLog(@"Performing operation");

    // do stuff

    operation = nil;
}];
```

Now the block keeps the object alive again. Notice that the `operation` variable must be declared as `__block` because you're changing its value inside the block.

Singletons

If your apps use singletons, their implementation may have these methods:

```
+ (id)allocWithZone:(NSZone *)zone
{
    return [[self sharedInstance] retain];
}

- (id)copyWithZone:(NSZone *)zone
{
    return self;
}

- (id)retain
{
    return self;
}

- (NSUInteger)retainCount
{
```

```
        return NSUIntegerMax;
    }

    - (oneway void)release
    {
        // empty
    }

    - (id)autorelease
    {
        return self;
    }
```

In this common singleton recipe, methods such as `retain` and `release` are overridden so that it is impossible to make more than one instance of this object. After all, that's what a singleton is, an object that can have no more than a single instance.

With ARC this will no longer work. Not only can you not call `retain` and `release`, but also you're not allowed to override these methods.

In my opinion, the above is not a very useful pattern anyway. How often does it happen that you truly want only a single instance of an object? It's easier to use a variation of the singleton pattern that I've heard someone call the "Interesting Instance Pattern". That is what Apple uses in their APIs as well. You typically access this preferred instance through a `sharedInstance` or `defaultInstance` class method, but if you wanted to you could make your own instances as well.

Whether that is a good thing or not for your own singletons can be documented or made a matter of convention. For certain singleton classes from the iOS API, having the ability to make your own instances is actually a feature, such as with **NSNotification-Center**.

To demonstrate the preferred way of making singletons, you're going to add one to our app. Add a new **NSObject subclass** to the project and name it **GradientFactory**.

Replace the contents of **GradientFactory.h** with:

```
@interface GradientFactory : NSObject

+ (id)sharedInstance;

- (CGGradientRef)newGradientWithColor1:(UIColor *)color1
                                color2:(UIColor *)color2
                                color3:(UIColor *)color3
                              midpoint:(CGFloat)midpoint;

@end
```

This class has a `sharedInstance` class method that is to be used to access it, and a `newGradient` method that returns a `CGGradientRef` object. You could still `[[alloc] init]` your own instance of `GradientFactory`, but convention says you shouldn't.

In GradientFactory.m, add the implementation of the `sharedInstance` method:

```
#import "GradientFactory.h"

@implementation GradientFactory

+ (id)sharedInstance
{
    static GradientFactory *sharedInstance;
    if (sharedInstance == nil)
    {
        sharedInstance = [[GradientFactory alloc] init];
    }
    return sharedInstance;
}
```

This is really all you need to do to make a singleton. The `sharedInstance` method uses a static local variable to track whether an instance already exists. If not, it makes one.

Note that you don't have to explicitly set the variable to nil:

```
static GradientFactory *sharedInstance = nil;
```

With ARC, all pointer variables are `nil` by default. Before ARC this was only true for instance variables and statics, not local variables. If you did something like this,

```
- (void)myMethod
{
    int someNumber;
    NSLog(@"Number: %d", someNumber);

    NSString *someString;
    NSLog(@"String: %p", someString);
}
```

then Xcode complained – "Variable is uninitialized when used here" – and the output would be random numbers:

```
Number: 67
String: 0x4babb5
```

With ARC, however, the output is:

```
Number: 10120117
String: 0x0
```

The int still contains some garbage value (and using it in this fashion issues a compiler warning) but the initial value of someString is nil. That's great because now it has become nearly impossible to use a pointer that doesn't point at a valid object.

Let's finish the implementation of GradientFactory. Add the following method:

```
- (CGGradientRef)newGradientWithColor1:(UIColor *)color1
                                color2:(UIColor *)color2
                                color3:(UIColor *)color3
                              midpoint:(CGFloat)midpoint
{
    NSArray *colors = @[ (id)color1.CGColor, (id)color2.CGColor,
                         (id)color3.CGColor ];

    const CGFloat locations[3] = { 0.0f, midpoint, 1.0f };

    CGColorSpaceRef colorSpace = CGColorSpaceCreateDeviceRGB();
    CGGradientRef gradient = CGGradientCreateWithColors(
            colorSpace, (__bridge CFArrayRef)colors, locations);
    CGColorSpaceRelease(colorSpace);

    return gradient;
}
```

This creates a gradient with three colors, two on the outer edges of the gradient and one in the middle. The position of the midpoint is flexible, and you'll use that to create a simple animation later.

The CGGradientCreateWithColors() function from Core Graphics is used to construct the gradient. This takes a pointer to a CGColorSpaceRef object, an array of CGColorRef objects, and an array of CGFloats. The colors array is a CFArrayRef object, but the locations array is a straight C-array. Creating the colorSpace object and the array of locations is pretty straightforward.

However, for the colors array it's much nicer to use an NSArray rather than a CFArrayRef. Thanks to toll-free bridging, you can write:

```
NSArray *colors = @[ (id)color1.CGColor, (id)color2.CGColor,
                     (id)color3.CGColor ];
```

The colors array should contain CGColorRef objects. The parameters to the newGradientWithColor… method are UIColor objects, so first you have to convert them. UIColor and CGColorRef are NOT toll-free bridged, so you cannot simply cast them. Instead, UIColor has a .CGColor property that returns a CGColorRef object.

Because NSArray can only hold Objective-C objects, not Core Foundation objects, you have to cast that CGColorRef back to an id. That works because all Core Foundation object types are toll-free bridged with `NSObject`, but only in regards to memory handling. So you can treat a `CGColor` as an `NSObject`, but not as a `UIColor`.

This might be terribly confusing, but that's what you get when you mix two different types of framework architectures.

Of course, the `CGGradientCreateWithColors()` function doesn't accept an `NSArray` so you need to cast colors to a `CFArrayRef` to do toll-free bridging the other way around. This time, however, a bridged cast is necessary. The compiler can't figure out by itself whether ownership of the object should change or not. In this case you still want to keep ARC responsible for releasing the `NSArray` object, so a simple `__bridge` cast serves to indicate that no transfer of ownership is taking place.

```
CGGradientRef gradient = CGGradientCreateWithColors(
        colorSpace, (__bridge CFArrayRef)colors, locations);
```

No `__bridge` statement was necessary when you casted the `CGColorRef` objects to `id` earlier. The compiler was able to figure out by itself what the proper rules were. (It will automatically retain the color objects for as long as the array exists, just like any object that you put into an `NSArray`.)

Finally, the app returns the new `CGGradientRef` object. Note that the caller of this method is responsible for releasing this gradient object. It is a Core Foundation object and therefore is not handled by ARC. Whoever calls the `newGradient` method is responsible for calling `CGGradientRelease()` on the gradient, or the app will leak memory. (And a lot of it too as you will be calling this method from the animation block that runs several times per second.)

The `newGradient` method has the word "new" in its name. That is not for nothing. The Cocoa naming rules say that methods whose name starts with `alloc`, `init`, `new`, `copy` or `mutableCopy` transfer ownership of the returned object to the caller.

To be honest, if your entire code base uses ARC then these naming conventions aren't important at all. The compiler will do the right thing anyway. But it's still a good idea to let the users of your classes and methods know that you expect them to release the objects manually if you're returning Core Foundation objects or `malloc()`'d buffers.

> Note: I still urge you to respect the Cocoa naming conventions, even though they are inconsequential when your entire project compiles as ARC. The names of methods are still important when *not* every file in your project is ARC, such as in this example project. For non-ARC code and ARC code to properly interoperate, sticking to the Cocoa naming conventions is essential.

Suppose you have a method in a non-ARC file that is named `newWidget` and it returns an autoreleased string rather than a retained one. If you use that method from ARC code then ARC will try to release the returned object and your app will crash on an over-release.

It's better to rename that method to `createWidget` or `makeWidget` so that ARC knows there is no need to release anything. (Alternatively, if you can't change the name, use the `NS_RETURNS_NOT_RETAINED` or `NS_RETURNS_RETAINED` annotations to tell the compiler about the non-standard behavior of these methods.)

You have to be really careful with mixing Core Foundation and Objective-C objects. Spot the bug in the following code snippet:

```
CGColorRef cgColor1 = [[UIColor alloc] initWithRed:1 green:0
                                            blue:0 alpha:1].CGColor;
CGColorRef cgColor2 = [[UIColor alloc] initWithRed:0 green:1
                                            blue:0 alpha:1].CGColor;
CGColorRef cgColor3 = [[UIColor alloc] initWithRed:0 green:0
                                            blue:1 alpha:1].CGColor;

NSArray *colors = @[ (__bridge id)cgColor1,
                     (__bridge id)cgColor2,
                     (__bridge id)cgColor3 ];
```

If you do this in your app it will crash. The reason is simple: you create a `UIColor` object that is not autoreleased but retained (because you call alloc + init). As soon as there are no strong pointers to this object, it gets deallocated. Because a `CGColorRef` is not an Objective-C object, the `cgColor1` variable does not qualify as a strong pointer. The new `UIColor` object is immediately released after it is created and `cgColor1` points at garbage memory. Yikes!

You can't solve it like this either:

```
CGColorRef cgColor1 = [UIColor colorWithRed:1 green:0 blue:0
                                     alpha:1].CGColor;
```

Because you now allocate the `UIColor` object using a method that appears to return an autoreleased object, you would think it stays alive until the autorelease pool is flushed. But there is no guarantee that the compiler actually gives you an autoreleased object, so you shouldn't depend on this.

> Note: The "getting a `CGColor` from a `UIColor` crashes my app" problem is probably the number one most common issue that people run into when switching an existing codebase to ARC. What's worse, the above code snippet appears to work fine on the simulator but crashes when run on a device!

The safest solution is to keep the `UIColor` object alive using a strong pointer:

```
UIColor *color1 = [UIColor colorWithRed:1 green:0 blue:0
                                  alpha:1];

. . . and use it later as color1.CGColor
```

If you don't want to worry about these weird situations, then mix and match as little with Core Foundation as possible. :-)

Enough theory. Let's put this `GradientFactory` to work in a silly animation example. Go to DetailViewController.m and add an import:

```
#import "GradientFactory.h"
```

Change `viewDidLoad` to:

```
- (void)viewDidLoad
{
    [super viewDidLoad];
    self.navigationBar.topItem.title = self.artistName;

    UIFont *font = [UIFont boldSystemFontOfSize:24.0f];
    CGSize textSize = [self.artistName sizeWithFont:font];

    float components[9];
    NSUInteger length = [self.artistName length];
    NSString* lowercase = [self.artistName lowercaseString];

    for (int t = 0; t < 9; ++t)
    {
        unichar c = [lowercase characterAtIndex:t % length];
        components[t] = ((c * (10 - t)) & 0xFF) / 255.0f;
    }

    UIColor *color1 = [UIColor colorWithRed:components[0]
            green:components[3] blue:components[6] alpha:1.0f];
    UIColor *color2 = [UIColor colorWithRed:components[1]
            green:components[4] blue:components[7] alpha:1.0f];
    UIColor *color3 = [UIColor colorWithRed:components[2]
            green:components[5] blue:components[8] alpha:1.0f];
```

```
    __weak DetailViewController *weakSelf = self;

    self.animatedView.block = ^(CGContextRef context, CGRect
        rect, CFTimeInterval totalTime, CFTimeInterval deltaTime)
    {
        DetailViewController *strongSelf = weakSelf;
        if (strongSelf != nil)
        {
            CGPoint startPoint = CGPointMake(0.0, 0.0);
            CGPoint endPoint = CGPointMake(0.0,
                                           rect.size.height);
            CGFloat midpoint = 0.5f + (sinf(totalTime))/2.0f;

            CGGradientRef gradient =
                [[GradientFactory sharedInstance]
                    newGradientWithColor1:color1 color2:color2
                            color3:color3 midpoint:midpoint];

            CGContextDrawLinearGradient(context, gradient,
                startPoint, endPoint,
                kCGGradientDrawsBeforeStartLocation |
                kCGGradientDrawsAfterEndLocation);

            CGGradientRelease(gradient);

            CGPoint textPoint = CGPointMake(
                (rect.size.width - textSize.width)/2,
                (rect.size.height - textSize.height)/2);

            [strongSelf.artistName drawAtPoint:textPoint
                                      withFont:font];
        }
    };
}
```

What happens here may look complicated but basically it takes the name of the artist and uses that to derive three colors. Each color contains three components (red, green, blue) so that makes nine color components in total. First it loops through the name of the artist, converted to lowercase, and transforms each character into a value between 0.0f and 1.0f using a basic formula:

```
    float components[9];
    NSUInteger length = [self.artistName length];
    NSString* lowercase = [self.artistName lowercaseString];

    for (int t = 0; t < 9; ++t)
    {
        unichar c = [lowercase characterAtIndex:t % length];
```

```
    components[t] = ((c * (10 - t)) & 0xFF) / 255.0f;
}
```

It then turns these color components into `UIColor` objects:

```
UIColor *color1 = [UIColor colorWithRed:components[0]
        green:components[3] blue:components[6] alpha:1.0f];
UIColor *color2 = [UIColor colorWithRed:components[1]
        green:components[4] blue:components[7] alpha:1.0f];
UIColor *color3 = [UIColor colorWithRed:components[2]
        green:components[5] blue:components[8] alpha:1.0f];
```

This can all be done outside of the block because it only needs to happen once. Inside the block it does the trick with `weakSelf` and `strongSelf` again and then calculates the start and end points for the gradient:

```
CGPoint startPoint = CGPointMake(0.0, 0.0);
CGPoint endPoint = CGPointMake(0.0,
                               rect.size.height);
CGFloat midpoint = 0.5f + (sinf(totalTime))/2.0f;
```

The midpoint moves up and down between the start and end points. The sine function is used to ease the animation in and out.

Now that the colors and the midpoint position are calculated, the new gradient object can be created:

```
CGGradientRef gradient =
    [[GradientFactory sharedInstance]
        newGradientWithColor1:color1 color2:color2
                    color3:color3 midpoint:midpoint];
```

The code accesses the `GradientFactory` object through the `sharedInstance` class method and then calls `newGradient`. Thanks to the singleton pattern, the very first time it does this a new instance of `GradientFactory` is created, but for every time after that the app simply re-uses that same instance.

Then a Core Graphics function draws that gradient between the start and end points:

```
CGContextDrawLinearGradient(context, gradient,
    startPoint, endPoint,
    kCGGradientDrawsBeforeStartLocation |
    kCGGradientDrawsAfterEndLocation);
```

And finally, the gradient object is released:

```
CGGradientRelease(gradient);
```

Remember that this release is necessary because ARC does not concern itself with Core Foundation objects, only Objective-C objects. You still need to do manual memory management when you're dealing with Core Foundation!

Here is an example of what the animation looks like. Every artist has its own colors:

If your singleton can be used from multiple threads then the simple `sharedInstance` accessor method does not suffice. A more sturdy implementation is this:

```
+ (id)sharedInstance
{
    static GradientFactory *sharedInstance;
    static dispatch_once_t done;

    dispatch_once(&done, ^
    {
        sharedInstance = [[GradientFactory alloc] init];
    });

    return sharedInstance;
}
```

Replace `sharedInstance` from `GradientFactory.m` with this method. This uses the `dispatch_once()` function from the Grand Central Dispatch library to ensure that `alloc` and `init` are truly executed only once, even if multiple threads at a time try to perform this block.

And that's it for singletons.

Autorelease

You have already seen that autorelease and the autorelease pool are still used with ARC, although it's now a language construct rather than a class (@autoreleasepool).

Methods basically always return an autoreleased object, except when the name of the method begins with alloc, init, new, copy or mutableCopy, in which case they return a retained object. That's still the same as it was with manual memory management. (It needs to be because ARC code needs to be able to play nice with non-ARC code.)

A retained object is deallocated as soon as there are no more variables pointing to it, but an autoreleased object is only deallocated when the autorelease pool is drained. Previously you had to call [drain] (or release) on the NSAutoreleasePool object, but now the pool is automatically drained at the end of the @autoreleasepool block:

```
@autoreleasepool
{
    NSString *s = [NSString stringWithFormat:. . .];
}

// the string object is deallocated when the code gets here
```

Contrast the above with this:

```
NSString *s;

@autoreleasepool
{
    s = [NSString stringWithFormat:. . .];
}

// the string object is still alive here
```

Even though the NSString object was created inside the @autoreleasepool block and was returned autoreleased from the stringWithFormat: method (it doesn't have alloc, init or new in its name), you store the string object in local variable s, and that is a strong pointer. As long as s is in scope, the string object stays alive.

There is a way to make the string object in the previous example be deallocated by the autorelease pool:

```
__autoreleasing NSString *s;
```

```
@autoreleasepool
{
    s = [NSString stringWithFormat:. . .];
}

// the string object is deallocated at this point

NSLog(@"%@", s);  // crash!
```

The special __autoreleasing keyword tells the compiler that this variable's contents may be autoreleased. Now it no longer is a strong pointer and the string object will be deallocated at the end of the @autoreleasepool block. Note, however, that s will keep its value and now points at a dead object. If you were to send a message to s afterwards, the app will crash.

You will hardly ever need to use __autoreleasing, but you might come across it in the case of out-parameters or pass-by-reference, especially with methods that take an (NSError **) parameter.

Let's add one last feature to the app to demonstrate this. When the user presses the Cool button you're going to capture the contents of the AnimatedView and save this image to a PNG file.

In DetailViewController.m, add the following method:

```
- (NSString *)documentsDirectory
{
    NSArray *paths = NSSearchPathForDirectoriesInDomains(
                    NSDocumentDirectory, NSUserDomainMask, YES);
    return [paths lastObject];
}
```

Also add an import for QuartzCore at the top:

```
#import <QuartzCore/QuartzCore.h>
```

And replace coolAction: with the following:

```
- (IBAction)coolAction
{
    UIGraphicsBeginImageContext(self.animatedView.bounds.size);
    [self.animatedView.layer renderInContext:
                                UIGraphicsGetCurrentContext()];
    UIImage *image =
                UIGraphicsGetImageFromCurrentImageContext();
    UIGraphicsEndImageContext();
```

```
NSData *data = UIImagePNGRepresentation(image);
if (data != nil)
{
    NSString *filename = [[self documentsDirectory]
                stringByAppendingPathComponent:@"Cool.png"];

    NSError *error;
    if (![data writeToFile:filename
                options:NSDataWritingAtomic error:&error])
    {
        NSLog(@"Error: %@", error);
    }
}

[self.delegate detailViewController:self
            didPickButtonWithIndex:0];
}
```

The revised coolAction: method is quite straightforward. First it captures the contents of the AnimatedView into a new UIImage object:

```
UIGraphicsBeginImageContext(self.animatedView.bounds.size);
[self.animatedView.layer renderInContext:
                            UIGraphicsGetCurrentContext()];
UIImage *image =
            UIGraphicsGetImageFromCurrentImageContext();
UIGraphicsEndImageContext();
```

Then it turns that image into a PNG file, which gives you an NSData object. It also creates the output filename, which is "Cool.png" inside the app's Documents folder.

```
NSData *data = UIImagePNGRepresentation(image);
if (data != nil)
{
    NSString *filename = [[self documentsDirectory]
                stringByAppendingPathComponent:@"Cool.png"];
```

The writeToFile method from NSData accepts a pointer to a variable for an NSError object, in other words an (NSError **). Yes, that is two stars! If there is some kind of error, the method will create a new NSError object and store that into your error variable. This is also known as an out-parameter and it's often used to return more than one value from a method or function.

In this case writeToFile already returns YES or NO to indicate success or failure. Upon failure, it also returns an NSError object with more information in the out-parameter.

```
NSError *error;
if (![data writeToFile:filename
```

```
                            options:NSDataWritingAtomic error:&error])
        {
            NSLog(@"Error: %@", error);
        }
```

If you type in the code by hand you'll get an auto-complete popup. There you'll see that this `NSError **` parameter is actually specified as `NSError *__autoreleasing *`:

```
    NSData *data = UIImagePNGRepresentation(image);
    if (data != nil)
    {
        NSString *filename = [[self documentsDirectory] stringByAppendingPathComponent:@"Cool.png"];

        NSError* error;
        if (![data writeToFile:(NSString *) options:(NSDataWritingOptions) error:(NSError *__autoreleasing *)
    }
        M  BOOL writeToFile:(NSString *) atomically:(BOOL)
    [self.d M  BOOL writeToFile:(NSString *) options:(NSDataWritingOptions) error:(NSError *__autoreleasing *) ?
}      M  BOOL writeToURL:(NSURL *) atomically:(BOOL)
- (IBAction M  BOOL writeToURL:(NSURL *) options:(NSDataWritingOptions) error:(NSError *__autoreleasing *)
{
    [self.delegate detailViewController:self didPickButtonWithIndex:1];
}
```

This is a common pattern for implementing out-parameters with ARC. It tells the compiler that the `NSError` object that is returned from `writeToFile` must be treated as an autoreleased object. Typically you don't have to worry about this. As you can see in the code above you've never actually used the `__autoreleasing` keyword anywhere. The compiler will figure this out automatically.

You only need to use `__autoreleasing` when you're writing your own method that needs to return an out-parameter, or when you have a performance problem.

When you write this:

```
NSError *error;
```

then you implicitly say that the error variable is `__strong`. However, if you then pass the address of that variable into the `writeToFile` method, you want to treat it as an `__autoreleasing` variable. These two statements cannot both be true; a variable is either strong or autoreleasing, not both at the same time.

To resolve this situation the compiler makes a new temporary variable. Under the hood the above code actually looks like this:

```
NSError *error;
__autoreleasing NSError *temp = error;
BOOL result = ![data writeToFile:filename
                    options:NSDataWritingAtomic error:&temp];
error = temp;

if (!result)
```

```
{
    NSLog(@"Error: %@", error);
}
```

Generally speaking, this extra temporary variable is no big deal. But if you want to avoid it you can write the code as follows:

```
__autoreleasing NSError *error;
if (![data writeToFile:filename options:NSDataWritingAtomic
                                   error:&error])
{
    NSLog(@"Error: %@", error);
}
```

Now the type of your local error variable is the same as the type of writeToFile's error parameter and no conversion is necessary. Personally, I wouldn't use the __autoreleasing keyword in situations such as these. Your code will work fine without it and in most cases the above is an unnecessary optimization.

To write your own method that needs to return an out-parameter, you would do something like this:

```
- (NSString *)fetchKeyAndValue:
                     (__autoreleasing NSNumber **)value
{
    NSString *theKey;
    NSString *theValue;

    // do whatever you need to do here

    *value = theValue;
    return theKey;
}
```

This returns an NSString object the regular way and places an NSNumber object in the out-parameter. You would call this method as follows:

```
NSNumber *value;
NSString *key = [self fetchKeyAndValue:&value];
```

The default ownership qualifier for out-parameters is __autoreleasing, by the way, so you could have written the method simply as follows:

```
- (NSString *)fetchKeyAndValue:(NSNumber **)value
{
    . . .
}
```

Note that you are not required to specify __autoreleasing for the out-parameter. If instead you did not want to put the object into the autorelease pool, you could declare the out-parameter __strong:

```
- (NSString *)fetchKeyAndValue:(__strong NSNumber **)value
{
    . . .
}
```

For ARC it doesn't matter whether out-parameters are autoreleased or strong, it will do the right thing anyway. However, if you want to use this method from non-ARC code, the compiler expects you to do a manual [release] on the returned object. Forgetting to do so will result in a memory leak, so be sure to document it properly when your methods return retained objects through out-parameters!

One thing to be aware of is that some API methods can use their own autorelease pool. For example, NSDictionary's enumerateKeysAndObjectsUsingBlock: method first sets up an autorelease pool before it calls your block. That means any autoreleased objects you create in that block will be released by NSDictionary's pool. That usually is exactly what you want to happen, except in the following situation:

```
- (void)loopThroughDictionary:(NSDictionary *)d
                        error:(NSError **)error
{
    [d enumerateKeysAndObjectsUsingBlock:^(
                                  id key, id obj, BOOL *stop)
    {
        // do stuff . . .

        if (there is some error && error != nil)
        {
            *error = [NSError errorWithDomain:@"MyError" code:1
                                    userInfo:nil];
        }
    }];
}
```

The error variable is intended to be autoreleased because it is an out-parameter. Because enumerateKeysAndObjectsUsingBlock: has its own autorelease pool, any new error object that you create will be deallocated long before the method returns.

To solve this problem you use a temporary strong variable to hold the NSError object:

```
- (void)loopThroughDictionary:(NSDictionary *)d
                        error:(NSError **)error
{
```

```
__block NSError *temp;

[d enumerateKeysAndObjectsUsingBlock:^(
                            id key, id obj, BOOL *stop)
    {
        // do stuff . . .

        if (there is some error)
        {
            temp = [NSError errorWithDomain:@"MyError" code:1
                            userInfo:nil];
        }
    }];

    if (error != nil)
        *error = temp;
}
```

Autoreleased objects may stick around for longer than you want. The autorelease pool is emptied after each UI event (e.g. tap on a button) but if your event handler does a lot of processing – for example in a loop that creates a lot of objects – you can set up your own autorelease pool to prevent the app from running out of memory:

```
for (int i = 0; i < 1000000; i++)
{
    @autoreleasepool
    {
        NSString *s = [NSString stringWithFormat:. . .];

        // do stuff . . .
    }
}
```

In older code you sometimes see special trickery to empty the autorelease pool every X iterations of the loop. That is because people believed that NSAutoreleasePool was slow (it wasn't) and that draining it on every iteration would not be very efficient. Well, that's no longer possible. Nor is it necessary because @autoreleasepool is about six times faster than NSAutoreleasePool was, so plugging an @autoreleasepool block into a tight loop should not slow down your app at all.

Note: If you're creating a new thread you also still need to wrap your code in an autorelease pool using the @autorelease syntax. The principle hasn't changed, just the syntax.

ARC has a bunch of further optimizations for autoreleased objects as well. Most of your code consists of methods that return autoreleased objects, but often there is no need for these objects to end up in the autorelease pool. Suppose you do something like this:

```
NSString *str = [NSString stringWithFormat:. . .];
```

The stringWithFormat method returns an autoreleased object. But str here is a strong local variable. When str goes out of scope, the string object can be destroyed. There is no need to also put the string object in the autorelease pool. ARC recognizes this pattern and through some magic will now not autorelease the object at all. So not only is @autoreleasepool faster, a lot fewer objects end up in it!

> **Note:** There is no such thing as autoreleasing a Core Foundation object. The principle of autorelease is purely an Objective-C thing. Some people have found ways to autorelease CF objects anyway by first casting them to an id, then calling autorelease, and then casting them back again:
>
> ```
> return (CGImageRef)[(id)myImage autorelease];
> ```
>
> That obviously won't work anymore because you cannot call autorelease with ARC. If you really feel like you need to be able to autorelease Core Foundation objects, then you can make your own CFAutorelease() function and put it in a file that gets compiled with -fno-objc-arc.

Cocos2D and Box2D

So far we've just talked about ARC and UIKit-based apps. The same rules apply to Cocos2D games, of course, but because the current version of Cocos2D is not 100% compatible with ARC I will explain how to put it into your ARC-based games.

For this part of the chapter I have prepared some starter code, based on the tutorial How to Create a Simple Breakout Game with Box2D and Cocos2D from raywenderlich.com. You can find the original tutorial here:

- Part 1: http://www.raywenderlich.com/475/how-to-create-a-simple-breakout-game-with-box2d-and-cocos2d-tutorial-part-12

- Part 2: http://www.raywenderlich.com/505/how-to-create-a-simple-breakout-game-with-box2d-and-cocos2d-tutorial-part-22

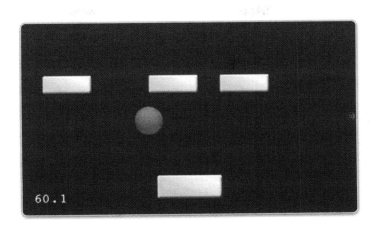

The code from this project is adapted to the latest available version of Cocos2D 1.x at the time of writing (v1.1 beta 2).

> **Note:** The previous edition of this book used the stable version 1.0.1 of Cocos2D, but that is out-of-date now and no longer compiles cleanly with the latest LLVM compiler and SDK. It also required extensive changes to the Cocos2D source itself to make it play nice with ARC.
>
> Fortunately, with v1.1 these changes are no longer necessary and integrating Cocos2D in your ARC-enabled games is much easier. There is also a new 2.x branch that is a complete rewrite of Cocos2D using OpenGL ES 2.0. For new projects, version 2.x is probably the version you would use, and the principles of putting Cocos2D v2.x into your ARC projects are the same as for v1.1.

You can find the starter code with this chapter's resources. This is a simple project that uses Cocos2D and Box2D to make a ball & paddle game. Because Box2D is written in C++, most of the game's source code files are Objective-C++ (they have a .mm file extension).

The starter code does not include Cocos2D, so first you need to install that. Download the complete package from:

- http://cocos2d-iphone.googlecode.com/files/cocos2d-iphone-1.1-beta2b.tar.gz

You may also download a newer version from the v1.x branch but there could be slight differences with the descriptions that follow.

After the download is complete, unzip the package. Inside the new Cocos2D folder you will find a file named `cocos2d-ios.xcodeproj`. Drag this file into Xcode so that the `cocos2d-ios` project becomes part of the Breakout project:

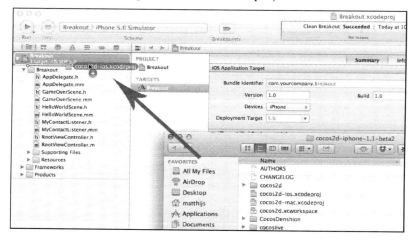

The result is a project inside a project:

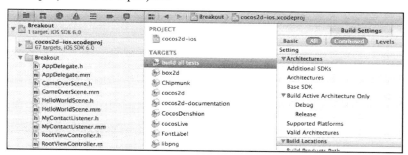

The cocos2d-ios project contains targets for a number of static libraries and tests. You will now add some of these libraries to the Breakout project.

Breakout already links with the following system frameworks:

- AVFoundation

- AudioToolbox

- CoreGraphics

- Foundation

- OpenAL

- OpenGLES

- QuartzCore

- UIKit

- libz

I mention this because you will also need to add these frameworks to your own game projects in order to use Cocos2D and the CocosDenshion audio library.

In the Project Settings for Breakout, under the Summary tab, there is a section Linked Frameworks and Libraries (you may have to scroll down to see it). Press the + button to add new libraries from the cocos2d project.

You only need these three:

- libbox2d.a

- libcocos2d.a

- libCocosDenshion.a

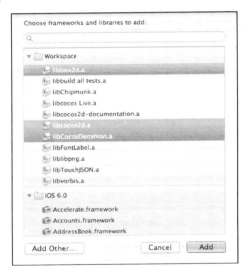

You are almost done. In order to make Xcode find the .h files from Cocos2D, you also have to tell it where these files are located. Go to the Build Settings tab, click on All, and search for "user". Under the Search Paths section, set Always Search User Paths to YES and add the path to where you unpacked the Cocos2D folder to the User Header Search Paths setting:

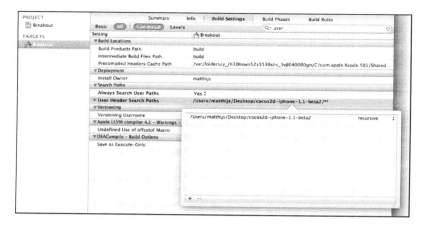

Make sure you select the Recursive option!

> Tip: If the path to the Cocos2D folder contains spaces, then put double quotes around it, otherwise Xcode gets confused.

Try and build the game. If the build succeeds, great! Unfortunately, v1.1-beta2 has some issues that prevented the build from completing for me. If the build also fails for you, then you will have to edit the Cocos2D source files. Don't worry, they are small changes. It is possible that these issues have been fixed in an update by the time you read this, in which case you can skip the next bit.

Go into the Search Navigator and click on Find to change the search mode to Replace and make it replace the text %08X with %p in all the source files. This will get rid of most of the "Format String Issue" errors that Xcode complains about.

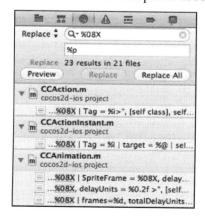

There are two more Format String Issue errors, in CCTMXXMLParser.m and in CCAnimation.m. Click on the error messages in the Issue Navigator and use Xcode's Fix-It suggestion to resolve both these problems.

The remaining compilation errors are in FontLabel.m and FontLabelString-Drawing.m. Both are the result of an incomplete switch-statement. Use the Issue Navigator to jump to these errors and add a default clause to the end of each switch:

```
default:
    break;
```

Now the Breakout project should compile with issues. There may still be some warning messages from Box2D, but that's no problem.

Run the game and play some breakout!

Converting to ARC

At this point, Xcode may suggest that you Validate Project Settings to update to the recommended settings. It's a good idea to do so, either by clicking the warning message in the Issue Navigator or the Validate Settings button in the Project Settings screen. Doing this will ensure the project is built with the latest LLVM compiler.

While you're in the Project Settings screen, it's also smart to set the Other Warning Flags to −Wall and Run Static Analyzer to YES.

Do Product\Clean to throw away all the files from the previous build, and compile & run the app again. You should get no new errors or warning messages. That's always a good sign. :-)

Cocos2D is a pretty big library. It would be insane to try and convert Cocos2D itself to ARC. That would probably take you a few weeks. It's smarter to convert the rest of the game but to leave Cocos2D as-is. It's very handy that Cocos2D already comes as a static library. That means you can tell Xcode to compile the Breakout project as ARC but keep the Cocos2D library as non-ARC.

Let's run the ARC conversion tool. Select the Breakout project and then choose Edit\Refactor\Convert to Objective-C ARC. Select all the files under Breakout.app, but none of the Cocos2D or Box2D ones:

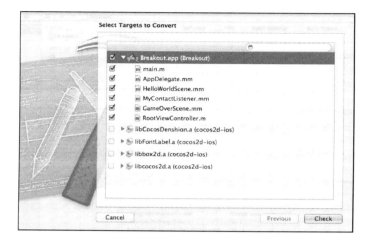

Press the Check button to perform the ARC readiness tests that determine whether the source code can be converted to ARC. Unsurprisingly, it finds a bunch of errors...

The first error in **HelloWorldScene.mm** is:

```
Assigning to 'void *' from incompatible type 'CCSprite
*__strong'
```

```
// Create ball body
b2BodyDef ballBodyDef;
ballBodyDef.type = b2_dynamicBody;
ballBodyDef.position.Set(100/PTM_RATIO, 100/PTM_RATIO);
ballBodyDef.userData = ball;                    Assigning to 'void *' from incompatible type 'CCSprite *__strong'
b2Body * ballBody = _world->CreateBody(&ballBodyDef);
```

It happens in the following bit of code:

```
b2BodyDef ballBodyDef;
ballBodyDef.type = b2_dynamicBody;
ballBodyDef.position.Set(100/PTM_RATIO, 100/PTM_RATIO);
ballBodyDef.userData = ball;       // <--- here is the error
b2Body * ballBody = _world->CreateBody(&ballBodyDef);
```

To explain what goes wrong here, we must take a slight detour into the world of C and C++. One of the new rules of ARC is that you can no longer put Objective-C objects into C structs. That makes it too hard for the compiler to figure out when and where it must insert retain and release statements. In order to avoid any nasty problems, the compiler gurus have simply decreed that pointers to objects can no longer be placed in structs.

There are a few workarounds. You can use a void * instead. If you haven't done much C programming before, then think of void * as being similar to Objective-C's id type.

"Void star" basically represents a pointer to anything. If C programmers need a pointer but they don't know in advance what datatype it will point to, they use a void *.

If you have this struct in your app,

```
typedef struct
{
    int someNumber;
    NSString *someString;
}
my_struct_t;
```

then you can change it to the following to make it compile under ARC:

```
typedef struct
{
    int someNumber;
    void *someString;
}
my_struct_t;
```

You can still store NSString objects into this struct, although you will have to cast them with a __bridge cast:

```
my_struct_t m;
m.someString = (__bridge void *)[NSString stringWithFormat:
                                 @"ARC is %@!", @"awesome"];
```

Not very pretty but at least it will still work. You can also do this, by the way:

```
typedef struct
{
    int someNumber;
    __unsafe_unretained NSString *someString;
}
my_struct_t;
```

The thing to remember is that you also need to keep strong pointers to those NSString objects somewhere else, or they will be deallocated. Putting them inside the struct is not enough to keep these objects alive.

Back to Breakout. In HelloWorldScene.mm the situation is slightly different because here you're dealing with C++, not regular C. b2BodyDef is a class and in Objective-C++ code, classes *are* allowed to store pointers to Objective-C objects.

The problem here is that the datatype of ballBodyDef.userData is void *, not CCSprite. The line with the error is:

```
ballBodyDef.userData = ball;
```

ARC doesn't like this because `ball` is a `CCSprite` object, not a `void *` pointer.

You can't simply do this to fix it:

```
ballBodyDef.userData = (void *)ball;
```

That's almost good enough, but now the compiler says: "Cast of Objective-C pointer type 'CCSprite *' to C pointer type 'void *' requires a bridged cast". This is similar to the situation you encountered before with toll-free bridging. The compiler needs to know who will be responsible for releasing the object.

In this case, the `b2BodyDef` should just have a pointer to the sprite so that the code can update the sprite's position when the Box2D body moves. The `CCSprite` object never changes owners, so the proper fix is:

```
ballBodyDef.userData = (__bridge void *)ball;
```

The next two errors in this source file have exactly the same fix.

The remaining errors are all in the `tick:` method:

```
156
157  - (void)tick:(ccTime)dt
158  {
159      bool blockFound = false;
160      _world->Step(dt, 10, 10);
161
162      for(b2Body *b = _world->GetBodyList(); b; b=b->GetNext())
163      {
164          if (b->GetUserData() != NULL)
165          {
166              CCSprite *sprite = (CCSprite *)b->GetUserData();
167              if (sprite.tag == 2)    Cast of C pointer type 'void *' to Objective-C pointer type 'CCSprite *' requires a brid...
168              {
169                  blockFound = true;
170              }
171
```

Here you do the reverse: you read the `userData` field from the `b2Body` object and cast it to a `CCSprite`. The code already performs the cast from the `void *` to `CCSprite *`, but the compiler again would like to know whether the ownership should transfer or not.

Again, adding a simple `__bridge` will suffice, also for the other errors in this method:

```
CCSprite *sprite = (__bridge CCSprite *)b->GetUserData();
```

Run the ARC conversion tool once more and now everything should check out.

Note: With Cocos2D version 1.1-beta2, the ARC conversion tool gives a couple of warnings on `ccArray.h`. The Cocos2D library itself is not converted to ARC, but because your own source files do include the Cocos2D header files, these .h files have to be ARC-compatible. This was not the case with earlier versions of Cocos2D (1.0.1 and before), which made it harder to embed those versions into ARC-enabled apps. With Cocos2D v1.1 and the 2.x branch, the headers are fully compatible with ARC. The warning in `ccArray.h` is harmless. If it bothers you, you can apply the Fix-Its that Xcode suggests to make it go away.

If you look at the proposed changes in the ARC conversion preview window you will see they are very similar to what happened with the Artists app. Properties go from `retain` to `strong`; `retain`, `release` and `autorelease` calls are dropped; `dealloc` is removed when no longer necessary. The changes in the code are minor.

Now you should be able to compile the app, and voila, you have a Cocos2D game running on ARC. Awesome!

More on C++

You've seen that you're not allowed to store object pointers in C-structs under ARC but that it is no problem with C++ classes. You can do the following and it will compile just fine:

```
class MyClass
{
public:
    CCSprite *sprite;
};

// elsewhere in your code:
CCSprite *ball = [CCSprite spriteWithFile:. . .];
MyClass *myObject = new MyClass;
myObject->sprite = ball;
```

ARC will automatically add the proper retain and release calls to the constructor and destructor of this C++ class. The `sprite` member variable is `__strong` because all variables are strong by default.

You can also use `__weak` if you must:

```
class MyClass
```

```
{
public:
    __weak CCSprite *sprite;
};
```

The same thing goes for structs in Objective-C++ code:

```
// in a .mm or .h file:
struct my_type_t
{
    CCSprite *sprite;
};

// elsewhere in your code:
static my_type_t sprites[10];
CCSprite *ball = [CCSprite spriteWithFile:. . .];
sprites[0].sprite = ball;
```

This is no problem whatsoever. It works because a C++ struct is much more powerful than a plain old C-struct. Just like a class it has a constructor and a destructor and ARC will use these to take care of the proper memory management.

You can also use Objective-C objects in vectors and other standard container templates:

```
std::vector<CCSprite *> sprites;
sprites.push_back(ball);
sprites.push_back(paddle);

for (std::vector<CCSprite *>::iterator i = sprites.begin();
                                      i != sprites.end(); ++i)
{
    NSLog(@"sprite %@", *i);
}
```

This creates a `std::vector` that keeps strong references to `CCSprite` objects.

Of course, you can also use weak references. In that case you must take care to use the __weak specifier on your iterators, or the compiler will shout at you:

```
std::vector<__weak CCSprite *> sprites;

for (std::vector<__weak CCSprite *>::iterator i =
                    sprites.begin(); i != sprites.end(); ++i)
{
    NSLog(@"sprite %@", *i);
}
```

It's not smart to put weak references into `NSArray`, because those pointers may become `nil` at any given time and `NSArray` doesn't allow `nil` values. But you can get away with zeroing weak references in C++ containers because unlike `NSArray`, `std::vector` can hold `NULL` objects just fine.

Making Your Own Static Library

Not all third-party libraries come bundled with a handy `.xcodeproj` file for building a static library. You could add the source files to your project and then disable ARC by hand on all of them with `-fno-objc-arc`, but that can be a bit of a chore.

To keep it clear which parts of your project are ARC and which aren't, it is handy to bundle these third-party components into one or more separate static libraries that are compiled with ARC disabled, just like you've done above with Cocos2D.

Creating your own static library is easy. In this section you will create one that includes all of the Cocos2D sources that are needed for the Breakout project.

First remove the `cocos2d-ios` project from the Breakout project. Don't move it to the trash, just choose Remove References.

Right-click the Breakout project in the Project Navigator and choose New Project... Pick the iOS\Framework & Library\Cocoa Touch Static Library project template:

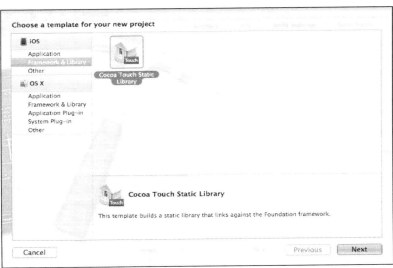

For Product Name choose "cocos2d". Disable Automatic Reference Counting. This will add a new static library project inside the Breakout project, with a few default files:

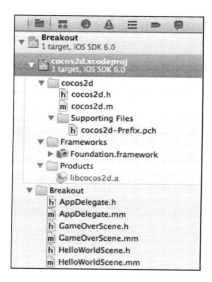

You can delete the cocos2d source group. Also delete it from Finder (it will delete the files but won't remove the cocos2d subfolder by default) so that you are just left with a cocos2d folder with a cocos2d.xcodeproj file inside.

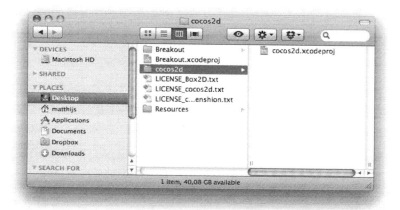

In Xcode, control-click the new cocos2d project in the Project Navigator and choose Add Files. Navigate to the folder where you unpacked Cocos2D and select the cocos2d folder. Make sure Copy items into destination group's folder is checked and that you're adding the sources to the new cocos2d target:

Repeat this for the CocosDenshion and external/FontLabel folders. Also add the files from external/Box2d/Box2D (that is two times Box2D, you don't want to add any of the Testbed files).

You need to change some build settings to make this all work. Select the cocos2d project and go the Build Settings tab.

• Search Paths\Always Search User Paths: Set to Yes

• Search Paths\User Header Search Paths: Set to ./**

This is necessary for Box2D to find its header files.

Just to make sure, the Skip Install setting should be Yes. If it isn't, you won't be able to make archives for distribution to the App Store because the static library will be installed inside the package too and that should not happen.

By default the iOS Deployment Target setting for the new library is set to 6.0 (or whatever version of the SDK you're using). Change this to 5.0 if you want the app to run on iOS 5 as well.

There's one more thing before you can build your new static library. The default Xcode static library template is configured to include a pre-compiled header file (Prefix file). But Cocos2D doesn't use one and you deleted the one from the template earlier, so you need to tell the compiler that it shouldn't use the Prefix file. Go into the Build Settings and search for "pch":

Simply delete the Prefix Header option.

Using the Scheme box at the top of the Xcode window, switch the active project to cocos2d and press Cmd+B to build it. If all went well you should get no build errors (but possibly some warnings). Congrats, you just built your own static library!

Switch the active project back to Breakout. In the Linked Frameworks and Libraries section, add libcocos2d.a. This is the static library that you've just created. You should be able to build and run the Breakout app now, using your custom version of Cocos2D.

> Note: If you are doing this in a real project, it may be a good idea to look at all the build settings from the official Cocos2D project and take these over to your own static library. That way you won't miss out on any important preprocessor flags and optimization settings.

Where To Go From Here?

I think ARC rocks! It's an important advancement for the Objective-C programming language. All the other new stuff in iOS 5 is cool too, but ARC completely changes – and improves – the way we write apps. Using ARC frees you up from having to think about unimportant bookkeeping details, so you can spend that extra brainpower on making your apps even more awesome.

One of the things I've shown you in this tutorial is how to convert existing apps to ARC. These instructions assumed that you were going to migrate most of the app but you still wanted to keep certain files – usually third-party libraries – out of it. If you want to migrate at a slower pace, you can also do it the other way around. Keep the project-wide ARC setting off and convert your files to ARC one-by-one. To do this, you can simply set the compiler flag -fobjc-arc on the files you have converted. From then on, only these files will be compiled with ARC.

If you maintain a reusable library and you don't want to switch it over to ARC (yet?), then you can use preprocessor directives to make it at least compatible with ARC where necessary. You can test for ARC with:

```
#if __has_feature(objc_arc)
// do your ARC thing here
#endif
```

Or even safer, if you also still want to support the old GCC compiler:

```
#if defined(__has_feature) && __has_feature(objc_arc)
// do your ARC thing here
#endif
```

The official documentation for ARC is "Transitioning to ARC Release Notes" that you can find in your Xcode documentation. Other good sources for information are WWDC 2011 video 323, Introducing Automatic Reference Counting, and video 322, Objective-C Advancements in Depth.

Chapter 4: Beginning Storyboards

By Matthijs Hollemans

Storyboarding is an exciting new feature in iOS 5 that will save you a lot of time building user interfaces for your apps. To show you what a storyboard is, I'll let a picture do the talking. This is the storyboard for the app that you will be making in this chapter and the next:

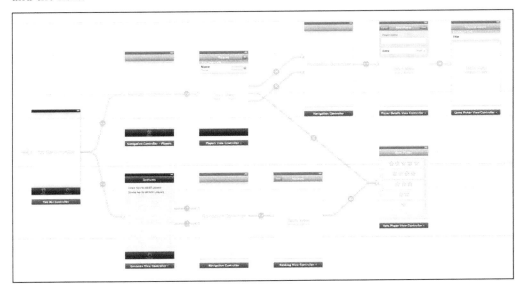

You may not know exactly yet what the app does but you can clearly see which screens it has and how they are related. That is the power of using storyboards.

If you have an app with many different screens then storyboards can help reduce the amount of glue code you have to write to go from one screen to the next. Instead of using a separate nib file for each view controller, your app uses a single storyboard that contains the designs of all of these view controllers and the relationships between them.

Storyboards have a number of advantages over regular nibs:

- With a storyboard you have a better conceptual overview of all the screens in your app and the connections between them. It's easier to keep track of everything because the entire design is in a single file, rather than spread out over many separate nibs.

- The storyboard describes the transitions between the various screens. These transitions are called "segues" and you create them by simply ctrl-dragging from one view controller to the next. Thanks to segues you need less code to take care of your UI.

- Storyboards make working with table views a lot easier with the new prototype cells and static cells features. You can design your table views almost completely in the storyboard editor, something else that cuts down on the amount of code you have to write.

Not everything is perfect, of course, and storyboards do have some limitations. The storyboard version of Interface Builder isn't as powerful as the old nib editor and there are a few handy things nibs can do that storyboards unfortunately can't. You also need a big monitor, especially when you write iPad apps.

If you're the type who hates Interface Builder and who really wants to create his entire UI programmatically, then storyboards are probably not for you. Personally, I prefer to write as little code as possible – especially UI code – so this tool is a welcome addition to my arsenal.

You can still use nibs with iOS 5. Nib files aren't suddenly frowned upon now that we have storyboards. If you want to keep using nibs then go right ahead, but know that you can also combine storyboards with nibs. It's not an either-or situation.

In this tutorial you'll take a look at what you can do with storyboards. You're going to build a simple app that lets you create a list of players and games, and rate their skill levels. In the process, you'll learn the most common tasks that you'll be using storyboards for on a regular basis.

Getting Started

Fire up Xcode 4.5 or better and create a new project. You'll use the Single View Application template as the starting point and then build up the app from there.

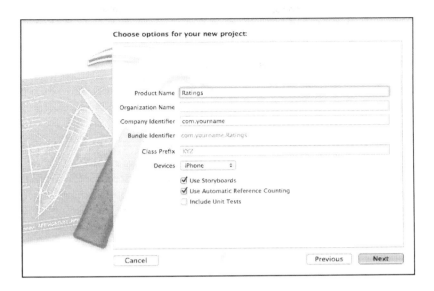

Fill in the template options as follows:

- **Product Name:** Ratings

- **Organization Name:** fill this in however you like

- **Company Identifier:** the identifier that you use for your apps, in reverse domain notation

- **Class Prefix:** leave this empty

- **Devices:** iPhone

- **Use Storyboards:** check this

- **Use Automatic Reference Counting:** check this

- **Include Unit Tests:** this should be unchecked

After Xcode has created the project, the main Xcode window looks like this:

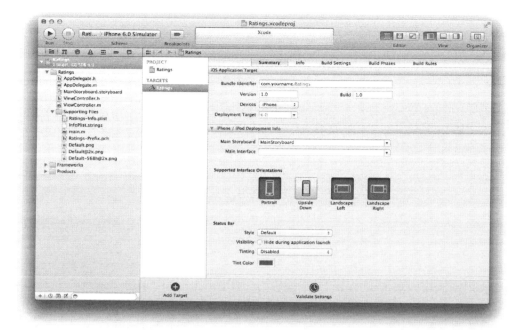

The new project consists of two classes, `AppDelegate` and `ViewController`, and the star of this tutorial, the `MainStoryboard.storyboard` file. Notice that there are no .xib files in the project, not even MainWindow.xib.

This is a portrait-only app, so before you continue, uncheck the **Landscape Left** and **Landscape Right** options under **Supported Interface Orientations**. Also set the Deployment Target to 5.0 to make this app run on iOS 5.0 and up.

Now let's take a look at that storyboard. Click the `MainStoryboard.storyboard` file in the Project Navigator to open it up in Interface Builder:

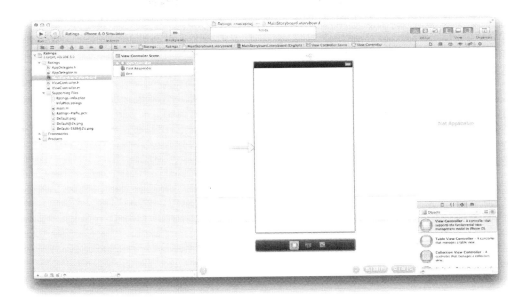

Editing storyboards in Interface Builder works pretty much the same way as editing nibs. You can drag new controls from the Object Library (see bottom-right corner) into your view controller to design its layout. The difference is that the storyboard doesn't contain just one view controller from your app, but all of them.

The official storyboard terminology for a view controller is "scene", but you can use the terms interchangeably. The scene simply represents the view controller in the storyboard. Previously you would use a separate nib for each scene / view controller, but now they are all combined into a single storyboard.

On the iPhone usually only one of these scenes is visible at a time, but on the iPad you can show several at once, for example the master and detail panes in a split-view, or the content of a popover.

> **Note:** Xcode 4.5 enables Auto Layout by default for storyboard and nib files. Auto Layout is a cool new technology for making flexible user interfaces that can easily resize, which is useful on the iPad and for supporting the new iPhone 5, but the downside is that it only works on iOS 6 and up. To learn more about Auto Layout, see our new book *iOS 6 by Tutorials*.

Disable Auto Layout from the File inspector for the storyboard:

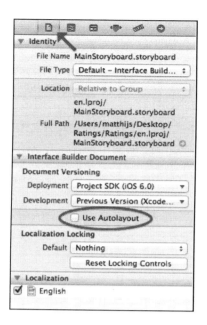

To get some feel for how the storyboard editor works, drag some controls into the blank view controller:

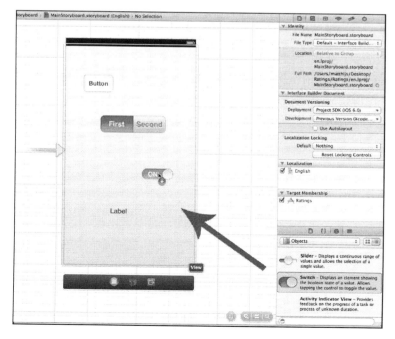

The sidebar on the left is the Document Outline:

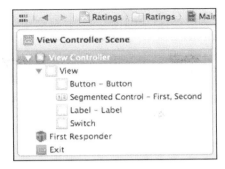

When editing a nib this area lists just the components from that one nib, but for a storyboard it shows the contents of all your view controllers. Currently there is only one view controller (or scene) in your storyboard but in the course of this tutorial you'll be adding several others.

There is a miniature version of this Document Outline below the scene, named the Dock:

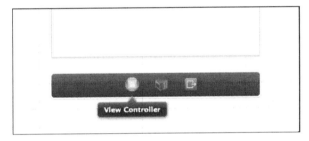

The Dock shows the top-level objects in the scene. Each scene has at least a View Controller object and a First Responder object, but it can potentially have other top-level objects as well. The Dock is convenient for making connections to outlets and actions. If you need to connect something to the view controller, you can simply drag to its icon in the Dock.

Note: You probably won't be using the First Responder very much. This is a proxy object that refers to whatever object has first responder status at any given time. It was also present in your nibs and you probably never had a need to use it then either. As an example, you can hook up the Touch Up Inside event from a button to First Responder's cut: selector. If at some point a text field has input focus then you can press that button to make the text field, which is now the first responder, cut its text to the pasteboard.

Run the app and it should look exactly like what you designed in the editor (shown here on the iPhone 5 simulator):

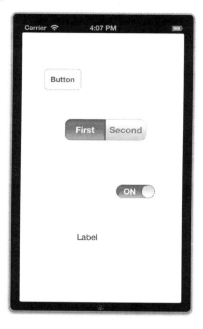

No more MainWindow.xib

If you've ever made a nib-based app before then you always had a MainWindow.xib file. This nib contained the top-level `UIWindow` object, a reference to the App Delegate, and one or more view controllers. When you put your app's UI in a storyboard, however, MainWindow.xib is no longer used.

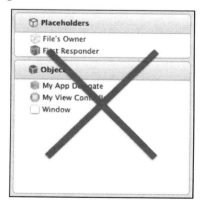

So how does the storyboard get loaded by the app if there is no MainWindow.xib file?

Let's take a peek at the application delegate. Open up AppDelegate.h and you'll see it looks like this:

```
#import <UIKit/UIKit.h>

@interface AppDelegate : UIResponder <UIApplicationDelegate>

@property (strong, nonatomic) UIWindow *window;

@end
```

It is a requirement for using storyboards that your application delegate inherits from UIResponder (previously it used to inherit directly from NSObject) and that it has a UIWindow property (unlike before, this is not an IBOutlet).

If you look into AppDelegate.m, you'll see that it does absolutely nothing. All the methods are practically empty. Even application:didFinishLaunchingWith-Options: simply returns YES. Previously, this method would either add the main view controller's view to the window or set the window's rootViewController property, but none of that happens here.

The secret is in the Info.plist file. Click on Ratings-Info.plist (you can find it in the Supporting Files group) and you'll see this:

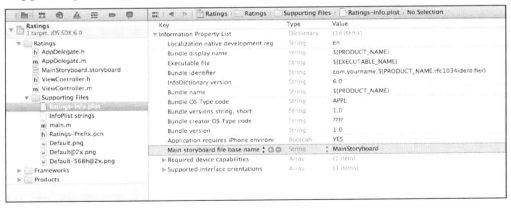

In nib-based projects there was a key in Info.plist named NSMainNibFile, or "Main nib file base name", that instructed UIApplication to load MainWindow.xib and hook it into the app. Your Info.plist no longer has that setting.

Instead, storyboard apps use the key UIMainStoryboardFile, or "Main storyboard file base name", to specify the name of the storyboard that must be loaded when the app starts. When this setting is present, UIApplication will load the "MainStoryboard

.storyboard" file and automatically instantiates the first view controller from that storyboard, then puts its view into a new **UIWindow** object. No programming necessary.

You can also see this in the Target Summary screen:

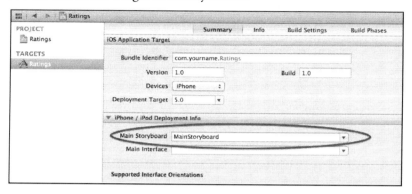

There is a new iPhone/iPod Deployment Info section that lets you choose between starting from a storyboard or from a nib file.

For the sake of completeness, also open **main.m** to see what's in there:

```
#import <UIKit/UIKit.h>

#import "AppDelegate.h"

int main(int argc, char *argv[])
{
    @autoreleasepool {
        return UIApplicationMain(argc, argv, nil,
                    NSStringFromClass([AppDelegate class]));
    }
}
```

Previously, the last parameter for **UIApplicationMain()** was simply **nil** but now it is the mouthful **NSStringFromClass([AppDelegate class])**.

A big difference with having a MainWindow.xib is that the app delegate is not part of the storyboard. Because the app delegate is no longer being loaded from a nib (nor from the storyboard), you have to tell the **UIApplicationMain()** function specifically what the name of your app delegate class is, otherwise it won't be able to find it.

Just Add It To My Tab

The Ratings app has a tabbed interface with two screens. With a storyboard it is easy to create tabs.

Switch back to MainStoryboard.storyboard and drag a Tab Bar Controller from the Object Library into the canvas. You may want to maximize your Xcode window first, because the Tab Bar Controller comes with two view controllers attached and you'll need some room to maneuver. You can zoom out using the little floating panel in the bottom-right corner of the canvas.

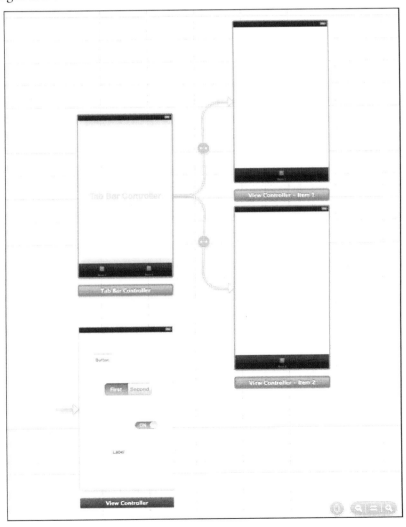

The new Tab Bar Controller comes pre-configured with two other view controllers, one for each tab. `UITabBarController` is a so-called *container* view controller because it contains one or more other view controllers. Two other common containers are the Navigation Controller and the Split View Controller (you'll see both of them later).

> **Note:** Another cool addition to iOS 5 is a new API for writing your own container controllers — and later on in this book, we have a chapter on that.

The container relationship is represented in the Storyboard Editor by the arrows between the Tab Bar controller and the view controllers that it contains.

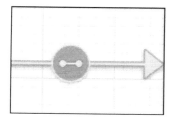

> **Tip:** If you want to move the Tab Bar controller and its attached view controllers as a group, you can Cmd-click (or shift-click) to select multiple scenes and then move them around together. (Selected scenes have a thick blue outline.)

Drag a label into the first view controller and give it the text "First Tab". Also drag a label into the second view controller and name it "Second Tab". This allows you to actually see something happen when you switch between the tabs.

> **Note:** You can't drag stuff into the scenes when the editor is zoomed out. You'll need to return to the normal zoom level first. You can do that quickly by double-clicking in the canvas.

Select the Tab Bar Controller and go to the Attributes inspector. Check the box that says Is Initial View Controller.

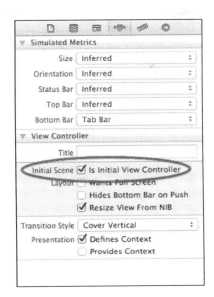

In the canvas the arrow that at first pointed to the regular view controller now points at the Tab Bar Controller:

This means that when you run the app, UIApplication will make the Tab Bar Controller the main screen. The storyboard always has a single view controller that is designated the *initial view controller*, that serves as the entry point into the storyboard.

> **Tip:** To change the initial view controller, you can also drag the arrow between view controllers.

Run the app and try it out. The app now has a tab bar and you can switch between the two view controllers with the tabs:

Xcode actually comes with a template for building a tabbed app (unsurprisingly called the Tabbed Application template) that you could have used, but it's good to know how this works so you can also create one by hand if you have to.

Remove the view controller that was originally added by the template, as you'll no longer be using it. The storyboard now contains just the tab bar and the two scenes for its tabs.

By the way, if you connect more than five scenes to the Tab Bar Controller, it automatically gets a More... tab when you run the app. Pretty neat!

Adding a Table View Controller

The two scenes that are currently attached to the Tab Bar Controller are both regular `UIViewControllers`. You are going to replace the scene from the first tab with a `UITableViewController` instead.

Click on that first view controller to select it, and then delete it. From the Object Library drag a new Table View Controller into the canvas in the place where that previous scene used to be:

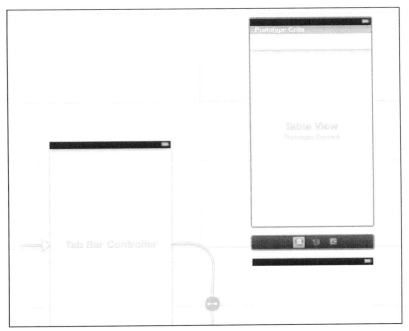

With the Table View Controller selected, choose Editor\Embed In\Navigation Controller from Xcode's menubar. This adds yet another view controller to the canvas:

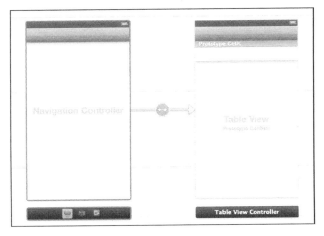

You could also have dragged in a Navigation Controller from the Object Library, but this Embed In command is just as easy.

Because the Navigation Controller is also a container view controller (just like the Tab Bar Controller), it has a relationship arrow pointing at the Table View Controller. You can also see these relationships in the Document Outline:

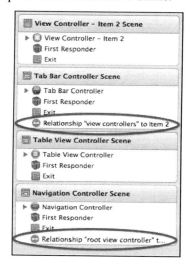

Notice that embedding the Table View Controller gave it a navigation bar. Interface Builder automatically put it there because this scene will now be displayed inside the Navigation Controller's frame. It's not a real UINavigationBar object but a simulated one.

If you look at the Attributes inspector for the Table View Controller, you'll see the Simulated metrics section at the top:

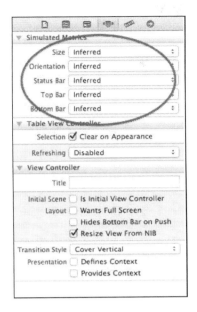

"Inferred" is the default setting for storyboards and it means the scene will show a navigation bar when it's inside of a Navigation Controller, a tab bar when it's inside of a Tab Bar Controller, and so on. You could override these settings if you wanted to, but keep in mind they are here only to help you design your screens. The Simulated Metrics aren't used during runtime; they're just a visual design aid that shows what your screen will end up looking like.

Let's connect these two new scenes to the Tab Bar Controller. Ctrl-drag from the Tab Bar Controller to the Navigation Controller:

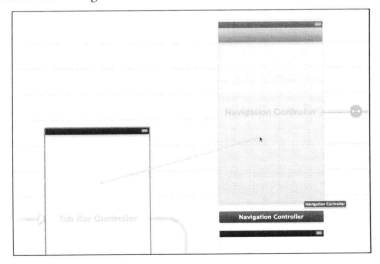

When you let go, a small popup menu appears:

Choose the Relationship Segue – view controllers option. This creates a new relationship arrow between the two scenes:

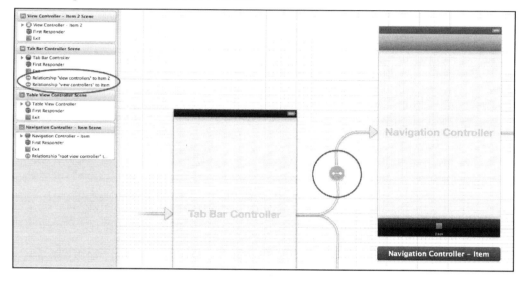

The Tab Bar Controller has two such relationships, one for each tab. The Navigation Controller itself has a relationship connection to the Table View Controller. There is also another type of arrow, the segue, that we'll talk about later.

When you made this new connection, a new tab was added to the Tab Bar Controller, simply named "Item". For this app, you want this new scene to be the first tab, so drag the tabs around to change their order:

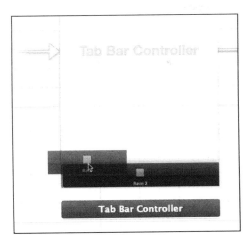

> **Note:** If Interface Builder doesn't let you drag to rearrange the tabs inside the Tab Bar Controller, then temporarily go to another file in the project and switch back to the storyboard again. That seems to fix it. Or follow the iOS developer's motto: When in doubt, restart Xcode.

Run the app and try it out. The first tab now contains a table view inside a navigation controller.

Before you put some actual functionality into this app, let's clean up the storyboard a little. You will name the first tab "Players" and the second "Gestures". Unlike what you may expect, you do not change this on the Tab Bar Controller itself, but in the view controllers that are connected to these tabs.

As soon as you connect a view controller to the Tab Bar Controller, it is given a Tab Bar Item object. You use the Tab Bar Item to configure the tab's title and image.

Select the Tab Bar Item inside the Navigation Controller, and in the Attributes inspector set its Title to "Players":

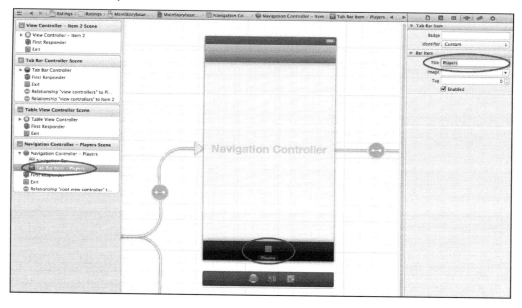

Rename the Tab Bar Item for the view controller from the second tab to "Gestures".

A well-designed app should also put some pictures on these tabs. The resources for this chapter contain a subfolder named Images. Add that folder to the project.

Then, in the Attributes inspector for the Players Tab Bar Item, choose the Players.png image. You probably guessed it, give the Gestures item the image Gestures.png.

A view controller that is embedded inside a Navigation Controller has a Navigation Item that is used to configure the navigation bar. Select the Navigation Item for the Table View Controller and change its title in the Attributes inspector to "Players".

Alternatively, you can double-click the navigation bar and change the title there. (Note: You should double-click the simulated navigation bar in the Table View Controller, not the actual Navigation Bar object in the Navigation Controller.)

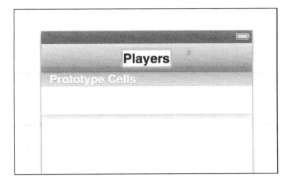

Run the app and marvel at your pretty tab bar, all without writing a single line of code!

Prototype Cells

You may have noticed that ever since you added the Table View Controller, Xcode has been complaining:

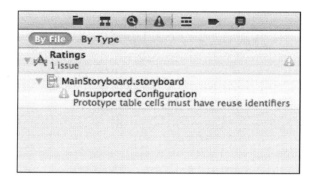

The warning message is, "Unsupported Configuration: Prototype table cells must have reuse identifiers". When you add a Table View Controller to a storyboard, it wants to use *prototype cells* by default but you haven't properly configured this yet, hence the warning.

Prototype cells allow you to easily design a custom layout for your cells directly from within the storyboard editor.

Note: Prior to iOS 5, if you wanted to use a table view cell with a custom design you either had to add your subviews to the cell programmatically, or create a new nib specifically for that cell and then load it from the nib with some magic. iOS 5 makes this much easier – you can use the prototype cell functionality built into the Storyboard editor, or the new NIB cell registration functionality you'll read about later in this book.

The Table View Controller comes with a blank prototype cell. Click on that cell to select it and in the Attributes inspector set the Style option to Subtitle. This immediately changes the appearance of the cell to include two labels.

If you've used table views before and created your own cells by hand, you may recognize this as the `UITableViewCellStyleSubtitle` style. With prototype cells you can either pick one of the built-in cell styles as you just did, or create your own custom design (which you'll do shortly).

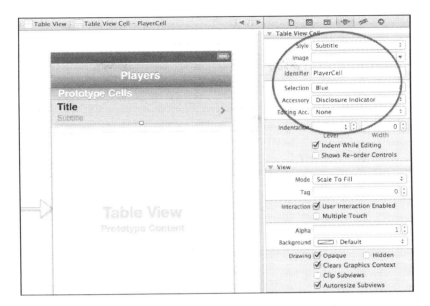

Set the Accessory attribute to Disclosure Indicator and give the cell the Reuse Identifier PlayerCell. That will make Xcode shut up about the warning. All prototype cells are still regular `UITableViewCell` objects and therefore should have a reuse identifier. Xcode is just making sure you don't forget (at least for those of us who pay attention to its warnings).

Run the app, and... nothing has changed. That's not so strange: you still have to make a data source for the table so it will know what rows to display.

Add a new file to the project. Choose the **Objective-C class** template. Name the class **PlayersViewController** and make it a subclass of **UITableViewController**. The **With XIB for user interface** option should be unchecked because you already have the design of this view controller in the storyboard. No nibs today!

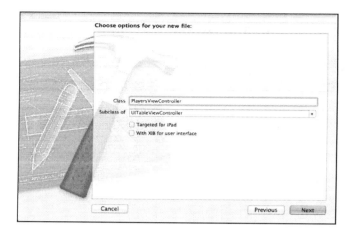

Go back to the storyboard and select the Table View Controller. In the Identity inspector, set its Class to PlayersViewController. That is the essential step for hooking up a scene from the storyboard with your own view controller subclass. Don't forget this or your class won't be used.

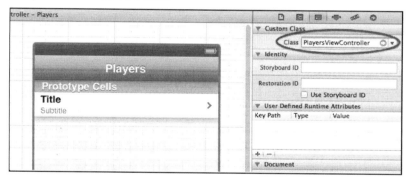

From now on when you run the app that table view controller from the storyboard is actually an instance of the PlayersViewController class.

Add a mutable array property to PlayersViewController.h:

```
#import <UIKit/UIKit.h>

@interface PlayersViewController : UITableViewController

@property (nonatomic, strong) NSMutableArray *players;

@end
```

This array will contain the main data model for the app, an array that contains `Player` objects. Add a new file to the project using the Objective-C class template. Name it Player, subclass of NSObject.

Change Player.h to the following:

```
@interface Player : NSObject

@property (nonatomic, copy) NSString *name;
@property (nonatomic, copy) NSString *game;
@property (nonatomic, assign) int rating;

@end
```

There's nothing special going on here. `Player` is simply a container object for these three properties: the name of the player, the game he's playing, and a rating of 1 to 5 stars.

> **Note:** Thanks to recent improvements to the LLVM compiler that ships with Xcode, it is no longer necessary to @synthesize your properties. Sweet!

You'll make the array of players and some test `Player` objects in the App Delegate and then assign it to the `PlayersViewController`'s `players` property. The reason you make this array inside `AppDelegate` and not inside `PlayersViewController` is that in the next chapter you will also pass the array to the view controller for the second tab.

In AppDelegate.m, add an #import for the `Player` and `PlayersViewController` classes at the top of the file, and add a new instance variable named _players:

```
#import "AppDelegate.h"
#import "Player.h"
#import "PlayersViewController.h"

@implementation AppDelegate
{
    NSMutableArray *_players;
}

. . .
```

Then change the `didFinishLaunchingWithOptions` method to:

```
- (BOOL)application:(UIApplication *)application
    didFinishLaunchingWithOptions:(NSDictionary *)launchOptions
{
```

```
_players = [NSMutableArray arrayWithCapacity:20];

Player *player = [[Player alloc] init];
player.name = @"Bill Evans";
player.game = @"Tic-Tac-Toe";
player.rating = 4;
[_players addObject:player];

player = [[Player alloc] init];
player.name = @"Oscar Peterson";
player.game = @"Spin the Bottle";
player.rating = 5;
[_players addObject:player];

player = [[Player alloc] init];
player.name = @"Dave Brubeck";
player.game = @"Texas Hold'em Poker";
player.rating = 2;
[_players addObject:player];

UITabBarController *tabBarController =
    (UITabBarController *)self.window.rootViewController;

UINavigationController *navigationController =
                [tabBarController viewControllers][0];

PlayersViewController *playersViewController =
                [navigationController viewControllers][0];

playersViewController.players = _players;

return YES;
}
```

This simply creates some Player objects and adds them to the _players array. But then it does the following:

```
UITabBarController *tabBarController =
    (UITabBarController *)self.window.rootViewController;

UINavigationController *navigationController =
                [tabBarController viewControllers][0];

PlayersViewController *playersViewController =
                [navigationController viewControllers][0];

playersViewController.players = _players;
```

Yikes, what is that? You want to assign the _players array to the players property of PlayersViewController so it can use this array for its data source. But the app delegate doesn't know anything about `PlayersViewController` yet, so it will have to dig through the storyboard to find it.

This is one of the annoying limitations of storyboards. With nibs you always had a reference to the App Delegate in your MainWindow.xib and you could make connections from your top-level view controllers to outlets on the App Delegate.

That is currently not possible with storyboards. You cannot make references to the app delegate from your top-level view controllers. That's unfortunate, but you can always get those references programmatically, which is what you do here.

Let's take it step-by-step:

```
UITabBarController *tabBarController =
        (UITabBarController *)self.window.rootViewController;
```

You know that the storyboard's initial view controller is a Tab Bar Controller, so you can look up the window's `rootViewController` and cast it.

The `PlayersViewController` sits inside a navigation controller in the first tab, so you first look up that `UINavigationController` object,

```
UINavigationController *navigationController =
                    [tabBarController viewControllers][0];
```

and then ask it for its root view controller, which is the `PlayersViewController` that you are looking for:

```
PlayersViewController *playersViewController =
                    [navigationController viewControllers][0];
```

It takes a bit of effort to dig through the storyboard to get the view controller you want, but that's the way to do it. Of course, if you change the order of the tabs, or change the app so that it no longer has a Tab Bar Controller at the root, then you will have to revise this logic as well.

> Note: The notation `[0]` is new with the latest versions of Xcode. Previously, in order to index an array you had to call `[array objectAtIndex:index]` but from now on you can simply type `[index]` to do the same thing.

Now that you have an array full of `Player` objects, you can continue building the data source for `PlayersViewController`. Open up PlayersViewController.m, and add an import at the top:

```
#import "Player.h"
```

Change the table view data source methods to the following:

```
#pragma mark - Table view data source

- (NSInteger)numberOfSectionsInTableView:
                            (UITableView *)tableView
{
    return 1;
}

- (NSInteger)tableView:(UITableView *)tableView
 numberOfRowsInSection:(NSInteger)section
{
    return [self.players count];
}
```

The real work happens in cellForRowAtIndexPath. Previously, this method typically looked something like this:

```
- (UITableViewCell *)tableView:(UITableView *)tableView
        cellForRowAtIndexPath:(NSIndexPath *)indexPath
{
    static NSString *CellIdentifier = @"Cell";

    UITableViewCell *cell = [tableView
            dequeueReusableCellWithIdentifier:CellIdentifier];

    if (cell == nil)
    {
        cell = [[UITableViewCell alloc]
                initWithStyle:UITableViewCellStyleDefault
                reuseIdentifier:CellIdentifier];
    }

    // Configure the cell...

    return cell;
}
```

You would ask the table view to dequeue a cell and if that returned nil because there were no free cells to reuse, you would create a new instance of the cell class. That is, no doubt, how you've been writing your own table view code all this time. Well, no longer!

Replace that method with:

```
- (UITableViewCell *)tableView:(UITableView *)tableView
        cellForRowAtIndexPath:(NSIndexPath *)indexPath
```

```
{
    UITableViewCell *cell = [tableView
            dequeueReusableCellWithIdentifier:@"PlayerCell"];

    Player *player = (self.players)[indexPath.row];
    cell.textLabel.text = player.name;
    cell.detailTextLabel.text = player.game;
    return cell;
}
```

That looks a lot simpler. The only thing you need to do to get a new cell is:

```
UITableViewCell *cell = [tableView
        dequeueReusableCellWithIdentifier:@"PlayerCell"];
```

If there is no existing cell that can be recycled, this will automatically make a new copy of the prototype cell and return it to you. All you need to do is supply the re-use identifier that you set on the prototype cell in the storyboard editor, in this case "PlayerCell". Don't forget to set that identifier, or this little scheme won't work.

> **Note:** When you create a UITableViewController class using the Xode template, it already puts some default code into `cellForRowAtIndexPath`. That code calls the method `dequeueReusableCellWithIdentifier:forIndexPath:` instead of just `dequeueReusableCellWithIdentifier:`. Be aware that this new method only works on iOS 6. For backwards compatibility with iOS 5, use the version without the `forIndexPath:` parameter.

Now you can run the app, and lo and behold, the table view has players in it:

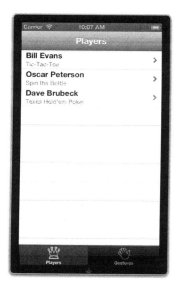

It just takes one line of code to use these newfangled prototype cells. I think that's just great!

Designing Your Own Prototype Cells

Using a standard cell style is OK for many apps, but for this app you want to add an image on the right-hand side of the cell that shows the player's rating (one to five stars). Having an image view in that spot is not supported by the standard cell styles, so you'll have to make a custom design.

Switch back to MainStoryboard.storyboard, select the prototype cell in the table view, and set its Style attribute to Custom. The default labels now disappear.

First make the cell a little taller. Either drag its handle at the bottom or change the Row Height value in the Size inspector. Make the cell 55 points high.

Drag two Label objects from the Objects Library into the cell and place them roughly where the standard labels were previously. Just play with the font and colors and pick something you like.

Set the Highlighted color of both labels to white. That will look better when the user taps the cell and the cell background turns blue.

Drag an Image View into the cell and place it on the right, next to the disclosure indicator. Make it 81 points wide, the height isn't very important. Set its Mode to Center (under View in the Attributes inspector) so that whatever image you put into this view is not stretched.

Resize the labels so they don't overlap with the image view (about 200 points wide). The final design for the prototype cell looks something like this:

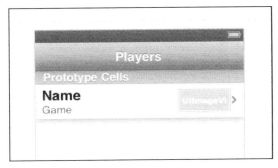

Because this is a custom designed cell, you can no longer use UITableViewCell's textLabel and detailTextLabel properties to put text into the labels. These properties refer to labels that aren't on this cell anymore; they are only valid for the standard cell types. Instead, you will use tags to find the labels.

Give the Name label tag 100, the Game label tag 101, and the Image View tag 102. You can do this in the Attributes inspector.

Then open PlayersViewController.m and change cellForRowAtIndexPath to:

```
- (UITableViewCell *)tableView:(UITableView *)tableView
        cellForRowAtIndexPath:(NSIndexPath *)indexPath
{
    UITableViewCell *cell = [tableView
            dequeueReusableCellWithIdentifier:@"PlayerCell"];

    Player *player = (self.players)[indexPath.row];

    UILabel *nameLabel = (UILabel *)[cell viewWithTag:100];
    nameLabel.text = player.name;
```

```
    UILabel *gameLabel = (UILabel *)[cell viewWithTag:101];
    gameLabel.text = player.game;

    UIImageView * ratingImageView = (UIImageView *)
                                    [cell viewWithTag:102];
    ratingImageView.image = [self imageForRating:player.rating];

    return cell;
}
```

This uses a new method, imageForRating:

```
- (UIImage *)imageForRating:(int)rating
{
    switch (rating)
    {
        case 1: return [UIImage imageNamed:@"1StarSmall"];
        case 2: return [UIImage imageNamed:@"2StarsSmall"];
        case 3: return [UIImage imageNamed:@"3StarsSmall"];
        case 4: return [UIImage imageNamed:@"4StarsSmall"];
        case 5: return [UIImage imageNamed:@"5StarsSmall"];
    }
    return nil;
}
```

That should do it. Now run the app again. It is possible that the app shows up like this:

Hmm, that doesn't look quite right, the cells appear to overlap one another. You did change the height of the prototype cell but the table view doesn't necessarily take that into consideration. There are two ways to fix it: you can change the table view's Row Height attribute or implement the heightForRowAtIndexPath method. The former is much easier, so let's do that.

Back in MainStoryboard.storyboard, in the Size inspector of the Table View, set Row Height to 55:

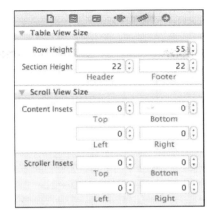

If you run the app now, it looks a lot better.

By the way, if you changed the height of the cell by dragging its handle rather than typing in the value, then the table view's Row Height property was automatically changed already. So it may have worked correctly for you the first time around.

Note: You would use `heightForRowAtIndexPath` if you did not know the height of your cells in advance, or if different rows can have different heights.

Using a Subclass for the Cell

The table view already works pretty well but I'm not a big fan of using tags to access the labels and other subviews of the prototype cell. It would be much more handy if you could connect these labels to outlets and then use the corresponding properties. As it turns out, you can.

Add a new file to the project, with the Objective-C class template. Name it PlayerCell and make it a subclass of UITableViewCell.

Change PlayerCell.h to:

```
@interface PlayerCell : UITableViewCell

@property (nonatomic, weak) IBOutlet UILabel *nameLabel;
@property (nonatomic, weak) IBOutlet UILabel *gameLabel;
@property (nonatomic, weak) IBOutlet UIImageView
                                  *ratingImageView;
```

```
@end
```

The class itself doesn't do much; it just adds properties for `nameLabel`, `gameLabel` and `ratingImageView`, all of which are `IBOutlets`.

Back in `MainStoryboard.storyboard`, select the prototype cell and change its Class to `PlayerCell` on the Identity inspector. Now whenever you ask the table view for a new cell with `dequeueReusableCellWithIdentifier:`, it returns a `PlayerCell` instance instead of a regular `UITableViewCell`.

Note that you gave this class the same name as its reuse identifier – they're both called "PlayerCell" – but whether you want to do that is a matter of personal preference (I like to keep things consistent). The class name and reuse identifier have nothing to do with each other, so you could name them differently if you wanted to.

Now connect the labels and the image view to these outlets. Either select the label and drag from its Connections inspector to the table view cell, or do it the other way around, ctrl-drag from the table view cell back to the label:

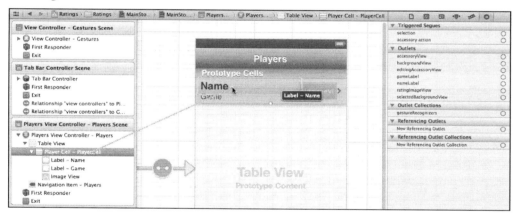

Important: You should hook up the controls to the table view cell, not to the view controller. You see, whenever your data source asks the table view for a new cell with `dequeueReusableCellWithIdentifier`, the table view doesn't give you the actual prototype cell but a *copy* (or one of the previous cells is recycled if possible).

This means there will be more than one instance of `PlayerCell` at any given time. If you were to connect a label from the cell to an outlet on the view controller, then several copies of the label will try to use the same outlet. That's just asking for trouble. (On the other hand, connecting the prototype cell to actions on the view controller is perfectly fine. You would do that if you had custom buttons or other UIControls on your cell that can trigger actions.)

Now that you've hooked up the properties, you can simplify the data source code one more time. First import the PlayerCell class in PlayersViewController.m:

```
#import "PlayerCell.h"
```

And then change cellForRowAtIndexPath to:

```
- (UITableViewCell *)tableView:(UITableView *)tableView
        cellForRowAtIndexPath:(NSIndexPath *)indexPath
{
    PlayerCell *cell = [tableView
              dequeueReusableCellWithIdentifier:@"PlayerCell"];

    Player *player = (self.players)[indexPath.row];

    cell.nameLabel.text = player.name;
    cell.gameLabel.text = player.game;
    cell.ratingImageView.image = [self
                                  imageForRating:player.rating];

    return cell;
}
```

That's more like it. You now cast the object that you receive from dequeueReusable-CellWithIdentifier: to a PlayerCell, and then you can simply use the properties that are wired up to the labels and the image view. Isn't it great how using prototype cells makes table views a whole lot less messy?

Run the app and try it out. It should still look the same as before, but behind the scenes it's now using your own table view cell subclass.

Here are some free design tips. There are a couple of things you need to take care of when you design your own table view cells. First, you should set the Highlighted color attribute of the labels so that they look good when the user taps the row:

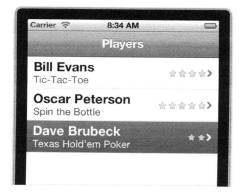

Second, you should make sure that the content you add is flexible so that when the table view cell resizes, the content sizes along with it. Cells will resize when you add the ability to delete or move rows, for example.

Add the following method to PlayersViewController.m:

```
- (void)tableView:(UITableView *)tableView
    commitEditingStyle:(UITableViewCellEditingStyle)editingStyle
    forRowAtIndexPath:(NSIndexPath *)indexPath
{
    if (editingStyle == UITableViewCellEditingStyleDelete)
    {
        [self.players removeObjectAtIndex:indexPath.row];
        [tableView deleteRowsAtIndexPaths:@[indexPath]
                withRowAnimation:UITableViewRowAnimationFade];
    }
}
```

When this method is present, swipe-to-delete is enabled on the table. Run the app and swipe a row to see what happens.

The Delete button slides into the cell but partially overlaps the stars image. What actually happens is that the cell resizes to make room for the Delete button, but the image view doesn't follow along.

To fix this, open `MainStoryBoard.storyboard`, select the image view in the table view cell, and in the Size inspector change the Autosizing so it sticks to its superview's right edge:

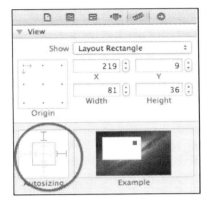

Autosizing for the labels should be set up as follows, so they'll shrink when the cell shrinks:

With those changes, the Delete button appears to push aside the stars:

You could also make the stars disappear altogether to make room for the Delete button, but that's left as an exercise for the reader. The important point is that you should keep these details in mind when you design your own table view cells.

Segues

It's time to add more view controllers to the storyboard. You're going to create a screen that allows users to add new players to the app.

Drag a Bar Button Item into the right slot of the navigation bar on the Players screen. In the Attributes inspector change its Identifier to Add to make it a standard + button. When you tap this button the app will make a new modal screen pop up that lets you enter the details for a new player.

Drag a new Navigation Controller into the canvas to the right of the Players screen. Remember that you can double-click the canvas to zoom out so you have more room to work. This new Navigation Controller comes with a Table View Controller attached, so that's handy.

Here's the trick: Select the + button that you just added on the Players screen and ctrl-drag to the new Navigation Controller:

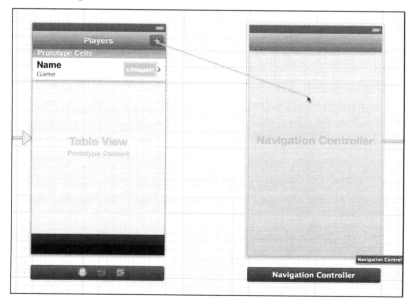

Release the mouse button and a small popup menu shows up:

Choose Modal. This places a new arrow between the Players screen and the Navigation Controller:

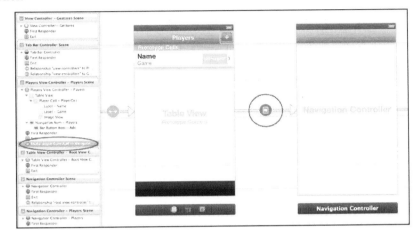

This type of connection is known as a *segue* (pronounce: seg-way) and represents a transition from one screen to another. The storyboard connections you've seen so far were relationships and they described one view controller containing another. A segue, on the other hand, changes what is on the screen. They are triggered by taps on buttons, table view cells, gestures, and so on.

The cool thing about using segues is that you no longer have to write any code to present the new screen, nor do you have to hook up your buttons to IBActions. What you just did, dragging from the Bar Button Item to the next screen, is enough to create the transition. (Note: If your control already had an IBAction connection, then the segue overrides that.)

Run the app and press the + button. A new table view will slide up the screen.

This is a so-called "modal" segue. The new screen completely obscures the previous one. The user cannot interact with the underlying screen until they close the modal screen first. Later on you'll also see "push" segues that push new screens on the navigation stack of a Navigation Controller.

The new screen isn't very useful yet – you can't even close it to go back to the main screen. That's because segues only go one way, from the Players screen to this new one. To go back, you have to use the delegate pattern. For that, you first have to give this new scene its own class. Add a new file to the project and name it PlayerDetailsViewController, subclass of UITableViewController.

To hook this new class up to the storyboard, switch back to MainStoryboard, select the new Table View Controller scene and in the Identity inspector, set its Class to PlayerDetailsViewController. I always forget this very important step, so to make sure you don't, I'll keep pointing it out.

While you're there, change the title of the screen to "Add Player" (by double-clicking in the navigation bar). Also add two Bar Button Items to the navigation bar. In the Attributes inspector, set the Identifier of the button to the left to Cancel, and the one on the right to Done.

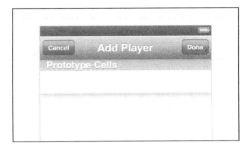

Then change PlayerDetailsViewController.h to the following:

```objc
@class PlayerDetailsViewController;

@protocol PlayerDetailsViewControllerDelegate <NSObject>
- (void)playerDetailsViewControllerDidCancel:
                    (PlayerDetailsViewController *)controller;
- (void)playerDetailsViewControllerDidSave:
                    (PlayerDetailsViewController *)controller;
@end

@interface PlayerDetailsViewController : UITableViewController

@property (nonatomic, weak) id
                <PlayerDetailsViewControllerDelegate> delegate;

- (IBAction)cancel:(id)sender;
- (IBAction)done:(id)sender;

@end
```

This defines a new delegate protocol that you'll use to communicate back from the Add Player screen to the main Players screen when the user taps Cancel or Done.

Switch back to Interface Builder, and hook up the Cancel and Done buttons to their respective action methods. One way to do this is to ctrl-drag from the bar button to the view controller and then picking the correct action name from the popup menu:

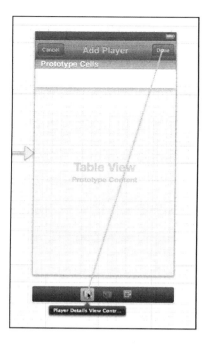

Make sure you pick the done: and cancel: actions from the Sent Actions section of the popup menu – don't create a new segue!

In PlayerDetailsViewController.m, add the following two methods at the bottom of the file:

```
- (IBAction)cancel:(id)sender
{
    [self.delegate playerDetailsViewControllerDidCancel:self];
}

- (IBAction)done:(id)sender
{
    [self.delegate playerDetailsViewControllerDidSave:self];
}
```

These are the action methods for the two bar buttons. For now, they simply let the delegate know what just happened. It's up to the delegate to close the screen. (That is not a requirement, but that's how I like to do it. Alternatively, you could make the Add Player screen close itself before or after it has notified the delegate.)

> Note: It is customary for delegate methods to include a reference to the object in question as their first (or only) parameter, in this case the `PlayerDetailsView-Controller`. That way the delegate always knows which object sent the message.

Now that you've given the `PlayerDetailsViewController` a delegate protocol, you still need to implement that protocol somewhere. Obviously, that will be in `PlayersViewController` since that is the view controller that presents the Add Player screen. Add the following to PlayersViewController.h:

```
#import "PlayerDetailsViewController.h"

@interface PlayersViewController : UITableViewController
                    <PlayerDetailsViewControllerDelegate>

. . .
```

And to the end of PlayersViewController.m:

```
#pragma mark - PlayerDetailsViewControllerDelegate

- (void)playerDetailsViewControllerDidCancel:
            (PlayerDetailsViewController *)controller
{
    [self dismissViewControllerAnimated:YES completion:nil];
}

- (void)playerDetailsViewControllerDidSave:
            (PlayerDetailsViewController *)controller
{
    [self dismissViewControllerAnimated:YES completion:nil];
}
```

Currently these delegate methods simply close the screen. Later you'll make them do more interesting things.

The `dismissViewControllerAnimated:completion:` method is new in iOS 5. You may have used `dismissModalViewControllerAnimated:` before. That method still works but the new version is the preferred way to dismiss view controllers from now on. (It also gives you the handy ability to execute additional code after the screen has been dismissed.)

There is only one thing left to do to make all of this work: the Players screen has to tell the `PlayerDetailsViewController` that it is now its delegate. That seems like something you could set up in Interface Builder just by dragging a line between the two.

Unfortunately, that is not possible. To pass data to the new view controller during a segue, you still need to write some code.

Add the following method to **PlayersViewController.m** (it doesn't really matter where):

```
- (void)prepareForSegue:(UIStoryboardSegue *)segue
                 sender:(id)sender
{
    if ([segue.identifier isEqualToString:@"AddPlayer"])
    {
        UINavigationController *navigationController =
                          segue.destinationViewController;

        PlayerDetailsViewController *playerDetailsViewController
            = [navigationController viewControllers][0];

        playerDetailsViewController.delegate = self;
    }
}
```

The `prepareForSegue` method is invoked whenever a segue is about to take place. The new view controller has been loaded from the storyboard at this point but it's not visible yet, and you can use this opportunity to send data to it.

> **Note:** You never call `prepareForSegue` yourself. It's a message from UIKit to let you know that a segue has just been triggered.

The destination of this particular segue is the Navigation Controller, because that is what you connected to the Bar Button Item. To get the `PlayerDetailsView-Controller` instance, you have to dig through the Navigation Controller's array of `viewControllers` to find it.

Run the app, press the + button, and try to close the Add Player screen. It still doesn't work!

That's because you never gave the segue an identifier. The code from `prepareForSegue` checks for that identifier ("AddPlayer"). It is recommended to always do such a check because you may have multiple outgoing segues from one view controller and you'll need to be able to distinguish between them (something that you'll do later in these chapters).

To fix this issue, open **MainStoryboard.storyboard** and click on the segue between the Players screen and the Navigation Controller. Notice that the Bar Button Item now lights up, so you can easily see which control triggers this segue.

In the Attributes inspector, set Identifier to **AddPlayer**:

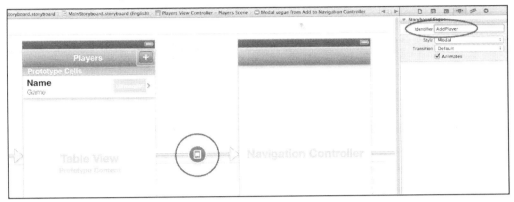

If you run the app again, tapping Cancel or Done will now properly close the screen and return you to the list of players.

> **Note:** It is perfectly possible to call `dismissViewControllerAnimated:completion:` from the modal screen. There is no requirement that says the delegate must do this. I personally prefer to let the delegate handle this but if you want the modal screen to close itself, then go right ahead.
>
> There's one thing you should be aware of. If you previously used,
>
> ```
> [self.parentViewController
>                 dismissModalViewControllerAnimated:YES]
> ```
>
> to close the screen, then that may no longer work because the "parent" view controller now means something else. Instead of using `self.parentView-Controller`, simply call the method on `self` or on `self.presentingView-Controller`, which is a new property that was introduced with iOS 5.

By the way, the Attributes inspector for the segue also has a Transition field. You can choose different animations:

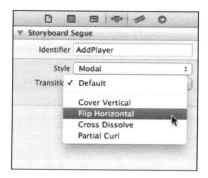

Play with them to see which one you like best. Don't change the Style setting, though. For this screen it should be Modal – any other option will crash the app!

You'll be using the delegate pattern a few more times in this tutorial. Here's a handy checklist for setting up the connections between two scenes:

4. Create a segue from a button or other control on the source scene to the destination scene. (If you're presenting the new screen modally, then often the destination will be a Navigation Controller.)

5. Give the segue a unique Identifier. (It only has to be unique in the source scene; different scenes can use the same identifier.)

6. Create a delegate protocol for the destination scene.

7. Call the delegate methods from the Cancel and Done buttons, and at any other point your destination scene needs to communicate with the source scene.

8. Make the source scene implement the delegate protocol. It should dismiss the destination view controller when Cancel or Done is pressed.

9. Implement the `prepareForSegue` method in the source view controller and do `destination.delegate = self;`.

Delegates are necessary because on iOS 5 there is no such thing as a "reverse segue". When a segue is triggered it always creates a new instance of the destination view controller. You can certainly make a segue back from the destination to the source, but that may not do what you expect.

If you were to make a segue back from the Cancel button to the Players screen, for example, then that wouldn't close the Add Player screen and return to Players, but it creates a new instance of the Players screen. You've started an infinite cycle of creating new view controllers over and over that only ends when the app runs out of memory.

Remember: Segues only go one way; they are only used to open a new screen. To go back you dismiss the screen (or pop it from the navigation stack), usually from a delegate. The segue is employed by the source controller only. The destination view controller doesn't even know that it was invoked by a segue.

> Note: Does creating a delegate protocol for each screen that you want to reach through a segue sound like a lot of work? That's what the creators of UIKit thought too, so in iOS 6 they introduced a new concept: the unwind segue. With this new feature you can create segues that close the screen and go back to the previous one. That is what the green Exit icon is for in the storyboard. Unfortunately, unwind segues are an iOS 6-only feature – it won't work on iOS 5 and therefore isn't covered in this book. If you want to learn more about unwind segues, we've dedicated a chapter to it in *iOS 6 by Tutorials*.

Static Cells

When you're finished with this section, the Add Player screen will look like this:

That's a grouped table view, of course, but the new thing is that you don't have to create a data source for this table. You can design it directly in Interface Builder – no need to write `cellForRowAtIndexPath` for this one. The new feature that makes this possible is *static cells*.

Select the table view in the Add Player screen and in the Attributes inspector change Content to Static Cells. Set Style to Grouped and Sections to 2.

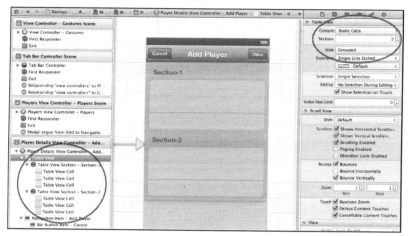

The Add Player screen will have only one row in each section, so select the superfluous cells and delete them.

Select the top-most section. In its Attributes inspector, give the Header field the value "Player Name".

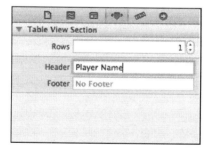

Drag a new Text Field into the cell for this section. Remove its border so you can't see where the text field begins or ends. Set the Font to System 17 and uncheck Adjust to Fit.

You're going to make an outlet for this text field on the `PlayerDetailsView-Controller` using the Assistant Editor feature of Xcode. Open the **Assistant Editor** with the button from the toolbar (the one that looks like a tuxedo / alien face). It should automatically open on **PlayerDetailsViewController.h**.

Select the text field and ctrl-drag into the .h file:

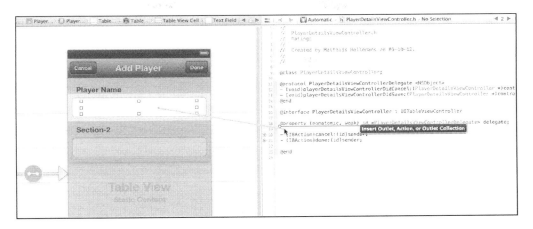

Let go of the mouse button and a popup appears:

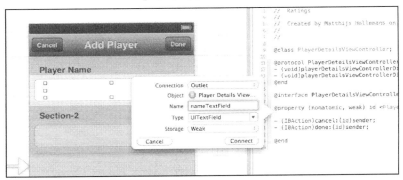

Name the new outlet `nameTextField` and choose Weak for storage. After you click Connect, Xcode will add the following property to PlayerDetailsViewController.h:

```
@property (weak, nonatomic) IBOutlet UITextField *nameTextField;
```

Note: When you make connections with the Assistant editor, the current version of Xcode also adds a `viewDidUnload` method to the .m file that sets the new outlet property to `nil`. This is no longer required. In fact, `viewDidUnload` is deprecated as of iOS 6 and Apple recommends that you no longer use it, even for iOS 5 apps. Feel free to remove this method from the code.

Creating outlets for views on your table cells is exactly the kind of thing I said you shouldn't try with prototype cells, but for static cells it is OK. There will be only one instance of each static cell (unlike prototype cells, they are never copied) and so it's perfectly acceptable to connect their subviews to outlets on the view controller.

Set the Style of the static cell in the second section to Right Detail. This gives you a standard cell style to work with. Change the label on the left to read "Game" and give the cell a disclosure indicator accessory. Make an outlet for the label on the right (the one that says "Detail") and name it detailLabel. The labels on this cell are just regular UILabel objects. Remove the header text for the section.

The final design of the Add Player screen looks like this:

Tip: The screens you have designed so far in this storyboard all have the height of the 4-inch screen of the iPhone 5, which is 568 points tall as opposed to the 480 points of the previous iPhone models. You can toggle between these two form factors using the left-most button from the little floating panel that sits at the bottom of the canvas.

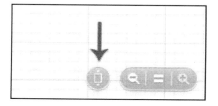

Obviously, your app should work properly with both screen sizes. You can accomplish this with autosizing masks or the new Auto Layout technology from iOS 6. For the Ratings app, you don't have to do anything fancy. It only uses table view controllers and they automatically resize to fit the extra screen space on the iPhone 5.

Back to the Add Player screen. When you use static cells, your table view controller does not need a data source. Because you used an Xcode template to create the `PlayerDetailsViewController` class, it still has some placeholder code for the data source and that will prevent the static cells from working properly. Delete anything between the lines,

```
#pragma mark - Table view data source
```

and:

```
#pragma mark - Table view delegate
```

That should silence Xcode about the warnings it has been giving ever since you added this class to the project.

Run the app and check out the new screen with the static cells. All without writing a line of code – in fact, you threw away a bunch of code!

You can't avoid writing code altogether, though. When you dragged the text field into the first cell, you probably noticed it didn't fit completely. There is a small margin of space around the text field. The user can't see where the text field begins or ends, so if they tap in the margin and the keyboard doesn't appear, they'll be confused.

To avoid that, you should let a tap anywhere in that row bring up the keyboard. That's pretty easy to do: just add or replace the `tableView:didSelectRowAtIndexPath:` method with the following:

```
- (void)tableView:(UITableView *)tableView
        didSelectRowAtIndexPath:(NSIndexPath *)indexPath
{
    if (indexPath.section == 0)
        [self.nameTextField becomeFirstResponder];
}
```

This just says that if the user tapped in the first cell, the app should activate the text field. There is only one cell in the section so you only need to test for the section index. Making the text field the "first responder" will automatically bring up the keyboard. It's just a little tweak, but one that can save users a bit of frustration.

You should also set the Selection Style for the cell to None (instead of Blue) in the Attributes inspector, otherwise the row becomes blue if the user taps in the margin around the text field.

All right, that's the design of the Add Player screen. Now let's actually make it work.

The Add Player Screen At Work

For now you will ignore the Game row and just let users enter the name of the player.

When the user presses the Cancel button the screen should close and whatever data they entered will be lost. That part already works. The delegate (the Players screen) receives the "did cancel" message and simply dismisses the view controller.

When the user presses Done, however, you should create a new Player object and fill in its properties. Then you should tell the delegate that you've added a new player, so it can update its own screen.

Inside PlayerDetailsViewController.m, first add an import:

```
#import "Player.h"
```

Then change the done: method to:

```
- (IBAction)done:(id)sender
{
    Player *player = [[Player alloc] init];
    player.name = self.nameTextField.text;
    player.game = @"Chess";
    player.rating = 1;
    [self.delegate playerDetailsViewController:self
                              didAddPlayer:player];
}
```

The done: method now creates a new Player instance and sends it to the delegate. The delegate protocol currently doesn't have this method, so change its definition in PlayerDetailsViewController.h file to:

```
@class PlayerDetailsViewController;
@class Player;

@protocol PlayerDetailsViewControllerDelegate <NSObject>

- (void)playerDetailsViewControllerDidCancel:
                    (PlayerDetailsViewController *)controller;
```

```
- (void)playerDetailsViewController:
                    (PlayerDetailsViewController *)controller
     didAddPlayer:(Player *)player;

@end
```

The "didSave" method declaration is gone. Instead, there is now a "didAddPlayer".

The last thing to do is to add the implementation for this method in PlayersViewController.m:

```
- (void)playerDetailsViewController:
                    (PlayerDetailsViewController *)controller
     didAddPlayer:(Player *)player
{
    [self.players addObject:player];

    NSIndexPath *indexPath = [NSIndexPath indexPathForRow:
                    ([self.players count] - 1) inSection:0];
    [self.tableView insertRowsAtIndexPaths:@[indexPath]
            withRowAnimation:UITableViewRowAnimationAutomatic];

    [self dismissViewControllerAnimated:YES completion:nil];
}
```

This first adds the new Player object to the array of players. Then it tells the table view that a new row was added (at the bottom), because the table view and its data source must always be in sync.

You could have just done a [self.tableView reloadData] but it looks nicer to insert the new row with an animation. UITableViewRowAnimationAutomatic is a new constant in iOS 5 that automatically picks the proper animation, depending on where you insert the new row. Very handy.

Try it out, you should now be able to add new players to the list.

If you're wondering about performance of these storyboards, then you should know that loading a whole storyboard at once isn't a big deal. The Storyboard doesn't instantiate all the view controllers right away, only the initial view controller. Because your initial view controller is a Tab Bar Controller, the two view controllers that it contains are also loaded (the Players scene from the first tab and the scene from the second tab).

The other view controllers are not instantiated until you segue to them. When you close these view controllers they are immediately deallocated, so only the actively used view controllers are in memory, just as if you were using separate nibs.

Let's see that in practice. Add these methods to PlayerDetailsViewController.m:

```
- (id)initWithCoder:(NSCoder *)aDecoder
{
    if ((self = [super initWithCoder:aDecoder]))
    {
        NSLog(@"init PlayerDetailsViewController");
    }
    return self;
}

- (void)dealloc
{
    NSLog(@"dealloc PlayerDetailsViewController");
}
```

You're overriding the `initWithCoder:` and `dealloc` methods and making them log a message to the Xcode Debug pane. Now run the app again and open the Add Player screen. You should see that this view controller did not get allocated until that point.

When you close the Add Player screen, either by pressing Cancel or Done, you should see the NSLog from `dealloc`. If you open the screen again, you should also see the message from `initWithCoder:` again. This should reassure you that view controllers are loaded on demand only, just as they would if you were loading nibs by hand.

One more thing about static cells, they only work in `UITableViewController`. Even though Interface Builder will let you add them to a Table View object inside a regular `UIViewController`, this won't work during runtime. The reason for this is that `UITableViewController` provides some extra magic to take care of the data source for the static cells. Xcode even prevents you from compiling such a project with the error message: "Illegal Configuration: Static table views are only valid when embedded in UITableViewController instances".

Prototype cells, on the other hand, work just fine in a table view that you place inside a regular view controller. Neither work for nibs, though. At the moment, if you want to use prototype cells or static cells, you'll have to use a storyboard.

It is not unthinkable that you might want to have a single table view that combines both static cells and regular dynamic cells, but this isn't very well supported by the SDK. If this is something you need to do in your own app, then see this post on the Apple Developer Forums [https://devforums.apple.com/message/505098] for a possible solution.

Note: If you're building a screen that has a lot of static cells – more than can fit in the visible frame – then you can scroll through them in Interface Builder with the scroll gesture on the mouse or trackpad (2 finger swipe). This might not be immediately obvious, but it works quite well.

The Game Picker Screen

Tapping the Game row in the Add Player screen should open a new screen that lets the user pick a game from a list. That means you'll be adding yet another table view controller, although this time you're going to push it on the navigation stack rather than show it modally.

Drag a new Table View Controller into the storyboard. Select the Game table view cell in the Add Player screen (be sure to select the entire cell, not one of the labels) and ctrl-drag to the new Table View Controller to create a segue between them. Make this a Push segue (under Selection Segue in the popup, not Accessory Action) and give it the identifier "PickGame".

Double-click the navigation bar and name this new scene "Choose Game". Set the Style of the prototype cell to Basic, and give it the reuse identifier GameCell. That's all you need to do for the design of this screen:

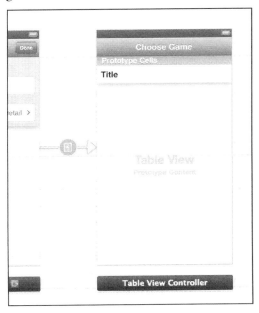

Add a new file to the project and name it GamePickerViewController, subclass of UITableViewController. Don't forget to set the Class in the storyboard so that your new GamePickerViewController object is associated with the Table View Controller.

First let's give this new screen some data to display. Add a new instance variable to GamePickerViewController.m:

```
@implementation GamePickerViewController
{
    NSArray *_games;
}
```

Fill up this array in viewDidLoad:

```
- (void)viewDidLoad
{
    [super viewDidLoad];

    _games = @[@"Angry Birds",
        @"Chess",
        @"Russian Roulette",
        @"Spin the Bottle",
        @"Texas Hold'em Poker",
        @"Tic-Tac-Toe"];
}
```

Note: This uses the new notation for creating array literals @[...] that was added to Objective-C recently. Another timesaver!

Replace the data source methods from the template with:

```
#pragma mark - Table view data source

- (NSInteger)numberOfSectionsInTableView:
                        (UITableView *)tableView
{
    return 1;
}

- (NSInteger)tableView:(UITableView *)tableView
  numberOfRowsInSection:(NSInteger)section
{
    return [_games count];
}

- (UITableViewCell *)tableView:(UITableView *)tableView
```

```
       cellForRowAtIndexPath:(NSIndexPath *)indexPath
{
    UITableViewCell *cell = [tableView
            dequeueReusableCellWithIdentifier:@"GameCell"];
    cell.textLabel.text = _games[indexPath.row];
    return cell;
}
```

That should do it as far as the data source is concerned. Run the app and tap the Game row. The new Choose Game screen will slide into view. Tapping the rows won't do anything yet, but because this screen is presented on the navigation stack you can always press the back button to return to the Add Player screen.

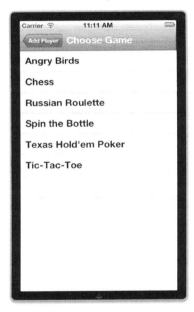

This is pretty cool, huh? You didn't have to write any code to invoke this new screen. You just ctrl-dragged from the static table view cell to the new scene and that was it.

Important: The table view delegate method didSelectRowAtIndexPath in PlayerDetailsViewController is still called when you tap the Game row, so make sure you don't do anything there that will conflict with the segue.

Of course, this new screen isn't very useful if it doesn't send any data back, so you'll have to add a new delegate for that. Replace GamePickerViewController.h with:

```
@class GamePickerViewController;

@protocol GamePickerViewControllerDelegate <NSObject>
- (void)gamePickerViewController:
                  (GamePickerViewController *)controller
      didSelectGame:(NSString *)game;
@end

@interface GamePickerViewController : UITableViewController

@property (nonatomic, weak) id
              <GamePickerViewControllerDelegate> delegate;
@property (nonatomic, strong) NSString *game;

@end
```

You've added a delegate protocol with just one method, and a property that will hold the name of the currently selected game.

Add a new instance variable, _selectedIndex, to GamePickerViewController.m:

```
@implementation GamePickerViewController
{
    NSArray *_games;
    NSUInteger _selectedIndex;
}
```

Then add the following line to the bottom of viewDidLoad:

```
    _selectedIndex = [_games indexOfObject:self.game];
```

The name of the selected game will be set in self.game. Here you figure out what the index is for that game in the list of games. You'll use that index to set a checkmark in the table view cell. For this to work, self.game must be filled in before the view is loaded. That will be no problem because you will do this in the caller's prepareForSegue, which takes place before viewDidLoad.

Change cellForRowAtIndexPath to:

```
- (UITableViewCell *)tableView:(UITableView *)tableView
        cellForRowAtIndexPath:(NSIndexPath *)indexPath
{
    UITableViewCell *cell = [tableView
              dequeueReusableCellWithIdentifier:@"GameCell"];
    cell.textLabel.text = _games[indexPath.row];

    if (indexPath.row == _selectedIndex)
        cell.accessoryType = UITableViewCellAccessoryCheckmark;
    else
```

```
    cell.accessoryType = UITableViewCellAccessoryNone;

    return cell;
}
```

This sets a checkmark on the cell that contains the name of the currently selected game. Small gestures such as these will be appreciated by the users of the app.

Replace the placeholder `didSelectRowAtIndexPath` method from the template with:

```
#pragma mark - Table view delegate

- (void)tableView:(UITableView *)tableView
        didSelectRowAtIndexPath:(NSIndexPath *)indexPath
{
    [tableView deselectRowAtIndexPath:indexPath animated:YES];

    if (_selectedIndex != NSNotFound)
    {
        UITableViewCell *cell = [tableView
            cellForRowAtIndexPath:[NSIndexPath
                indexPathForRow:_selectedIndex inSection:0]];
        cell.accessoryType = UITableViewCellAccessoryNone;
    }

    _selectedIndex = indexPath.row;
    UITableViewCell *cell = [tableView
                            cellForRowAtIndexPath:indexPath];
    cell.accessoryType = UITableViewCellAccessoryCheckmark;

    NSString *game = _games[indexPath.row];
    [self.delegate gamePickerViewController:self
                            didSelectGame:game];
}
```

First this deselects the row after it was tapped. That makes it fade from the blue highlight color back to the regular white. Then it removes the checkmark from the cell that was previously selected, and puts it on the row that was just tapped. Finally, the method returns the name of the chosen game to the delegate.

Run the app now to test that this works. Tap the name of a game and its row will get a checkmark. Tap the name of another game and the checkmark moves along with it. The screen ought to close as soon as you tap a row but that doesn't happen yet because you haven't actually hooked up the delegate.

In PlayerDetailsViewController.h, add an import:

```
#import "GamePickerViewController.h"
```

And add the delegate protocol to the @interface line:

```
@interface PlayerDetailsViewController : UITableViewController
    <GamePickerViewControllerDelegate>
```

In PlayerDetailsViewController.m, add the prepareForSegue method:

```
- (void)prepareForSegue:(UIStoryboardSegue *)segue
               sender:(id)sender
{
    if ([segue.identifier isEqualToString:@"PickGame"])
    {
        GamePickerViewController *gamePickerViewController =
                                    segue.destinationViewController;
        gamePickerViewController.delegate = self;
        gamePickerViewController.game = _game;
    }
}
```

This is similar to what you did before. This time the destination view controller is the game picker screen. Remember that this happens after GamePickerViewController is instantiated but before its view is loaded.

The _game variable is new. This is a new instance variable:

```
@implementation PlayerDetailsViewController
{
    NSString *_game;
}
```

You use this variable to remember the selected game so you can store it in the Player object later. It should get a default value. The initWithCoder: method is a good place for that:

```
- (id)initWithCoder:(NSCoder *)aDecoder
{
    if ((self = [super initWithCoder:aDecoder]))
    {
        NSLog(@"init PlayerDetailsViewController");
        _game = @"Chess";
    }
    return self;
}
```

If you've worked with nibs before, then initWithCoder: will be familiar. That part has stayed the same with storyboards; initWithCoder:, awakeFromNib, and viewDidLoad are still the methods to use. You can think of a storyboard as a collection of nibs with additional information about the transitions and relationships between them. But the views and view controllers inside the storyboard are still encoded and decoded in the same way.

Change `viewDidLoad` to display the name of the game in the cell:

```
- (void)viewDidLoad
{
    [super viewDidLoad];
    self.detailLabel.text = _game;
}
```

All that remains is to implement the delegate method:

```
- (void)gamePickerViewController:
                (GamePickerViewController *)controller
    didSelectGame:(NSString *)game
{
    _game = game;
    self.detailLabel.text = _game;

    [self.navigationController popViewControllerAnimated:YES];
}
```

This is pretty straightforward: you put the name of the new game into the _game instance variable and also the cell's label, and then close the Choose Game screen. Because it's a push segue, you have to pop this screen off the navigation stack to close it.

The `done:` method can now put the name of the chosen game into the new `Player` object, rather than the hardcoded value you've been using so far:

```
- (IBAction)done:(id)sender
{
    Player *player = [[Player alloc] init];
    player.name = self.nameTextField.text;
    player.game = _game;
    player.rating = 1;

    [self.delegate playerDetailsViewController:self
                                  didAddPlayer:player];
}
```

Awesome. You now have a functioning Choose Game screen!

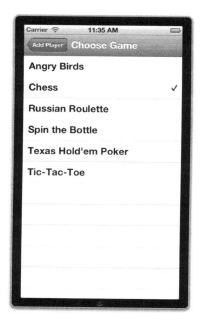

Where To Go From Here?

Congratulations. You now know the basics of using storyboards, and can create apps with multiple view controllers transitioning between each other with segues.

If you want to learn more about storyboards in iOS 5, keep reading the next chapter, where we'll cover:

- How to change the PlayerDetailsViewController so that it can also edit existing Player objects.

- How to have multiple outgoing segues to other scenes, and how to make your view controllers re-usable so they can handle multiple incoming segues.

- How to perform segues from disclosure buttons, gestures, and any other event you can think of.

- How to make custom segues – you don't have to be limited to the standard Push and Modal animations!

- How to use storyboards on the iPad, with a split-view controller and popovers.

- And finally, how to manually load storyboards and use more than one storyboard inside an app.

Chapter 5: Intermediate Storyboards

By Matthijs Hollemans

In the last chapter, you got some basic experience with storyboarding. You learned how to add view controllers into a storyboard, transition between them with segues, and even create custom table view cells quite easily.

In this chapter, you're going to learn even more cool things you can do with storyboards in iOS 5. We'll show you how to modify the app to edit players, add multiple segues between scenes, implement custom segue animations, use storyboards on the iPad, and much more.

This chapter picks up where you left off last time. Open up your Ratings project in Xcode and let's get started!

Editing Existing Players

It's always a good idea to give users of your app the ability to edit the data they've added. In this section you will extend the PlayerDetailsViewController so that besides adding new players it can also edit existing ones.

Ctrl-drag from the prototype cell in the Players screen to the Navigation Controller that is attached to the Add Player screen and add a new modal segue. Name this segue EditPlayer.

There are now two segues between these scenes:

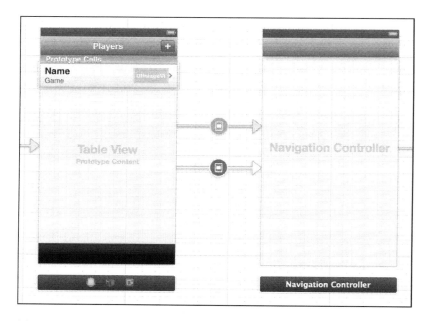

It is possible to distinguish between these two segues because you've given them unique names, AddPlayer and EditPlayer. If you get confused as to which one is which, you can simply click on the segue icon and the control that triggers it will be highlighted with a blue box. That is the + button for the AddPlayer segue, and the prototype cell for the EditPlayer segue.

In PlayersViewController.m, extend prepareForSegue to:

```objc
- (void)prepareForSegue:(UIStoryboardSegue *)segue
             sender:(id)sender
{
    if ([segue.identifier isEqualToString:@"AddPlayer"])
    {
        UINavigationController *navigationController =
                              segue.destinationViewController;
        PlayerDetailsViewController *playerDetailsViewController
            = [navigationController viewControllers][0];
        playerDetailsViewController.delegate = self;
    }
    else if ([segue.identifier isEqualToString:@"EditPlayer"])
    {
        UINavigationController *navigationController =
                              segue.destinationViewController;
        PlayerDetailsViewController *playerDetailsViewController
            = [navigationController viewControllers][0];
        playerDetailsViewController.delegate = self;
```

```
                NSIndexPath *indexPath = [self.tableView
                                     indexPathForCell:sender];
                Player *player = self.players[indexPath.row];
                playerDetailsViewController.playerToEdit = player;
        }
    }
```

The if-statement that checks for the "EditPlayer" segue is new. What happens is very similar to the "AddPlayer" segue, except that you now pass along a `Player` object in the new `playerToEdit` property.

To find the index-path for the cell that was tapped, you do:

```
            NSIndexPath *indexPath = [self.tableView
                                 indexPathForCell:sender];
```

The "sender" parameter from `prepareForSegue` contains a pointer to the control that initiated the segue. In the case of the AddPlayer segue that is the + UIBarButtonItem, but for EditPlayer it is a table view cell. Because you put the segue on the prototype cell, it can be triggered from any cell that is copied from the prototype, and you use `sender` to tell which particular cell that was.

Add the new `playerToEdit` property to PlayerDetailsViewController.h:

```
 @property (strong, nonatomic) Player *playerToEdit;
```

In PlayerDetailsViewController.m, change `viewDidLoad` to:

```
 - (void)viewDidLoad
 {
     [super viewDidLoad];

     if (self.playerToEdit != nil)
     {
         self.title = @"Edit Player";
         self.nameTextField.text = self.playerToEdit.name;
         _game = self.playerToEdit.game;
     }

     self.detailLabel.text = _game;
 }
```

If the `playerToEdit` property is set, then this screen no longer functions as the Add Player screen but it becomes Edit Player. It also fills in the text field and the game label with the values from the existing `Player` object.

Run the app and tap on a player to open the Edit Player screen:

Of course, you're not quite done with the changes. If you were to press Done now, a new Player object would still be added to the list. You have to change that part of the logic to update the existing Player object instead.

Add a new method to the delegate protocol in PlayerDetailsViewController.h:

```objectivec
- (void)playerDetailsViewController:
                    (PlayerDetailsViewController *)controller
    didEditPlayer:(Player *)player;
```

Then in PlayerDetailsViewController.m change the done: action to call this new delegate method when the user is editing an existing player object:

```objectivec
- (IBAction)done:(id)sender
{
    if (self.playerToEdit != nil)
    {
        self.playerToEdit.name = self.nameTextField.text;
        self.playerToEdit.game = _game;

        [self.delegate playerDetailsViewController:self
                            didEditPlayer:self.playerToEdit];
    }
    else
    {
        Player *player = [[Player alloc] init];
```

```
    player.name = self.nameTextField.text;
    player.game = _game;
    player.rating = 1;

    [self.delegate playerDetailsViewController:self
                            didAddPlayer:player];
    }
}
```

Finally, implement the delegate method in PlayersViewController.m:

```
- (void)playerDetailsViewController:
                    (PlayerDetailsViewController *)controller
        didEditPlayer:(Player *)player
{
    NSUInteger index = [self.players indexOfObject:player];
    NSIndexPath *indexPath = [NSIndexPath indexPathForRow:index
                                            inSection:0];
    [self.tableView reloadRowsAtIndexPaths:@[indexPath]
            withRowAnimation:UITableViewRowAnimationAutomatic];

    [self dismissViewControllerAnimated:YES completion:nil];
}
```

This simply reloads the cell for that player so that its labels get updated and then closes the Edit Player screen.

That's all there is to it. With a few small changes you were able to re-use the existing PlayerDetailsViewController class to also edit Player objects. There are two segues going to this scene, AddPlayer and EditPlayer, and which mode is used, adding or editing, depends on which segue is triggered.

Remember that performing a segue always creates a new instance of the destination view controller, so if you do Add Player first and then Edit Player some time later, you are interacting with separate instances of this class.

I have mentioned a few times that prepareForSegue is called before viewDidLoad. Here you use that to your advantage to set the playerToEdit property on the destination view controller. In viewDidLoad you read the values from playerToEdit and put them into the labels.

Note: There is no such thing as a "didPerformFromSegue" method on the destination scene that lets the scene know it was invoked by a segue. In fact, the new view controller doesn't know anything about the segue at all.

To tell the destination view controller that it was launched from a segue, or to perform additional configuration, you'll need to set a property or call a method from prepareForSegue.

You can also override the setter for your data object in the destination view controller. For example:

```
- (void)setPlayerToEdit:(Player *)newPlayerToEdit
{
    if (playerToEdit != newPlayerToEdit)
    {
        playerToEdit = newPlayerToEdit;

        // do additional configuration here
        // ...

        self.invokedFromSegue = YES;
    }
}
```

The Rating Screen

The app is called Ratings but so far you haven't done much with those ratings except show a few stars here and there. You will now add a new screen that lets you pick a rating for a player:

Drag a new View Controller into the canvas and put it below the Add Player screen. This is a regular view controller, not a table view controller.

There is a bit of a problem, you need to invoke this new Rate Player screen from the list of players, but tapping a row in that table already brings up the Edit Player screen. So first there needs to be a way to distinguish between rating a player and editing a player.

The way you're going to do it is as follows: tapping a row will now bring up the Rate Player screen, but tapping the detail disclosure button goes to the Edit Player screen.

Select the prototype cell in the Players view controller. Change its accessory to Detail Disclosure so it becomes a blue button instead of just a chevron.

Delete the existing EditPlayer segue. The idea is that you should make a new segue from the detail disclosure button to the Add/Edit Player screen. Here's the rub: making segues from the detail disclosure button is not supported on iOS 5, but as of version 4.5, Xcode does provide a means to do so.

If you ctrl-drag from the table view cell to the Navigation Controller, Xcode gives you the option to create a "Selection Segue" or an "Accessory Action". The last one sounds like what you need, but it works on iOS 6 only and it will crash the app on iOS 5 with the following error message:

```
*** Terminating app due to uncaught exception
'NSUnknownKeyException', reason: '[<PlayerCell 0x6d35530>
```

```
setValue:forUndefinedKey:]: this class is not key value coding-
compliant for the key accessoryActionSegueTemplate.'
```

So instead, because this app should be backwards compatible to iOS 5, what you'll do is put the segue on the view controller itself and then trigger it programmatically.

Ctrl-drag from the view controller icon in the dock to the Navigation Controller and add a new Modal segue. As before, give it the identifier **EditPlayer**. Note that this segue is connected to the Players view controller itself, not to any specific control inside it. There is no button or other control that you can tap to trigger the segue.

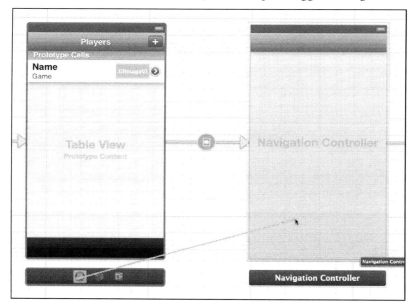

While you're here, ctrl-drag from the prototype cell to the new view controller that you just added. Make this a push segue named **RatePlayer**. There are now three outgoing segues from the Players screen.

Double-click its navigation bar to title the new screen "Rate Player".

Back to the disclosure button. If you've worked with these before you know that there is a special table view delegate method for handling taps on disclosure buttons. You're going to add this method to **PlayersViewController.m** and trigger the EditPlayer segue manually.

```
- (void)tableView:(UITableView *)tableView
      accessoryButtonTappedForRowWithIndexPath:
                                  (NSIndexPath *)indexPath
{
```

```
[self performSegueWithIdentifier:@"EditPlayer"
                          sender:indexPath];
}
```

That's all you have to do. This will load the `PlayerDetailsViewController` from the storyboard (and the Navigation Controller that contains it), and present it modally on the screen.

Of course, before the new screen is displayed, `prepareForSegue` is still called. You need to make a small change to that method. Previously, the `sender` parameter contained the `UITableViewCell` object that triggered the segue. Now, however, the segue is not being triggered from the table view cell, so instead you're sending along an `NSIndexPath` (because that's what you just put in the `sender` parameter of the call to `performSegue-WithIdentifier:sender:`).

In `prepareForSegue` the line,

```
NSIndexPath *indexPath = [self.tableView
                             indexPathForCell:sender];
```

now simply becomes:

```
NSIndexPath *indexPath = sender;
```

If you trigger a segue programmatically by calling `performSegueWithIdentifier`, then you can pass along anything you want as the `sender`. I chose to send the `NSIndexPath` because that was the least amount of work. (You could also have sent the `Player` object from that row, for example, or look up the `UITableViewCell` and send that.)

Run the app. Tapping the blue disclosure button now brings up the Edit Player screen (modally, sliding up from below) and tapping the row slides in the Rate Player screen from the side (pushed on the navigation stack).

Let's finish building the Rate Player screen. Add a new file for a `UIViewController` subclass to the project and name it RatePlayerViewController (remember, this is a regular view controller, not a table view controller).

Set the Class for the Rate Player screen in the Identity inspector. This is something I always forget and then I spend five minutes puzzling over why my screen doesn't do the things it's supposed to – until I realize I didn't actually tell the storyboard to use my subclass. Don't be as foolish as me and remember to fill in the Class field!

Replace the contents of RatePlayerViewController.h with:

```
@class RatePlayerViewController;
@class Player;
```

```
@protocol RatePlayerViewControllerDelegate <NSObject>
- (void)ratePlayerViewController:
            (RatePlayerViewController *)controller
        didPickRatingForPlayer:(Player *)player;
@end

@interface RatePlayerViewController : UIViewController

@property (nonatomic, weak) id
                <RatePlayerViewControllerDelegate> delegate;
@property (nonatomic, strong) Player *player;

- (IBAction)rateAction:(UIButton *)sender;

@end
```

This should look familiar by now. Again you're using the delegate pattern to communicate back to the source view controller.

Add an import at the top of RatePlayerViewController.m:

```
#import "Player.h"
```

Change viewDidLoad to:

```
- (void)viewDidLoad
{
    [super viewDidLoad];
    self.title = self.player.name;
}
```

This sets the name of the chosen player in the navigation bar title (instead of the text "Rate Player").

The interesting part in this view controller is the rateAction method, so add it next:

```
- (IBAction)rateAction:(UIButton *)sender
{
    self.player.rating = sender.tag;
    [self.delegate ratePlayerViewController:self
                didPickRatingForPlayer:self.player];
}
```

This puts the new rating into the Player object and then lets the delegate know about it. The rating comes from sender.tag, where the sender is a UIButton.

What you're going to do is add five UIButton objects to the view controller – one star, two stars, three stars, etc. – and give each of them a tag value that corresponds to the number of stars on the button. All of these buttons will be connected to the same action method. That's a quick 'n' easy way to make this work.

Drag five Buttons into the Rate Player screen and make the layout look like this:

The images for the buttons have already been added to the project (they are inside the Images folder). Use "1Star.png", "2Stars.png", and so on.

Connect each button's Touch Up Inside event to the rateAction: method. Set the tag attribute for the 5-stars button to 5, for the 4-stars button to 4, etc. The tag value should correspond to the number of stars on the button.

Make the background color for the scene's main view light gray so the buttons stand out a bit more. When placing the buttons, keep in mind that the screen has to work both on the new iPhone 5 and the smaller older models. Under Simulated Metrics, you can toggle the form factor for how this view controller appears in Interface Builder, which will help you make a layout that fits on all screen sizes:

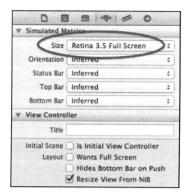

This screen doesn't need Cancel or Done buttons in the navigation bar because it's pushed on the navigation stack.

The final step is to set the delegate so that the buttons actually have somewhere to send their messages. Here are the changes to PlayersViewController.h:

```
#import "RatePlayerViewController.h"

@interface PlayersViewController : UITableViewController
    <PlayerDetailsViewControllerDelegate,
    RatePlayerViewControllerDelegate>
```

And PlayersViewController.m:

```
#pragma mark - RatePlayerViewControllerDelegate

- (void)ratePlayerViewController:
            (RatePlayerViewController *)controller
        didPickRatingForPlayer:(Player *)player
{
    NSUInteger index = [self.players indexOfObject:player];
    NSIndexPath *indexPath = [NSIndexPath indexPathForRow:index
                                              inSection:0];
    [self.tableView reloadRowsAtIndexPaths:@[indexPath]
            withRowAnimation:UITableViewRowAnimationAutomatic];

    [self.navigationController popViewControllerAnimated:YES];
}
```

Again, you simply redraw the table view cell for the player that was changed, but this time you pop the Rate Player screen off the navigation stack rather than dismiss it.

Of course, you can't forget prepareForSegue:

```objc
- (void)prepareForSegue:(UIStoryboardSegue *)segue
              sender:(id)sender
{
    // ...existing code...

    else if ([segue.identifier isEqualToString:@"RatePlayer"])
    {
        RatePlayerViewController *ratePlayerViewController =
                                    segue.destinationViewController;
        ratePlayerViewController.delegate = self;

        NSIndexPath *indexPath = [self.tableView
                                    indexPathForCell:sender];
        Player *player = self.players[indexPath.row];
        ratePlayerViewController.player = player;
    }
}
```

Because this scene has three outgoing segues, there are also three if-statements in `prepareForSegue`.

Run the app and verify that you can now pick ratings for the players.

Gestures

We've been neglecting the second tab of the app. Let's give it something to do. The project has a class named `ViewController` that was originally generated by the Xcode template, but you haven't used it until now. Using Xcode's **Edit\Refactor\Rename** menu, rename that class to **GesturesViewController**.

In the storyboard, go to the view controller that is hooked up to the second tab and set its Class field to **GesturesViewController**.

Drag in some labels and a Navigation Bar to make it look somewhat like this:

You're not going to push any screens on the navigation stack here, so you don't need to embed this scene inside a Navigation Controller. Just putting a Navigation Bar subview at the top is enough.

As the text on the labels indicates, you're going to add gestures to this screen. A swipe to the right will pop up a new screen that lists all the best players (5 stars); a double-tap will list the worst players (1 star) instead. The app needs some place to list those best/worst players, and you'll add a new table view controller for that.

Drag a Navigation Controller from the Object Library into the canvas and place it to the right of the Gestures screen. This actually gives you two new scenes: the Navigation Controller itself and a default Root View Controller attached to it. Humor me and delete that Root View Controller. There's nothing wrong with it, but I want to show you how you can connect your own view controller to the Navigation Controller.

Now drag a new Table View Controller into the canvas, next to that new Navigation Controller. Ctrl-drag from the Navigation Controller to the Table View Controller and choose Relationship Segue – root view controller to connect the two. You may need to reshuffle your scenes a bit to make this all fit.

We will designate this new Table View Controller the Ranking screen. Give it that title in its Navigation Item, so you don't get confused as to which scene is which. The storyboard is already getting quite big!

Back to the Gestures scene. Triggering a segue based on a gesture is actually pretty simple. In the Object Library there are several gesture recognizer objects:

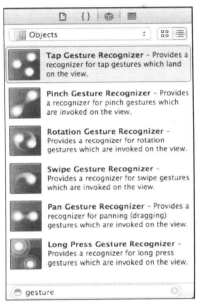

Drag the Swipe Gesture Recognizer into the Gestures screen. This will add an icon for the gesture recognizer to the dock:

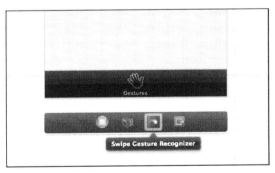

Now ctrl-drag from this icon into the Navigation Controller next door and pick the Modal segue option. Give this segue the identifier BestPlayers.

Also drag in a Tap Gesture Recognizer. Create a segue for that one too and name it WorstPlayers. In the Attributes inspector for the tap gesture recognizer, set the number of taps to 2 so it will detect double taps.

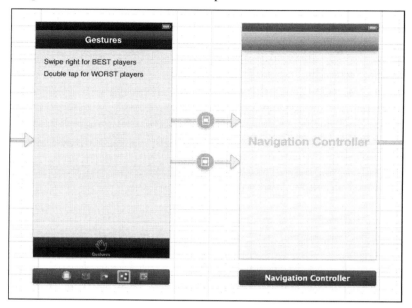

Run the app, perform the gesture, and the segue should either happen – or the app may actually crash. ☹

There is a bug in iOS 5 where adding a gesture recognizer to a view controller inside a Tab Bar Controller crashes the app. As a workaround, you can connect the gesture recognizer objects to a strong outlet in order to keep them alive.

Add the following properties to GesturesViewController.h:

```
@interface GesturesViewController : UIViewController

@property (nonatomic, strong) IBOutlet UISwipeGestureRecognizer
                                    *swipeGestureRecognizer;
@property (nonatomic, strong) IBOutlet UITapGestureRecognizer
                                    *tapGestureRecognizer;

@end
```

In the storyboard, ctrl-drag from the Gestures View Controller to the two gesture recognizer symbols in the dock to connect them to these properties. Try the app again: the crash should be history.

Now that you can make it appear, let's make the Ranking screen do something. Create a new `UITableViewController` subclass named RankingViewController.

Replace RankingViewController.h with:

```
@interface RankingViewController : UITableViewController

@property (nonatomic, strong) NSMutableArray *rankedPlayers;

- (IBAction)done:(id)sender;

@end
```

Set the Class for the Ranking screen in the storyboard to RankingViewController. Add a Done bar button to its navigation bar and connect it to the `done:` action.

Tip: You can simply ctrl-drag from the Done button to the status bar. That will always select the view controller as the target.

Delete the prototype cell from the table view. For this view controller you're going to build cells the old fashioned way. The old method of making table view cells still works, and you can even combine them with prototype cells if you want to. Some of the cells in your table view can be based on prototype cells while others are old school handmade cells. (Combining static cells with your own is also possible, but kinda tricky.)

The final design of the Ranking screen is about as simple as it gets:

For the changes in RankingViewController.m, first import the Player header:

```
#import "Player.h"
```

Replace the table view data source methods with the following:

```
#pragma mark - Table view data source

- (NSInteger)numberOfSectionsInTableView:
                          (UITableView *)tableView
{
    return 1;
}

- (NSInteger)tableView:(UITableView *)tableView
 numberOfRowsInSection:(NSInteger)section
{
    return [self.rankedPlayers count];
}

- (UITableViewCell *)tableView:(UITableView *)tableView
        cellForRowAtIndexPath:(NSIndexPath *)indexPath
{
    static NSString *CellIdentifier = @"Cell";

    UITableViewCell *cell = [tableView
             dequeueReusableCellWithIdentifier:CellIdentifier];
    if (cell == nil)
    {
        cell = [[UITableViewCell alloc]
                initWithStyle:UITableViewCellStyleSubtitle
                reuseIdentifier:CellIdentifier];
    }

    Player *player = self.rankedPlayers[indexPath.row];
    cell.textLabel.text = player.name;
    cell.detailTextLabel.text = player.game;

    return cell;
}
```

Finally, add the implementation of the done: action method:

```
- (IBAction)done:(id)sender
{
    [self dismissViewControllerAnimated:YES completion:nil];
}
```

There is no delegate for this screen. We don't really have anything useful to send back to the view controller that invoked the Ranking screen, so it simply dismisses itself when the user presses Done.

Run the app. You should be able to open and close the Ranking screen, even though it doesn't display anything yet. You still need to give it the list of ranked players.

Add the following property to GesturesViewController.h:

```
@property (nonatomic, strong) NSArray *players;
```

GesturesViewController.m needs these additional imports:

```
#import "RankingViewController.h"
#import "Player.h"
```

Add a new `prepareForSegue` method for setting up the segues in response to the gestures:

```
- (void)prepareForSegue:(UIStoryboardSegue *)segue
               sender:(id)sender
{
    if ([segue.identifier isEqualToString:@"BestPlayers"])
    {
        UINavigationController *navigationController =
                            segue.destinationViewController;
        RankingViewController *rankingViewController =
                    [navigationController viewControllers][0];
        rankingViewController.rankedPlayers =
                            [self playersWithRating:5];
        rankingViewController.title = @"Best Players";
    }
    else if ([segue.identifier isEqualToString:@"WorstPlayers"])
    {
        UINavigationController *navigationController =
                            segue.destinationViewController;
        RankingViewController *rankingViewController =
                    [navigationController viewControllers][0];
        rankingViewController.rankedPlayers =
                            [self playersWithRating:1];
        rankingViewController.title = @"Worst Players";
    }
}
```

For both segues this first gets the Navigation Controller that is on the other end of the segue, and from that you can obtain the `RankingViewController` instance. Then you give it the list of ranked players and a title.

The `playersWithRating:` method is also new:

```
- (NSMutableArray *)playersWithRating:(int)rating
{
    NSMutableArray *rankedPlayers = [NSMutableArray
                      arrayWithCapacity:[self.players count]];

    for (Player *player in self.players)
    {
        if (player.rating == rating)
            [rankedPlayers addObject:player];
    }

    return rankedPlayers;
}
```

This simply loops through the list of players and only adds those with the specified rating to a new array.

Now the question is, where does GesturesViewController get its own list of players from in the first place? From AppDelegate, of course. The App Delegate is the owner of the data model for this app.

Add the following import to AppDelegate.m:

```
#import "GesturesViewController.h"
```

Add the following to the bottom of didFinishLaunchingWithOptions:

```
- (BOOL)application:(UIApplication *)application
    didFinishLaunchingWithOptions:(NSDictionary *)launchOptions
{
    // ...existing code...

    GesturesViewController *gesturesViewController =
                      [tabBarController viewControllers][1];
    gesturesViewController.players = _players;

    return YES;
}
```

Now all the data model stuff is hooked up and you can run the app. Doing a swipe right will show all the players with 5 stars, double-tapping shows all the players with 1 star.

You're not done yet. You are also going to connect the Ranking screen to the Rate Player screen. Not for any good reason, but simply because you can.

In the storyboard, ctrl-drag from the Ranking view controller to the Rate Player screen and create a Push segue. Name it RatePlayer. There are now two segues going to the Rate Player scene, both named "RatePlayer", from different source view controllers:

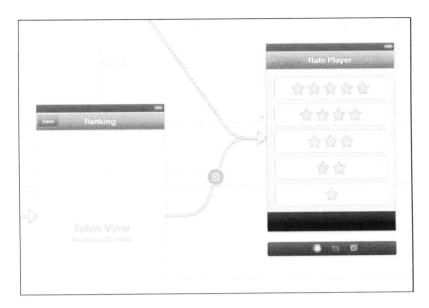

To the `RatePlayerViewController`, it doesn't really matter how many incoming segues it has or which classes are at the other ends of those segues. It just expects to receive a `Player` object in its `player` property, and then uses a delegate to communicate back to the view controller that invoked it. In fact, it doesn't even know (or care) that it was invoked by a segue.

Note: If instead of using a delegate you had hardcoded the relationship between `RatePlayerViewController` and `PlayersViewController` then it would have been much harder to also segue to it from the `RankingViewController` or any other screen.

But `RatePlayerViewController` doesn't see `PlayersViewController` or `RankingViewController` at all. It only knows that there is some object that conforms to the `RatePlayerViewControllerDelegate` protocol that it can send messages to. This kind of design keeps your code modular, reusable, and free of unwanted side effects.

Because there is no prototype cell in the Ranking screen, you'll have to perform the segue manually.

In RankingViewController.m, change `didSelectRowAtIndexPath` to the following:

```
#pragma mark - Table view delegate

- (void)tableView:(UITableView *)tableView
        didSelectRowAtIndexPath:(NSIndexPath *)indexPath
{
    Player *player = self.rankedPlayers[indexPath.row];
    [self performSegueWithIdentifier:@"RatePlayer"
                              sender:player];
}
```

First this finds the Player object in question and then sends it along as the sender parameter of performSegueWithIdentifier. That may be abusing the intent of the "sender" parameter a little (it's supposed to contain the object that initiated the segue), but it works just fine in practice.

Of course you also need a prepareForSegue method:

```
- (void)prepareForSegue:(UIStoryboardSegue *)segue
                 sender:(id)sender
{
    if ([segue.identifier isEqualToString:@"RatePlayer"])
    {
        RatePlayerViewController *ratePlayerViewController =
                            segue.destinationViewController;
        ratePlayerViewController.delegate = self;
        ratePlayerViewController.player = sender;
    }
}
```

In RankingViewController.h, add an import and make the class conform to the delegate:

```
#import "RatePlayerViewController.h"

@interface RankingViewController : UITableViewController
    <RatePlayerViewControllerDelegate>
```

Finally, add the delegate method to RankingViewController.m. It just closes the screen:

```
#pragma mark - RatePlayerViewControllerDelegate

- (void)ratePlayerViewController:
            (RatePlayerViewController *)controller
        didPickRatingForPlayer:(Player *)player
{
    [self.navigationController popViewControllerAnimated:YES];
}
```

Run the app. You should now be able to rate a player from the Ranking screen.

> **Note:** You can also use `performSegueWithIdentifier` to trigger segues based on input from the accelerometer or gyroscope, or for any other events that cannot be expressed by Interface Builder. Your imagination is the limit (but don't take it too far or your users may start to question your sanity.)

To let this app make at least some sense, it has to remove the player from the Ranking screen if the rating changes, because when that happens he or she by definition is no longer a best (5-star) or worst (1-star) player.

Add a new property to the RankingViewController.h:

```
@property (nonatomic, assign) int requiredRating;
```

For the list of best players this property's value will be set to 5, for the list of worst players it will be set to 1.

Change the implementation of the `RatePlayerViewControllerDelegate` method to the following:

```
- (void)ratePlayerViewController:
            (RatePlayerViewController *)controller
         didPickRatingForPlayer:(Player *)player
{
    if (player.rating != self.requiredRating)
    {
        NSUInteger index = [self.rankedPlayers
                                    indexOfObject:player];
        [self.rankedPlayers removeObjectAtIndex:index];

        NSIndexPath *indexPath = [NSIndexPath
                            indexPathForRow:index inSection:0];
        [self.tableView deleteRowsAtIndexPaths:@[indexPath]
                withRowAnimation:UITableViewRowAnimationFade];
    }
    [self.navigationController popViewControllerAnimated:YES];
}
```

If the rating of the selected Player changed, this removes the Player object from the array and from the table.

GesturesViewController.m has to set `requiredRating` to the proper value before it transitions to the new screen:

```objc
- (void)prepareForSegue:(UIStoryboardSegue *)segue
                 sender:(id)sender
{
    if ([segue.identifier isEqualToString:@"BestPlayers"])
    {
        // ...existing code...
        rankingViewController.requiredRating = 5;
    }
    else if ([segue.identifier isEqualToString:@"WorstPlayers"])
    {
        // ...existing code...
        rankingViewController.requiredRating = 1;
    }
}
```

Try it out and see what happens.

> Note: The app should really refresh the contents of the Players screen too, but that's left as an exercise for the reader.

Custom Segues

You've seen two types of segues already: Modal and Push. These will do fine for most apps but you have to admit they are a little boring. Fortunately, you can also create your own segue animations to liven things up a little.

Let's replace the transition from the Gestures screen to the Ranking screen with a transition of our own. Select the BestPlayers segue and set its Style to Custom. This lets you enter the name for the segue class that you're going to write in a moment. Set Segue Class to **SuperCoolSegue**. Do the same thing for the WorstPlayers segue.

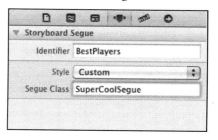

To create your own segue, you have to extend the `UIStoryboardSegue` class. Add a new Objective-C class file to the project, named SuperCoolSegue, subclass of UIStoryboardSegue.

All you need to add to this class is a "perform" method. To start, add the simplest possible implementation inside SuperCoolSegue.m:

```objc
#import "SuperCoolSegue.h"

@implementation SuperCoolSegue

- (void)perform
{
    [self.sourceViewController
        presentViewController:self.destinationViewController
        animated:NO completion:nil];
}

@end
```

This immediately presents the destination view controller on top of the source controller (modally), without an animation of any sort.

> **Note:** Previously you may have used the `presentModalViewController:animated:` method for showing modal screens, but as of iOS 5 the new method `presentViewController:animated:completion:` is the preferred way to modally present view controllers.

Try it out. When you perform the gesture, the Ranking screen appears as before, but without the usual animation. That's not much fun, and a little abrupt, so let's give it a cool animated effect.

Replace the contents of SuperCoolSegue.m with:

```objc
#import <QuartzCore/QuartzCore.h>
#import "SuperCoolSegue.h"

@implementation SuperCoolSegue

- (void)perform
{
    UIViewController *source = self.sourceViewController;
    UIViewController *destination =
                        self.destinationViewController;
```

```objc
    // Create a UIImage with the contents of the destination
    UIGraphicsBeginImageContext(destination.view.bounds.size);
    [destination.view.layer renderInContext:
                            UIGraphicsGetCurrentContext()];
    UIImage *destinationImage = UIG
                    raphicsGetImageFromCurrentImageContext();
    UIGraphicsEndImageContext();

    // Add this image as a subview to the tab bar controller
    UIImageView *destinationImageView = [[UIImageView alloc]
                            initWithImage:destinationImage];
    [source.parentViewController.view
                            addSubview:destinationImageView];

    // Scale the image down and rotate it 180 degrees
    // (upside down)
    CGAffineTransform scaleTransform =
                        CGAffineTransformMakeScale(0.1, 0.1);
    CGAffineTransform rotateTransform =
                        CGAffineTransformMakeRotation(M_PI);
    destinationImageView.transform =
        CGAffineTransformConcat(scaleTransform, rotateTransform);

    // Move the image outside the visible area
    CGPoint oldCenter = destinationImageView.center;
    CGPoint newCenter = CGPointMake(oldCenter.x -
        destinationImageView.bounds.size.width, oldCenter.y);
    destinationImageView.center = newCenter;

    // Start the animation
    [UIView animateWithDuration:0.5f delay:0
        options:UIViewAnimationOptionCurveEaseOut
        animations:^(void)
        {
            destinationImageView.transform =
                                CGAffineTransformIdentity;
            destinationImageView.center = oldCenter;
        }
        completion: ^(BOOL done)
        {
            // Remove the image as we no longer need it
            [destinationImageView removeFromSuperview];

            // Properly present the new screen
            [source presentViewController:destination
                    animated:NO completion:nil];
        }];
}

@end
```

The trick is to make a snapshot of the new view controller's view hierarchy before starting the animation, which gives you a `UIImage` with the contents of the screen, and then animate that `UIImage`. It's possible to do the animation directly on the actual views but that may be slower and it doesn't always give the results you would expect. Built-in controllers such as the navigation controller don't lend themselves very well to these kinds of manipulations.

You add that `UIImage` as a temporary subview to the Tab Bar Controller, so that it will be drawn on top of everything else. The initial state of the image view is scaled, rotated, and outside of the visible screen, so that it will appear to tumble into view when the animation starts.

After the animation is done, you remove the image view again and properly present the view controller. This transition from the image to the actual view is seamless and unnoticeable to the user because they both contain the same content.

Give it a whirl. If you don't think this animation is cool enough, then have a go at it yourself. See what kind of effects you can come up with. It can be a lot of fun to play with this stuff. If you also want to animate the source view controller to make it fly out of the screen, then I suggest you make a `UIImage` for that view as well.

When you close the Ranking screen, it still uses the regular sink-to-the-bottom animation. It's perfectly possible to perform a custom animation there as well, but remember that this transition is not a segue. The delegate is responsible for handling this, but the same principles apply. Set the `animated` flag to `NO` and do your own animation instead.

> **Note:** With the new unwind segues in iOS 6 you can also create your own `UIStoryboardSegue` subclass to perform the closing animation. You can read more about that in the book *iOS 6 by Tutorials*.

Storyboards and the iPad

You're going to make the Ratings app universal so that it also runs on the iPad.

In the project's Target Summary screen, under **iOS Application Target**, change the **Devices** setting to **Universal**. That adds a new iPad Deployment Info section to the screen.

Add a new Storyboard file to the project. Create a new file, and from the User Interface section choose the Storyboard template, and set the Device Family to iPad. Save it in the en.lproj folder as MainStoryboard~ipad.storyboard.

Open this new storyboard in the editor and drag a View Controller into it. Notice that this is now an iPad-sized view controller. Drag a Label into this new view controller and give it some text, just for testing.

Note: Disable Auto Layout in the storyboard's File inspector to make sure this app can still run on iOS 5.

Back in your target settings, in the iPad Deployment Info section on the Target Summary screen, choose MainStoryboard~ipad as the Main Storyboard:

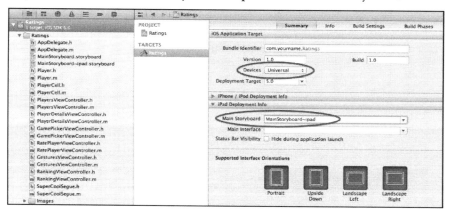

Also make sure to enable all interface orientations, because iPad apps are expected to support both portrait and landscape.

Then change AppDelegate.m to the following:

```
- (BOOL)application:(UIApplication *)application
    didFinishLaunchingWithOptions:(NSDictionary *)launchOptions
{
    _players = [NSMutableArray arrayWithCapacity:20];

    // ...existing code...

    if (UI_USER_INTERFACE_IDIOM() != UIUserInterfaceIdiomPad)
    {
        UITabBarController *tabBarController =
```

```
                (UITabBarController *)self.window.rootViewController;
        UINavigationController *navigationController =
                        [tabBarController viewControllers][0];

        PlayersViewController *playersViewController =
                        [navigationController viewControllers][0];
        playersViewController.players = _players;

        GesturesViewController *gesturesViewController =
                        [tabBarController viewControllers][1];
        gesturesViewController.players = _players;
    }

    return YES;
}
```

The new if-statement checks whether the app runs on a regular iPhone or iPod touch, and then proceeds to do the things it did before, i.e. passing the _players array to the two view controllers inside the Tab Bar Controller. The if-statement is necessary because you don't want to do any of that stuff on the iPad version, because the iPad storyboard doesn't have a Players or Gestures view controller (yet).

Now run the app on the iPad Simulator. Instead of the tab bar interface from before, you should see the new view controller with the test label from the new storyboard. The iPad version of the app successfully loaded its own storyboard.

There really aren't that many differences between making storyboards for the iPhone and the iPad, except that the iPad storyboards will be a lot bigger. You also have two additional segue types: Popover and Replace.

Let's get serious with this iPad stuff. Get rid of the view controller from the iPad storyboard and drag a new Split View Controller into the canvas. The Split View Controller comes with three other scenes attached... I told you, you need a big monitor!

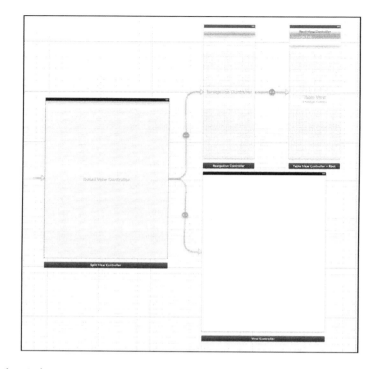

By default this Split View Controller is oriented in portrait, but if you set the Orientation field from its Simulated Metrics to Landscape, then you can see both the master and detail panes.

Note that the arrows between these scenes are all relationship connections. Just like the Navigation and Tab Bar Controllers, a Split View Controller is a container of other view controllers. On the iPhone only one scene from the storyboard is visible at a time when you run the app, but on the iPad several scenes may be visible simultaneously. The master and detail panes of the Split View Controller are an example of that.

If you run the app now it doesn't work very well yet. All you get is a white screen that doesn't rotate when you flip the device (or the simulator) over.

Add a new file to the project and name it DetailViewController, subclass of UIViewController. This is the class for the big scene that goes into the right pane of the Split View Controller.

Change DetailViewController.h to:

```
@interface DetailViewController : UIViewController
    <UISplitViewControllerDelegate>

@property (nonatomic, weak) IBOutlet UIToolbar *toolbar;
```

```
@end
```

You're making this object the delegate for the Split View Controller so it will be notified whenever the device is rotating.

Replace the contents of DetailViewController.m with:

```objc
#import "DetailViewController.h"

@implementation DetailViewController
{
    UIPopoverController *_masterPopoverController;
}

- (BOOL)shouldAutorotateToInterfaceOrientation:
        (UIInterfaceOrientation)interfaceOrientation
{
    return YES;
}

#pragma mark - UISplitViewControllerDelegate

- (void)splitViewController:
                    (UISplitViewController *)splitViewController
  willHideViewController:(UIViewController *)viewController
  withBarButtonItem:(UIBarButtonItem *)barButtonItem
  forPopoverController:(UIPopoverController *)popoverController
{
    barButtonItem.title = @"Master";
    NSMutableArray *items = [[self.toolbar items] mutableCopy];
    [items insertObject:barButtonItem atIndex:0];
    [self.toolbar setItems:items animated:YES];
    _masterPopoverController = popoverController;
}

- (void)splitViewController:
                    (UISplitViewController *)splitController
  willShowViewController:(UIViewController *)viewController
  invalidatingBarButtonItem:(UIBarButtonItem *)barButtonItem
{
    NSMutableArray *items = [[self.toolbar items] mutableCopy];
    [items removeObject:barButtonItem];
    [self.toolbar setItems:items animated:YES];
    _masterPopoverController = nil;
}

@end
```

This is the minimum you need to do to support a Split View Controller in your app.

In the storyboard, set the Class of the big scene to DetailViewController. Drag a Toolbar into this scene, at the top. The toolbar comes with a default Bar Button Item named simply Item. Rename it to "Menu" (this is for a popover you'll be adding later) and add a flexible space in front of it.

The design should look like this:

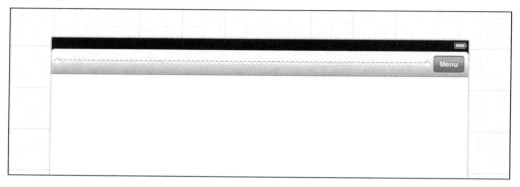

Connect the Toolbar to the view controller's toolbar outlet. Also make sure the autosizing for the toolbar is set up as follows:

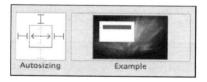

By default, toolbars are made to stick to the bottom of the screen but you want this one to sit at the top at all times, or it won't look right when the device is rotated.

You're not done yet. You also have to make a class for the "master" view controller (the Table View Controller inside the Navigation Controller), i.e. what goes on the left pane of the split-view. The only reason for doing this is so you can override the shouldAutorotateToInterfaceOrientation method and make it return YES. On the iPad all visible view controllers need to agree on the rotation or the app won't rotate properly.

Create a new UITableViewController subclass and name it MasterViewController. Add the method to MasterViewController.m:

```objc
- (BOOL)shouldAutorotateToInterfaceOrientation:
            (UIInterfaceOrientation)interfaceOrientation
{
    return YES;
}
```

Open MainStoryboard-ipad.storyboard again, select the scene named Root View Controller in the storyboard and set its Class to MasterViewController. Xcode will give some warnings about the missing data source methods from this new class, but you don't have to worry about that.

There is one more thing to do. The DetailViewController class is the delegate for the split view controller, but you haven't set up that delegate relationship anywhere yet. As you know you cannot make these kinds of connections directly in Interface Builder (unfortunately!) so you'll have to write some code in the App Delegate.

Switch to AppDelegate.m, and change the didFinishLaunchingWithOptions method to:

```
- (BOOL)application:(UIApplication *)application
    didFinishLaunchingWithOptions:(NSDictionary *)launchOptions
{
    // ...existing code...

    if (UI_USER_INTERFACE_IDIOM() != UIUserInterfaceIdiomPad)
    {
        // ...existing code...
    }
    else
    {
        UISplitViewController *splitViewController =
        (UISplitViewController *)self.window.rootViewController;

        splitViewController.delegate =
                [splitViewController.viewControllers lastObject];
    }

    return YES;
}
```

Run the app and you should now have a fully functional split view controller.

You can configure the popover size for the master view controller in the Storyboard Editor. The Attributes inspector for the Split View Controller has a setting for the popover size:

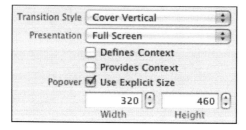

As of iOS 5.1, the master pane no longer appears in a popover but is a full-height panel that slides in from the left:

Xcode comes with a Master-Detail Application template that already sets all of this up for you, but it's good to know how to do it from scratch as well.

> Note: The way autorotation works has changed a bit on iOS 6. The trick with making the `MasterViewController` class to override the `shouldAutorotate-ToInterfaceOrientation` method is no longer necessary if your app is meant for iOS 6 and up.

Popovers

You can also easily create your own popovers. You add a new scene to the storyboard and then simply link a "Popover" segue to it.

Drag a new View Controller into the canvas. This will become the content controller of the popover. It's a little too big so under Simulated Metrics change its Size from Inferred to Freeform. Also remove the simulated status bar.

Now you can resize its view in the Size inspector. Make it 400 by 400 points. Just so you can see that the popover actually works, change the Background Color of the view to something other than white (for example Scroll View Textured Background).

Ctrl-drag from the Menu bar button item on the Detail View Controller to this new view controller and choose the Popover segue. Name it ShowPopover. Notice that the

Attributes inspector for a popover segue has quite a few options that correspond to the properties that you can set on `UIPopoverController`:

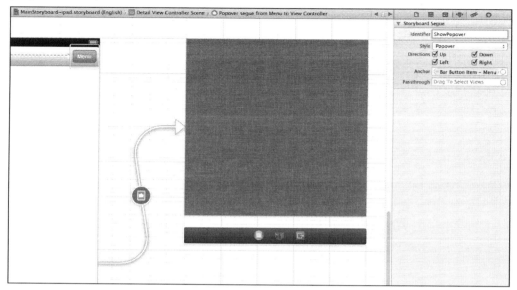

Run the app and you have a working popover! Talk about easy...

The segue that presents a popover is the `UIStoryboardPopoverSegue`, a subclass of `UIStoryboardSegue`. It adds a new property to the segue object, `popoverController`, that refers to the `UIPopoverController` that manages the popover. You should really capture that `popoverController` object in an instance variable so that you can dismiss it later if necessary.

Add the `UIPopoverControllerDelegate` protocol to the `@interface` declaration in DetailViewController.h:

```
@interface DetailViewController : UIViewController
    <UISplitViewControllerDelegate, UIPopoverControllerDelegate>
```

In DetailViewController.m, add a new instance variable:

```
@implementation DetailViewController
{
    UIPopoverController *_masterPopoverController;
    UIPopoverController *_menuPopoverController;
}
```

Add the by now very familiar `prepareForSegue` method:

```objc
- (void)prepareForSegue:(UIStoryboardSegue *)segue
                 sender:(id)sender
{
    if ([segue.identifier isEqualToString:@"ShowPopover"])
    {
        _menuPopoverController =
            ((UIStoryboardPopoverSegue *)segue).popoverController;

        _menuPopoverController.delegate = self;
    }
}
```

Here you put the value from the segue's `popoverController` property into your own `_menuPopoverController` variable and make the `DetailViewController` the delegate for the popover controller.

Add the delegate method:

```objc
#pragma mark - UIPopoverControllerDelegate

- (void)popoverControllerDidDismissPopover:
        (UIPopoverController *)popoverController
{
    _menuPopoverController.delegate = nil;
    _menuPopoverController = nil;
}
```

It simply sets the instance variable back to `nil` when the popover is dismissed.

Now that you have an instance variable that refers to the segue's popover controller when it is visible, you can dismiss the popover when the device rotates with the following method:

```objc
- (void)willAnimateRotationToInterfaceOrientation:
            (UIInterfaceOrientation)toInterfaceOrientation
        duration:(NSTimeInterval)duration
{
    if (_menuPopoverController != nil &&
                    _menuPopoverController.popoverVisible)
    {
        [_menuPopoverController dismissPopoverAnimated:YES];
        _menuPopoverController = nil;
    }
}
```

Try it out.

You may have noticed a small problem: every time you tap the Menu button, a new popover is opened but the previous one isn't closed. Tap repeatedly on the button and you end up with a whole stack of popovers. This is annoying (and might even cause your app to be rejected if you ship with this) but fortunately the workaround is easy.

It is not possible to cancel a segue once it has started so that is not an option, but when a popover is open you do have a reference to it in the _menuPopoverController variable. Change prepareForSegue to:

```
- (void)prepareForSegue:(UIStoryboardSegue *)segue
            sender:(id)sender
{
    if ([segue.identifier isEqualToString:@"ShowPopover"])
    {
        if (_menuPopoverController != nil &&
            _menuPopoverController.popoverVisible)
        {
            [_menuPopoverController dismissPopoverAnimated:NO];
        }

        _menuPopoverController =
            ((UIStoryboardPopoverSegue *)segue).popoverController;

        _menuPopoverController.delegate = self;
    }
}
```

No matter how many times you tap the Menu button now, only one popover is ever visible.

> Note: On iOS 6 it is a little easier to prevent multiple instances of the popover from showing using the new method shouldPerformSegueWithIdentifier: sender: that is called just before the segue happens. For example:
>
> ```
> - (BOOL)shouldPerformSegueWithIdentifier:(NSString *)identifier
>                                   sender:(id)sender
> {
>     if ([identifier isEqualToString:@"ShowPopover"] &&
>             _menuPopoverController != nil &&
>             _menuPopoverController.popoverVisible)
>         return NO;
>     else
>         return YES;
> }
> ```

Besides the Popover segue, iPad storyboards can also have a "Replace" segue. You use this to replace the master or detail view controllers in a Split View Controller. Like the built-in Settings app, you could have a table view in the master pane with each row having its own detail view. You can put a Replace segue between each row and its associated detail scene, to swap out the detail controller when you tap such a row.

You can also use segues for presenting modal form sheets and page sheets. To do this you simply set the Presentation attribute for the destination view controller to the style you want to use:

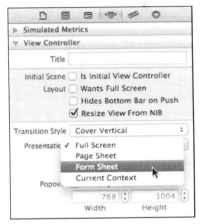

Manually Loading Storyboards

The iPad version of the Ratings app doesn't have a lot to do with ratings yet, so let's put the screens from the iPhone storyboard into the master pane of the Split View Controller. You're going to do that programmatically as there is no way you can link from one storyboard to another.

> Note: I'm not saying that this is what you should do in your own universal apps. It may make more sense to keep the storyboards for the iPhone and iPad apps completely separate. However, for the purposes of this tutorial it is a good demonstration of how to load additional storyboards by hand, just in case you ever need to write an app that uses more than one storyboard.

Delete the Navigation Controller and Root View Controller scenes from the iPad storyboard. You can also delete the `MasterViewController` class files from the project if you want. The storyboard now looks like this:

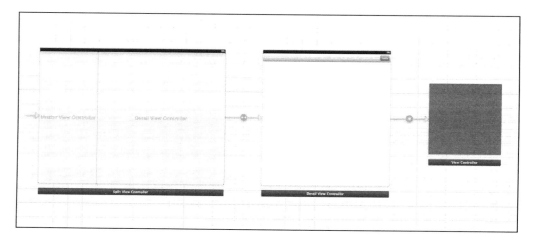

You're going to load the iPhone storyboard in the App Delegate and then put its Tab Bar Controller into the master pane of the Split View Controller.

Storyboards are represented by the UIStoryboard class. The main storyboard file is loaded automatically when your app starts, but you can load additional storyboards by calling [UIStoryboard storyboardWithName:bundle:].

There is only one problem. If you attempt to load the iPhone storyboard using,

```
UIStoryboard *storyboard = [UIStoryboard
          storyboardWithName:@"MainStoryboard" bundle:nil];
```

then this will actually load the MainStoryboard~ipad file. Even though you only specified "MainStoryboard" as the filename, the app will automatically append "~ipad" to it because this is a universal app running in iPad mode. The app will get totally confused. For this section of the chapter you'd better rename the iPad storyboard file. Call it iPadMainStoryboard.storyboard instead.

Don't forget to change the Main Storyboard setting in the iPad Deployment Info section under Target Summary. (It's also a good idea to do a clean build and to remove the app from the Simulator before you continue just to make sure it doesn't use a cached version of the old storyboard.)

In AppDelegate.m, change didFinishLaunchingWithOptions to:

```
- (BOOL)application:(UIApplication *)application
    didFinishLaunchingWithOptions:(NSDictionary *)launchOptions
{
    // ...code to make the Player objects...

    UITabBarController *tabBarController;
```

```objc
if (UI_USER_INTERFACE_IDIOM() != UIUserInterfaceIdiomPad)
{
    tabBarController = (UITabBarController *)
                       self.window.rootViewController;
}
else
{
    UISplitViewController *splitViewController =
                    (UISplitViewController *)
                        self.window.rootViewController;
    id detailViewController =
            [splitViewController.viewControllers lastObject];

    UIStoryboard *storyboard = [UIStoryboard
            storyboardWithName:@"MainStoryboard" bundle:nil];
    tabBarController = [storyboard
                        instantiateInitialViewController];

    NSArray *viewControllers = @[tabBarController,
                                detailViewController];
    splitViewController.viewControllers = viewControllers;
    splitViewController.delegate = detailViewController;
}

UINavigationController *navigationController =
                [tabBarController viewControllers][0];
PlayersViewController *playersViewController =
                [navigationController viewControllers][0];
playersViewController.players = _players;

GesturesViewController *gesturesViewController =
                [tabBarController viewControllers][1];
gesturesViewController.players = _players;

return YES;
}
```

The new part is this:

```objc
UIStoryboard *storyboard = [UIStoryboard
        storyboardWithName:@"MainStoryboard" bundle:nil];

tabBarController = [storyboard
                    instantiateInitialViewController];
```

This loads the MainStoryboard file into a new UIStoryboard object and then calls instantiateInitialViewController to load its initial view controller, which in your case is the Tab Bar Controller.

Once you have the Tab Bar Controller, you need to put it into the Split View Controller's master pane. Currently the split-view only contains the Detail View Controller, so you add the Tab Bar Controller to its viewControllers property:

```
NSArray *viewControllers = @[tabBarController,
                             detailViewController];

splitViewController.viewControllers = viewControllers;
```

Run the app and you should see the screens from the iPhone version of the app in the split-view popover:

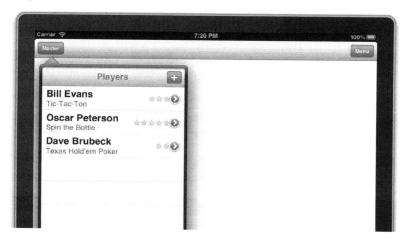

If you start tapping on stuff you'll notice the integration isn't as seamless as it could be. That's because you never configured the scenes from your original storyboard to work on the iPad.

Go through the .m files for all the view controllers and add the shouldAutorotateTo-InterfaceOrientation method:

```
- (BOOL)shouldAutorotateToInterfaceOrientation:
        (UIInterfaceOrientation)interfaceOrientation
{
    if (UI_USER_INTERFACE_IDIOM() == UIUserInterfaceIdiomPad)
        return YES;

    return (interfaceOrientation !=
            UIInterfaceOrientationPortraitUpsideDown);
}
```

Now the app will properly rotate to landscape mode.

> Note: Overriding `shouldAutorotateToInterfaceOrientation:` in all your view controllers is no longer necessary on iOS 6. But if you still want your app to be compatible with iOS 5, then doing so is unavoidable.

Interface Builder doesn't let you set the popover size for view controllers in an iPhone storyboard (which is understandable because the iPhone doesn't have popovers), so you'll have to do that in code. Add to `application:didFinishLaunchingWith-Options:`

```
tabBarController.contentSizeForViewInPopover = CGSizeMake(
                                         320, 460);
```

Now the popover from the Split View Controller is just as big as the contents of the iPhone screen. This setting only has an effect on iOS 5.0. As of 5.1, the split-view master pane is no longer a popover but a panel that always takes up the full height of the screen.

There is one more minor problem with the app and that is that the modal view controllers are being presented full screen, which looks a little weird when you tap the + button to add a new player. This is related to the modal presentation style setting of the view controllers.

For example, if in PlayersViewController.m in `prepareForSegue`, you do,

```
navigationController.modalPresentationStyle =
                        UIModalPresentationCurrentContext;
playerDetailsViewController.contentSizeForViewInPopover =
                                  CGSizeMake(320, 423);
```

then the modal scene doesn't take over the whole screen – the modal view will appear in the master controller only.

`UIStoryboard`'s `instantiateInitialViewController` method is not the only way to load a view controller from a storyboard. You can also ask for a specific view controller using `instantiateViewControllerWithIdentifier:`. That is useful if you don't have a segue to that view controller in the storyboard.

To demonstrate this feature, open the iPhone storyboard and delete the EditPlayer segue from the Players scene. This segue was formerly triggered by the disclosure button.

Replace the `accessoryButtonTappedForRowWithIndexPath:` method in PlayersViewController.m with the following:

```objc
- (void)tableView:(UITableView *)tableView
    accessoryButtonTappedForRowWithIndexPath:
                        (NSIndexPath *)indexPath
{
    UINavigationController *navigationController =
        [self.storyboard instantiateViewControllerWithIdentifier:
            @"PlayerDetailsNavigationController"];

    PlayerDetailsViewController *playerDetailsViewController =
                    [navigationController viewControllers][0];
    playerDetailsViewController.delegate = self;

    Player *player = self.players[indexPath.row];
    playerDetailsViewController.playerToEdit = player;

    [self presentViewController:navigationController
                    animated:YES completion:nil];
}
```

This is very similar to what you did in `prepareForSegue`, except for the first line:

```objc
UINavigationController *navigationController =
    [self.storyboard instantiateViewControllerWithIdentifier:
        @"PlayerDetailsNavigationController"];
```

The `self.storyboard` property refers to the `UIStoryboard` object that this view controller was loaded from. You can ask this `UIStoryboard` object to instantiate a specific view controller, in this case the Navigation Controller that contains the Player Details scene.

In order for this to work, you have to set an identifier (PlayerDetailsNavigation-Controller) on the view controller in its Identity inspector:

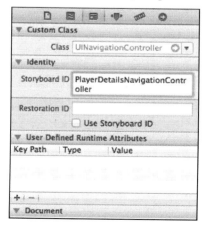

> **Note:** You want to instantiate the Navigation Controller, so set this identifier on the Navigation Controller, not on the Player Details view controller.

Run the app (from the iPhone simulator) and try editing a player. You'll see that this still works even though the storyboard no longer has the EditPlayer segue.

Last Words

Localizing your storyboards is pretty easy; it works just like localizing any other resource. Simply select the storyboard and under Localization in the File inspector you add a new language. Done.

You've seen that each scene in the storyboard has a dock area that contains the top-level objects for that scene, usually just the First Responder, the View Controller, and an Exit icon that is used with unwind segues on iOS 6. Gesture recognizers and table view sections are also added to the dock.

In theory you can drag any other view objects that you want into the dock, just like you can with nibs. The problem is that the Interface Builder doesn't give you any means to edit these objects.

For example, if you want to change the background image for a static cell, you can drag a `UIImageView` into the dock and hook it up to the cell's `backgroundImage` property. That works but you can only edit that Image View through the inspectors. It is not visible in the canvas anywhere. I hope the storyboard team adds in this functionality because it's really handy to load extra objects that way.

Another thing that storyboards don't support very well is custom container view controllers. Having a `UITabBarController` or `UINavigationController` is fine and dandy, but what if you want to make your own "tab bar" or some other container using the new view containment APIs?

As of iOS 6 you can use the Container View element to embed the contents of one view controller inside another in your storyboards (see the book *iOS 6 by Tutorials* for more info), but that's only half a solution and it obviously doesn't work on iOS 5. For the time being, you will have to handle view controller containment programmatically and not in your storyboards.

Tip: You can put the standard view controllers such as the UIImagePicker-Controller and MFMailComposeViewController in your storyboards with a little trick. Drag a regular view controller onto the canvas and set its class to UIImagePickerController. In prepareForSegue, set the properties on the new controller and off you go. I'm not really sure if this is supported behavior, but it seems to work fairly well. ;-)

Where To Go From Here?

Congratulations on making it through – you now have a lot of hands-on experience with using storyboards to create an app. I think storyboards are a great addition to iOS and I look forward to using them in my new projects. Prototype cells and static cells especially are bound to be big time savers.

Should you change your existing projects to use Storyboards? Probably not, but for any new apps that you want to make iOS 5+ only it's a good idea.

In case you want to migrate your existing projects anyway, it is possible to copy the contents of your nibs into the storyboard. First drag a new View Controller into the storyboard and delete its main view. Then open your nib file in a new window and drag its view into the new View Controller on the storyboard. This will take over the existing design and save you some time recreating it. You may need to reconnect the outlets and actions, though.

Have fun storyboarding!

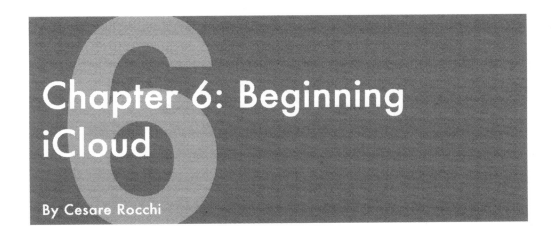

Chapter 6: Beginning iCloud

By Cesare Rocchi

iCloud is meant to solve a big problem which affects our daily lives as users of multiple devices: data synchronization. We all have stuff we use on our devices regularly like documents, pictures, videos, emails, calendars, music, and address books. Now that mobile devices are becoming more and more common, we often find our stuff scattered in many places. Some might be on our PC, some on our iPhone, and some on our iPad. How many times have you tried to quickly open a document and realized "argh, I have it saved on another device"?

A common workaround is to keep data you need often on some shared folder (like Dropbox) or send yourself emails with recent versions of documents. There are ways to address these issues, but they are, as I said, workarounds that require some effort, like remembering to send yourself an email or to upload recently changed documents to the shared folder.

iCloud is a service to which you can delegate this "remembering". It is a set of central servers that store your documents, and make the latest version available to every device/app compatible with iCloud (iPhone, iPod, iPad, Mac, or even PC).

Here is a common scenario: you enter an appointment in the calendar on the Mac, you forget to synch it with the iPhone, pick up your iPhone and get out of the office. When will you see the notification? When you get back to the office, it might be too late! Before iCloud you'd be in trouble, but now the calendar app on the iPhone is integrated with iCloud! iCloud will automatically pick changes to your calendar and push them to all the other devices connected to your account. It is all in one place (the cloud) and anywhere (your devices) at the same time!

To some extent this is a solution very similar to the IMAP protocol, which allows keeping emails in synch on different devices, due to the flexibility of the protocol and the fact that messages are stored on a central server and copied on clients upon request.

Before the release of iOS5, iTunes has been a sort of solution to the "synchronization problem", with the huge drawback mentioned above: you have to remember to physically connect your device to your Mac or PC and hit the synch button. Moreover, you have to repeat the operation for each of your devices. Now iCloud solves everything automatically without the need to remember, because some magic process takes care of synchronizing documents, pictures, preferences, contacts and calendars.

iCloud is great news for developers. By using a set of new APIs, you can configure your app to store and retrieve data on iCloud as well. Can you think of the advantages? The possibilities are just endless!

In this tutorial, you'll investigate iCloud by implementing a set of simple applications that interact with cloud servers to read, write and edit documents. In the process, you'll learn about the new `UIDocument` class, querying iCloud for files, autosaving, and much more!

To get the most out of this tutorial, you will need two physical devices for testing, such as an iPhone and an iPad. The simulator does not currently have iCloud support.

Note: There's an important note about Apple's data saving policy and iCloud that you should be aware of. Whether or not you enable iCloud in your application, all the contents stored in local "Documents" directory of your application are automatically backed up on iCloud if the user chooses to enable backup for applications.

If your data can be recreated somehow, don't store it in "Documents", otherwise backups are not efficient and your app wastes user's iCloud storage space. In fact, Apple is getting more strict about checking for this kind of thing, and your app might be rejected if you do this.

Temporary data can be stored in <Application_Home>/tmp. Data that can be downloaded again, like copies of magazines, can be stored in <Application_Home>/Library/Caches.

Under the hood

Before you begin, let's talk about how iCloud works.

In iOS each application has its data stored in a local directory, and can only access data in its own directory. This prevents apps from reading or modifying data from other apps.

iCloud allows you to upload your local data to central servers on the network, and receive updates from other devices. The replication of content across different devices is achieved by means of a continuous background process (referred to as *daemon*), which detects changes to a resource (document) and uploads them to the central storage.

If you ever tried to create something like this on your own, you know there are several major challenges when implementing this:

1. **Conflict resolution.** What happens if you modify a document on your iPhone, and modify the same document on your iPad at the same time? Somehow you have to reconcile these changes. iCloud allows you to break your documents into chunks to prevent many merge conflicts from being a problem (because if you change chunk A on device 1, and chunk B on device 2, since chunk A and B are different you can just combine them). For cases when it truly is a problem, it allows you as a developer fine-grained control over how to handle the problem (and you can always ask the user what they would like to do).

2. **Background management.** iOS apps only have limited access to running tasks in the background, but keeping your documents up-to-date is something you want to always be doing. The good news is that, since iCloud synchronization is running in a background daemon, it's always active!

3. **Network bandwidth costs.** Continuously pushing documents between devices can take a lot of network bandwidth. As mentioned above, iCloud helps reduce the costs by breaking each document into chunks. When you first create a document, every chunk is copied to the cloud. When subsequent changes are detected only the chunks affected are uploaded to the cloud, to minimize the usage of bandwidth and processing. A further optimization is based on a peer-to-peer solution. That happens when two devices are connected to the same iCloud account and the same wireless network. In this case data take a shortcut and move directly between devices.

The mechanisms described so far are enabled by a smart management of metadata like file name, size, modification date, version etc. This metadata is aggressively pushed to the servers, and iCloud uses this information to determine what needs to be pulled down to each device.

Note that devices pull data from the cloud when "appropriate". The meaning of this depends on the OS and platform. For example an iPhone has much less power and "battery dependency" than an iMac plugged into a wall. In this case iOS might decide to notify just the presence of a new file, without downloading it, whereas Mac OS X might start the download immediately after the notification.

The important aspect is that an application is always aware of the existence of a new file, or changes to an already existing file, and through an API the developer is free to implement the synchronization policy. In essence the API allows an app to know the "situation" on iCloud even if the files are not yet local, leaving the developer free to choose whether (and when) to download an updated version.

Note. While you're going through this tutorial, if you get stuck with a bug or unexpected behavior it is suggested to start from scratch with a fresh app install and make sure no previous data is on your device. This is because previous versions of the app (especially if you use the same provisioning and bundle id) might conflict with the version you are working on.

To do this, uninstall the application from your device and delete the data stored by your app from Settings/iCloud/Storage & Backup/Manage Storage. Most of the examples create an "Unknown" item in this list.

Configuring iCloud

When you first set up an iOS device, you'll be asked to configure an iCloud account by providing or creating an Apple ID. Configuration steps will also allow you to set which services you want to synchronize (calendar, contacts, etc.). Those configurations are also available under Settings\iCloud on your device.

Before you proceed any further with this tutorial, make sure that you have two test devices, and that iCloud is working properly on both devices. One easy way to test this is to add a test entry into your calendar, and verify that it synchronizes properly between your various devices. You can also visit http://www.icloud.com to see what's in your calendar.

Once you're sure iCloud is working on your device, you'll try it out in an app of your own creation!

Enabling iCloud in your application

In this tutorial, you'll be creating a simple app that manages a shared iCloud document called "dox". The app will be universal and will be able to run on both iPhone and iPad, so you can see changes made on one device propagated to the other.

There are three steps to use iCloud in an app, so let's try them out as you start this new project.

1. Create an iCloud-enabled App ID

To do this, visit the iOS Developer Center and log onto the iOS Provisioning Portal. Create a new App ID for your app similar to the below screenshot (but replace the bundle identifier with a unique name of your own).

Note. Be sure to end your App ID with "dox" in this tutorial, because that is what you will be naming the project. For example, you could enter `com.yourname.dox`.

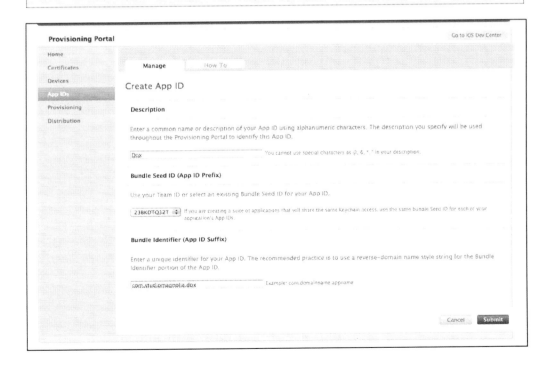

After you create the App ID, you will see that Push Notifications and Game Center are automatically enabled, but iCloud requires you to manually enable it. Click the Configure button to continue.

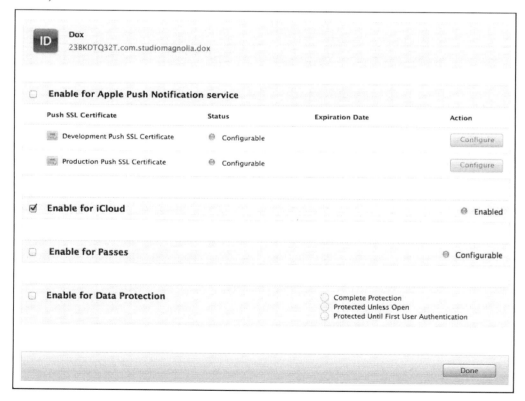

On the next screen, click the checkbox next to Enable for iCloud and click OK when the popup appears. If all works well, you will see a green icon next to the word Enabled. Then just click Done to finish.

2. Create a provisioning profile for the App ID

Still in the iOS Provisioning Portal, switch to the Provisioning section, and click New Profile. Select the App ID you just created from the dropdown, and fill out the rest of the information, similar to the screenshot below.

After creating the profile, refresh the page until it is ready for download, and then download it to your machine. Once it's downloaded, double click it to bring it into Xcode, and verify that it is visible in Xcode's Organizer.

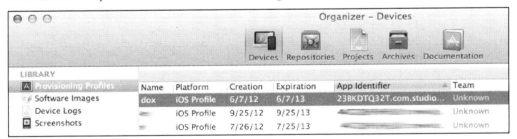

3. Configure your Xcode project for iCloud

Start up Xcode and create a new project with the iOS\Application\Master-Detail Application template. Enter dox for the product name, enter the company identifier you used when creating your App ID, enter SM for the class prefix, set the device family to Universal, and make sure Use Automatic Reference Counting and Use Storyboards are checked (but leave the other checkboxes unchecked).

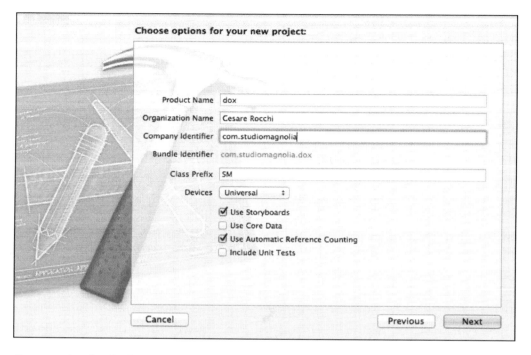

Once you've finished creating the project, select your project in the Project Navigator and select the dox target. Select the Summary tab, and scroll way down to the Entitlements section.

Once you're there, check the **Entitlements** and **Enable iCloud** checkboxes, and populate the fields based on your App ID, as shown below.

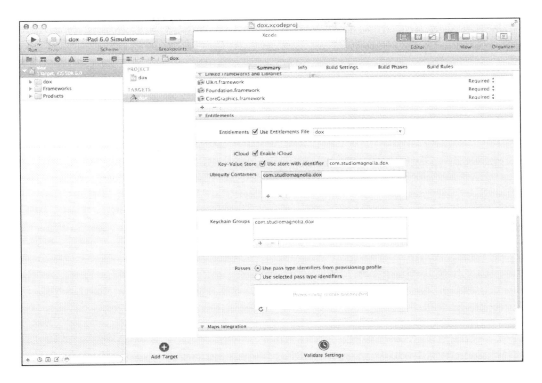

This is what the fields here mean:

- The Entitlements File points to a property list file which, much like the info.plist file, includes specifications about application entitlements.

- The iCloud Key-Value Store represents the unique identifier which points to the key-value store in iCloud. You will learn more about the key-value store more in the next chapter.

- The Ubiquity Containers section represents "directories" in the cloud in which your applications can read/write documents. Yes, you have read correctly, I said applications (plural), for a user's container can be managed by more than one application. The only requirement is that applications have to be created by the same team (as set up in the iTunes Developer Center).

- The Keychain Groups includes keys needed by applications that are sharing keychain data. The keychain is beyond the scope of this chapter.

You don't have to change anything from the defaults for this tutorial, so you are ready to go! If you like you can edit the same settings by editing the file dox.entititlements that is included in your project.

Checking for iCloud availability

When building an application that makes use of iCloud, the best thing to do is to check the availability of iCloud as soon as the application starts. Although iCloud is available on all iOS 5 and iOS 6 devices, the user might not have configured it. To avoid possible unintended behaviors or crashes, you should check if iCloud is available before using it. Let's see how this works.

Open up the SMAppDelegate.m file of the project you have just created and add the following code at the bottom of `application:didFinishLaunchingWithOptions` (before the return statement).

```
id currentToken = [[NSFileManager defaultManager]
    ubiquityIdentityToken];
if (currentToken) {
    NSLog(@"iCloud access on with id %@", currentToken);
} else {
    NSLog(@"No iCloud access");
}
```

Here you use a new method you haven't seen yet called `ubiquityIdentityToken`. This method allows you to retrieve the token associated with the user's iCloud account. If this token is `nil` that means the user has not activated iCloud on his device, otherwise you are good to go and you can use iCloud features in your app.

> Note: The token identifies a single user account, so if the user switches accounts by entering new iCloud's credentials, you'll get a separate token. You can use this to tweak you application accordingly.

Compile and run your project (on a device, because iCloud does not work on the simulator), and if all works well, you should see a message in your console like this:

```
iCloud access on with id <1b10b44e 0cc644b0 63843d43 976b46b5
0189c5d3>
```

Note that this method is new to iOS 6 - unlike iOS 5, there no need to call `URLForUbiquityContainerIdentifier` and pass the id of the ubiquity container.

> Note: The project up to this point is in the resources for this chapter as dox-00.

iCloud API overview

Before you go on with the code, let's take a few minutes to give an overview of the APIs you'll be using to work with iCloud documents.

To store documents in iCloud, you can do things manually if you'd like, by moving files to/from the iCloud directory with new methods in `NSFileManager` and the new `NSFilePresenter` and `NSFileCoordinator` classes. However doing this is fairly complex and unnecessary in most cases, because iOS5 has introduced a new class to make working with iCloud documents much easier: `UIDocument`.

`UIDocument` acts as middleware between the file itself and the actual data (which in your case will be the text of a note). In your apps, you'll usually create a subclass of `UIDocument` and override a few methods on it that we'll discuss below.

`UIDocument` implements the `NSFilePresenter` protocol for you and does its work in the background, so the application is not blocked when opening or saving files, and the user can continue working with it. Such a behavior is enabled by a double queue architecture.

The first queue, the main thread of the application, is the one where your code is executed. Here you can open, close and edit files. The second queue is on the background and it is managed by UIKit.

For example let's say you want to open a document, which has been already created on iCloud. You'd send a message to an instance of `UIDocument` like the following:

```
[doc openWithCompletionHandler:^(BOOL success) {
    // Code to run when the open has completed
}];
```

This triggers a 'read' message into the background queue. You can't call this method directly, for it gets called when you execute `openWithCompletionHandler:`. Such an operation might take some time (for example, the file might be very big, or not downloaded locally yet).

In the meantime you can do something else on the user application so the application is not blocked. Once the reading is done you are free to load the data returned by the read operation.

This is exactly where `UIDocument` comes in handy, because you can override the `loadFromContents:ofType:error:` method to read the data into your `UIDocument` subclass. Here's a simplified version what it will look like for your simple notes app:

```
- (BOOL)loadFromContents:(id)contents
```

```
                          ofType:(NSString *)typeName
                          error:(NSError **)outError
    {

        self.noteContent = [[NSString alloc]
                            initWithBytes:[contents bytes]
                            length:[contents length]
                            encoding:NSUTF8StringEncoding];

        return YES;

    }
```

This method is called by the background queue whenever the read operation has been completed. The most important parameter here is contents, which is typically an NSData containing the actual data which you can use to create or update your model. You'd typically override this method to parse the NSData and pull out your document's information, and store it in some instance variables in your UIDocument subclass, like shown here.

After loadFromContents:ofType:error: completes, you'll receive the callback you provided in the openWithCompletionHandler: block, as shown in the diagram below.

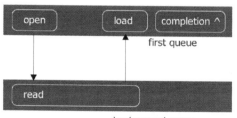

To sum up, when you open a file you receive two callbacks: first in your UIDocument subclass when data has been read, and secondly when open operation is completely finished.

The write operation is pretty similar and it exploits the same double queue. The difference is that when opening a file you have to parse an NSData instance, but while closing you have to convert your document's data to NSData and provide it to the background queue.

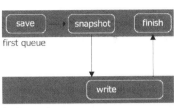

To save a document, you can either manually initiate the process by writing code, or via the auto saving feature implemented in `UIDocument` (more on this below).

If you want to save manually, you'd call a method like this:

```
[doc saveToURL:[doc fileURL]
  forSaveOperation:UIDocumentSaveForCreating
  completionHandler:^(BOOL success) {
    // Code to run when the save has completed
}];
```

Just like when opening a file, there is a completion handler that is called when the writing procedure is done. When asked to write, the background queue asks for a snapshot of the contents of your `UIDocument` subclass. This is accomplished by overriding another method of `contentsForType:error:`.

Here you should return an `NSData` instance that describes the current model to be saved. In your notes application, you'll be returning an `NSData` representation of a string as follows:

```
- (id)contentsForType:(NSString *)typeName
                error:(NSError **)outError
{

    return [NSData dataWithBytes:[self.noteContent UTF8String]
                         length:[self.noteContent length]];

}
```

The rest is taken care of in the background queue, which manages the storing of data. Once done the code in the completion handler will be executed.

For sake of completeness I should mention that in both reading and writing, instead of `NSData` you can use `NSFileWrapper`. While `NSData` is meant to manage flat files `NSFileWrapper` can handle **packages**, that is a directory with files treated as a single file. You'll learn how to use `NSFileWrapper` in the next chapter.

As I mentioned earlier, the save operation can be called explicitly via code or triggered automatically. The UIDocument class implements a saveless model, where data is saved automatically at periodic intervals or when certain events occur. This way there is no need for the user to tap a 'save' button anymore, because the system manages that automatically, e.g. when you switch to another document.

Under the hood the UIKit background queue calls a method on UIDocument called hasUnsavedChanges, which returns whether the document is "dirty" and needs to be saved. In case of positive response the document is automatically saved. There is no way to directly set the value for such a method but there are two ways to influence it.

The first way is to explicitly call the updateChangeCount: method. This notifies the background queue about changes. As an alternative you can use the undo manager, which is built in the UIDocument class. Each instance of this class (or subclasses) has in fact a property undoManager. Whenever changes are registered via an undo or redo action the updateChangeCount: is called automatically. You'll learn about this topic later in the chapter.

It is important to remember that in either case the propagation of changes might not be immediate. By sending these messages you are only providing 'hints' to the background queue, which will start the update process when it's appropriate according to the device and the type of connection.

Subclassing UIDocument

Now that you have a good overview of UIDocument, let's create a subclass for your note application and see how it works!

Create a new file with the iOS\Cocoa Touch\Objective-C class template. Name the class SMNote, and make it a subclass of UIDocument.

To keep things simple, your class will just have a single property to store the note as a string. To add this, replace the contents of SMNote.h with the following:

```
@interface SMNote : UIDocument
@property (strong) NSString * noteContent;
@end
```

As you have learned above you have two override points, one when you read and one when you write. Add the implementation of these by replacing SMNote.m with the following:

```
#import "SMNote.h"
```

```objc
@implementation SMNote

// Called when the application reads data from the file system
- (BOOL)loadFromContents:(id)contents
  ofType:(NSString *)typeName error:(NSError **)outError
{

    if ([contents length] > 0) {
        self.noteContent = [[NSString alloc]
                            initWithBytes:[contents bytes]
                            length:[contents length]
                            encoding:NSUTF8StringEncoding];
    } else {
        // When the note is created, assign default content
        self.noteContent = @"Empty";
    }

    [[NSNotificationCenter defaultCenter]
     postNotificationName:@"noteModified"
     object:self];

    return YES;
}

// Called when the application (auto)saves the content of a note
- (id)contentsForType:(NSString *)typeName
  error:(NSError **)outError
{

    if ([self.noteContent length] == 0) {
        self.noteContent = @"Empty";
    }

    return [NSData dataWithBytes:[self.noteContent UTF8String]
                         length:[self.noteContent length]];

}

@end
```

When you load a file you need a procedure to 'transform' the NSData contents returned by the background queue into a string. Conversely, when you save you have to encode your string into an NSData object. In both cases you do a quick check and assign a default value in case the string is empty. This happens the first time that the document is created.

Believe it or not, the code you need to model the document is already over! Now you can move to the code related to loading and updating.

Opening an iCloud file

First of all you should decide a file name for your document. For this tutorial, you'll start by creating a single filename. Add the following #define at the top of SMMasterViewController.m:

```
#define kFILENAME @"mydocument.dox"
```

Next, let's extend the class to keep track of your document, and a metadata query to look up the document in iCloud. Modify SMMasterViewController.h to look like the following:

```
#import "SMNote.h"

@class SMDetailViewController;

@interface SMMasterViewController : UITableViewController

@property (strong, nonatomic)
  SMDetailViewController *detailViewController;
@property (strong, nonatomic) SMNote * doc;
@property (strong, nonatomic) NSMetadataQuery *query;

- (void)loadDocument;
- (void)loadData:(NSMetadataQuery *)query;

@end
```

When the view is loaded you want to call the method loadDocument, In SMMasterViewController.m you add the following as the last row of viewDidLoad.

```
[self loadDocument];
```

Next you define the loadDocument method. Let's put it together bit by bit so you can uderstand the code one piece at a time. Start by adding the following:

```
- (void)loadDocument {

    NSMetadataQuery *query = [[NSMetadataQuery alloc] init];
    _query = query;

}
```

Note that before you can load a document from iCloud, you first have to check what's there. If you ever worked with the Spotlight API on the Mac, you'll be familiar with the class NSMetadataQuery. It is a class to represent results of a query related to the properties of an object, such as a file.

In building such a query you have the possibility to specify parameters and scope, i.e. what you are looking for and where. In the case of iCloud files the scope is always NSMetadataQueryUbiquitousDocumentsScope. You can have multiple scopes, so you have to build an array containing just one item.

So continue loadDocument as follows:

```
- (void)loadDocument {

    NSMetadataQuery *query = [[NSMetadataQuery alloc] init];
    _query = query;
    [query setSearchScopes:[NSArray arrayWithObject:
      NSMetadataQueryUbiquitousDocumentsScope]];

}
```

Now you can provide the parameters of the query. If you ever worked with Core Data or even arrays you probably know the approach. Basically, you build a predicate and set it as parameter of a query/search.

In your case you are looking for a file with a particular name, so the keyword is NSMetadataItemFSNameKey, where 'FS' stands for file system. Add the code to create and set the predicate next:

```
- (void)loadDocument {

    NSMetadataQuery *query = [[NSMetadataQuery alloc] init];
    _query = query;
    [query setSearchScopes:[NSArray arrayWithObject:
      NSMetadataQueryUbiquitousDocumentsScope]];

    NSPredicate *pred = [NSPredicate predicateWithFormat:
                          @"%K == %@",
                          NSMetadataItemFSNameKey,
                          kFILENAME];
    [query setPredicate:pred];

}
```

You might not have seen the %K substitution before. It turns out predicates treat formatting characters a bit differently than you might be used to with NSString's stringWithFormat:. When you use %@ in predicates, it wraps the value you provide in quotes. You don't want this for keypaths, so you use %K instead to avoid wrapping it in quotes. For more information, see the Predicate Format String Syntax in Apple's documentation here:

- https://developer.apple.com/library/mac/#documentation/Cocoa/Conceptual/Predicat es/Articles/pSyntax.html

Now the query is ready to be run, but since it is an asynchronous process you need to set up an observer to catch a notification when it completes. The specific notification you want has a long name: NSMetadataQueryDidFinishGatheringNotification. This is posted when the query has finished gathering info from iCloud.

```objc
- (void)loadDocument {

    NSMetadataQuery *query = [[NSMetadataQuery alloc] init];
    _query = query;
    [query setSearchScopes:[NSArray arrayWithObject:
        NSMetadataQueryUbiquitousDocumentsScope]];

    NSPredicate *pred = [NSPredicate predicateWithFormat:
                         @"%K == %@",
                         NSMetadataItemFSNameKey,
                         kFILENAME];
    [query setPredicate:pred];

    [[NSNotificationCenter defaultCenter]
      addObserver:self
      selector:@selector(queryDidFinishGathering:)
      name:NSMetadataQueryDidFinishGatheringNotification
      object:query];

    [query startQuery];

}
```

Now that this is in place, add the code for the method that will be called when the query completes:

```objc
- (void)queryDidFinishGathering:(NSNotification *)notification {

    NSMetadataQuery *query = [notification object];
    [query disableUpdates];
    [query stopQuery];

    [[NSNotificationCenter defaultCenter]
      removeObserver:self
      name:NSMetadataQueryDidFinishGatheringNotification
      object:query];

    _query = nil;
```

```
    [self loadData:query];

}
```

Note that once you run a query, if you don't stop it, it runs forever or until you quit the application. Especially in a cloud environment things can change often. It might happen that while you are processing the results of a query, due to live updates, the results change! So it is important to stop this process by calling `disableUpdates` and `stopQuery`. In particular the first prevents live updates and the second allows you to stop a process without deleting already collected results.

You then remove ourselves as an observer to ignore further notifications, and finally call a method to load the document, passing the **NSMetadataQuery** as a parameter.

Add the starter implementation of this method next (add this above `queryDidFinishGathering:`):

```
- (void)loadData:(NSMetadataQuery *)query {

    if ([query resultCount] == 1) {

        NSMetadataItem *item = [query resultAtIndex:0];

    }
}
```

As you can see here, a **NSMetadataQuery** wraps an array of **NSMetadataItems** which contain the results. In your case, you are working with just one file so you are just interested in the first element.

An **NSMetadataItem** is like a dictionary, storing keys and values. It has a set of predefined keys that you can use to look up information about each file:

- NSMetadataItemURLKey

- NSMetadataItemFSNameKey

- NSMetadataItemDisplayNameKey

- NSMetadataItemIsUbiquitousKey

- NSMetadataUbiquitousItemHasUnresolvedConflictsKey

- NSMetadataUbiquitousItemIsDownloadedKey

- NSMetadataUbiquitousItemIsDownloadingKey

- NSMetadataUbiquitousItemIsUploadedKey

- NSMetadataUbiquitousItemIsUploadingKey

- NSMetadataUbiquitousItemPercentDownloadedKey

- NSMetadataUbiquitousItemPercentUploadedKey

In your case, you are interested in NSMetadataItemURLKey, which points to the URL that you need to build your Note instance. Continue the loadData: method as follows:

```objc
- (void)loadData:(NSMetadataQuery *)query {

    if ([query resultCount] == 1) {

        NSMetadataItem *item = [query resultAtIndex:0];
        NSURL *url = [item
                    valueForAttribute:NSMetadataItemURLKey];

        SMNote *doc = [[SMNote alloc] initWithFileURL:url];
        self.doc = doc;

    }
}
```

When you create a UIDocument (or a subclass of UIDocument like SMNote), you always have to use the initWithFileURL: initializer and give it the URL of the document to open. You call that here, passing in the URL of the located file, and store it away in an instance variable.

Now you are ready to open the note. As explained previously you can open a document with the openWithCompletionHandler: method, so continue loadData: as follows:

```objc
- (void)loadData:(NSMetadataQuery *)query {

    if ([query resultCount] == 1) {

        NSMetadataItem *item = [query resultAtIndex:0];
        NSURL *url = [item
                    valueForAttribute:NSMetadataItemURLKey];

        SMNote *doc = [[SMNote alloc] initWithFileURL:url];
        self.doc = doc;

        [self.doc openWithCompletionHandler:^(BOOL success) {
            if (success) {
                NSLog(@"iCloud document opened");
                [self.tableView reloadData];
            } else {
                NSLog(@"failed opening document from iCloud");
            }
        }];

    }
}
```

```
    }
```

You can run the app now, and it seems to work, except it never prints out either of the above messages! This is because there is currently no document in your container in iCloud, so the search isn't finding anything (and the result count is 0).

Since the only way to add a document on the iCloud is via an app, you need to write some code to create a document. You will append this to the `loadData:` method that you defined a few seconds ago. When the query returns zero results, you should:

1. Retrieve the local iCloud directory

2. Initialize an instance of document in that directory

3. Call the `saveToURL:forSaveOperation:completionHandler:` method

4. When the save is successful you can call `openWithCompletionHandler:`.

So add an `else` case in `loadData:` as follows:

```
else {

    NSURL *ubiq = [[NSFileManager defaultManager]
                    URLForUbiquityContainerIdentifier:nil];
    NSURL *ubiqPackage = [[ubiq
        URLByAppendingPathComponent:@"Documents"]
        URLByAppendingPathComponent:kFILENAME];

    SMNote *doc = [[SMNote alloc] initWithFileURL:
                    ubiqPackage];
    self.doc = doc;

    [doc saveToURL:[doc fileURL]
        forSaveOperation:UIDocumentSaveForCreating
        completionHandler:^(BOOL success) {
            if (success) {
                [doc openWithCompletionHandler:^(BOOL success) {
                    NSLog(@"newly created document opened");
                    [self.tableView reloadData];
                }];
            }
        }];
}
```

Compile and run your app, and you should see the "new document" message arrive the first time you run it, and "iCloud document opened" in subsequent runs. Big success!

You can even try this on a second device (I recommend temporarily commenting out the else case first though to avoid creating two documents due to timing issues), and you should see the "iCloud document opened" message show up on the second device (because the document already exists on iCloud now!)

Now your application is almost ready. The iCloud part is over, and you just need to set up the user interface!

Setting up the user interface

The Xcode project template you chose already set up a bunch of stuff for us. There are two storyboards (both for iPhone and iPad) and the navigation logic is already in place. So whenever you tap a note in the table, its details are shown. You will add some code to show the a single note in SMMasterViewController and you will add a UITextView to show the content of the note in SMDetailViewController.

Let's start by modifying the **SMMasterViewController.m**. Tweak the table view data source methods to display the note as follows:

```objc
- (NSInteger)numberOfSectionsInTableView:
   (UITableView *)tableView
{
    return 1;
}

- (NSInteger)tableView:(UITableView *)tableView
 numberOfRowsInSection:(NSInteger)section
{
    return 1;
}

- (UITableViewCell *)tableView:(UITableView *)tableView
        cellForRowAtIndexPath:(NSIndexPath *)indexPath
{
    UITableViewCell *cell = [tableView
dequeueReusableCellWithIdentifier:@"Cell"
forIndexPath:indexPath];

    cell.textLabel.text = self.doc.noteContent;
    return cell;

}

- (void)tableView:(UITableView *)tableView
didSelectRowAtIndexPath:(NSIndexPath *)indexPath
{
```

```
    if ([[UIDevice currentDevice] userInterfaceIdiom] ==
UIUserInterfaceIdiomPad) {
        self.detailViewController.detailItem = self.doc;
    }

}
- (void)prepareForSegue:(UIStoryboardSegue *)segue
                sender:(id)sender
{
    if ([[segue identifier] isEqualToString:@"showDetail"]) {

        [[segue destinationViewController]
            setDetailItem:self.doc];
    }

}
```

Now you can quickly check if the application is working. Compile and run on one device and you should see that the table is populated with an empty note.

This is the note created by default the first time you run the application. Next you need to tweak the detail view to show the content's note. Open the SMDetailViewController.h and edit as follows.

```
#import <UIKit/UIKit.h>
```

```
#import "SMNote.h"

@interface SMDetailViewController : UIViewController
<UISplitViewControllerDelegate>

@property (strong, nonatomic) SMNote *detailItem;
@property (weak, nonatomic) IBOutlet UITextView *noteTextView;

@end
```

With respect to the generated code you have simply specified that detailItem is of type SMNote and you have added an outlet for a text view to display the note's content.

Next switch to SMDetailViewController.m and refactor two methods as follows:

```
- (void)setDetailItem:(SMNote *)newDetailItem
{
    if (_detailItem != newDetailItem) {
        _detailItem = newDetailItem;
        [self configureView];
    }

    if (self.masterPopoverController != nil) {
        [self.masterPopoverController
            dismissPopoverAnimated:YES];
    }
}

- (void)configureView
{
    if (self.detailItem) {
        self.noteTextView.text = self.detailItem.noteContent;
    }
}
```

Let's now configure the storyboard. Open MainStoryboard_iPhone.storyboard and scroll right to see the detail view controller. Delete the existing label and drag a Text View as follows:

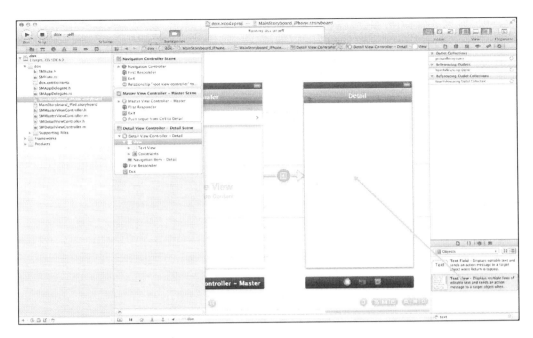

Don't forget to link the outlet to the code. Select the controller from the scene on the left and connect the noteTextView outlet to the text view.

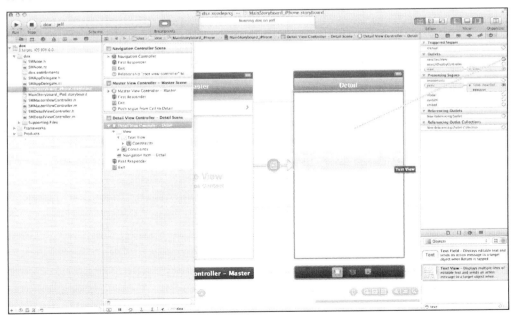

Repeat the same steps for MainStoryboard_iPad.storyboard. Now you are ready for the first real run of your application!

> Note: At this point, for testing purposes you should start from a clean configuration.
>
> If you still have data from the previous run of the app you should delete them from Settings/iCloud/Storage & Backup/Manage Storage. Select the item dox and then tap "Edit" on the top right to enable the deletion of items.

After making sure you're at a clean state, install the application on your iPhone. As previously the application will generate the file from scratch. If you tap the note you'll see its content in the detail view controller:

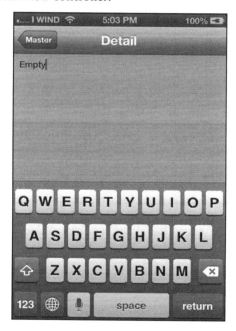

Now install the app on the iPad and run. This time the file won't be created because it's already on iCloud and the application will populate the table view with your item. If you select it the text view will show its content.

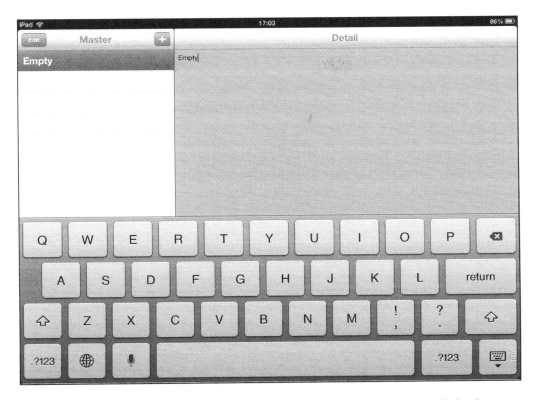

If you change the text, it will not synchronize to the other device yet – you'll do that later.

Another way to check the result is to browse the list of files in your iCloud Console, which is a bit hidden in the menu. Here is the sequence: Settings -> iCloud -> Storage and Backup -> Manage Storage -> Documents & Data -> dox. Here you will see the file as you have named it and the quota it takes on iCloud.

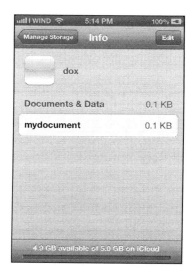

A third way to check the storage on iCloud is to visit: developer.icloud.com. Enter your credentials and you'll see (read only) all the data stored on iCloud by the applications you have installed.

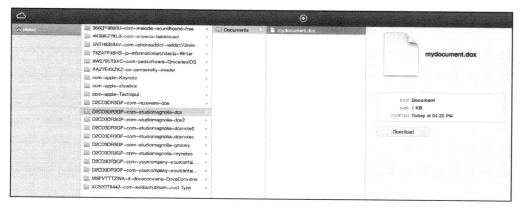

Congrats! You have built your first iCloud-enabled application!

Note: The project up to this point is in the resources for this chapter as dox-01.

Handling multiple documents

Cool, your example works and you are a bit more acquainted with the capabilities of iCloud. But what you have right now isn't enough to impress your users, or build an application that makes sense. Who wants to manage just one document?!

Next you are going to extend your application to manage more than one document at a time. The most natural development of your current prototype is to transform it into a notes application, as follows:

• Each note will have a unique id

• The table will show a list of notes

• Users can then edit the content

• The list of notes is updated when you launch the application

To do this, you will have to reorganize your code a bit. The architecture of view controllers will be the same, one master and one detail view. Let's start with the master controller.

You add an array to keep track of all the notes. Open SMMasterViewController.h and replace the contents with the following:

```
#import <UIKit/UIKit.h>
#import "SMNote.h"

@class SMDetailViewController;

@interface SMMasterViewController : UITableViewController

@property (strong, nonatomic)
    SMDetailViewController *detailViewController;
@property (strong, nonatomic) NSMetadataQuery *query;
@property (strong, nonatomic) NSMutableArray *notes;

- (void)loadDocument;

@end
```

You have added an array to store the notes, while the rest is unchanged. Next switch over to SMMasterViewController.m and change viewDidLoad like this:

```
- (void)viewDidLoad
{
    [super viewDidLoad];
```

```
        self.navigationItem.leftBarButtonItem = self.editButtonItem;

        UIBarButtonItem *addButton =
          [[UIBarButtonItem alloc]
            initWithBarButtonSystemItem:UIBarButtonSystemItemAdd
            target:self
            action:@selector(insertNewObject:)];
        self.navigationItem.rightBarButtonItem = addButton;

        self.detailViewController = (SMDetailViewController *)
          [[self.splitViewController.viewControllers lastObject]
          topViewController];

        self.notes = [NSMutableArray array];

        [[NSNotificationCenter defaultCenter]
          addObserver:self
          selector:@selector(loadDocument)
          name:UIApplicationDidBecomeActiveNotification
          object:nil];

}
```

Here you have added the initialization for the new array and an observer to listen when the application becomes active, so that each time you resume it notes get reloaded.

Unlike the previous project that had just one document (so always used the same filename each time), this time you're storing multiple documents (one for each note created), so you need a way to generate unique file names. As an easy solution, you will use the creation date of the file and prepend the 'Note_' string.

So change the implementation of insertNewObject: as follows:

```
- (void)insertNewObject:(id)sender
{
    NSDateFormatter *formatter = [[NSDateFormatter alloc] init];
    [formatter setDateFormat:@"yyyyMMdd_hhmmss"];

    NSString *fileName = [NSString stringWithFormat:@"Note_%@",
      [formatter stringFromDate:[NSDate date]]];

    NSURL *ubiq = [[NSFileManager defaultManager]
                    URLForUbiquityContainerIdentifier:nil];

    NSURL *ubiquitousPackage =
    [[ubiq URLByAppendingPathComponent:@"Documents"]
      URLByAppendingPathComponent:fileName];

    SMNote *doc = [[SMNote alloc]
```

```
      initWithFileURL:ubiquitousPackage];

    [doc saveToURL:[doc fileURL]
      forSaveOperation:UIDocumentSaveForCreating
      completionHandler:^(BOOL success) {

    if (success) {
        [self.notes addObject:doc];
        [self.tableView reloadData];
    }
  }];
}
```

You should be pretty familiar with this code. The file name is generated by combining the current date and hour. You call the saveToURL:forSaveOperation:complectionHandler: method and, in case of success, you add the newly created note to the array which populates the table view.

> Note: If you target from iOS6 up, instead of using date and hour, you can use the new class **NSUUID** to generate a unique id.

Almost done with the ability to add notes - just need to add the code to populate the table view with the contents of the notes array. Implement the table view data source and delegate methods like the following:

```
- (NSInteger)numberOfSectionsInTableView:(UITableView *)
  tableView
{
    return 1;
}

- (NSInteger)tableView:(UITableView *)tableView
  numberOfRowsInSection:(NSInteger)section
{
    return self.notes.count;
}

- (UITableViewCell *)tableView:(UITableView *)tableView
  cellForRowAtIndexPath:(NSIndexPath *)indexPath
{
    UITableViewCell *cell = [tableView
      dequeueReusableCellWithIdentifier:@"Cell"
      forIndexPath:indexPath];
    SMNote * note = self.notes[indexPath.row];
    cell.textLabel.text = note.fileURL.lastPathComponent;
    return cell;
```

```
    }

  - (void)tableView:(UITableView *)tableView
    didSelectRowAtIndexPath:(NSIndexPath *)indexPath
  {
      if ([[UIDevice currentDevice] userInterfaceIdiom] ==
          UIUserInterfaceIdiomPad)
      {
          SMNote *selectedNote = self.notes[indexPath.row];
          self.detailViewController.detailItem = selectedNote;
      }
  }

  - (void)prepareForSegue:(UIStoryboardSegue *)segue
    sender:(id)sender
  {
      if ([[segue identifier] isEqualToString:@"showDetail"]) {

          NSIndexPath *indexPath = [self.tableView
                                    indexPathForSelectedRow];
          SMNote *selectedNote = self.notes[indexPath.row];
          self.detailViewController.detailItem = selectedNote;
          [[segue destinationViewController]
            setDetailItem:selectedNote];

      }
  }
```

Now it's time to tweak the loading methods to deal with the new data model. Still in the
SMMasterViewController.m let's go to the `loadDocument` method. You will
follow a similar strategy to what you did earlier when loading a single note. However,
this time you don't know the exact file name, so you have to tweak your search predicate
to look for a file name like "Note_*".

```
  - (void)loadDocument {

      NSURL *ubiq = [[NSFileManager defaultManager]
                  URLForUbiquityContainerIdentifier:nil];

      if (ubiq) {

          self.query = [[NSMetadataQuery alloc] init];
          [self.query setSearchScopes:
            [NSArray arrayWithObject:
              NSMetadataQueryUbiquitousDocumentsScope]];

          NSPredicate *pred = [NSPredicate predicateWithFormat:
                          @"%K like 'Note_*'",
```

```
                            NSMetadataItemFSNameKey];
    [self.query setPredicate:pred];
    [[NSNotificationCenter defaultCenter]
     addObserver:self
     selector:@selector(queryDidFinishGathering:)
     name:NSMetadataQueryDidFinishGatheringNotification
     object:self.query];

    [self.query startQuery];

} else {

    NSLog(@"No iCloud access");

}

}
```

You might be tempted to place a call to this method in `viewDidLoad`. That would be correct, but that is executed on initial app startup. You want to reload data really each time the app is opened (even from the background), and you have already added the observer to listen when the application becomes active.

Next you need to tweak the `loadData:` method.

```
- (void)loadData:(NSMetadataQuery *)query {

    [self.notes removeAllObjects];

    for (NSMetadataItem *item in [query results]) {

        NSURL *url = [item
                    valueForAttribute:NSMetadataItemURLKey];
        SMNote *doc = [[SMNote alloc] initWithFileURL:url];

        [doc openWithCompletionHandler:^(BOOL success) {
            if (success) {

                [self.notes addObject:doc];
                [self.tableView reloadData];

            } else {
                NSLog(@"failed to open from iCloud");
            }

        }];
    }
}
```

This method populates the array of notes according to the results of the query. The implementation here fully reloads the list of notes as returned by iCloud.

The last step is to add a "Save" button to the detail view so the user can store changes to the selected note. Open SMDetailViewController.m and change viewDidLoad as follows:

```objc
- (void)viewDidLoad
{
    [super viewDidLoad];
    [self configureView];
    self.noteTextView.backgroundColor =
                                    [UIColor lightGrayColor];

    UIBarButtonItem *saveButton = [[UIBarButtonItem alloc]
        initWithBarButtonSystemItem:UIBarButtonSystemItemSave
                        target:self
                        action:@selector(saveEdits:)];

    self.navigationItem.rightBarButtonItem = saveButton;

}
```

This will add a button named "Save" on the top right of the detail view. Add the method that it will call when you tap it next:

```objc
- (void) saveEdits:(id)sender {

    self.detailItem.noteContent = self.noteTextView.text;

    [self.detailItem saveToURL:[self.detailItem fileURL]
            forSaveOperation:UIDocumentSaveForOverwriting
            completionHandler:nil];

    if ([[UIDevice currentDevice] userInterfaceIdiom] ==
                                    UIUserInterfaceIdiomPad) {
        self.detailItem = nil;
        self.noteTextView.text = @"";
    } else {
        [self.navigationController popViewControllerAnimated:YES];
    }
}
```

Note to save the edits here, you call the saveToURL:forSaveOperation:completeHandler method on UIDocument. There is another way to get it to save automatically which you'll learn about in the next chapter.

That's it! Compile and run the app on one device, and create a few notes. Then edit one or two of them, and be sure to tap Save when you're done. Then start the app on another device, and see that the table is correctly populated with the same notes!

> **Note:** The project up to this point is in the resources for this chapter as dox-02.

Where to go from here?

Congratulations, you now have hands-on experience with the basics of using iCloud and the new UIDocument class to create an iCloud-enabled app with multi-document support.

You've just scratched the surface of iCloud - stay tuned for the next chapter, where you'll learn how to handle conflict resolution, use NSFileWrapper, store simple key-value pairs, and use Core Data with iCloud!

Chapter 7: Intermediate iCloud

By Cesare Rocchi

In the last chapter, you learned the basics of synchronizing your application data with iCloud using the new `UIDocument` class. You also learned how to work with multiple documents and search the current documents on iCloud with `NSMetadataQuery`.

In this chapter, you're going to learn a lot more about iCloud, such as:

- How to switch between iCloud and local storage
- How to handle multi-file documents with `NSFileWrapper`
- How to easily store key-value information on iCloud
- How to delete files from iCloud
- How to deal with file changes and conflicts
- How to use the undo manager with iCloud
- How to export data (via URLs) with iCloud
- How wo use Core Data with iCloud

By the time you are done with this chapter, you will have a great overview of most of the ways to use iCloud, and will be ready to put this to use in your own apps!

This chapter begins with the project that you created in the previous chapter. If you don't have this project already, you can start from the one in the resources for this chapter, named **dox-02**.

Toggling iCloud Support

So far you have assumed that your users are willing to use iCloud and that it is available when the application runs.

However, it could be the case that a user has iCloud disabled. Or you might want to give the user a choice whether to save their data locally or on iCloud (even if iCloud is enabled). For example, a user might want to start using your application by just saving notes locally. Later he might change his mind and turn iCloud on. How do you cope with this case? Let's see.

First, you have to update your user interface by adding a switch button that activates iCloud storage. You will place it in the toolbar at the bottom of the master view controller. The intended result is shown in the following screenshot:

To achieve this you have to refactor your code a bit.

Let's first add a boolean property to keep track when the iCloud functionality is enabled. Add the following properties to SMMasterViewController.h:

```
@property (strong, nonatomic) UISwitch *cloudSwitch;
@property (nonatomic) BOOL useiCloud;
```

Next in SMMasterViewController.m add a static string to use as a key for storing the switch button value (right after the @implementation statement):

```
static NSString * const useiCloudKey = @"useiCloud";
```

Next, add the following code to the beginning of `viewDidLoad` (after the call to `[super viewDidLoad]`) to initialize the `_useiCloud` Boolean and to add the switch to the toolbar:

```
_useiCloud = [[NSUserDefaults standardUserDefaults]
                              boolForKey:useiCloudKey];

self.cloudSwitch = [[UISwitch alloc]
                    initWithFrame:CGRectMake(40, 4, 80, 27)];
self.cloudSwitch.on = _useiCloud;

[self.cloudSwitch addTarget:self
                action:@selector(enableDisableiCloud:)
        forControlEvents:UIControlEventValueChanged];

UIBarButtonItem *flexSpace1 = [[UIBarButtonItem alloc]
initWithBarButtonSystemItem:UIBarButtonSystemItemFlexibleSpace
                     target:nil
                     action:NULL];

UIBarButtonItem *iCloudSwitchItem = [[UIBarButtonItem alloc]
                           initWithCustomView:self.cloudSwitch];

UIBarButtonItem *flexSpace2 = [[UIBarButtonItem alloc]
initWithBarButtonSystemItem:UIBarButtonSystemItemFlexibleSpace
                     target:nil
                     action:NULL];

self.toolbarItems = @[flexSpace1,iCloudSwitchItem, flexSpace2];
```

When the view is loaded you retrieve the value previously selected by the user and assign it to the boolean (you'll see how to store it later). To make the switch button centered you surround it with two flexible spaces (`flexSpace1` and `flexSpace2`).

Next write the method that will get called when the switch is toggled:

```
- (void) enableDisableiCloud: (id) sender {
    self.useiCloud = [sender isOn];
}
```

The navigation controller's toolbar is hidden by default, so implement `viewWillAppear` to make it visible:

```
- (void) viewWillAppear:(BOOL)animated {
    [super viewWillAppear:animated];
    [self.navigationController setToolbarHidden:NO];
```

```
}
```

The last step for your first milestone is to persist the value of the switch button. You can do this by overriding the setter of the boolean property, as follows:

```
- (void) setUseiCloud:(BOOL)val {
    if (_useiCloud != val) {
        _useiCloud = val;
        [[NSUserDefaults standardUserDefaults]
          setBool:_useiCloud
          forKey:useiCloudKey];
        [[NSUserDefaults standardUserDefaults] synchronize];
    }
}
```

Build and run, and you'll see the switch button now appears at the bottom of the app, its value is persisted even when you quit or restart the application.

You can play with the application to verify that the value of both the switch button and the _useiCloud variable are the same values set before quitting of putting the application in background.

Now that the user interface is in place, let's move on to the iCloud logic.

Working Off-cloud

Describing the application from now on can be quite complex since code is pretty intertwined to cover both iCloud-on and iCloud-off cases. To make things simpler, you will start with the case where the user starts working on notes without synching to iCloud.

You are about to write two helper methods to make managing this easier:

- localNotesURL: this will return the URL of the directory where local notes are stored (the Documents directory).

- ubiquitousNotesURL: this will return the URL of the local iCloud directory (outside of the app directory), used by the daemon to synch with the remote location.

This is an extremely important distinction. When you switch on iCloud the notes will be moved from a local folder (e.g. Documents) to another iCloud-enabled local folder. On the contrary, when you switch off iCloud the notes will be moved from the iCloud-enabled folder to the local one.

It is important to stress that there is no way to change a property of a directory to make it iCloud enabled/disabled. So you need to have two separate URLs to cover both the off and the on case.

Add the implementations for these methods at the bottom of SMMasterViewController.m:

```objc
- (NSURL *) localNotesURL {
    return [[[NSFileManager defaultManager]
            URLsForDirectory:NSDocumentDirectory
            inDomains:NSUserDomainMask] lastObject];
}

- (NSURL *) ubiquitousNotesURL {
    return [[[NSFileManager defaultManager]
            URLForUbiquityContainerIdentifier:nil]
            URLByAppendingPathComponent:@"Documents"];
}
```

The first returns a URL pointing to the Documents directory inside your application sandbox. The second returns the ubiquity container that you are already familiar with.

So let's get back to your use case. The user starts the application, iCloud is off and the list of notes is empty. In the last chapter you already implemented a method to add a note. You just have to modify it a bit to cover the iCloud-off case. To do this, you change the base URL according to the value of the _useiCloud boolean property.

By default you initialize it as local and you change it if iCloud is enabled. The rest of the method is the same of the previous project.

```objc
- (void)insertNewObject:(id)sender
{
    NSDateFormatter *formatter = [[NSDateFormatter alloc] init];
    [formatter setDateFormat:@"yyyyMMdd_hhmmss"];

    NSString *fileName = [NSString stringWithFormat:@"Note_%@",
                            [formatter stringFromDate:
                                [NSDate date]]];

    NSURL *baseURL = [self localNotesURL];

    if (_useiCloud) {
        baseURL = [self ubiquitousNotesURL]; // iCloud url
    }

    NSURL *noteFileURL = [baseURL
                        URLByAppendingPathComponent:fileName];
    SMNote *doc = [[SMNote alloc] initWithFileURL:noteFileURL];

    [doc saveToURL:[doc fileURL]
  forSaveOperation:UIDocumentSaveForCreating
 completionHandler:^(BOOL success) {

        if (success) {

            [self.notes addObject:doc];
            [self.tableView reloadData];

        }

    }];
}
```

Now you can do a first test. Run the application, make sure iCloud storage is off and add a note. Then check your iCloud storage on your device (via Settings/iCloud/Storage & Backup/Manage Storage) and verify the note is not saved. Cool, first goal achieved!

However there's still a problem. If you quit and reopen the application you won't see the document you added (but you will see anything that might be in iCloud). Where'd your file go?

The local file is still there but in the loadDocument method you are searching for iCloud documents, whether iCloud is enabled or not by the switch. You need to rework the method to cover the iCloud-off case. Modify the method so it looks like the following:

```objc
- (void)loadDocument {

    NSURL *ubiq = [[NSFileManager defaultManager]
                        URLForUbiquityContainerIdentifier:nil];

    if (ubiq && _useiCloud) { // iCloud is on

        self.query = [[NSMetadataQuery alloc] init];
        [self.query setSearchScopes:[NSArray arrayWithObject:
                        NSMetadataQueryUbiquitousDocumentsScope]];

        NSPredicate *pred = [NSPredicate predicateWithFormat:
                            @"%K like 'Note_*'",
                            NSMetadataItemFSNameKey];
        [self.query setPredicate:pred];
        [[NSNotificationCenter defaultCenter]
      addObserver:self
        selector:@selector(queryDidFinishGathering:)
            name:NSMetadataQueryDidFinishGatheringNotification
          object:self.query];

        [self.query startQuery];

    } else { // iCloud switch is off or iCloud not available

        [self.notes removeAllObjects];
        NSArray *arr = [[NSFileManager defaultManager]
                    contentsOfDirectoryAtURL:[self localNotesURL]
                includingPropertiesForKeys:nil
                                    options:0
                                      error:NULL];

        for (NSURL *filePath in arr) {

            SMNote *doc = [[SMNote alloc]
                            initWithFileURL:filePath];
            [self.notes addObject:doc];
            [self.tableView reloadData];

        }

    }
}
```

In the "iCloud off" case the retrieval is not asynchronous, so you can just cycle over the returned array, build instances of notes according to the array and reload the content of the table view.

Build and run the application, and this time you should see the note you created earlier in local storage!

At this point, you have an application that allows you to store documents locally or in iCloud. However, there's no way to move the local documents to iCloud (or vice versa). So let's tackle that next!

Turning on iCloud

In theory this last step is simple, since to move a document to/from the local iCloud directory is just a matter of calling a single method:

```
- (BOOL)setUbiquitous:(BOOL)flag
            itemAtURL:(NSURL *)url
       destinationURL:(NSURL *)destinationURL
                error:(NSError **)error
```

The idea is that you want to call this method whenever the user toggles the switch, to move documents between local and iCloud storage.

However, there is a complication. If you check out the documentation for this method, it clearly says "Do not call this method from your application's main thread. This method performs a coordinated write operation on the file you specify, and calling this method from the main thread can trigger a deadlock with the file presenter." Ouch, sounds like a problem you want to avoid!

To resolve this problem, the documentation suggests performing this operation on a secondary thread. Here you have two options: using a Grand Central Dispatch (GCD) queue or an NSOperationQueue. You use GCD in many other places within this book, so to switch things up you'll use NSOperationQueue this time.

In essence you will run some code in the background to move all the notes from the local folder to the ubiquity container that the iCloud daemon keeps in synch with data on the cloud. You do this when the user taps the switch.

So modify the setUseiCloud: method to the following:

```
- (void) setUseiCloud:(BOOL)val {
    if (_useiCloud != val) {
        _useiCloud = val;

        [[NSUserDefaults standardUserDefaults]
                        setBool:_useiCloud
                         forKey:useiCloudKey];
        [[NSUserDefaults standardUserDefaults] synchronize];

        NSOperationQueue *iCloudQueue = [NSOperationQueue new];
        NSInvocationOperation *oper =
```

```
            [[NSInvocationOperation alloc]
                initWithTarget:self
                    selector:@selector(setNotesUbiquity)
                        object:nil];

        [iCloudQueue addOperation:oper];
    }
}
```

Here you instantiate a `NSOperationQueue` and you add to that an instance of
`NSInvocationOperation`. The operation has the controller as target and a selector
(`setNotesUbiquity`) where the actual moving of files is performed. By adding this
operation to the queue, it will run in the background.

Next implement `setNotesUbiquity` as the following:

```
- (void) setNotesUbiquity {

    NSURL *baseUrl = [self localNotesURL];

    if (_useiCloud)
        baseUrl = [self ubiquitousNotesURL];

    for (SMNote *note in self.notes) {
        NSURL *destUrl = [baseUrl URLByAppendingPathComponent:
                            [note.fileURL lastPathComponent]];
        NSLog(@"note.fileURL = %@", note.fileURL);
        NSLog(@"destUrl = %@", destUrl);

        [[NSFileManager defaultManager]
            setUbiquitous:_useiCloud
                itemAtURL:note.fileURL
            destinationURL:destUrl
                    error:NULL];
    }

    [self performSelectorOnMainThread:@selector(ubiquityIsSet)
                        withObject:nil
                        waitUntilDone:YES];

}
```

As previously discussed, you have to assign a different folder according to the value of
the `_useiCloud` boolean. Then you cycle over the list of notes and for each one you call
the `NSFileManager` method described above.

You should remember to notify the main thread that the operation on the secondary
thread is complete. For now, just implement the callback to log out the results as
follows:

```
- (void) ubiquityIsSet {
    NSLog(@"notes are now ubiq? %i", _useiCloud);
}
```

In your apps, you might want to display a spinner to indicate ongoing activity, and then you could hide it in this callback.

In the implementation of setNotesUbiquity you have included two log statements to show both the current and the destination URL of each note, so you can see in the console that they are different. A local document not synced with iCloud has a URL like this (a subdirectory of the application's folder):

```
file://localhost/var/mobile/Applications/75C93597-DD34-4F33-
BE1D-DA092EBCF1E2/Documents/Note_20121020_121016
```

A document synced with iCloud has a different URL (outside of the application's directory):

```
file://localhost/private/var/mobile/Library/Mobile%20Documents/D
2CD3DR3GP~com~studiomagnolia~dox/Documents/Note_20121020_121016
```

Build and run the application on one device, create a few notes and turn on iCloud. Notice the user interface is not locked and you can continue to work. Then run the app on another device. Turn on iCloud, put the app in background and then reopen it. You'll see the notes you created locally are correctly synchronized!

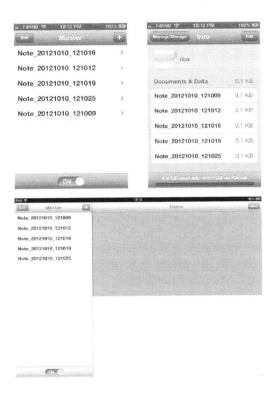

But what happens if you turn iCloud off? Of course, notes are moved to the local directory. What happens to those on the iCloud account? They are gone!

Turning off iCloud within an application does not mean to unhook the synchronization, as if you were offline. It means that all the documents stored by your application on the iCloud account get deleted, though they still persist on the local directory.

The user might not expect this (because it would mean that other devices would no longer have access to the shared files). So it's a good idea to notify the user before making that choice, by means of an alert view.

Let's go for a quick refactoring. Edit SMMasterViewController.h to mark the interface as implementing the UIAlertViewDelegate protocol:

```
@interface SMMasterViewController : UITableViewController
                                            <UIAlertViewDelegate>
```

Then switch to SMMasterViewController.m and add a new method to wrap the "migration" procedure, which will be performed on a secondary thread:

```
- (void) startMigration {

    NSOperationQueue *iCloudQueue = [NSOperationQueue new];
    NSInvocationOperation *oper =
      [[NSInvocationOperation alloc]
                 initWithTarget:self
                       selector:@selector(setNotesUbiquity)
                         object:nil];
    [iCloudQueue addOperation:oper];

}
```

The next step is to refactor setUseiCloud: one more time to show an alert view if the user tries to turn off iCloud:

```
- (void) setUseiCloud:(BOOL)val {

    if (_useiCloud != val) {

        _useiCloud = val;
        [[NSUserDefaults standardUserDefaults]
                              setBool:_useiCloud
                               forKey:useiCloudKey];
        [[NSUserDefaults standardUserDefaults] synchronize];

        if (!_useiCloud ) {

            UIAlertView *iCloudAlert =
            [[UIAlertView alloc]
              initWithTitle:@"Attention"
                    message:@"This will delete notes from your
iCloud account. Are you sure?"
                   delegate:self
          cancelButtonTitle:@"No"
          otherButtonTitles:@"Yes", nil];

            [iCloudAlert show];

        } else {

            [self startMigration];

        }
    }
}
```

Finally you implement the callback from the alert view:

```
- (void)alertView:(UIAlertView *)alertView
  clickedButtonAtIndex:(NSInteger)buttonIndex {
```

```
    if (buttonIndex == 0) {
        [self.cloudSwitch setOn:YES animated:YES];
        _useiCloud = YES;
    } else {
        [self startMigration];
    }
}
```

From now on, when the user wants to turn off iCloud synchronization, she will receive an alert as in the following screenshot:

Congratulations, you now know how to turn iCloud on and off within an application, allowing the user to choose whether to store locally or with iCloud (and change their mind at any point!)

Note: The project up to this point is in the resources for this chapter as dox-03.

Now is a good time to take a break because you're about to move on to a new topic. But don't go away, as there's a lot left to explore - such as multi-file documents, key-value pairs, conflict resolution, Core Data, and more!

Custom Documents

In the examples so far you have always opted for a one-to-one mapping, one note per file. Although this might seem natural to developers, end users might not be comfortable with that. For example, let's say a user wants to delete your application's data using the iCloud storage editor in Settings, but your application list is crowded with tons of weirdly named small files. That might be quite annoying to have to delete each one individually!

In this part you are going to create an alternate version of your app that stores all of the notes in a single file on iCloud. In the process of doing this, you'll also learn how you can create a document that consists of multiple files using `NSFileWrapper` (such as perhaps notes data plus image data) and how to register your app as the owner of a custom document type.

Rather than refactoring your existing app, I have prepared a starter project, called **dox-4-starter**. It is a very basic project that includes:

- A project configured with an iCloud-enabled application id and its related settings (as explained in the previous chapter).

- A check in `application:didFinishLaunchingWithOptions:` to see if iCloud is enabled

- Two storyboards for iPhone and iPad, using the same user interface hierarchy of previous projects: `UINavigatorController`, `SMMasterViewController`, `SMDetailViewController`

- The "+" action to add a new note from the master view controller

- The loading of notes triggered when the application becomes active

- The `saveEdit:` action in the detail view controller at the top right

- A text field in detail view controller to show or edit the content of a note.

- `SMNote` as an empty class, extending `NSObject`.

This is all you need to build an app to focus on iCloud features. Have a look at the code, and update the Bundle identifier and entries in the Entitlements section to match your App ID. Moreover, make sure there are no notes on iCloud from previous runs, because you want to start from a clean situation.

Then run it and play with it a bit to get familiar with the structure of the application!

Modeling a Custom Document

Now it's time to focus on the way you model data. Unlike previous projects here you need two classes: one to manage the single note, and one to manage both iCloud interaction and the list of notes.

We will call the first class SMNote. It is a simple class just to store data. Since data will have to persist on disk (and then iCloud) the class has to implement the NSCoding protocol. By implementing this protocol you can encode and decode information into a data buffer. For each note you will keep track of the following properties:

- id

- content

- creation date

- update date

Open SMNote.h and replace the contents of the file with the following:

```objc
@interface SMNote : NSObject <NSCoding>

@property (copy, nonatomic) NSString *noteId;
@property (copy, nonatomic) NSString *noteContent;
@property (strong, nonatomic) NSDate *createdAt;
@property (strong, nonatomic) NSDate *updatedAt;

@end
```

Next switch to SMNote.m and replace it with the following implementation:

```objc
#import "SMNote.h"

@implementation SMNote

- (id) init {
    if (self = [super init]) {
        NSDateFormatter *formatter =
        [[NSDateFormatter alloc] init];
        [formatter setDateFormat:@"yyyyMMdd_hhmmss"];
        _noteId = [NSString stringWithFormat:@"Note_%@",
                  [formatter stringFromDate:[NSDate date]]];
    }
    return self;
}

#pragma mark NSCoding methods
```

```objc
- (id)initWithCoder:(NSCoder *)aDecoder {
    if ((self = [super init])) {
        _noteId = [aDecoder decodeObjectForKey:@"noteId"];
        _noteContent = [aDecoder
                        decodeObjectForKey:@"noteContent"];
        _createdAt = [aDecoder decodeObjectForKey:@"createdAt"];
        _updatedAt = [aDecoder decodeObjectForKey:@"updatedAt"];
    }
    return self;
}

- (void)encodeWithCoder:(NSCoder *)aCoder {
    [aCoder encodeObject:self.noteId
                forKey:@"noteId"];
    [aCoder encodeObject:self.noteContent
                forKey:@"noteContent"];
    [aCoder encodeObject:self.createdAt
                forKey:@"createdAt"];
    [aCoder encodeObject:self.updatedAt
                forKey:@"updatedAt"];
}

@end
```

This assigns an id automatically built according to the creation time. The two methods needed by the NSCoding allow the decoding and encoding of the object when loading/saving.

Next you'll create another class to keep track of all the notes created. Since this class will manage the interaction with iCloud, it will extend UIDocument.

Create a file with the iOS\Cocoa Touch\Objective-C class template, name the class SMNotesDocument and make it a subclass of UIDocument. Then replace SMNotesDocument.h with the following:

```objc
#import <UIKit/UIKit.h>
#import "SMNote.h"

@interface SMNotesDocument : UIDocument

@property (nonatomic, strong) NSMutableArray *entries;
@property (nonatomic, strong) NSFileWrapper *fileWrapper;

- (NSInteger ) count;
- (void) addNote:(SMNote *) note;
- (SMNote *)entryAtIndex:(NSUInteger)index;

@end
```

Here you create an **NSFileWrapper** so you can build up a single document from potentially many files, and declare some methods to manage the array of notes.

Next switch to **SMNotesDocument.m** and replace it with the following:

```
#import "SMNotesDocument.h"

@implementation SMNotesDocument

- (id)initWithFileURL:(NSURL *)url {
    if ((self = [super initWithFileURL:url])) {
        _entries = [[NSMutableArray alloc] init];
        [[NSNotificationCenter defaultCenter]
          addObserver:self
             selector:@selector(noteChanged)
                 name:@"com.studiomagnolia.noteChanged"
               object:nil];

    }
    return self;
}

@end
```

Here you override the **initWithFileURL:** method to initialize the array of entries, and you set up an observer to wait for a notification when a note has changed. The notification will trigger a selector, which in turn will save the document. Add the code for this next:

```
- (void) noteChanged {
  [self saveToURL:[self fileURL]
 forSaveOperation:UIDocumentSaveForOverwriting
completionHandler:^(BOOL success) {
    if (success) {
      NSLog(@"note updated");
    }
  }];
}
```

Next you need to add a couple methods to wrap the notes array:

```
- (SMNote *)entryAtIndex:(NSUInteger)index{
    if (index < _entries.count) {
        return [_entries objectAtIndex:index];
    } else {
        return nil;
    }
}
```

```
- (NSInteger ) count {
    return self.entries.count;
}
```

The entryAtIndex: method will be needed when you populate the table view. It simply returns the entry at a given index in the notes array. The count method is even simpler; it just returns the count of the array.

Next add the addNote: method, which you'll use to add a note instance to the array and save the document:

```
- (void) addNote:(SMNote *) note {
    [_entries addObject:note];
    [self saveToURL:[self fileURL]
    forSaveOperation:UIDocumentSaveForOverwriting
  completionHandler:^(BOOL success) {
        if (success) {
            NSLog(@"note added and doc updated");
            [self openWithCompletionHandler:^ (BOOL success) {}];
        }
    }];
}
```

Now you are left with the two methods to manage reading and writing on iCloud. This is the crucial step for this application.

Unlike the previous chapter, where you stored just a string, here you have a more complex data model: an array of SMNote instances. To encode this set of objects you will use an NSKeyedArchiver, which allows converting objects that implement the NSCoding protocol into NSData, which can be then stored in a file. To use an NSKeyedArchiver, you perform the following steps:

1. Create a buffer of mutable data.

2. Initialize an archiver with the buffer.

3. Call encodeObject:forKey: on the archiver, passing in the objects to encode. It will convert the objects into the mutable data.

Here's what the code would look like to encode your list of note entries into an NSMutableData:

```
NSMutableData *data = [NSMutableData data];
NSKeyedArchiver *arch =
    [[NSKeyedArchiver alloc] initForWritingWithMutableData:data];
[arch encodeObject:_entries forKey:@"entries"];
[arch finishEncoding];
```

Once you have the NSMutableData, its time to pass the buffer to an NSFileWrapper.
This class manages attributes related to a file. Moreover NSFileWrappers can be nested
(so you can contain documents with multiple files inside).

For example, you might want to store notes and perhaps images in two separate
wrappers, which are in turn wrapped by a 'root' NSFileWrapper. To do this you need
to:

1. Create a mutable dictionary.

2. Initialize a wrapper with the buffer data of notes

3. Add the wrapper to the dictionary with a key.

4. Build another "root" file wrapper initialized with the dictionary.

Now you have enough information to build the method to generate your file wrapper, so
add the following new method:

```
- (id)contentsForType:(NSString *)typeName
                error:(NSError **)outError {

    NSMutableDictionary *wrappers =
    [NSMutableDictionary dictionary];

    NSMutableData *data = [NSMutableData data];
    NSKeyedArchiver *arch =
      [[NSKeyedArchiver alloc]
        initForWritingWithMutableData:data];
    [arch encodeObject:_entries forKey:@"entries"];
    [arch finishEncoding];

    NSFileWrapper *entriesWrapper =
    [[NSFileWrapper alloc] initRegularFileWithContents:data];

    [wrappers setObject:entriesWrapper forKey:@"notes.dat"];
    // here you could add another wrapper for other resources,
    // like images
    NSFileWrapper *res =
    [[NSFileWrapper alloc]
                initDirectoryWithFileWrappers:wrappers];

    return res;

}
```

In this app you only need the document to contain a single set of files, but this shows
you how you could easily add multiple files if you need to.

Be sure to remember the keys used to encode objects ("entries" and "notes.dat"), since you'll need them when it is time to read and decode data.

Now it's time to write the `loadFromContents:ofType:error:` method, which will be called when you read data. It does the exact opposite of the previous method:

1. Unfolds the main wrapper in a dictionary.

2. Retrieves the wrapper of notes by using the same key ('notes.dat').

3. Builds a data buffer from the wrapper.

4. Initializes an `NSKeyedUnarchiver` with the buffer.

5. Decodes the buffer into the array of entries.

Implement the method as follows:

```
- (BOOL)loadFromContents:(id)contents
                  ofType:(NSString *)typeName
                   error:(NSError **)outError
{
    NSFileWrapper *wrapper = (NSFileWrapper *)contents;
    NSDictionary *children = [wrapper fileWrappers];

    NSFileWrapper *entriesWrap =
                    [children objectForKey:@"notes.dat"];
    NSData *data = [entriesWrap regularFileContents];
    NSKeyedUnarchiver *arch = [[NSKeyedUnarchiver alloc]
                                 initForReadingWithData:data];
    _entries = [arch decodeObjectForKey:@"entries"];

    [[NSNotificationCenter defaultCenter]
        postNotificationName:@"com.studiomagnolia.notesLoaded"
                      object:self];

    return YES;
}
```

Whenever notes are (re)loaded you also post a notification to trigger the reload of data in the user interface.

We are almost done with the iCloud part, but there is another crucial step to make: the registration of a custom document type.

Declaring a Custom Document

To build a custom document it is not enough to specify its structure and the way data is encoded and decoded. The iCloud requires the application to register its custom document type in the Info.plist file.

In this section you are going to create a new UTI (Uniform Type Identifier) for your app's custom data format. An UTI is a string that uniquely identifies a class of objects (in your case an array of notes), which you can refer to as a 'type', much like a jpg image.

To add a new UTI, select the Supporting Files\dox-Info.plist file in the project tree. Select one of the items shown and click +. This will display a menu from which you can add new metadata for the application. Select Document types, as shown below

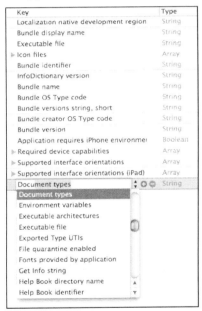

If you click the down arrow to expand Document Types and the dictionary inside, you'll see it's created a dictionary with two elements inside: Document Type Name and Handler rank.

Document Type Name is the descriptive name for the document, so set it to Dox Package. Set the Handler rank to Owner.

Then select the dictionary and click the + button to add another entry. Set the key to Document is a package or bundle, and it will set itself up as a Boolean. Set the value to YES.

Add another entry to the dictionary, set the key to Document Content Type UTIs, and it will set itself up as an array. This is the list of unique IDs for the document, so set the first entry to something unique like 'com.studiomagnolia.dox.package'.

At this point your dox-Info.plist should look like the following:

▼ Document types	Array	(1 item)
▼ Item 0 (Dox Package)	Dictionary	(4 items)
Document Type Name	String	Dox Package
Handler rank	String	Owner
▼ Document Content Type UTIs	Array	(1 item)
Item 0	String	com.studiomagnolia.dox.package
Document is a package or bur	Boolean	YES

Now you might think you are done, but you are not! It is not enough to declare a new UTI, you have also to export it. You have to add another property to the plist file, called 'Exported Type UTIs'. Essentially you have to recreate a structure as in the following picture:

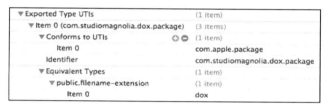

The identifier has to be the same provided above and 'dox' will be the extension of your file.

You should also check that all the information entered in the plist are replicated in the info section of your target application. Select the project in the tree, then the target, select the Info tab, and unfold both 'Document Types' and ' Exported UTIs'. The settings have to look as in the following screenshot:

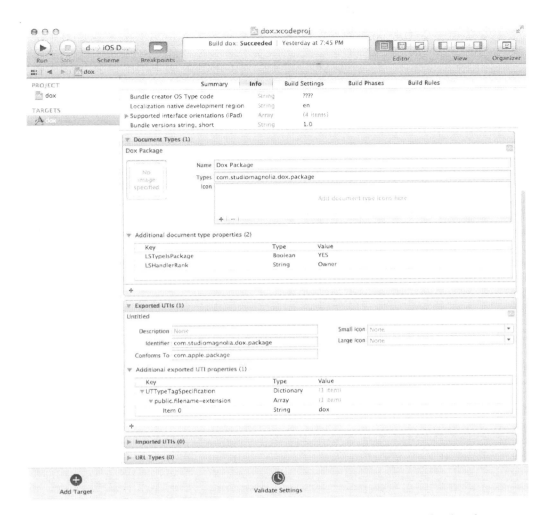

Congrats! Now the iCloud setup is done and you are ready to connect the dots by hooking up the model with the user interface!

Showing Notes in the Table View

To display notes in the table view you will follow an approach similar to last chapter. Replace **SMMasterViewController.h** with the following:

```
#import <UIKit/UIKit.h>
#import "SMNotesDocument.h"
```

```
@class SMDetailViewController;

@interface SMMasterViewController : UITableViewController

@property (strong, nonatomic) SMDetailViewController
*detailViewController;
@property (strong, nonatomic) NSMetadataQuery *query;
@property (strong, nonatomic) SMNotesDocument *document;

- (void)loadDocument;

@end
```

The document property is a reference to the SMNotesDocument instance that manages the array of notes and iCloud functionality.

Next switch to SMMasterViewController.m and modify viewDidLoad to add a listener when notes are reloaded. You add this at the bottom of the method.

```
[[NSNotificationCenter defaultCenter]
    addObserver:self
    selector:@selector(notesLoaded:)
    name:@"com.studiomagnolia.notesLoaded"
    object:nil];
```

Next add the implementation of insertNewObject:, which is pretty trivial:

```
- (void)insertNewObject:(id)sender {
    SMNote *doc = [[SMNote alloc] init];
    doc.noteContent = @"Test";
    [self.document addNote:doc];
}
```

This simply creates a new SMNote with some default content and adds it to the SMNotesDocument.

Then add the selector triggered when notes are reloaded, which is simple as well:

```
- (void) notesLoaded:(NSNotification *) notification {
    self.document = notification.object;
    [self.tableView reloadData];
}
```

This notification passes the document as a parameter, so you store it in your instance variable and reload the table view to display the new data.

The loadDocument method is triggered when the application becomes active. Impelment that as follows:

```objc
- (void)loadDocument {

    NSURL *ubiq = [[NSFileManager defaultManager]
                    URLForUbiquityContainerIdentifier:nil];

    if (ubiq) {

        NSMetadataQuery *query = [[NSMetadataQuery alloc] init];
        _query = query;
        [query setSearchScopes:[NSArray arrayWithObject:
                    NSMetadataQueryUbiquitousDocumentsScope]];
        NSPredicate *pred = [NSPredicate predicateWithFormat:
                        @"%K == %@",
                        NSMetadataItemFSNameKey, kFILENAME];
        [query setPredicate:pred];

        [[NSNotificationCenter defaultCenter]
        addObserver:self
          selector:@selector(queryDidFinishGathering:)
            name:NSMetadataQueryDidFinishGatheringNotification
          object:query];

        [query startQuery];

    } else {
        NSLog(@"No iCloud access");
    }
}
```

You should be pretty familiar with this code. You check if iCloud is available and you run a query to look for a file in the cloud. Before you forget, declare kFILENAME at the top of the file as follows:

```objc
#define kFILENAME @"notes.dox"
```

Next add the callback for when the query has finished gathering data, which is pretty simple as well:

```objc
- (void)queryDidFinishGathering:(NSNotification *)notification {

    NSMetadataQuery *query = [notification object];
    [query disableUpdates];
    [query stopQuery];

    [self loadData:query];

    [[NSNotificationCenter defaultCenter]
    removeObserver:self
            name:NSMetadataQueryDidFinishGatheringNotification
```

```
                    object:query];

    _query = nil;

}
```

This simply stops the updates and calls `loadData:`.

The `loadData:` method behaves as in previous projects: if the document exists it gets opened, if it doesn't it is created.

```objc
- (void)loadData:(NSMetadataQuery *)query {

    if ([query resultCount] == 1) {
        NSMetadataItem *item = [query resultAtIndex:0];
        NSURL *url = [item
                        valueForAttribute:NSMetadataItemURLKey];
        SMNotesDocument *doc =
        [[SMNotesDocument alloc] initWithFileURL:url];
        self.document = doc;

        [doc openWithCompletionHandler:^ (BOOL success) {
            if (success) {
                NSLog(@"doc opened from cloud");
                [self.tableView reloadData];
            } else {
                NSLog(@"failed to open");
            }
        }];

    } else { // No notes in iCloud
        NSURL *ubiqContainer = [[NSFileManager defaultManager]
            URLForUbiquityContainerIdentifier:nil];
        NSURL *ubiquitousPackage = [[ubiqContainer
            URLByAppendingPathComponent:@"Documents"]
            URLByAppendingPathComponent:kFILENAME];
        SMNotesDocument *doc = [[SMNotesDocument alloc]
            initWithFileURL:ubiquitousPackage];
        self.document = doc;

        [doc saveToURL:[doc fileURL]
          forSaveOperation:UIDocumentSaveForCreating
        completionHandler:^(BOOL success) {
            NSLog(@"new document saved to iCloud");
            [doc openWithCompletionHandler:^(BOOL success) {
                NSLog(@"new document was opened from iCloud");
            }];
        }];
    }
}
```

As the last step, select your **dox** Project entry, select the **dox** Target, and click the **Summary** tab. Scroll down to the **Entitlements** section, and click the **Enable iCloud** checkbox to enable iCloud (if it's not alrready). The default entries will be fine. You should be able to use the same provisioning profile you created in the last chapter, since your project name (hence bundle ID) should be the same.

Buid and run, and you should see a message in the console that says "new document saved to iCloud." The document has been correctly created, for this is the first time you run the application. The notes array is obviously empty.

Now you have to just to integrate the mechanism to render the view correctly according to the iCloud document. Add the following code to **SMMasterViewController.m**:

```
- (NSInteger)numberOfSectionsInTableView:(UITableView *)
  tableView
{
    return 1;
}

- (NSInteger)tableView:(UITableView *)tableView
 numberOfRowsInSection:(NSInteger)section
{
    return self.document.entries.count;
}

- (UITableViewCell *)tableView:(UITableView *)tableView
        cellForRowAtIndexPath:(NSIndexPath *)indexPath
{
    static NSString *CellIdentifier = @"Cell";

    SMNote *n = [self.document entryAtIndex:indexPath.row];

    UITableViewCell *cell = [tableView
            dequeueReusableCellWithIdentifier:CellIdentifier];

    if (cell == nil) {

        cell = [[UITableViewCell alloc]
            initWithStyle:UITableViewCellStyleDefault
          reuseIdentifier:CellIdentifier];

        if ([[UIDevice currentDevice] userInterfaceIdiom] ==
            UIUserInterfaceIdiomPhone) {

            cell.accessoryType =
                UITableViewCellAccessoryDisclosureIndicator;

        }
```

```
    }

    cell.textLabel.text = n.noteId;
    return cell;

}
```

Run the application again and add a few notes:

As you can see in the figure the table is correctly populated. If you like you can also check out the iCloud panel on your device to verify the presence of a new package file. Although you have created multiple notes they are all wrapped in a single file.

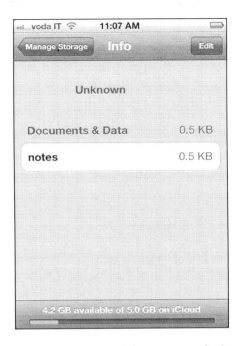

You can also run the application on a second device to verify that notes are correctly loaded:

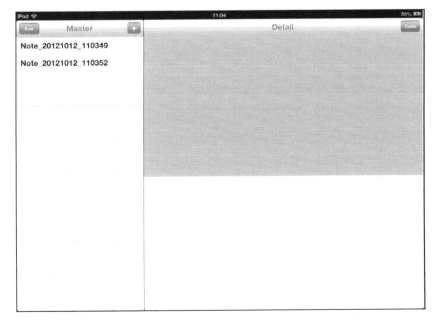

If you have any issues, you might want to change your kFilename constant to a different filename in case you have a corrupted file saved.

Now you are left with the last step: to show the content of a single note and save it when it is edited. Let's add the code to present the detail view when a note is tapped in the list. Open SMMasterViewController.m and add the following.

```
- (void)tableView:(UITableView *)tableView
didSelectRowAtIndexPath:(NSIndexPath *)indexPath
{
    if ([[UIDevice currentDevice] userInterfaceIdiom] ==
                                   UIUserInterfaceIdiomPad)
    {

        SMNote *selectedNote = [self.document
                                 entryAtIndex:indexPath.row];
        self.detailViewController.detailItem = selectedNote;

    }
}

- (void)prepareForSegue:(UIStoryboardSegue *)segue
              sender:(id)sender
{
    if ([[segue identifier] isEqualToString:@"showDetail"]) {

        NSIndexPath *indexPath = [self.tableView
                                   indexPathForSelectedRow];
        SMNote *selectedNote = [self.document
                                 entryAtIndex:indexPath.row];
        self.detailViewController.detailItem = selectedNote;
        [[segue destinationViewController]
                            setDetailItem:selectedNote];

    }
}
```

Next you tweak a bit the detail view controller. Open SMDetailViewController.h and change as follows.

```
#import <UIKit/UIKit.h>
#import "SMNote.h"

@interface SMDetailViewController : UIViewController
<UISplitViewControllerDelegate, UITextViewDelegate>

@property (strong, nonatomic) SMNote *detailItem;
@property (weak, nonatomic) IBOutlet UITextView *noteTextView;
@property BOOL isChanged;
```

@end

Here you made the class implement the UITextViewDelegate and added a new property called isChanged.

Let's move onto the implementation file, SMDetailViewController.m. Add these two lines at the end of viewDidLoad:

```
self.noteTextView.delegate = self;
self.isChanged = NO;
```

This is just to initialize the property and set the class as delegate of the text field. The only method triggered by the text view that you are interested in is textViewDidChange:. Implement it as follows:

```
- (void)textViewDidChange:(UITextView *)textView
{
    self.isChanged = YES;
}
```

Then change the configureView method to display the note's content, as follows.

```
- (void)configureView
{
    if (self.detailItem) {
        self.noteTextView.text = self.detailItem.noteContent;
    }
}
```

And implement saveEdits: as follows:

```
- (void) saveEdits:(id)sender {

    if (self.isChanged) {
        self.detailItem.noteContent = self.noteTextView.text;
        [[NSNotificationCenter defaultCenter]
          postNotificationName:@"com.studiomagnolia.noteChanged"
                      object:nil];
    }

    if ([[UIDevice currentDevice] userInterfaceIdiom] ==
                                    UIUserInterfaceIdiomPad) {

        self.detailItem = nil;
        self.noteTextView.text = @"";

    } else {
```

```
        [self.navigationController
                            popViewControllerAnimated:YES];
    }

}
```

Here when the user taps save button, you update the content of the note and post a "note changed" notification and pop or clean the detail view controller.

This notification will be caught by the UIDocument subclass which will trigger the save procedure.

Well done again! You have a whole new project where notes are not scattered in files but all wrapped in a single package, and have demonstrated how you can build up a single document consisting of multiple files.

Try it out on multiple devices to see how changes to note list and single notes are propagated correctly to the cloud.

> Note: The project up to this point is in the resources for this chapter as dox-04-final.

That concludes this topic, so it's time for another break if you need one! Next up, you'll cover how you can easily store small amounts of key-value data in iCloud!

Storing Key-value Information in iCloud

If you have a very small amount of data you want to save in your app, like the current page number for an eBook reading app, or the last game level number you've unlocked, iCloud provides an extremely simple way to do so in the form of a key-value store.

You can think of the key-value store as an iCloud-enabled NSUserDefaults. It lets you easily store small pieces of data like NSNumber, NSString, NSDate, NSData, NSArray, or NSDictionary.

Before you think to refactor your application and store all the notes using this simple API, you should know that this part of iCloud is meant to share small amount of data, like preferences. The maximum amount of data an app can store in the key-value store was just 64KB in iOS 5 and is 1024KB for iOS 6.

One way that you could use the key-value in your app is to keep track of the current note you're editing. This would come in handy if you have a ton of notes in your application, and you're editing a note on the iPhone and you close the application. You might like to edit it on your iPad later, but you might not remember the note title or id.

If you kept track of the current note you're editing in the key-value store, the app could look this up when you open the app and start you off on the same note. This is exactly the feature that you are going to build next!

In this case you will store a simple and small piece of information: the id of the last edited note. In general the iCloud key-value store is perfect for this kind of usage.

The class that manages the iCloud key-value store is `NSUbiquitousKeyValueStore`. You can create a store, or a reference to the default one, set some objects and synchronize. Here's what the code might look like:

```
[[NSUbiquitousKeyValueStore defaultStore]
        setString:@"YOUR_VALUE"
           forKey:@"YOUR_KEY"];
[[NSUbiquitousKeyValueStore defaultStore] synchronize];
```

To retrieve a value you can use the message corresponding to the data type you stored, in your case `stringForKey`:

```
[[NSUbiquitousKeyValueStore defaultStore]
        stringForKey:@"YOUR_KEY"];
```

As with `NSFileManager` the key-value store works asynchronously so you have to set up an observer to find out about changes. The notification to listen for has a pretty long name, `NSUbiquitousKeyValueStoreDidChangeExternallyNotification`.

```
[[NSNotificationCenter defaultCenter]
   addObserver:self
     selector:@selector(YOURSELECTOR:)
    name:NSUbiquitousKeyValueStoreDidChangeExternallyNotification
       object:nil];
```

The pattern to work with key-value stores is pretty simple:

1. Register for updates from the iCloud key-value store

2. React accordingly in the callback

You will extend the project developed during the previous section. If you don't have it it's called `dox-04-final` in the resources for this chapter.

Let's update the app to work with the key-value store. Here are the changes you'll make:

1. Store a key-value entry when a single note is displayed and the user closes an application

2. Listen for key-value changes in `SMMasterViewController`

3. When notified, push a new view controller showing the note stored as the last edited

Before writing any code you should check that entitlements for iCloud key-value store are correctly set in the project as in the following figure (i.e. there is a iCloud key-value store entry):

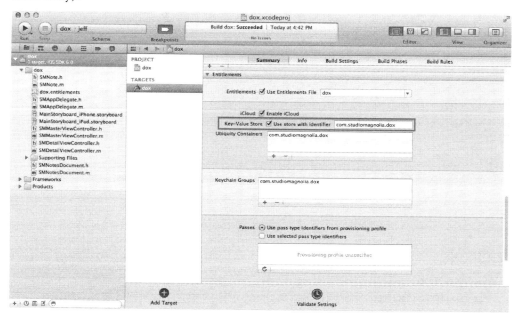

Let's start by modifying SMDetailViewController.m. Add the following code to the bottom of `viewDidLoad`:

```
[[NSNotificationCenter defaultCenter]
    addObserver:self
        selector:@selector(saveNoteAsCurrent)
            name:UIApplicationDidEnterBackgroundNotification
          object:nil];
```

Here you start listening to see if the application enters the background when the user is editing a note. Next implement the `saveNoteAsCurrent` callback:

```
- (void) saveNoteAsCurrent {
```

```
[[NSUbiquitousKeyValueStore defaultStore]
    setString:self.detailItem.noteId
        forKey:@"com.studiomagnolia.currentNote"];

[[NSUbiquitousKeyValueStore defaultStore] synchronize];
}
```

This uses the iCloud key-value store to store the note id of the current note. It stores it under the key "com.studiomagnolia.currentNote", and you will use the very same key to look up the value later.

Now let's modify SMMasterViewController.m. Add the following at the bottom of viewDidLoad:

```
NSUbiquitousKeyValueStore* store =
    [NSUbiquitousKeyValueStore defaultStore];

[[NSNotificationCenter defaultCenter]
  addObserver:self
    selector:@selector(updateCurrentNodeIfNeeded:)
   name:NSUbiquitousKeyValueStoreDidChangeExternallyNotification
      object:store];

[store synchronize];
```

When you receive an update notification, you'll behave as if the user had tapped the cell corresponding to the note with that identifier. You will retrieve the note using the key and you push an instance of SMDetailViewController, as shown below:

```
- (void) updateCurrentNodeIfNeeded:(NSNotification *)
  notification {
    NSLog(@"updateCurrent");

    NSString *currentNoteId =
    [[NSUbiquitousKeyValueStore defaultStore] stringForKey:
      @"com.studiomagnolia.currentNote"];
    SMNote *note = [self.document noteById:currentNoteId];
    if (note == nil) return;

    if ([[UIDevice currentDevice] userInterfaceIdiom] ==
        UIUserInterfaceIdiomPhone) {

        int row = [self.document.entries indexOfObject:note];
        NSIndexPath * indexPath = [NSIndexPath
          indexPathForRow:row inSection:0];
        [self.tableView selectRowAtIndexPath:indexPath
          animated:YES
          scrollPosition:UITableViewScrollPositionBottom];
        [self performSegueWithIdentifier:@"showDetail"
```

```
                sender:nil];

    } else {
        self.detailViewController.detailItem = note;
    }
}
```

Also call this method inside `loadData`, right after calling `reloadData` on the table view:

```
[self updateCurrentNodeIfNeeded:nil];
```

Next you just need to add a little helper method, `noteById:`, to SMNotesDocument.h:

```
- (SMNote *) noteById:(NSString *)noteId;
```

And add the implementation in SMNotesDocument.m:

```
- (SMNote *) noteById:(NSString *)noteId {

    SMNote *res = nil;

    for (SMNote *n in _entries) {
        if ([n.noteId isEqualToString:noteId]) {
            res = n;
        }
    }

    return res;
}
```

Run this app on a device, open a note, and tap the home button to enter the background. Then run the app on a second device, and after the notes are loaded it will automatically open the note you were editing last.

Pretty cool eh? A nicer experience for the user, and you can see how easy `NSUbiquitousKeyValueStore` is to use!

> **Note:** The project up to this point is in the resources for this chapter as **dox-05-kvs**.

How to Delete a File

You have seen how to add a local file to iCloud and how to remove a file from iCloud and just keep a local copy. But how can you just delete a file from iCloud (without necessarily having to keep a local copy)?

To delete a file completely, from the local directory and the iCloud, you can simply use the method `removeItemAtURL:error:`

```
NSError *err;
[[NSFileManager defaultManager] removeItemAtURL:
                                [self.document fileURL]
                                error:&err];
```

Note: There is no undo for this action so it's best to ask the user for confirmation beforehand.

Let's see how to integrate this in your application. You will start from a basic version of the project that you created earlier – the one that stores notes in separate files.

You can find this in the resources for this chapter as **dox-02**. Open it in Xcode, update your Bundle Identifier and Entitlement settings, and verify it works by installing on one device and creating a few notes. Then install on another device and check that the same notes appear as well.

To implement deletion from the table view you have to implement `tableView:commitEditingStyle:forRowAtIndexPath:` Here you define what happens to the cell that the user choses to delete. The selected note has to be deleted from three places: the table view, the array that populates the table and the file system.

Open **SMMasterViewController.m** and replace the implementation of the method as follows:

```
- (void)tableView:(UITableView *)tableView
commitEditingStyle:(UITableViewCellEditingStyle)editingStyle
 forRowAtIndexPath:(NSIndexPath *)indexPath
{

    if (editingStyle == UITableViewCellEditingStyleDelete) {

        SMNote *n = [self.notes objectAtIndex:indexPath.row];
        NSError *err;
        [[NSFileManager defaultManager] removeItemAtURL:
```

```
                                              [n fileURL]
                                                 error:&err];
        [self.notes removeObjectAtIndex:indexPath.row];
        [tableView deleteRowsAtIndexPaths:
                     [NSArray arrayWithObject:indexPath]
             withRowAnimation:UITableViewRowAnimationFade];

    }

}
```

Now you are ready to test the application. The ideal test is the following:

1. Run the app, add a few notes, and quit.

2. Reopen to check that notes are stored.

3. Delete a note, and quit again.

4. Reopen the app and verify that the deleted note is no longer there.

It all works fine, but what happens on other devices when you delete a note? Let's see in the following section.

Handling Deletion From Other Devices

Now try the following test script:

1. Add a few notes on one device.

2. Wait a little bit and start up the second device, verify the new notes appear.

3. Don't quit or put in background either app.

4. Delete a note on one device.

What happens on the other device? Nothing at all unfortunately!

The only way you can re-synchronize the devices is by putting the application in the background and making it active again to trigger the refresh of the list.

But shouldn't you handle that in real-time? Yes indeed - and that's the feature that you are going to add now!

One of the advantages of iCloud is that it can make applications aware of changes in remote resources on the fly. You just have to listen and react accordingly.

When there's a change in the cloud, a `UIDocumentStateChangedNotification` notification will be sent. That is the only notification available in the `UIDocument` class but it is enough to handle all the cases.

Besides notifications you can also keep track of the state of a document. Sometimes you might experience problems in reading or writing, e.g. the disk is full, the file has been edited, etc.

`UIDocument` has a key property, called `documentState`, which indicates how safe it is to allow a change in a document. This is a read-only property whose value is managed by the iCloud daemon. Possible values are the following:

- `UIDocumentStateNormal`: Everything is fine. Changes are persisted to disk and ready to be uploaded.

- `UIDocumentStateClosed`: When you have not yet opened the document.

- `UIDocumentStateInConflict`: There are conflicts (yes plural), in the document. For example when a document has been saved almost at the same time on two devices with different content.

- `UIDocumentStateSavingError`: There was an error in saving the document, e.g. no permission on the file, file already in use, etc.

- `UIDocumentStateEditingDisabled`: E.g. in the middle of a revert or whenever it is not safe to edit the document.

Now you are going to use the notification combined with these document states to handle the following use case: detecting when a note has been deleted and allowing the user to reinstate it.

Let's start by preparing `SMMasterViewController` to be ready to react to a deletion. The first step you want to achieve is to reload the list of notes in the table in case of change. Open up **SMMasterViewController.m** and add the following at the bottom of `viewDidLoad` to listen for a document change notification:

```
[[NSNotificationCenter defaultCenter]
    addObserver:self
       selector:@selector(noteHasChanged:)
           name:UIDocumentStateChangedNotification
         object:nil];
```

It is important to notice that this notification is posted whenever there is a change, including when you open a file or when you add a new note.

So add this method to make the table view reload when the document state is
UIDocumentStateSavingError. This is the state of a document when it has been
deleted on the cloud but it is still present locally.

```
- (void)noteHasChanged:(id)sender {
    SMNote *d = [sender object];
    if ([d documentState] == UIDocumentStateSavingError) {
        [self.tableView reloadData];
    }
}
```

Now you can run the application on the two devices and verify the same list of
documents appears. Now keep on device connected to the Mac and delete a document
on the other. After a few seconds you should see the following:

The note has been deleted from the cloud and you have a sort of temporary version
locally, without the previous id and file URL. If you tap the note you can see that also
the content is still there. The console should also show an error message, like the
following.

```
[Switching to process 8195 thread 0x2003]
[Switching to process 7171 thread 0x1c03]
2011-11-04 14:05:41.108 dox[2974:220f] Foundation called mkdir("/var/mobile/Library/Mobile Documents/.ubd/peer-98B230AE-135F-
D571-D757-E25E258309F8-v23/ftr/(A Document Being Saved By dox)"), it didn't return 0, and errno was set to 1.
```

This is due to the fact that the note is not a 'legal' document anymore. It is not on the
cloud anymore and it is not even a 'classic' local file stored in the documents directory. It
is just in a sort of limbo.

In such a situation, you can offer the user the opportunity to reinstate the note and its content. It will not be possible to reinstate a file with the same name as before, but you can create a new document with the content attached to the 'limbo note'.

To achieve this you have to refactor **SMDetailViewController.m** a bit. You have to change the label and action of the **UIBarButtonItem** on the top right according to the state of the document. Here is the new **viewDidLoad**.

```objc
- (void)viewDidLoad
{
    [super viewDidLoad];
    [self configureView];
    self.noteTextView.backgroundColor =
                                [UIColor lightGrayColor];


    UIBarButtonItem *saveButton = [[UIBarButtonItem alloc]
            initWithBarButtonSystemItem:UIBarButtonSystemItemSave
                                 target:self
                                 action:@selector(saveEdits:)];
    self.navigationItem.rightBarButtonItem = saveButton;

    if (self.detailItem.documentState ==
                    UIDocumentStateSavingError) {

        UIBarButtonItem *reinstateNoteButton =
            [[UIBarButtonItem alloc]
                    initWithTitle:@"Reinstate"
                            style:UIBarButtonItemStylePlain
                           target:self
                           action:@selector(reinstateNote)];

        self.navigationItem.rightBarButtonItem =
                                        reinstateNoteButton;
    }

}
```

If the document is in a saving error state the button on the right has the label "Reinstate" and the action **reinstateNote**. For the iPad to work correctly you also have to refactor the **configureView** method.

```objc
- (void)configureView
{
    if (self.detailItem) {
        self.noteTextView.text = self.detailItem.noteContent;

        if (self.detailItem.documentState ==
                            UIDocumentStateSavingError) {
```

```
        UIBarButtonItem *reinstateNoteButton =
        [[UIBarButtonItem alloc]
              initWithTitle:@"Reinstate"
                     style:UIBarButtonItemStylePlain
                    target:self
                    action:@selector(reinstateNote)];

        self.navigationItem.rightBarButtonItem =
                                    reinstateNoteButton;
     }
   }
}
```

If you run the application now and tap a 'limbo' note, the view should appear with the reinstate button as in the figure below:

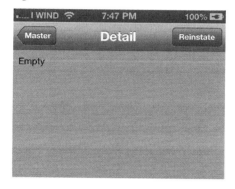

Tapping the button will cause the app to crash since you haven't implemented the associated action yet, so let's do that next.

The method is pretty similar to the one used to create a new note. In fact, you have to instantiate a new note with a new URL and save it on disk. If the save operation is successful you can pop the view controller and post a notification to tell the table view that a note has been reinstated.

```
- (void) reinstateNote {

    // Generate new filename for note based on date
    NSDateFormatter *formatter = [[NSDateFormatter alloc] init];
    [formatter setDateFormat:@"yyyyMMdd_hhmmss"];

    NSString *fileName = [NSString stringWithFormat:@"Note_%@",
                    [formatter stringFromDate:
                        [NSDate date]]];

    NSURL *ubiq = [[NSFileManager defaultManager]
```

```
                        URLForUbiquityContainerIdentifier:nil];
    NSURL *ubiquitousPackage =
    [[ubiq URLByAppendingPathComponent:@"Documents"]
     URLByAppendingPathComponent:fileName];

    // Create new note and save it
    SMNote *n = [[SMNote alloc]
                    initWithFileURL:ubiquitousPackage];
    n.noteContent = self.noteTextView.text;

    [n saveToURL:[n fileURL]
    forSaveOperation:UIDocumentSaveForCreating
completionHandler:^(BOOL success) {
        if (success) {
            [[NSNotificationCenter defaultCenter]
             postNotificationName:
             @"com.studiomagnolia.noteReinstated"
             object:self];

            if ([[UIDevice currentDevice] userInterfaceIdiom] ==
                UIUserInterfaceIdiomPad) {
                self.detailItem = nil;
                self.noteTextView.text = @"";
            } else {
                [self.navigationController
                 popViewControllerAnimated:YES];
            }
        } else {
            NSLog(@"error in saving reinstated note");
        }
    }];
}
```

We have now to catch the notification in SMMasterViewController.m. Add the following to the bottom of viewDidLoad:

```
[[NSNotificationCenter defaultCenter]
    addObserver:self
      selector:@selector(loadDocument)
          name:@"com.studiomagnolia.noteReinstated"
        object:nil];
```

This way, whenever a note is reinstated, the application loads a fresher list of notes from iCloud.

Since you have two view controllers, you have to manage the "note has been deleted" scenario also in SMDetailViewController. Add the following to the bottom of viewDidLoad in SMDetailViewController.m:

```
[[NSNotificationCenter defaultCenter]
    addObserver:self
        selector:@selector(noteHasChanged:)
            name:UIDocumentStateChangedNotification
          object:nil];
```

The selector is pretty similar to the previous one: you change the title and you show the "Reinstate" button.

```
- (void)noteHasChanged:(id)sender {

    if (self.detailItem.documentState ==
                              UIDocumentStateSavingError) {
        self.title = @"Limbo note";
        UIBarButtonItem *reinstateNoteButton =
            [[UIBarButtonItem alloc]
              initWithTitle:@"Reinstate"
                      style:UIBarButtonItemStylePlain
                     target:self
                     action:@selector(reinstateNote)];

        self.navigationItem.rightBarButtonItem =
                                     reinstateNoteButton;

    }

}
```

Build and run to test it. Now the 'Reinstate' button appears also when a note is opened and gets deleted on another device. Use the button to bring a deleted note back up to life!

Note: The project up to this point is in the resources for this chapter as dox-06.

Now that you know how to create and delete notes, let's see how to handle changes.

Handling Changes

So far you took care of situations where files are created or deleted. But you also need to handle the case where the content of a file changes. In particular, what happens if you are editing a note on two devices at about the same time?

In your current implementation, nothing happens because although you observe for document changes, you filter for only the `UIDocumentStateSavingError` case.

In the scenario of concurrent editing there is no save error, because the daemon on different devices pushes changes to the cloud at discrete intervals after the `updateChangeCount:` method is called. If you are editing a note and the daemon pulls new changes from the cloud, although there is no conflict at document level, there is a conflict at the user interface level, because you are editing a note whose content has changed. At this point you need a policy to handle the situation.

There is no golden policy perfect for every situation, but there is a good policy according to the aim of your application and the goal that the user is trying to achieve. Some examples of policies in conflict situations are:

• The most recent version wins;

• The current version on the device in usage wins

• The user is asked to pick a version

• The user is asked to manually merge changes

Before implementing a policy let's see where the best place is to apply it. In your current implementation (project **dox-06**) you are already listening for changes to the `documentState` property. Add the following code to the bottom of the `noteHasChanged:` method in **SMDetailViewController.m** as follows:

```
if (self.detailItem.documentState ==
                UIDocumentStateEditingDisabled) {

    self.navigationItem.leftBarButtonItem.enabled = NO;
    NSLog(@"document state is
                        UIDocumentStateEditingDisabled");

}

if (self.detailItem.documentState == UIDocumentStateNormal) {

    self.navigationItem.leftBarButtonItem.enabled = YES;
    NSLog(@"old content is %@", self.noteTextView.text);
    NSLog(@"new content is %@", self.detailItem.noteContent);

}
```

Now run the app on two devices, and make sure the second is connected to Xcode so you can see the output on the console. Then run the following test:

1. On one device, connected to the debugger, tap a note as if you are going to edit it.

2. On the other device, open the same note, change it and close the single note view.

After a few minutes, the console should show something like this:

```
2011-11-04 15:55:28.964 dox[1351:707] document state is UIDocumentStateEditingDisabled
2011-11-04 15:55:29.508 dox[1351:707] old content is This is a note
2011-11-04 15:55:29.508 dox[1351:707] new content is This is an edited note
```

As you can see you receive two notifications. In the first case the state of the document is UIDocumentStateEditingDisabled. As explained above, while the document is in this state, it is not suggested to edit and save it. That is why you have temporarily disabled the 'back' button to prevent the user from closing the view, and thus saving the file. The document has been put in this state because new content is being received from the other device.

Right after that (depends on the length of the content to be saved), you receive a new notification, where the state of the document is back to normal.

We have also traced the new content of the current note, which is different with respect to the string populating your text view. This is the key point to implement your policy. Update the code in noteHasChanged: so that the latest version wins, by updating the UIDocumentStateNormal case to the following:

```
if (self.detailItem.documentState == UIDocumentStateNormal) {

    self.navigationItem.leftBarButtonItem.enabled = YES;
    NSLog(@"old content is %@", self.noteTextView.text);
    NSLog(@"new content is %@", self.detailItem.noteContent);
    self.noteTextView.text = self.detailItem.noteContent;

}
```

Build and run to test it out - now when you edit a note on one device and have it open on a second, the second will automatically update to the latest content!

Note that if you want the old version to win you can just ignore the notification and don't update the view.

If you want the user to pick a version then you need a new view controller which shows both versions so the user can choose which one to continue with. Let's try this out to see how it works.

We will call this new class SMVersionPicker. It will have a view controller that displays two versions of a note, with two buttons to let the user pick, as in the following screenshot.

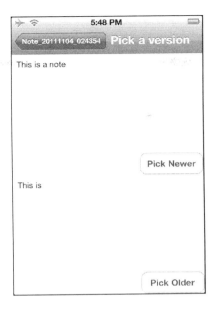

This view will be pushed when the user taps a 'Resolve' button, which will appear in case of conflict between local and iCloud content.

Update the `UIDocumentStateNormal` case in `noteHasChanged:` to change the top right button when needed. Here is the new version of the method in SMDetailViewController.m.

```objc
- (void)noteHasChanged:(id)sender {

    if (!self.detailItem)
        return;

    if (self.detailItem.documentState ==
                          UIDocumentStateSavingError) {
        self.title = @"Limbo note";
        UIBarButtonItem *reinstateNoteButton =
                [[UIBarButtonItem alloc]
                      initWithTitle:@"Reinstate"
                            style:UIBarButtonItemStylePlain
                            target:self
                            action:@selector(reinstateNote)];

        self.navigationItem.rightBarButtonItem =
                                      reinstateNoteButton;

    }
```

```
if (self.detailItem.documentState ==
                    UIDocumentStateEditingDisabled) {

    self.navigationItem.leftBarButtonItem.enabled = NO;
    NSLog(@"document state is
                    UIDocumentStateEditingDisabled");

}

if (self.detailItem.documentState == UIDocumentStateNormal)
{

    self.navigationItem.leftBarButtonItem.enabled = YES;
    NSLog(@"old content is %@", self.noteTextView.text);
    NSLog(@"new content is %@",
                        self.detailItem.noteContent);

    if (![self.noteTextView.text
        isEqualToString:self.detailItem.noteContent]) {

        UIBarButtonItem * resolveButton =
            [[UIBarButtonItem alloc]
                initWithTitle:@"Resolve"
                        style:UIBarButtonItemStylePlain
                        target:self
                        action:@selector(resolveNote)];

        self.navigationItem.rightBarButtonItem =
                                resolveButton;

    }

}

}
```

In the project dox-07 in the resources for this chapter, I have made a view controller for you called SMVersionPicker that is ready to use, because creating the user interface itself is out of the scope of this chapter. Drag SMVersionPicker.h, SMVersionPicker.m, SMVersionPicker_iPad.xib, and SMVersion_iPhone.xib into your project.

It has xib files for both iPhone and iPad already configured, including two text views and two buttons to allow the user picking the version. To give you an idea of how it works, here is its header file:

```
#import <UIKit/UIKit.h>
#import "SMNote.h"
```

```objc
@interface SMVersionPicker : UIViewController

@property (strong, nonatomic) IBOutlet UITextView
                            *oldContentTextView;
@property (strong, nonatomic) IBOutlet UITextView
                            *newerContentTextView;
@property (strong, nonatomic) NSString *oldNoteContentVersion;
@property (strong, nonatomic) NSString *newerNoteContentVersion;
@property (strong, nonatomic) SMNote *currentNote;

- (IBAction)pickNewerVersion:(id)sender;
- (IBAction)pickOldVersion:(id)sender;

@end
```

And here are the relevant parts of its implementation:

```objc
- (void) viewWillAppear:(BOOL)animated {

    [super viewWillAppear:animated];

    self.oldContentTextView.text = self.oldNoteContentVersion;
    self.newerContentTextView.text =
                            self.newerNoteContentVersion;

}

- (IBAction)pickNewerVersion:(id)sender {

    self.currentNote.noteContent =
                        self.newerContentTextView.text;

    [self.currentNote
        saveToURL:[self.currentNote fileURL]
 forSaveOperation:UIDocumentSaveForOverwriting
completionHandler:^(BOOL success) {

        if (success) {

            [self.navigationController
                        popViewControllerAnimated:YES];

        }

    }];

}

- (IBAction)pickOldVersion:(id)sender {
```

```
      self.currentNote.noteContent = self.oldContentTextView.text;

    [self.currentNote
        saveToURL:[self.currentNote fileURL]
  forSaveOperation:UIDocumentSaveForOverwriting
completionHandler:^(BOOL success) {

        if (success) {

            [self.navigationController
                            popViewControllerAnimated:YES];

        }

    }];

}
```

When the controller appears it sets both old and new contents in the text views. Once a button is tapped it updates the content of the note with the value of the corresponding text are and saves the note.

After adding the files into your project, all you have to do is add the code to display it in SMDetailViewController.m. First import the header at the top of the file:

```
#import "SMVersionPicker.h"
```

Then add the code for the resolveNote button tap callback to display the new view controller:

```
- (void) resolveNote {
    SMVersionPicker *picker = nil;
    if (UI_USER_INTERFACE_IDIOM() == UIUserInterfaceIdiomPad) {
        picker = [[SMVersionPicker alloc]
                    initWithNibName:@"SMVersionPicker_iPad"
                    bundle:nil];
    } else {
        picker = [[SMVersionPicker alloc]
                    initWithNibName:@"SMVersionPicker_iPhone"
                    bundle:nil];
    }

    picker.newerNoteContentVersion =
                            self.detailItem.noteContent;
    picker.oldNoteContentVersion = self.noteTextView.text;
    picker.currentNote = self.detailItem;

    [self.navigationController pushViewController:picker
                                    animated:YES];
```

```
    }
```

The final touch is to refresh the detail view when a version has been picked. To do this, implement `viewWillAppear:` as follows:

```
- (void) viewWillAppear:(BOOL)animated {

    self.noteTextView.text = self.detailItem.noteContent;

    if (self.detailItem.documentState == UIDocumentStateNormal)
    {

        UIBarButtonItem *saveButton =
            [[UIBarButtonItem alloc]
             initWithBarButtonSystemItem:UIBarButtonSystemItemSave
                                  target:self
                                  action:@selector(saveEdits:)];

        self.navigationItem.rightBarButtonItem = saveButton;

    }

}
```

Here you are, finally! Build and run, edit a document while you're viewing it on another, and you'll see your application is now able to detect changes to documents and to show the "Resolve" button when there are two versions of a note. By tapping the button the user is shown a view that helps choosing the version to keep on iCloud.

> **Note:** The project up to this point is in the resources for this chapter as **dox-07**.

Handling Conflicts

Earlier in this chapter you saw the list of available states, and one of them was `UIDocumentStateInConflict`. This state is assigned to documents that are being updated almost at the same time from different devices.

At this point it is difficult to define the 'almost'. In many cases this scenario is usually reproducible by triggering the save actions on two different devices, both connected to the web, with a lag of 1-2 seconds.

Let's see how to deal with such a situation. First let's update your **dox-07** project so you can get an indication of when you have a conflict.

Inside SMMasterViewController.m, refactor noteHasChanged: as follows:

```
- (void)noteHasChanged:(id)sender {
    [self.tableView reloadData];
}
```

Then refactor tableView:cellForRowAtIndexPath: to color a cell red when it is in conflict, like this:

```
- (UITableViewCell *)tableView:(UITableView *)tableView
        cellForRowAtIndexPath:(NSIndexPath *)indexPath
{
    UITableViewCell *cell = [tableView
                dequeueReusableCellWithIdentifier:@"Cell"
                                forIndexPath:indexPath];

    SMNote * note = self.notes[indexPath.row];
    if ([note documentState] == UIDocumentStateInConflict) {
        cell.textLabel.textColor = [UIColor redColor];
    } else {
        cell.textLabel.textColor = [UIColor blackColor];
    }

    cell.textLabel.text = note.fileURL.lastPathComponent;
    return cell;
}
```

Then try out this scenario by running the following test:

1. Run the app on two devices.

2. Open the same note on both devices.

3. Edit the note so that the content is different on each device.

4. Tap the save button on both applications almost at the same time.

If you wait for a while (usually 10-15 seconds depending on the size of the file saved and the speed of the connection) both devices should receive a notification and the table should show a red note as in the following screenshot:

Unlike previously explored states, this kind of conflict is 'permanent'. That is, if you restart the application you will continue to see a red label. In previous examples, a reload of the application would make the last version win over the rest, but in this case the conflict is detected by iCloud itself and requires user intervention to be resolved.

To resolve an iCloud-detected conflict, there is a handy set of APIs you can use. NSFileVersion is a very helpful class that represents 'snapshots' of a file at a given point. You can retrieve an array of NSFileVersion snapshots of the document that conflict with each other using the unresolvedConflictVersionsOfItemAtURL: method. You can access each documents data, modification time, and URL, and use this information resolve the conflicts automatically, or allow the user to decide.

To experiment with what we've got access to, refactor a bit the tableView:cellForRowAtIndexPath: method to display some properties of a version:

```objc
- (UITableViewCell *)tableView:(UITableView *)tableView
         cellForRowAtIndexPath:(NSIndexPath *)indexPath
{

    UITableViewCell *cell = [tableView
                  dequeueReusableCellWithIdentifier:@"Cell"
                                      forIndexPath:indexPath];

    SMNote * note = self.notes[indexPath.row];

    if ([note documentState] == UIDocumentStateInConflict) {
```

```
        cell.textLabel.textColor = [UIColor redColor];

        NSArray *conflicts = [NSFileVersion
            unresolvedConflictVersionsOfItemAtURL:note.fileURL];
        for (NSFileVersion *version in conflicts) {
            NSLog(@"- - - - - -");
            NSLog(@"name = %@", version.localizedName);
            NSLog(@"date = %@", version.modificationDate);
            NSLog(@"device = %@",
                        version.localizedNameOfSavingComputer);
            NSLog(@"url = %@", version.URL);
            NSLog(@"- - - - - -");
        }
    } else {
        cell.textLabel.textColor = [UIColor blackColor];
    }

    cell.textLabel.text = note.fileURL.lastPathComponent;
    return cell;
}
```

Run your project again, and you should see something like the following in the console:

```
All Output ⬍                                                    ( Clear ) ▢ ▣ ▢
2012-10-21 13:24:46.020 dox[9563:907] - - - - -
2012-10-21 13:24:46.022 dox[9563:907] name = Note_20121020_042145
2012-10-21 13:24:46.024 dox[9563:907] date = 2012-10-21 17:22:17 +0000
2012-10-21 13:24:46.025 dox[9563:907] device = iPad
2012-10-21 13:24:46.026 dox[9563:907] url = file://localhost/private/var/mobile/Library/
Application%20Support/Ubiquity/genstore/peer-66B3BA01-9A0D-B5D1-CD7F-61E955D3F07A/66B3BA01-9A0D-
B5D1-CD7F-61E955D3F07A-0x000000000000013d/Note_20121020_042145.92312F70-CF3B-49CE-
B924-00A684C02E74
2012-10-21 13:24:46.028 dox[9563:907] - - - - - -
```

Notice that the URL of the document in conflict is a very long and unique address. This helps avoiding filename conflicts, much like in git or other source code management systems, where each commit has a project unique reference id.

One possible solution to resolve this conflict is to show the version picker when the user taps a red note. In this case you assume there will be just two competing versions of a document but you can easily adapt it to allow more complex cases.

To handle this case I have prepared a refactored version of the SMVersionPicker, which is included in the project named **dox-08** in the resources for this chapter. Remove the old version of SMVersionPicker from your project and drag the new files in.

Also, open **SMDetailViewController.m** and comment out resolveNote:, as you will not need that for this section.

This version of the class has slightly different names to match this new scenario, plus a new method called cleanConflicts. Here is the header:

```objc
#import <UIKit/UIKit.h>
#import "SMNote.h"

@interface SMVersionPicker : UIViewController

@property (strong, nonatomic) IBOutlet UITextView
                                *thisDeviceContentTextView;
@property (strong, nonatomic) IBOutlet UITextView
                                *otherDeviceContentTextView;
@property (strong, nonatomic) NSString
                                *thisDeviceContentVersion;
@property (strong, nonatomic) NSString
                                *otherDeviceContentVersion;
@property (strong, nonatomic) SMNote *currentNote;

- (IBAction)pickOtherDeviceVersion:(id)sender;
- (IBAction)pickThisDeviceVersion:(id)sender;

- (void) cleanConflicts;

@end
```

The methods to pick the version have been refactored as follows.

```objc
- (IBAction)pickOtherDeviceVersion:(id)sender {

    self.currentNote.noteContent =
                        self.otherDeviceContentTextView.text;
    [self cleanConflicts];

    [self.currentNote saveToURL:[self.currentNote fileURL]
            forSaveOperation:UIDocumentSaveForOverwriting
            completionHandler:^(BOOL success) {

        if (success) {

            [self.navigationController
                        popViewControllerAnimated:YES];

            [[NSNotificationCenter defaultCenter]
    postNotificationName:@"com.studiomagnolia.conflictResolved"
                object:self];

        }

    }];
```

```
}

- (IBAction)pickThisDeviceVersion:(id)sender {

    self.currentNote.noteContent =
                            self.thisDeviceContentTextView.text;
    [self cleanConflicts];

    [self.currentNote saveToURL:[self.currentNote fileURL]
            forSaveOperation:UIDocumentSaveForOverwriting
            completionHandler:^(BOOL success) {

        if (success) {

            [self.navigationController
                            popViewControllerAnimated:YES];

            [[NSNotificationCenter defaultCenter]
        postNotificationName:@"com.studiomagnolia.conflictResolved"
                object:self];

        }

    }];

}
```

Besides storing the selected value you also call the cleanConflicts method, you save the URL as usual, and you post a notification before popping the view controller. The cleanConflicts method is defined like this:

```
- (void) cleanConflicts {
    NSArray *conflicts =[NSFileVersion
                        unresolvedConflictVersionsOfItemAtURL:
                            [self.currentNote fileURL]];

    for (NSFileVersion *c in conflicts) {
        c.resolved = YES;
    }

    NSError *error = nil;
    BOOL ok = [NSFileVersion
                removeOtherVersionsOfItemAtURL:
                        [self.currentNote fileURL]
                                    error:&error];

    if (!ok) {
        NSLog(@"Can't remove other versions: %@", error);
    }
```

```
}
```

As stated earlier a conflict is 'permanent' until it is marked as resolved. To resolve a conflict you have to perform two steps:

1. Mark each unresolved conflict as resolved

2. Remove the other versions of the file.

The code above performs both of theses tasks. Once you have met these conditions the conflict is fully resolved and a reload of the note list will show the normal black labeled titles!

In the next step you have to present the version picker if the document is in conflict. To do so, import the file at the top of SMMasterViewController.m:

```
#import "SMVersionPicker.h"
```

Then modify `tableView:didSelectRowAtIndexPath:` as follows:

```
- (void)tableView:(UITableView *)tableView
  didSelectRowAtIndexPath:(NSIndexPath *)indexPath
{
    SMNote *selectedNote = self.notes[indexPath.row];
    if (selectedNote.documentState == UIDocumentStateInConflict)
    {
        SMVersionPicker *picker = nil;

        if (UI_USER_INTERFACE_IDIOM() ==
                                    UIUserInterfaceIdiomPad) {
            picker = [[SMVersionPicker alloc]
                    initWithNibName:@"SMVersionPicker_iPad"
                            bundle:nil];
        } else {
            picker = [[SMVersionPicker alloc]
                    initWithNibName:@"SMVersionPicker_iPhone"
                            bundle:nil];
        }

        picker.currentNote = selectedNote;

        NSArray *conflicts =
        [NSFileVersion unresolvedConflictVersionsOfItemAtURL:
                                    selectedNote.fileURL];

        for (NSFileVersion *version in conflicts) {

            SMNote *otherDeviceNote = [[SMNote alloc]
                            initWithFileURL:version.URL];
```

```
                    [otherDeviceNote openWithCompletionHandler:^(BOOL
  success) {

              if (success) {
                  picker.thisDeviceContentVersion =
                                        selectedNote.noteContent;
                  picker.otherDeviceContentVersion =
                                        otherDeviceNote.noteContent;
                  [self.navigationController
                        pushViewController:picker
                                    animated:YES];
              }

          }];
      }
  }

  if (selectedNote.documentState == UIDocumentStateNormal) {
      if ([[UIDevice currentDevice] userInterfaceIdiom] ==
                                      UIUserInterfaceIdiomPad)
      {
          self.detailViewController.detailItem = selectedNote;

      } else {
          SMDetailViewController *detailViewController =
          [self.storyboard
                  instantiateViewControllerWithIdentifier:
                  @"SMDetailViewControllerID"];
          detailViewController.detailItem = selectedNote;
          [self.navigationController
                  pushViewController:detailViewController
                              animated:YES];
      }
  }
}
```

Here you have hijacked a bit the flow of the storyboard. The easiest way to fix this is to import the new storyboards from the dox-08 project (or you could tweak yours to 'unlink' the master and detail view controller and to assign to the detail view the storyboard id "SMDetailViewControllerID").

The last step is to listen for the "com.studiomagnola.conflictResolved" notification in SMMasterViewController to correctly update the list of notes and revert to black those previously red. Add the following to end of viewDidLoad:

```
[[NSNotificationCenter defaultCenter]
    addObserver:self
      selector:@selector(conflictResolved)
```

```
        name:@"com.studiomagnolia.conflictResolved"
   object:nil];
```

Then implement the associated selector, which simply reloads the table view data:

```
- (void) conflictResolved {
   [self.tableView reloadData];
}
```

Let's try it out! Run the application on two devices (d1 and d2) and perform the following steps:

1. Create a conflicted file if you don't have one already (following the instructions earlier)

2. On d1 tap the red note and pick one version

3. Notice on d1 the reloaded list of notes with no conflict

4. Wait to see the update also on d2

Your knowledge of iCloud is growing more and more. you are now able to create, edit, delete documents and even resolve version conflicts!

> **Note:** The project up to this point is in the resources for this chapter as **dox-08**.

There's still a lot left to explore with iCloud - still to cover is working with undo and redo, exporting data for download, and working with Core Data.

Using the Undo Manager

In all the examples so far, to save a document you have used either `saveToURL:forSaveOperation:completionHandler:` or a simple `updateChangeCount:`. Both of these methods are basically telling iCloud "I am done editing this file, so you can send updates to the remote location."

In this section, you'll learn about a third way to trigger this mechanism: using the undo manager.

`NSUndoManager` is a class available since iOS 3 (!) and it helps you keep track of undo (and redo) changes to properties. It is quite simple to use, and allows you to register a set of operations related to an object together with the method to be invoked if the user chooses to undo.

So if you want to use the undo manager, whenever you modify an object, you should call this method to tell the undo manager how to undo the modification:

```
- (void)registerUndoWithTarget:(id)target
                selector:(SEL)selector
                object:(id)anObject;
```

Let's go over these parameters one by one:

1. `target`: The object to which the selector belongs.

2. `selector`: The method called to revert the modification.

3. `object`: Here you can pass an object to be passed to the selector. Often you'll pass the "old state" here so the undo method can switch back to the old state.

The manager keeps also track whenever you move back in the history of states. For example if you undo an action the manager does not delete current state, but keeps it so you can reinstate it by means of a redo.

It is important to note that all the actions collected in the undo stack are related to the main run loop, so if you quit and restart the application you lose memory of the stack.

Whenever you use an undo manager, there is no need to call `updateChangeCount:`, because is automatically called for you when you send an undo or redo message. Moreover, Apple engineers have been kind enough to integrate an undo manager in `UIDocument`, so each instance of this class (and subclasses) has a property called `undoManager` which allows developers to build their stack of changes for each iCloud-enabled file.

Let's see how you can integrate an undo manager in your application. You can start from project `dox-08`, which you have finished in the previous section. It is included in the resources for the chapter.

Open up `SMDetailViewController.h` and add two new properties and methods, as shown below:

```
@property (strong, nonatomic) IBOutlet UIButton *undoButton;
@property (strong, nonatomic) IBOutlet UIButton *redoButton;
```

Then open the storyboard and add two `UIButtons` for undo and redo:

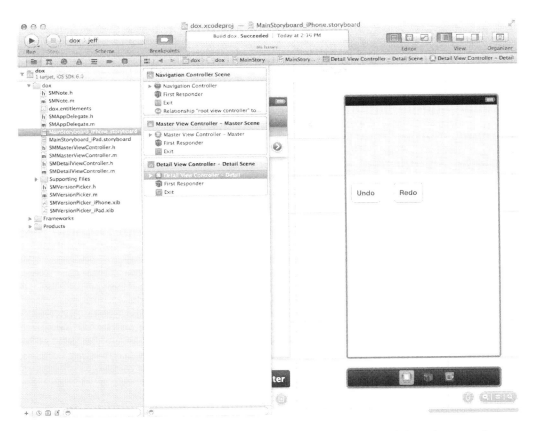

Note you should put the buttons high enough so that the keyboard doesn't cover them up when it appears. Remember to connect the buttons to their outlets. Finally, repeat this entire process for the iPad storyboard.

Now that your user interface is hooked up with the view controller you need to refactor its logic. Open SMDetailViewController.m and add the following at the bottom of viewDidLoad:

```
[self.undoButton addTarget:self
             action:@selector(performUndo:)
     forControlEvents:UIControlEventTouchUpInside];

[self.redoButton addTarget:self
             action:@selector(performRedo:)
     forControlEvents:UIControlEventTouchUpInside];
```

Then implement the methods that get called when these buttons are tapped as follows:

```
- (void)performUndo:(id)sender {
```

```
        if ([self.detailItem.undoManager canUndo]) {
            [self.detailItem.undoManager undo];
        }
    }

- (void)performRedo:(id)sender {
    if ([self.detailItem.undoManager canRedo]) {
        [self.detailItem.undoManager redo];
    }
}
```

Then change the saveEdits: method associated to the 'save' button like this:

```
- (void) saveEdits:(id)sender {
    [self saveNoteWithContent:self.noteTextView.text];
}
```

Finally implement the method saveNoteWithContent: as follows:

```
- (void) saveNoteWithContent:(NSString *)newContent {

    NSString *currentText = self.detailItem.noteContent;

    if (newContent != currentText) {

        [self.detailItem.undoManager
            registerUndoWithTarget:self

                    selector:@selector(saveNoteWithContent:)
                      object:currentText];

        self.detailItem.noteContent = newContent;
        self.noteTextView.text = self.detailItem.noteContent;

    }

    self.undoButton.enabled =
                        [self.detailItem.undoManager canUndo];
    self.redoButton.enabled =
                        [self.detailItem.undoManager canRedo];

}
```

This method updates the content of the note and the text view, but before that it registers itself with the undo manager built in the SMNote class (inherited from UIDocument). After that it updates the states of buttons according to the stack of changes.

This way, whenever and undo or redo is triggered that action will be registered as a change and the user will be free to move back and forth new or old versions of the note.

Compile and run on two different devices, and run through the following test case:

- Open a note on device 1, edit the text and save.

- Then you can tap the undo and redo buttons to see the text changing.

This is a new tool that you can exploit to build user-friendly applications, which enable the user to review changes to the content of notes. And as you can see – it's pretty easy to add, eh?

Exporting Data From iCloud

You an export a URL for your data you save in iCloud, so that users or non-iCloud applications can access the data just by downloading it at the given URL.

To do this, you just call the following method on NSFileManager:

```
- (NSURL *)
    URLForPublishingUbiquitousItemAtURL:(NSURL *)url
                        expirationDate:(NSDate **)outDate
                                error:(NSError **)error;
```

This method returns a URL like the following:

```
https://www.icloud.com/documents/dl/?p=2&t=BAJJZKAKzzXMg7o4tC8BO
DEIOzkOd6UN2q0A
```

This is a temporary URL and is not indexed by search engines. Whoever has the URL can download the file unless it is expired. This is what it looks like when you open the URL:

Let's see how you can integrate this functionality in your application.

In this section you will add an export button when a note is opened. Tapping the button will send en email containing the URL of the exported note.

In this section, you will start from the project **dox-07** completed previously. Grab it from the resources for this chapter, update the bundle identifier and entitlements, and run it to check that everything is ok.

Then open **SMDetailViewController.h** and modify the file to the following:

```objc
#import <UIKit/UIKit.h>
#import "SMNote.h"
#import <MessageUI/MessageUI.h>

@interface SMDetailViewController : UIViewController
<UISplitViewControllerDelegate,
MFMailComposeViewControllerDelegate>

@property (strong, nonatomic) SMNote *detailItem;
@property (weak, nonatomic) IBOutlet UITextView *noteTextView;

- (NSURL *) generateExportURL;

@end
```

This imports the MessageUI framework, implements the compose delegate, and adds the method generateExportURL.

Since you're using the MessageUI framework you have to import it into your project as well. So select the project, then the target and finally the **Build Phases** tab. Expand the list of linked libraries, click on the + sign, select **MessageUI.framework**, and click **Add**.

Next, open up **SMDetailViewController**.m and change viewWillAppear: like this:

```
- (void) viewWillAppear:(BOOL)animated {

    self.noteTextView.text = self.detailItem.noteContent;

    UIBarButtonItem *exportButtonItem =
        [[UIBarButtonItem alloc]
                initWithTitle:@"Export"
                        style:UIBarButtonItemStylePlain
                       target:self
                       action:@selector(sendNoteURL)];

    self.navigationItem.rightBarButtonItem = exportButtonItem;

}
```

Then implement the callback as follows:

```
- (void) sendNoteURL {

    NSURL *url = [self generateExportURL];

    MFMailComposeViewController *mailComposer;
    mailComposer = [[MFMailComposeViewController alloc] init];
    mailComposer.mailComposeDelegate = self;
    [mailComposer
        setModalPresentationStyle:UIModalPresentationFormSheet];
    [mailComposer setSubject:@"Download my note"];
    [mailComposer setMessageBody:[NSString stringWithFormat:
            @"The note can be downloaded at the following url:\n
 %@ \n \n It will expire in one hour.", url]
                        isHTML:NO];

    [self presentViewController:mailComposer
                       animated:YES
                     completion:nil];

}
```

This creates a view controller similar to the one used by the mail application in iOS. you set the subject and the body of the email.

Next, add the following method to generate the URL:

```
- (NSURL *) generateExportURL {

    NSTimeInterval oneHourInterval = 3600.0;
    NSDate *expirationInOneHourSinceNow =
    [NSDate dateWithTimeInterval:oneHourInterval
                    sinceDate:[NSDate date]];
    NSError *err;

    NSURL *url = [[NSFileManager defaultManager]
                 URLForPublishingUbiquitousItemAtURL:
                 [self.detailItem fileURL]
                 expirationDate:&expirationInOneHourSinceNow
                 error:&err];
    if (err)
        return nil;
    else
        return url;

}
```

Here you create an interval of one hour to calculate the expiration date of the download link. Then you pass it as a parameter to the URLForPublishingUbiquitousItemAtURL:expirationDate:error: method, which instructs iCloud to make the file downloadable for a given time. If you are not interested in an expiration date you can pass nil as parameter.

The final touch is to implement the delegate method to dismiss the mail compose view when done:

```
- (void)mailComposeController:
(MFMailComposeViewController*)controller
        didFinishWithResult:(MFMailComposeResult)result
                    error:(NSError*)error {

    if (result == MFMailComposeResultSent) {

        [self dismissViewControllerAnimated:YES
                            completion:nil];

    }

}
```

Build and run the app, and when you tap the Export button you should see something like this:

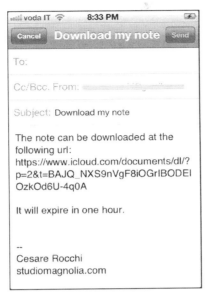

Try sending the email to yourself, and verify you can access the note by clicking the link. Pretty cool, eh?

Note: The project up to this point is in the resources for this chapter as **dox-09**.

Congrats, you have now covered almost everything you might want to do with loading and saving data with the UIDocument class. Next up you're going to switch gears, and dive into using iCloud with Core Data!

What is Core Data?

Besides files, either single or packaged, iCloud allows storing information in a relational form. That means you can use iCloud in your applications as a backend database! You can store objects that are related to others, push changes on one device and receive them on another.

All this enabled by Core Data, which has been extended in iOS5 to support iCloud. Core Data is a technology introduced in iOS 3 to manage relational data. In such a model, objects can be described in terms of attributes and can be related to other objects by means of relations.

For example, a commonly known domain used to represent relational data is a company. There are different types of objects like employees, departments, offices and each is related to each other in some way. An employee has attributes like name, surname, phone number; he belongs to a department and has an office. An office, in turn, can host more than one employee and so on.

All this structured information can be stored in different ways: xml files, binary form or even SQLite. Core Data abstracts the way you usually work with such kind of model. Instead of writing sql queries to interact with your objects you will write actual Objective-C code. For example to create a new employee and assign him to a department you will use the following way (pseudo-code):

```
Department *dep ... // a department
Employee *newEmployee = [[Employe alloc] init];
newEmployee.name = "Cesare"
newEmployee.surname = "Rocchi"
newEmployee.department = dep;
```

You might be tempted to say that Core Data is an ORM (Object Relational Mapping) system. It is not, for data are not related to a database schema. Core Data is an "object graph management framework", where data are kept in memory and, when needed, persisted on disk. An object graph is a set of interrelated instances, which describes your domain. If Core Data were an ORM it would just store information in SQLite form. Instead, it allows dumping a graph in xml and binary format as well.

Apart from this, Core Data includes many features to manage relational information like:

- validation of attributes (values for properties have to be correctly typed)

- migration of schemas (when you add new objects or relations)

- support to the tracking of changes (when you update objects or relations)

- fetching, filtering and sorting (to retrieve the data you need)

- user interface integration (to notify the view of changes to the data model)

- merging (to resolve conflicts in data, especially in iCloud)

In writing a Core Data enabled application there are three key elements to deal with: model, context and coordinator. Now you will see in details their respective roles.

Model

You might be already familiar with the notion of **model**. For example, the applications built so far have been 'modeled' in terms of notes, which were defined by attributes like identifier, title, content, creation date and so on.

XCode allows defining a model graphically, much like a xib. The model defines the objects of your domain in terms of properties and relationships. It's like a schema for databases.

Objects are often referred to as **entities**, which usually correspond to classes. In your example, employees, offices and departments are entities of the company domain. Depending on the way entities are persisted on disk, entities are represented as subclasses of NSManagedObject or UIManagedDocument.

Entities are described in terms of **attributes**, which correspond to instance variables. For example, name and surname of an employee are attributes describing that entity. The fillers of attributes can be of many types like strings, numbers, dates, etc.

Relationships are the way to describe how two entities are connected. Relationships have a cardinality which can be:

• one-to-one (one employee has one office and each office can host just one employee)

• one-to-many (one employee has one office and one office can host more than one employee)

Finally, there is concept similar to relationships called **fetched properties**. An example of fetched property in plain English is "all the employees of department a whose name starts with 'F'". Although this example relates two entities (employees and departments) it is not a relationship defined in the schema but a sort of 'temporary' relation defined in terms of rules or constraints applied to the domain.

Context

A **context**, short for managed object context, is a sort of mediator between managed objects and the functionalities of Core Data. Whenever there is change in a domain (e.g. an employee changes department) such a variation is not stored directly in the database but it is first written on "scratch paper", the context.

So whenever you write some code to change information in your domain, those variations are not immediately persisted to disk. Indeed, to make them persistent you have to explicitly tell the context: "please store all the changes I have made so far". At this point the context performs a lot of tasks such as:

- validating values (for example a filler for the name property has to be a string)

- managing undo and redo

To some extent a context is a gateway: no changes to the databases are committed if they are not first annotated into a context. This is why a context plays a central role in Core Data architecture and you will use it a lot.

Coordinator

The **coordinator**, short for persistent store coordinator, is the mediator between a store and a context. The changes temporarily included in a context are persisted on disk by means of a coordinator, which serializes all the changes and updates the information on the disk.

While the context deals with changes at an abstract level, with data kept in memory, the coordinator performs the dirty work to store those changes according to the store type. So a coordinator has "competence" in SQLite, XML and binary format. It is a façade that acts as a bridge between the context and the specific behaviors of the persistent store type.

I should mention that a coordinator can manage multiple contexts and stores at a time. The following image shows the interplay between model, context and coordinator.

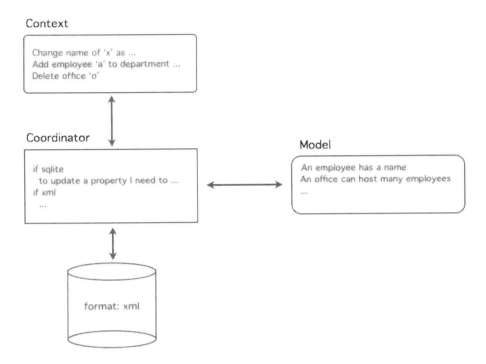

Before digging into iCloud features you will build a simple example to show how information can be persisted on disk by means of Core Data.

Porting the Dox Application to Core Data

Since Core Data is ideal for relational information you are going to extend your model a bit. Now, each note will have one or more tags attached. This way you will have two entities in your domain, note and tag, related by a many-to-many relationship (each note can have multiple tags, and each tag can be assigned to multiple notes). The user interface will be pretty similar, but under the hood there are many changes to do.

If you are new to Core Data, you might want to run through the next few sections so you get some experience with Core Data and see how it fits together. But if you are already experienced with Core Data, you might want to skip to the "Porting a Core Data Application with iCloud" section later on in this chapter.

Creating A Model For Notes And Tags

In this section you will start with the **dox-10-starter-project** in the resources for this chapter, so create a copy and edit your bundle ID, entitlements, and code signing profile as usual. It is a barebones master/detail project, with the storyboards configured correctly but nothing more. Run it on your device to check that everything works fine.

Next, create a new file with the **iOS\Core Data\Data Model** template, and name it **doxModel.xcdatamodeld**. Select the file, and you'll see the following view:

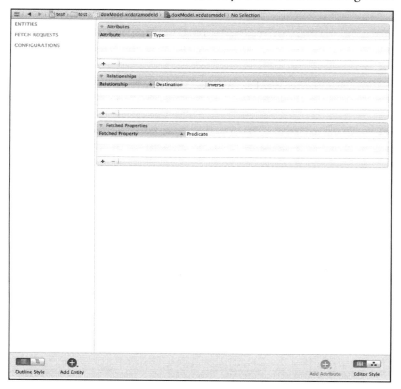

This is where you can define the entities you'll use in your project and their relationships. At the bottom there is a button **Add Entity**. Click it and call the new entity **SMNote**.

Next add two properties to the class. Click on the '+' sign in the attributes section and add two entries named `noteContent` and `noteTitle`, and set them as strings.

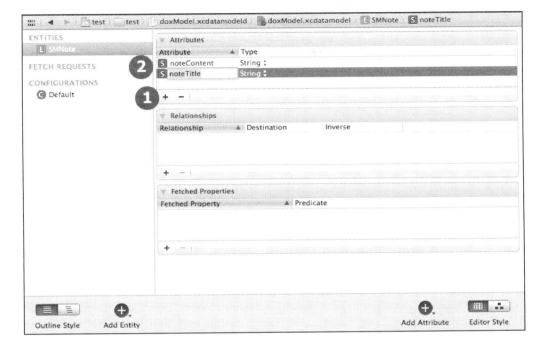

Next add another entity, called **SMTag**, with just one attribute, `tagContent` as a string. This is the name of the tag that will be displayed on the user interface.

Now it is time to relate these new entities that you have created. As you saw above there is a many-to-many relationship between them. First select **SMNote** and click on the + in the **Relationships** section. Name the relation `tags` and set **SMTag** as the destination.

Then you should specify that the relation is of type **To-Many**. With the relation selected you open the panel on the right and you select the corresponding option.

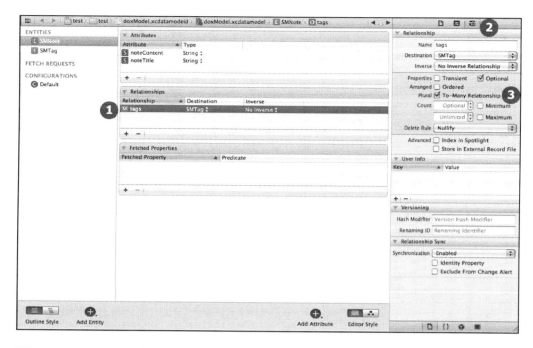

This is just one part of relation, from a note to a tag. You should also model its counterpart.

Select the **SMTag** entity and add a new relationship, named **notes**, with the destination **SMNote**, whose inverse relation is **tags** (the one defined previously). Also mark this as a **To-Many** relation. The inverse relationship will help Core Data keep the consistency in the model.

Now if you switch the **Editor Style** to **Graph** (click the button in the bottom right of the Core Data editor), you'll see a diagram of entities as the following:

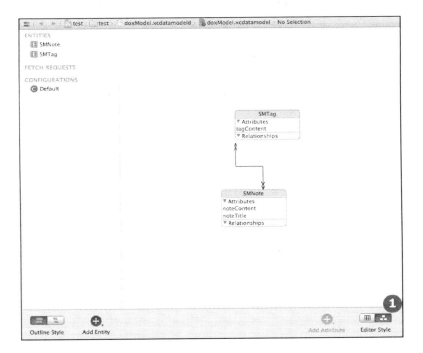

This view can be a nice way to visualize the relationships between the entities. All the classes have the attributes and the relations specified previously.

Now you can generate classes for the entities you created in the Core Data editor. To do this, drag a rectangle on the diagram to select all the boxes and then from the main menu select **Editor\Create NSManagedObject Subclass**, and click **Create**. XCode will generate header and implementation files for both of your entities: **SMTag** and **SMNote**.

You will notice that each class extends **NSManagedObject**, which is an abstract class that helps to interact with Core Data storage. Also relationships are modeled. The **SMNote** class will contain the following helper methods, which are needed to add/remove single or multiple tags.

```
- (void)addTagsObject:(SMTag *)value;
- (void)removeTagsObject:(SMTag *)value;
- (void)addTags:(NSSet *)values;
- (void)removeTags:(NSSet *)values;
```

For example, when you will need to assign a tag to a note the corresponding code will be pretty simple.

```
SMNote *note ... // a note instance
```

```
SMTag *tag ... // a tag instance
[note addTagsObject:tag];
// save context
```

The data model for your application is ready. Now it is time to load the model in the application and prepare it to manage Core Data functionalities.

Integrating Core Data

As you learned earlier there are three elements that interplay in the Core Data-based application: the model, the context and the coordinator. But before you can add these elements to the project you have to import the Core Data framework.

To do this, select the root element of the project, then the target and open the Link Binary with Libraries section in the Build Phases tab. Click the + sign to add a new framework. You can use the search bar to look for the CoreData.framework. Select it and click to add it.

Now you can include the Core Data classes without any complaint from the compiler. It is better to place these elements in the application delegate so whenever the application starts up or gets reactivated you can perform the actions needed to refresh data. The three classes that you need are: NSManagedObjectModel, NSPersistentStoreCoordinator and NSManagedObjectContext.

Go ahead and update SMAppDelegate.h as follows:

```
#import <UIKit/UIKit.h>
#import <CoreData/CoreData.h>

@interface SMAppDelegate : UIResponder <UIApplicationDelegate>

@property (strong, nonatomic) UIWindow *window;
@property (strong, nonatomic) NSManagedObjectContext
                                        *managedObjectContext;
@property (strong, nonatomic) NSManagedObjectModel
                                        *managedObjectModel;
@property (strong, nonatomic)
        NSPersistentStoreCoordinator *persistentStoreCoordinator;

- (void)saveContext;
- (NSURL *)applicationDocumentsDirectory;

@end
```

In addition to adding the Core Data classes you need, here you also added two helper methods to retrieve the documents directory and to save changes.

Now let's start by defining the model. Switch to SMAppDelegate.m and add the following method:

```objc
- (NSManagedObjectModel *)managedObjectModel
{
    if (_managedObjectModel != nil)
    {
        return _managedObjectModel;
    }

    NSURL *modelURL = [[NSBundle mainBundle]
                        URLForResource:@"doxModel"
                        withExtension:@"momd"];

    _managedObjectModel = [[NSManagedObjectModel alloc]
                           initWithContentsOfURL:modelURL];

    return _managedObjectModel;
}
```

The task of this method is to load the schema that you have defined graphically to provide all the rules and constraints needed to verify the consistency. The model needs a URL that you build from the main bundle file of the application.

You might wonder why you are loading a file with extension "momd". The model defined in doxModel.xcdatamodeld is not copied as-is in the application folder. Instead, each file corresponding to an entity gets "compiled" into a file whose extension is .mom (which stands for managed object model). In a second step all the mom files are wrapped into a .momd file, which is the one you have to load from the bundle of the application.

Now you can use the model to create a coordinator:

```objc
- (NSPersistentStoreCoordinator *)persistentStoreCoordinator
{
    if (_persistentStoreCoordinator != nil)
    {
        return _persistentStoreCoordinator;
    }

    NSURL *storeURL = [[self applicationDocumentsDirectory]
                        URLByAppendingPathComponent:@"dox.sqlite"];

    NSError *error = nil;
    _persistentStoreCoordinator =
        [[NSPersistentStoreCoordinator alloc]

            initWithManagedObjectModel:[self managedObjectModel]];

    if (![_persistentStoreCoordinator
```

```
                    addPersistentStoreWithType:NSSQLiteStoreType
                                configuration:nil
                                          URL:storeURL
                                      options:nil
                                        error:&error])
        {

            NSLog(@"Core Data error %@, %@", error,
                    [error userInfo]);
            abort();
        }

        return _persistentStoreCoordinator;

    }
```

In your case you are going to use a SQLite store type so you need to provide a name for the file where the database will be stored, in your case 'dox.sqlite'. The coordinator is initialized with the model created above.

Once you have an instance of the coordinator, you can add the persistent store by specifying the type and the store URL. You could also provide a configuration and some options. To keep things simple, for the moment you will pass nil as a parameter. You will come back to options when you will configure Core Data for iCloud.

Next add the helper method applicationDocumentsDirectory as follows:

```
- (NSURL *)applicationDocumentsDirectory
{
    return [[[NSFileManager defaultManager]
            URLsForDirectory:NSDocumentDirectory
                  inDomains:NSUserDomainMask]
            lastObject];
}
```

And implement the method to return the context, which is initialized and associated to the coordinator:

```
- (NSManagedObjectContext *)managedObjectContext
{
    if (_managedObjectContext != nil)
    {
        return _managedObjectContext;
    }

    NSPersistentStoreCoordinator *coordinator =
        [self persistentStoreCoordinator];

    if (coordinator != nil)
```

```
    {
        _managedObjectContext =
                [[NSManagedObjectContext alloc] init];
        [_managedObjectContext
            setPersistentStoreCoordinator:coordinator];
    }

    return _managedObjectContext;

}
```

The last thing to implement in the application delegate is the saveContext method:

```
- (void)saveContext {
    NSError *error = nil;

    if ([self.managedObjectContext hasChanges] &&
        ![self.managedObjectContext save:&error])
    {
        NSLog(@"Core Data error %@, %@",
            error, [error userInfo]);
        abort();
    }
}
```

This method calls the save method of the context if there are changes. It can be useful to place a call to such a method when the application is put in background or quit.

```
- (void)applicationDidEnterBackground:
                            (UIApplication *)application
{
    [self saveContext];
}


- (void)applicationWillTerminate:(UIApplication *)application
{
    [self saveContext];
}
```

Now the application is ready to interact with a database persisted on disk and based on the model you have defined previously. Let's see how you can retrieve and store notes in your new data structure.

Adding and Retrieving Notes

As mentioned above, the interaction with the data store is managed by the context. So you can use the context to get or modify the list of notes.

The first task is to show the list of notes retrieved from the store into the table view. This is done by using a `NSFetchedResultsController`, which allows defining a query which is managed by the context to fetch data.

Replace SMMasterViewController.h with the following:

```
#import <UIKit/UIKit.h>
#import "SMNote.h"
#import "SMTag.h"

@class SMDetailViewController;

@interface SMMasterViewController :
UITableViewController<NSFetchedResultsControllerDelegate>

@property (strong, nonatomic) SMDetailViewController
                              *detailViewController;
@property (strong, nonatomic) NSFetchedResultsController
                              *fetchedResultsController;
@property (strong, nonatomic) NSManagedObjectContext
                              *managedObjectContext;

@end
```

We have added a result controller and a managed object context, along with a protocol to manage callbacks from the result controller.

There are a few steps to create a fetched results controller:

1. Create a fetch request.

2. Create an entity description for the entity to be fetched (in your case, `SMNote`).

3. Assign the entity description to the request.

4. Create a sort descriptor to specify how the results should be sorted.

5. Assign the sort descriptor to the request.

6. Create a fetched results controller with the fetch request and the context.

7. Perform a fetch request to retrieve the data!

Here's the code corresponding to these steps - go ahead and add it to SMMasterViewController.m:

```
- (NSFetchedResultsController *)fetchedResultsController
{
    if (_fetchedResultsController != nil) {
        return _fetchedResultsController;
    }
```

```objc
    // 1) Create a fetch request.
    NSFetchRequest *fetchRequest =
    [[NSFetchRequest alloc] init];

    // 2) Create an entity description for the entity to be
    // fetched.
    NSEntityDescription *entity = [NSEntityDescription
                              entityForName:@"SMNote"
                              inManagedObjectContext:
                              self.managedObjectContext];

    // 3) Assign the entity description to the request.
    [fetchRequest setEntity:entity];

    // 4) Create a sort descriptor to specify how the results
    // should be sorted.
    NSSortDescriptor *sortDescriptor = [[NSSortDescriptor alloc]
                                initWithKey:@"noteTitle"
                                ascending:NO];
    NSArray *sortDescriptors =
    [NSArray arrayWithObjects:sortDescriptor, nil];

    // 5) Assign the sort descriptor to the request.
    [fetchRequest setSortDescriptors:sortDescriptors];

    // 6) Create a fetched results controller with the fetch
    // request and the context.
    NSFetchedResultsController *aFetchedResultsController =
    [[NSFetchedResultsController alloc]
     initWithFetchRequest:fetchRequest
     managedObjectContext:self.managedObjectContext
     sectionNameKeyPath:nil
     cacheName:@"Master"];

    aFetchedResultsController.delegate = self;
    self.fetchedResultsController = aFetchedResultsController;

    // 7) Perform a fetch request to retrieve the data!
    NSError *error = nil;
    if (![self.fetchedResultsController performFetch:&error]) {

        NSLog(@"Unresolved error %@, %@", error, [error
userInfo]);

    }

    return _fetchedResultsController;

}
```

To keep things simple, in creating the controller you did not provide any section path (see the Core Data documentation for more details) and you specified a name for the cache to quicken the retrieval time.

Finally you called `performFetch:` to load data when the instance variable is created. You might have noticed that you have specified 'self' as the delegate of the controller.

Next you are going to implement the fetched result controller delegate's `controllerDidChangeContent:` method, which is called when the result controller has processed some change to data. Implement it to reload data in the table view:

```
- (void)controllerDidChangeContent:
                    (NSFetchedResultsController *)controller {

    NSLog(@"something has changed");
    [self.tableView reloadData];

}
```

Next, replace `insertNewObject:` with the following:

```
- (void)insertNewObject:(id)sender
{
    SMNote *newNote =
    [NSEntityDescription
     insertNewObjectForEntityForName:@"SMNote"
            inManagedObjectContext:self.managedObjectContext];

    NSDateFormatter *formatter = [[NSDateFormatter alloc] init];
    [formatter setDateFormat:@"yyyyMMdd_hhmmss"];

    NSString *noteTitle = [NSString stringWithFormat:@"Note_%@",
                            [formatter stringFromDate:[NSDate
                                                        date]]];
    newNote.noteTitle = noteTitle;
    newNote.noteContent = @"New note content";

    NSError *error = nil;
    if (![self.managedObjectContext save:&error]) {
        NSLog(@"Core Data error %@, %@",
              error, [error userInfo]);
    }
}
```

Unlike previous examples, notes populating the table view are not stored in an array inside the class, but rather the Core Data the store itself. So when you add a new note you instantiate it in the context, you set its properties and you save the context.

Here the note is not created via the usual alloc/init, but instead with
`NSEntityDescription`'s
`insertNewObjectForEntityForName:inManagedObjectContext:` method (this is
what you have to do with Core Data).

Once you have an instance you have access to its properties as usual. The save: method
of the context, once done, will trigger `controllerDidChangeContent:` which will
reload data in the table. Finally, you have just to implement the table view delegates to
use the data returned by the fetched results controller:

```objc
- (NSInteger)numberOfSectionsInTableView:
                              (UITableView *)tableView
{
    return 1;
}

- (NSInteger)tableView:(UITableView *)tableView
 numberOfRowsInSection:(NSInteger)section
{
    id <NSFetchedResultsSectionInfo> sectionInfo =
      [[self.fetchedResultsController sections]
                              objectAtIndex:section];
    return [sectionInfo numberOfObjects];
}

- (UITableViewCell *)tableView:(UITableView *)tableView
        cellForRowAtIndexPath:(NSIndexPath *)indexPath
{

    NSManagedObject *managedObject =
                 [self.fetchedResultsController
                     objectAtIndexPath:indexPath];

    UITableViewCell *cell =
        [tableView dequeueReusableCellWithIdentifier:@"Cell"
                                      forIndexPath:indexPath];

    cell.textLabel.text = [managedObject
                     valueForKey:@"noteTitle"];

    return cell;

}
```

This way data persisted on disk will be displayed in the table view as in previous
examples. As a final step, open SMAppDelegate.m and
`application:didFinishLaunchingWithOptions:` to this:

```objc
- (BOOL)application:(UIApplication *)application
  didFinishLaunchingWithOptions:(NSDictionary *)launchOptions
{
    if ([[UIDevice currentDevice] userInterfaceIdiom] ==
                              UIUserInterfaceIdiomPad) {
        UISplitViewController *splitViewController =
         (UISplitViewController*)self.window.rootViewController;
        UINavigationController*navigationController =
              [splitViewController.viewControllers lastObject];
        splitViewController.delegate =
              (id)navigationController.topViewController;

        UINavigationController *masterNavigationController =
                    splitViewController.viewControllers[0];
        SMMasterViewController *controller =
          (SMMasterViewController *)
          masterNavigationController.topViewController;
        controller.managedObjectContext =
                                  self.managedObjectContext;
    } else {
        UINavigationController *navigationController =
         (UINavigationController *)self.window.rootViewController;
        SMMasterViewController *controller =
          (SMMasterViewController *)
          navigationController.topViewController;
        controller.managedObjectContext =
                                  self.managedObjectContext;
    }

    id currentToken =
         [[NSFileManager defaultManager] ubiquityIdentityToken];
    if (currentToken) {
        NSLog(@"iCloud access on with id %@", currentToken);
    } else {
        NSLog(@"No iCloud access");
    }
    return YES;
}
```

Phew, finally done! Run the application and add a few notes:

As you can see in the screenshot, the table view is correctly populated after each new addition. If you quit and restart the application, the data is properly reloaded from the Core Data SQLite database. Nice!

If you want to show a single note you have to push an instance of SMDetailViewController. So open SMMasterViewController.m and add the implementation for tableView:didSelectRowAtIndexPath: and prepareForSegue:sender: methods as follows:

```objc
- (void)tableView:(UITableView *)tableView
didSelectRowAtIndexPath:(NSIndexPath *)indexPath
{
    if ([[UIDevice currentDevice] userInterfaceIdiom] ==
                                        UIUserInterfaceIdiomPad)
    {
        SMNote *n = (SMNote *)[self.fetchedResultsController
                            objectAtIndexPath:indexPath];
        self.detailViewController.detailItem = n;

    }
}

- (void)prepareForSegue:(UIStoryboardSegue *)segue
                sender:(id)sender
{
    if ([[segue identifier] isEqualToString:@"showDetail"]) {
```

```
        NSIndexPath *indexPath = [self.tableView
                                    indexPathForSelectedRow];
        SMNote *n = (SMNote *)[self.fetchedResultsController
                                objectAtIndexPath:indexPath];
        self.detailViewController.detailItem = n;
        [[segue destinationViewController] setDetailItem:n];

    }
}
```

Now let's move on to the visualization of a single note and its tags.

Single Note and Tags

Now it is time to rework the user interface of SMDetailViewController to show the tags in a label. Replace SMDetailViewController.h with the following:

```
#import <UIKit/UIKit.h>
#import "SMNote.h"
#import "SMTag.h"

@interface SMDetailViewController : UIViewController
<UISplitViewControllerDelegate>

@property (strong, nonatomic) SMNote *detailItem;
@property (weak, nonatomic) IBOutlet UITextView *noteTextView;
@property (weak, nonatomic) IBOutlet UILabel *tagsLabel;

@end
```

You have to squeeze the text view a bit to accommodate a new label to show tags related to a note. Open the storyboards, resize the text view, and add a new label at the bottom. Then connect the label to tagsLabel outlet declared in the header file, as shown in the following screenshot:

The next step is to show the note content and the tags when a note is selected from the list. In the case of the iPhone you do it in `viewWillAppear:`, to be added in SMDetailViewController.m:

```objc
- (void)viewWillAppear:(BOOL)animated {
    [super viewWillAppear:animated];

    NSArray *tagsArray = [self.detailItem.tags allObjects];
    NSMutableArray *tagNames =
    [NSMutableArray arrayWithCapacity:tagsArray.count];

    for (SMTag *t in tagsArray) {
        [tagNames addObject:t.tagContent];
    }

    if (tagNames.count == 0) {
        self.tagsLabel.text = @"Tap to add tags";
    } else {
        NSString *s = [tagNames componentsJoinedByString:@","];
        self.tagsLabel.text = s;
    }
    [self.noteTextView becomeFirstResponder];
}
```

With the iPad you do it in `configureView`.

```
- (void)configureView
{
    if (self.detailItem) {

        self.noteTextView.text = self.detailItem.noteContent;
        self.title = self.detailItem.noteTitle;

        NSArray *tagsArray = [self.detailItem.tags allObjects];
        NSMutableArray *tagNames =
            [NSMutableArray arrayWithCapacity:tagsArray.count];

        for (SMTag *t in tagsArray) {
            [tagNames addObject:t.tagContent];
        }

        NSString *s = [tagNames componentsJoinedByString:@","];
        self.tagsLabel.text = s;
        [self.noteTextView becomeFirstResponder];
    }
}
```

In both cases this view controller does not need a fetch result controller, because it deals with only one note. Tags, although stored in the persistent store, are referenced as a property of a note. If you check the code generated for the class **SMNote** you will notice the following property.

```
@property (nonatomic, retain) NSSet *tags;
```

This is exactly the way the has-tags relation is modeled, by means of a set. This set is populated with the instances of tags related to a note. To populate the label you have transformed the set in an array and concatenated its elements with commas.

A note gets saved when the user taps the 'save' button. Unlike previous example, here you call the save: method of the context to store changes. Add the implementation of saveEdits: as following:

```
- (void) saveEdits:(id)sender {
    self.detailItem.noteContent = self.noteTextView.text;

    NSError *error = nil;
    if (![self.detailItem.managedObjectContext save:&error]) {
        NSLog(@"Core data error %@, %@",
            error, [error userInfo]);
        abort();
    }
}
```

A new note comes with no tags, so you have to create a way to assign one of more tags to a note. In the next step you will build a tag picker controller. Since you are editing the single note controller let's add the code to show the picker at the end of `viewDidLoad`. The action is triggered when the user taps the tags label. You associate this action once the view is loaded.

```
self.tagsLabel.userInteractionEnabled = YES;
UITapGestureRecognizer *tapGesture =
    [[UITapGestureRecognizer alloc]
                initWithTarget:self
                        action:@selector(tagsTapped)];
[self.tagsLabel addGestureRecognizer:tapGesture];
```

The action `tagsTapped` creates an instance of a new controller (which you are going to create in a bit), assign it the current note and push it onto the navigation stack. As usual you have to make the difference between the iPhone and the iPad version.

```
- (void) tagsTapped {
    SMTagPickerViewController *tagPicker = nil;
    if ([[UIDevice currentDevice] userInterfaceIdiom] ==
                                    UIUserInterfaceIdiomPhone) {
        tagPicker =
            [[SMTagPickerViewController alloc]
                initWithNibName:@"SMTagPickerViewController_iPhone"
                        bundle:nil];
    } else {
        tagPicker =
            [[SMTagPickerViewController alloc]
                initWithNibName:@"SMTagPickerViewController_iPad"
                        bundle:nil];
    }
    tagPicker.currentNote = self.detailItem;
    [self.navigationController pushViewController:tagPicker
                                        animated:YES];

}
```

Of course for this to work you have to import the header you'll write in a minute at the top of the file:

```
#import "SMTagPickerViewController.h"
```

Let's now define the behavior of the tag picker.

Building The Tag Picker

This component is meant to show the list of available tags so that the user can pick one or more and associated them to a note.

Create a new file with the iOS\Cocoa Touch\Objective-C class template. Name the class SMTagPickerViewController, make it a subclass of UITableViewController, and make sure that With XIB for user interface is checked.

Rename the newly created xib to SMTagPickerViewController_iPhone.xib, and create a xib for the iPad as well named SMTagPickerViewController_iPad.xib, with a table view like the one of the iPhone.

Next replace SMTagPickerViewController.h with the following:

```objc
#import <UIKit/UIKit.h>
#import "SMNote.h"
#import "SMTag.h"

@interface SMTagPickerViewController : UITableViewController

@property (nonatomic, strong) SMNote *currentNote;
@property (nonatomic, strong) NSMutableSet *pickedTags;
@property (strong, nonatomic) NSFetchedResultsController
                                    *fetchedResultsController;

@end
```

The currentNote will keep a reference to the note shown in the previous view controller, the set will store selected tags and the result controller will contain all the tags available in your domain.

Switch to SMTagPickerViewController.m to implement the fetch controller. This will perform a different query, focused on the SMTag entity. The pattern is exactly the same presented above: create a request, set some properties on it, and initialize a fetched results controller with the request and the context.

```objc
- (NSFetchedResultsController *)fetchedResultsController
{

    if (_fetchedResultsController != nil) {
        return _fetchedResultsController;
    }

    NSFetchRequest *fetchRequest =
                            [[NSFetchRequest alloc] init];
```

```
    NSEntityDescription *entity =
            [NSEntityDescription
          entityForName:@"SMTag"
inManagedObjectContext:self.currentNote.managedObjectContext];

    [fetchRequest setEntity:entity];

    NSSortDescriptor *sortDescriptor =
            [[NSSortDescriptor alloc]
                            initWithKey:@"tagContent"
                            ascending:NO];
    NSArray *sortDescriptors =
                [NSArray arrayWithObjects:sortDescriptor, nil];
    [fetchRequest setSortDescriptors:sortDescriptors];

    NSFetchedResultsController *aFetchedResultsController =
                [[NSFetchedResultsController alloc]
      initWithFetchRequest:fetchRequest
    managedObjectContext:self.currentNote.managedObjectContext
      sectionNameKeyPath:nil
                cacheName:@"Master"];

    self.fetchedResultsController = aFetchedResultsController;

    NSError *error = nil;
    if (![self.fetchedResultsController performFetch:&error]) {

        NSLog(@"Core data error %@, %@",
        error, [error userInfo]);
        abort();

    }

    return _fetchedResultsController;

}
```

In this specific case you do not need a reference to the context created in the application delegate, because each class generated from the schema contains a reference to that exact context. So in this case you use `self.currentNote.managedObjectContext`.

To keep things simple, you want to avoid creating another view controller to enter new tags. So you will populate your application with a static list of tags if none are present. You will perform this task when the tag picker has loaded.

First you perform a query and if that is empty you create a few tags and save them in the context. After saving them you reload tags from the persistent store.

```objc
- (void)viewDidLoad
{
    [super viewDidLoad];
    self.pickedTags = [[NSMutableSet alloc] init];
    self.title = @"Tag your note";

    // Retrieve tags
    NSError *error;
    if (![self.fetchedResultsController performFetch:&error]) {
        NSLog(@"Unresolved error %@, %@",
            error, [error userInfo]);
        abort();
    }

    // in case there are no tags,
    // presumably it's the first time you run the application
    if (self.fetchedResultsController.fetchedObjects.count == 0)
    {
        for (int i = 1; i < 6; i++) {

            SMTag *t = [NSEntityDescription
                        insertNewObjectForEntityForName:@"SMTag"
                        inManagedObjectContext:
                            self.currentNote.managedObjectContext];
            t.tagContent =
            [NSString stringWithFormat:@"tag%i", i];

        }

        // Save to new tags
        NSError *error = nil;
        if (![self.currentNote.managedObjectContext
             save:&error]) {
            NSLog(@"Unresolved error %@, %@", error,
                [error userInfo]);
            abort();
        } else {
            // Retrieve tags again
            NSLog(@"new tags added");
            [self.fetchedResultsController performFetch:&error];
        }
    }

    // Each tag attached to the note should be included
    // in the pickedTags array
    for (SMTag *tag in self.currentNote.tags) {
        [self.pickedTags addObject:tag];
    }
}
```

This code is executed each time the tag picker is loaded but new tags are added just once, the first time the application is run. You will assign the tag selected when the user is about to close the picker, in the `viewWillDisappear:` method.

```objc
- (void) viewWillDisappear:(BOOL)animated {

    [super viewWillDisappear:animated];
    self.currentNote.tags = self.pickedTags;

    NSError *error = nil;
    if (![self.currentNote.managedObjectContext save:&error]) {
        NSLog(@"Core data error %@, %@",
        error, [error userInfo]);
        abort();
    }
}
```

Now you have the entire infrastructure needed to create the tag picker. You are left with connecting the user interface with the result controller. As previously the table is populated by the result of the fetch controller.

```objc
- (NSInteger)numberOfSectionsInTableView:
                            (UITableView *)tableView
{
    return 1;
}

- (NSInteger)tableView:(UITableView *)tableView
 numberOfRowsInSection:(NSInteger)section
{
    id <NSFetchedResultsSectionInfo> sectionInfo =
        [[self.fetchedResultsController sections]
                        objectAtIndex:section];
    return [sectionInfo numberOfObjects];
}
```

Each cell will show the string stored in the `tagContent` property of each tag. The cell will also display a checkmark if the tag is selected (associated with the note).

```objc
- (UITableViewCell *)tableView:(UITableView *)tableView
 cellForRowAtIndexPath:(NSIndexPath *)indexPath
{
    static NSString *CellIdentifier = @"Cell";
    UITableViewCell *cell =
        [tableView
        dequeueReusableCellWithIdentifier:CellIdentifier];

    if (cell == nil) {
        cell = [[UITableViewCell alloc]
```

```
                     initWithStyle:UITableViewCellStyleDefault
                     reuseIdentifier:CellIdentifier];
    }

    cell.accessoryType = UITableViewCellAccessoryNone;
    SMTag *tag = (SMTag *)[self.fetchedResultsController
                     objectAtIndexPath:indexPath];
    if ([self.pickedTags containsObject:tag]) {
        cell.accessoryType = UITableViewCellAccessoryCheckmark;
    }
    cell.textLabel.text = tag.tagContent;
    return cell;
}
```

Finally when you tap a cell you will add or remove the tag from the array of picked tags.

```
- (void)tableView:(UITableView *)tableView
didSelectRowAtIndexPath:(NSIndexPath *)indexPath
{
    SMTag *tag = (SMTag *)[self.fetchedResultsController
                     objectAtIndexPath:indexPath];
    UITableViewCell * cell = [self.tableView
                     cellForRowAtIndexPath:indexPath];
    [cell setSelected:NO animated:YES];

    if ([self.pickedTags containsObject:tag]) {

        [self.pickedTags removeObject:tag];
        cell.accessoryType = UITableViewCellAccessoryNone;

    } else {

        [self.pickedTags addObject:tag];
        cell.accessoryType = UITableViewCellAccessoryCheckmark;

    }
}
```

w00t - finally time to build and run the application! Go ahead and try adding a few notes, editing the text, and assigning one or more tags. Note that to save a tag selection you have to dismiss the tag picker view, and to save note edits you have to put the application in background or quit it.

Here are a few screenshots of the application at work:

Congrats, you have built a good old Core Data application!

Note: The project up to this point is in the resources for this chapter as **dox-10**.

Now it is time to see how to port it to iCloud, so that all the modifications made to the persistent store are propagated to the cloud and other devices.

Porting a Core Data Application to iCloud

In iOS 5 Core Data was extended to support iCloud. One key addition is related to the event that happens when you push new changes to the store. Each change is saved into a transaction, which in turn is pushed to iCloud.

Much like `UIDocument`, only changes are propagated to the cloud, making the mechanism much more efficient than pushing a whole new file at each change, especially if the database is large.

In a Core Data scenario, changes are propagated to iCloud when you call the save method of a context. The steps needed to get this working are:

1. Provide a location to store transaction operations in iCloud

2. Observe new notifications coming from iCloud to correctly update the local persistent store.

3. Update the user interface according to new changes in the persistent store.

We will adapt the project created in the previous section (called dox-10 if you jumped here from earlier) to enable iCloud synchronization.

There are two fundamental changes to make: one is related to the configuration of the persistent store and the other deals with the context. Both elements have to be made iCloud-aware.

Another important aspect is that, unlike in the previous project, you are in an asynchronous situation, since data from the cloud might take a while to be downloaded. That's why you have to use a secondary thread to instantiate the store coordinator.

Let's proceed step by step. In the previous example, in the SMAppDelegate, you provided no options to the addPersistentStoreWithType:configuration:URL:options:error: method. In this case you have to create an array of options, in which you specify the features to be enabled in the persistent store. Three are the options you are interested in:

- NSPersistentStoreUbiquitousContentNameKey: A unique name that identifies the store in the ubiquity container

- NSPersistentStoreUbiquitousContentURLKey: The path to store log transactions to the persistent store

- NSMigratePersistentStoresAutomaticallyOption: A boolean value to allow automatic migrations in the store if needed

The key is arbitrary so you can provide the name you like, such as @"com.studiomagnolia.coredata.notes".

The URL for transaction logs is built by creating a subdirectory in the ubiquity container, as follows (you don't need to add this quite yet, you'll add the complete method soon):

```
NSFileManager *fileManager = [NSFileManager defaultManager];
NSURL *transactionLogsURL =
          [fileManager URLForUbiquityContainerIdentifier:nil];
NSString* coreDataCloudContent = [[transactionLogsURL path]
                  stringByAppendingPathComponent:@"dox_data"];
transactionLogsURL = [NSURL
                  fileURLWithPath:coreDataCloudContent];
```

So the resulting array of options can be defined like this:

```
NSDictionary* options =
    [NSDictionary dictionaryWithObjectsAndKeys:
      @"com.studiomagnolia.coredata.notes",
      NSPersistentStoreUbiquitousContentNameKey,
      transactionLogsURL,
      NSPersistentStoreUbiquitousContentURLKey,
      [NSNumber numberWithBool:YES],
      NSMigratePersistentStoresAutomaticallyOption,
nil];
```

The final step is to add the store to the coordinator as in the previous project but there is a catch. You are in a threaded situation so it is preferable to prevent other threads executions by adding a lock mechanism as follows.

```
// psc is an instance of persistent store coordinator
NSError *error = nil;
[psc lock];
if (![psc addPersistentStoreWithType:NSSQLiteStoreType
                       configuration:nil
                                 URL:storeUrl
                             options:options
                               error:&error]) {

    NSLog(@"Core data error %@, %@", error, [error userInfo]);
    abort();
}
[psc unlock];
```

Once the store has been added you can post a notification to refresh the user interface.

```
dispatch_async(dispatch_get_main_queue(), ^{

    NSLog(@"persistent store added correctly");
    [[NSNotificationCenter defaultCenter]
        postNotificationName:@"com.studiomagnolia.refetchNotes"
                      object:self
                    userInfo:nil];

});
```

Here is the complete code for the new `persistentStoreCoordinator` method, with comments. Replace the current implementation in SMAppDelegate.m with the following:

```
- (NSPersistentStoreCoordinator *)persistentStoreCoordinator {

    if (_persistentStoreCoordinator != nil) {
```

```objectivec
        return _persistentStoreCoordinator;
}

_persistentStoreCoordinator =
[[NSPersistentStoreCoordinator alloc]
 initWithManagedObjectModel: [self managedObjectModel]];

NSPersistentStoreCoordinator* psc =
_persistentStoreCoordinator;
NSURL *storeUrl = [[self applicationDocumentsDirectory]
  URLByAppendingPathComponent:@"dox.sqlite"];

// done asynchronously since it may take a while
// to download preexisting iCloud content
dispatch_async(dispatch_get_global_queue(
  DISPATCH_QUEUE_PRIORITY_DEFAULT, 0), ^{

    // building the path to store transaction logs
    NSFileManager *fileManager = [NSFileManager
                                    defaultManager];
    NSURL *transactionLogsURL = [fileManager
      URLForUbiquityContainerIdentifier:nil];
    NSString* coreDataCloudContent = [[transactionLogsURL
                                        path]
      stringByAppendingPathComponent:@"dox_data"];
    transactionLogsURL = [NSURL
      fileURLWithPath:coreDataCloudContent];

    // Building the options array for the coordinator
    NSDictionary* options =
    [NSDictionary dictionaryWithObjectsAndKeys:
     @"com.studiomagnolia.coredata.notes",
     NSPersistentStoreUbiquitousContentNameKey,
     transactionLogsURL,
     NSPersistentStoreUbiquitousContentURLKey,
     [NSNumber numberWithBool:YES],
     NSMigratePersistentStoresAutomaticallyOption,
     nil];

    NSError *error = nil;
    [psc lock];
    if (![psc addPersistentStoreWithType:NSSQLiteStoreType
                        configuration:nil
                                  URL:storeUrl
                              options:options
                                error:&error]) {
        NSLog(@"Core data error %@, %@",
            error, [error userInfo]);
    }
    [psc unlock];
```

```
    // post a notification to tell the main thread
    // to refresh the user interface
    dispatch_async(dispatch_get_main_queue(), ^{
        NSLog(@"persistent store added correctly");
        [[NSNotificationCenter defaultCenter]
          postNotificationName:
            @"com.studiomagnolia.refetchNotes"
          object:self
          userInfo:nil];
    });
  });

    return _persistentStoreCoordinator;
}
```

The next step is to revise the implementation of the context. In an iCloud-enabled scenario the context has to be initialized according to a concurrency type, that is the way the context is bound to threads. Since views and controllers are already bound with the main thread it is appropriate to adopt the same for the context, by choosing a NSMainQueueConcurrencyType as follows:

```
NSManagedObjectContext* moc =
    [[NSManagedObjectContext alloc]
            initWithConcurrencyType:NSMainQueueConcurrencyType];
```

This means that all the code executed by the context will be performed on the main thread. When you send messages to a context which implements a queue like this you have to use either the performBlock: or the performBlockAndWait: method. This is due to the new queue-based nature of the context. The first method is synchronous, while the second is asynchronous. For example to set the coordinator you can use:

```
[moc performBlockAndWait:^{

    [moc setPersistentStoreCoordinator: coordinator];
    // other configurations

}];
```

As you learned above, one of the keys to an iCloud-enabled Core Data application is to listen for notifications about changes to the persistent store. This step has to be performed when you define the context. In this case the notification has a very long name: NSPersistentStoreDidImportUbiquitousContentChangesNotification. You can set up an observer like this:

```
[[NSNotificationCenter defaultCenter]
```

```
                    addObserver:self
                selector:@selector(mergeChangesFrom_iCloud:)
                        name:
    NSPersistentStoreDidImportUbiquitousContentChangesNotification
                    object:coordinator];
```

Summing up the final implementation of managedObjectContext is the following:

```objc
- (NSManagedObjectContext *)managedObjectContext
{
    if (_managedObjectContext != nil) {
        return _managedObjectContext;
    }

    NSPersistentStoreCoordinator *coordinator =
    [self persistentStoreCoordinator];

    if (coordinator != nil) {
        // choose a concurrency type for the context
        NSManagedObjectContext* moc =
        [[NSManagedObjectContext alloc]
         initWithConcurrencyType:NSMainQueueConcurrencyType];

        [moc performBlockAndWait:^{
            // configure context properties
            [moc setPersistentStoreCoordinator: coordinator];
            [[NSNotificationCenter defaultCenter]
             addObserver:self
             selector:@selector(mergeChangesFrom_iCloud:)
             name:

    NSPersistentStoreDidImportUbiquitousContentChangesNotification
             object:coordinator];

        }];
        _managedObjectContext = moc;
    }
    return _managedObjectContext;
}
```

The selector associated to the notification is defined as follows. To go back to the main thread you use the performBlock: API.

```objc
- (void)mergeChangesFrom_iCloud:(NSNotification *)notification {

    NSManagedObjectContext* moc = [self managedObjectContext];
    [moc performBlock:^{
        [self mergeiCloudChanges:notification
                      forContext:moc];
    }];
```

```
    }
```

You should remember to add this method signature to the header file.

```
- (void)mergeiCloudChanges:(NSNotification*)note
                forContext:(NSManagedObjectContext*)moc;
```

The actual method that performs the merging is defined as follows.

```
- (void)mergeiCloudChanges:(NSNotification*)note
                forContext:(NSManagedObjectContext*)moc {

    [moc mergeChangesFromContextDidSaveNotification:note];
    //Refresh view with no fetch controller if any

}
```

The method `mergeChangesFromContextDidSaveNotification:` does some sort of magic by updating the objects that have been notified as changed, inserted or deleted. If you need to have a higher control on the merging, as you will learn below.

Once this code is executed all the views that embed a fetch controller do not need any notification, because each instance of a fetch controller listens for changes by means of the context. In case there are views with no instance of `NSFetchedResultsController`, here you should post a notification and hook up those view with the same notification name.

You might remember you have setup a notification when you add the persistent store to the coordinator. It is important to catch it and refresh the user interface.

In SMMasterViewController.m, once the view has loaded, you listen for such a notification. Add this at the bottom of `viewDidLoad`:

```
[[NSNotificationCenter defaultCenter]
    addObserver:self
      selector:@selector(reloadNotes)
          name:@"com.studiomagnolia.refetchNotes"
        object:nil];
```

The method triggered by the notification performs a retrieval and reloads data in the table view as follows:

```
- (void) reloadNotes {
    NSLog(@"refetching notes");
    NSError *error = nil;
    if (![[self fetchedResultsController] performFetch:&error])
    {
        NSLog(@"Core data error %@, %@", error, [error userInfo]);
```

```
    } else {
        NSLog(@"reloadNotes - results are %i",
        self.fetchedResultsController.fetchedObjects.count);
        [self.tableView reloadData];
    }
}
```

The rest of the code is untouched, since all the views are already populated by Core Data contents.

Believe it or not, you are done! As you can see, it's really easy to make your Core Data applications synch with iCloud.

Build and run and test out the application. You should follow the usual protocol: install on two devices and see changes propagated from one to another.

The code for this section is in the repository under the name "dox-11".

Merging Conflicts in Core Data Apps

In the last application you have seen that merging can be done by means of a simple call to the mergeChangesFromContextDidSaveNotification: method. For sake of completeness I should mention that, if you like to dig deeper, there are many more aspects that you might want to consider.

In this section I won't guide you through the process of building an application, for conflict resolution is very specific to the purpose of the application. You will provide an explanation of the capabilities of iCloud when it comes to merging conflicting data.

For example, a context can have different merge policies. As long as the user changes different fields on the same note, the application raises no issues and merges changes. For example, if you edit a note's content on one device and the same note's tags on another, after a while changes will be propagated on both devices with no issues. In this case Core Data is smart enough to "make the sum" of edits. Problems arise when you edit the same property of the same note.

The first way to approach this issue is by adopting a merge policy in the context. You did not mention before that the default policy for a context is NSErrorMergePolicy, meaning that an error is thrown when you try to save a context that includes conflicts. Alternative policies are the following:

NSMergeByPropertyStoreTrumpMergePolicy: If there is a conflict between the persistent store and the in-memory version of an object, external changes win over the in-memory ones.

NSMergeByPropertyObjectTrumpMergePolicy: Similar to the above, but in-memory changes win.

NSOverwriteMergePolicy: Changes are overwritten in the persistent store.

NSRollbackMergePolicy: In-memory changes to conflicting objects are discarded.

In all these policies the conflict resolution is made for each record, in your case for each note. If you are happy with one of these you can just change the declaration of the context and leave the rest unchanged.

Otherwise, you can actually unfold what is being in conflict and try to resolve it by adopting a custom policy. All this happens in the mergeiCloudChanges:forContext: method. For example, when you add a note, if you print out the notification object

```
- (void)mergeiCloudChanges:(NSNotification*)notification
            forContext:(NSManagedObjectContext*)moc {

    NSLog(@"%@", notification);

}
```

we should see in the console a message like the following:

```
NSConcreteNotification 0x37fec0 {name =
    com.apple.coredata.ubiquity. importer.didfinishimport;
object = <NSPersistentStoreCoordinator: 0x353f30>;
userInfo = {
        deleted = "{(\n)}";
        inserted = "{(\n     0x36d050 <x-coredata://9F154E9E-
658A-4653-8981-
        F3619AE5FE18/SMNote/p5>\n)}";
        updated = "{(\n)}";
}}
```

Here the key is that the userInfo array contains keyed lists of changes categorized in deletions, insertions and updates. You receive this notification each time you update, delete or create a new note. The userInfo is a dictionary directly attached to the notification, so if you want to unfold its content you can use the key corresponding to the change you are keeping track of, as in the following code.

```
- (void)mergeiCloudChanges:(NSNotification*)note
            forContext:(NSManagedObjectContext*)moc {

    NSDictionary *noteInfo = [note userInfo];
    NSMutableDictionary *localUserInfo =
                            [NSMutableDictionary dictionary];
    NSSet* allInvalidations = [noteInfo
```

```
                                objectForKey:NSInvalidatedAllObjectsKey];

    NSLog(@"insertions = %@",
          [noteInfo objectForKey:NSInsertedObjectsKey]);
    NSLog(@"deletions = %@",
          [noteInfo objectForKey:NSDeletedObjectsKey]);
                          NSLog(@"updates = %@",
          [noteInfo objectForKey:NSUpdatedObjectsKey]);

}
```

At this point you have all the elements to detect which objects are in conflict. The output result of you policy has to be another dictionary that you pass to the mergeChangesFromContextDidSaveNotification: method. So a schema of a custom policy for conflict resolution might be like this.

```
- (void)mergeiCloudChanges:(NSNotification*)note
              forContext:(NSManagedObjectContext*)moc {

    NSMutableDictionary *mergingPolicyResult =
    [NSMutableDictionary dictionary];

    // do something with insertions
    // do something with deletions
    // do something with updates

    NSNotification *saveNotification = [NSNotification
    notificationWithName:NSManagedObjectContextDidSaveNotification
              object:self
          userInfo:mergingPolicyResult];

    [moc mergeChangesFromContextDidSaveNotification:
          saveNotification];
    [moc processPendingChanges];

}
```

Once you have established the content of mergingPolicyResult you build a notification object wrapping that dictionary and a NSManagedObjectContextDidSaveNotification notification type. To force the context to update the object graph you call processPendingChanges. The "do something" part is pretty trivial. Each objectForKey: call returns a set of objects, that you can include or not in the mergingPolicyResult.

```
// do something with updates
NSDictionary *noteInfo = [note userInfo];
```

```
NSSet *updatedObjects = [noteInfo
                        objectForKey:NSUpdatedObjectsKey];
NSMutableSet *objectsToBeAccepted = [NSMutableSet set];

for (NSManagedObjectID *updatedObjectID in updatedObjects) {

    [objectsToBeAccepted addObject:
                        [moc objectWithID:updatedObjectID]];
}

[mergingPolicyResult setObject:objectsToBeAccepted
                    forKey:NSUpdatedObjectsKey];
```

This way you have the opportunity to filter out insertions and deletions. The same mechanism can be applied to deletions and modifications.

During development and debugging you might end up with some warning or error due to lo loading to Core Data changes in iCloud. To avoid that you might want to refresh sometimes the URL of transaction logs.

Prevent Synching With iCloud

As a final note, there are scenarios in which your application stores data that have to be kept permanent on disk but are not needed to be synched with iCloud. In this case there is an attribute, available since iOS 5.0.1, which allows you to mark a file to be skipped for backup. Here is the code if you need it:

```
#include <sys/xattr.h>

- (BOOL)addSkipBackupAttributeToItemAtURL:(NSURL *)URL
{
    const char* filePath = [[URL path]
                            fileSystemRepresentation];
    const char* attrName = "com.apple.MobileBackup";
    u_int8_t attrValue = 1;

    int result = setxattr(filePath, attrName, &attrValue,
                          sizeof(attrValue), 0, 0);
    return result == 0;

}
```

If you are targeting iOS5.1 or later there is a shorter way to do it.

```
NSError *error = nil;
```

```
BOOL success = [URL setResourceValue:
                    [NSNumber numberWithBool: YES]
                    forKey: NSURLIsExcludedFromBackupKey
                    error: &error];
if(!success){

    NSLog(@"Error excluding %@ from backup %@",
        [URL lastPathComponent], error);

}
```

Where To Go From Here?

Wow, this was a long journey - but now you have a lot of experience working with iCloud that you can leverage in your own apps.

iCloud is probably the biggest feature introduced in iOS 5. Including iCloud support in you new or existing applications is your call. Nonetheless it is undeniable that your application (and your income!) will likely profit from such a cool new tool.

As a general rule, you should add iCloud support only if you foresee benefits for the end users of your application. In case your are building an 'ecosystem', e.g. an iOS and MacOS application, it is very likely that you can leverage all the power of iCloud to enrich the experience of your apps.

We hope to see an iCloud-enabled app from you soon! :]

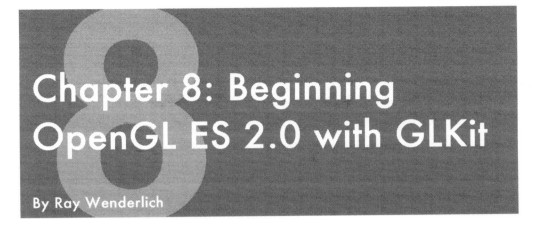

Chapter 8: Beginning OpenGL ES 2.0 with GLKit

By Ray Wenderlich

OpenGL ES is the lowest level graphics API on the iPhone that you can use to draw things to the screen quickly and efficiently, leveraging the power of the graphics card. It is most commonly used in games, and many libraries you may know and love such as Cocos2D, Corona, or Unity3D are built on top of OpenGL ES.

Prior to iOS 5, there were a lot of common frustrations when making OpenGL ES apps or games:

- **Tons of boilerplate.** Creating the simplest possible OpenGL ES app that rendered a triangle to the screen took a ton of code – things like setting up render buffers, compiling shaders, and more. This made it extremely difficult to get started, since there was so much prerequisite code and knowledge required.

- **Hard to load textures.** Although you'd think it would be simple to load a texture to use in an OpenGL ES app, it wasn't – you had to write a ton of code yourself to get this working. The worst part was this code was quite complicated and easy to get wrong.

- **No math libraries.** Writing apps or games that use OpenGL ES use a lot of math, and you commonly need functions to work with vectors and matrices. But since there was no vector and matrix math libraries included with the library, each project would add their own implementation, adding extra work to the project and making project less reusable.

- **No easy transition to OpenGL ES 2.0.** In the old days, people wrote games for the iPhone using OpenGL ES 1.0, but the latest and most powerful graphics API on the iPhone is OpenGL ES 2.0. It's best to use OpenGL ES 2.0 these days when possible, but if you had an app already written in OpenGL ES 1.0 it wasn't very easy to transition to OpenGL ES 2.0.

But since iOS 5, Apple has introduced a new set of APIs known as GLKit that makes developing with OpenGL ES much easier than it used to be.

GLKit contains four main sections:

1. **GLKView/GLKViewController**: These classes abstract out much of the boilerplate code it used to take to set up a basic OpenGL ES project.

2. **GLKTextureLoader**: This class makes it much easier to load images as textures to be used in OepnGL. Rather than having to write a complicated method dealing with tons of different image formats, loading a texture is now a single method call.

3. **GLKMath**: Now instead of each project having to include its own math library, GLKMath contains the most common math routines for you.

4. **GLKEffects**: These classes implement common shading behaviors used in OpenGL ES 1.0, to make transitioning to OpenGL ES 2.0 easier. They're also a handy way to get some basic lighting and texturing working.

The goal of this tutorial is to get you quickly up-to-speed with the basics of using OpenGL ES 2.0 with GLKit, from the ground up, assuming that you have no experience with OpenGL ES 2.0 or GLKit whatsoever. You will build a simple app from scratch that draws a cube to the screen and makes it rotate around.

In the process, you'll learn the basics of using each of these new APIs. It should be a good introduction to GLKit, whether you've already used OpenGL ES in the past, or if you're a complete beginner.

> **Note:** This chapter is split into two parts. The first part teaches you about `GLKView` and `GLKViewController` by building a simple GLKit project from scratch – basically a very simple version of the OpenGL game template that comes with Xcode.
>
> If you don't care much about how the template works and want to jump straight to writing OpenGL ES code, feel free to skip to the "Creating vertex data for a simple square" section later in this chapter – there's a starter project there where you can pick up where we left off.

What is OpenGL ES?

Before you get started, let's talk a bit more about what OpenGL ES is for those of you who are unfamiliar with it.

As I mentioned earlier, OpenGL ES is the lowest level API available on iOS to let you interact with the graphics card to draw to the screen. It is most typically used for games, since games often require heavy graphics processing and effects.

If you are familiar with other game frameworks such as Cocos2D, Corona, or Unity3D, these are built on top of OpenGL ES. Programmers often prefer working with one of these higher level game frameworks instead of using OpenGL ES directly, because they are easier to learn and are often faster to write code with.

However, OpenGL ES is still good to know for several reasons:

• **It has the most power.** OpenGL ES gives you full control and power, while the other game frameworks often have limitations. If you have a game where you want to push the boundaries of what can be done, OpenGL ES may be the way to go.

• **It's a great learning experience.** Learning OpenGL ES is a great learning experience – it will teach you a lot about how graphics cards work, how game engines work, a lot about math, and more.

• **You'll be able to better understand and extend game frameworks.** Even if you decide to use a game framework, understanding OpenGL ES will help you better understand of what the game frameworks do for you. This can help you increase the performance of your games, and extend the game frameworks a low level – such as creating some special effects for Cocos2D games.

• **It's much easier than it used to be.** Thanks to the new GLKit framework in iOS that you'll learn about in this book, making OpenGL ES apps and games is much easier than it used to be. Especially with this book to guide you through, there's no reason not to get started learning OpenGL ES. ☺

The "ES" at the end of "OpenGL ES" stands for "Embedded Systems", and is there to distinguish the API from the plain-old OpenGL (without the "ES") used on desktops. Basically, OpenGL ES is a stripped down/simplified version of the plain-old OpenGL API designed for devices with less powerful graphics processing capabilities - such as your iPhone. If you're familiar with plain-old OpenGL, you will notice a few differences here and there – but overall it's fairly similar.

Finally, note that OpenGL ES is a C-based API. If you do not know C (and only know Objective-C), this chapter might be a struggle for you, as some of the code might look unfamiliar. I will not be covering the C synatax here, so if you are new to C I recommend getting a C reference book to help get you used to the syntax.

OpenGL ES 1.0 vs OpenGL ES 2.0

Note that this book will be focusing on OpenGL ES 2.0 – not OpenGL ES 1.0.

Here is the difference between OpenGL ES 1.0 and OpenGL ES 2.0:

- OpenGL ES 1.0 uses a fixed pipeline, which is a fancy way of saying you use built-in functions to set lights, vertices, colors, and more.

- OpenGL ES 2.0 uses a programmable pipeline, which is a fancy way of saying all those built-in funcitons go away, and you have to write everything yourself.

"OMG!" you may think , "Why would I ever want to learn OpenGL ES 2.0 then, if it's just extra work?" Although it does add some extra work, with OpenGL ES 2.0 you can make some really cool effects that wouldn't be possible in OpenGL ES 1.0, such as this toon shader by Imagination Technologies:

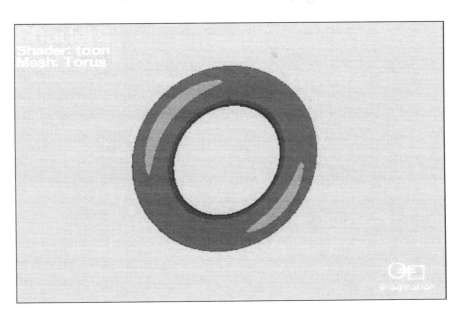

Or these amazing lighting and shadow effects by Fabien Sanglard:

Pretty cool, eh?

OpenGL ES 2.0 is only available on the iPhone 3GS+, iPod Touch 3G+, and all iPads. But the overwhelming majority of your customers are using these devices these days, so OpenGL ES 2.0 is well worth using.

OpenGL ES 2.0 does have a bit of a higher learning curve than OpenGL ES 1.0, but now with GLKit the learning curve is much easier, because the GLKEffect and GLKMath APIs allow you to easily do a lot of the stuff that was built into OpenGL ES 1.0.

I'd say if you're new to OpenGL ES programming, it's probably best to jump straight into OpenGL ES 2.0 rather than trying to learn OpenGL ES 1.0 and then upgrading, especially now that GLKit is available. This book will show you the basics and help you get started.

Getting started

Create a new project in Xcode with the iOS\Application\Empty Application template. You're choosing the Empty Application template (not the OpenGL Game template!) so you can put everything together from scratch and get a better understanding of how it works.

Set the Product Name to HelloGLKit, make sure Devices is set to iPhone, and make sure Use Automatic Reference Counting is selected. Click Next, choose a location for your project, and click Create.

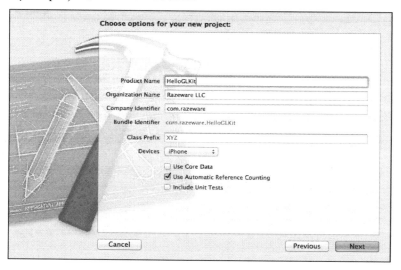

Build and run your app, and you should see a blank Window:

The project contains almost no code at this point, but let's take a look to see how it all fits together. If you went through the Storyboard tutorial earlier in this book, this should be a good review.

Open `main.m`, and you'll see the first function that is called when the app starts up, unsurpsisingly called `main`:

```
int main(int argc, char *argv[])
{
    @autoreleasepool {
        return UIApplicationMain(argc, argv, nil,
            NSStringFromClass([AppDelegate class]));
    }
}
```

The last parameter to this method tells `UIApplication` the class to create an instance of and use as its delegate – in this case, a class called `AppDelegate`.

So let's check that out. Open `AppDelegate.m` and take a look at the method that gets called when the app starts up:

```
- (BOOL)application:(UIApplication *)application
    didFinishLaunchingWithOptions:(NSDictionary *)launchOptions
```

```
{
    self.window = [[UIWindow alloc] initWithFrame:
        [[UIScreen mainScreen] bounds]];
    // Override point for customization after application
launch.
    self.window.backgroundColor = [UIColor whiteColor];
    [self.window makeKeyAndVisible];
    return YES;
}
```

This programmatically creates the main window for the app and makes it visible. And that's it! This is about as "from scratch" as you can get.

Introducing GLKView

To get started with OpenGL ES 2.0, the first thing you need to do is add a new subview to the window that does its drawing with OpenGL. If you've programmed with OpenGL ES 2.0 before, you know that there used to be a ton of boilerplate code to get this working – things like creating a render buffer and frame buffer, etc.

But now it's nice and easy with a new GLKit class called GLKView. Whenever you want to use OpenGL ES rendering inside a view, you simply add a GLKView (which is a normal subclass of UIView) and configure a few properties on it.

You can then set a class as the GLKView's delegate, and it will call a method on that class when it needs to be drawn. And that's where you can put in your OpenGL ES commands.

Let's see how this works. First things first – you need to add a few frameworks to your project to use GLKit. Select your HelloGLKit project in the Project Navigator, select the HelloGLKit target, select the Build Phases tab, expand the Link Binary with Libraries section, and click the + button. From the drop-down list, select the following frameworks and click Add:

• QuartzCore.framework

• OpenGLES.framework

• GLKit.framework

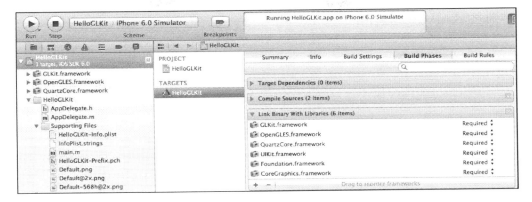

Switch to AppDelegate.h, and at the top of the file import the header file for GLKit as follows:

```
#import <GLKit/GLKit.h>
```

Next switch to AppDelegate.m and modify the application:didFinishLaunchingWithOptions: method to add a new GLKView as a subview of the main window:

```
- (BOOL)application:(UIApplication *)application
  didFinishLaunchingWithOptions:(NSDictionary *)launchOptions
{
    self.window = [[UIWindow alloc] initWithFrame:
      [[UIScreen mainScreen] bounds]];

    EAGLContext * context = [[EAGLContext alloc]
      initWithAPI:kEAGLRenderingAPIOpenGLES2]; // 1
    GLKView * view = [[GLKView alloc] initWithFrame:
      [[UIScreen mainScreen] bounds] context:context]; // 2
    view.delegate = self; // 3
    [self.window addSubview:view]; // 4

    self.window.backgroundColor = [UIColor whiteColor];
    [self.window makeKeyAndVisible];
    return YES;
}
```

The lines marked with comments are the new lines – so let's go over them one by one.

1. **Create an OpenGL context.** To do anything with OpenGL ES, you need to create an EAGLContext.

   An EAGLContext manages all of the information iOS needs to draw with OpenGL. It's similar to how you need a CGContextRef to do anything with Core Graphics.

When you create a context, you specify which version of the OpenGL ES API you want to use. Here, you specify that you want to use OpenGL ES 2.0. If this version of the API is not available (such as if the app was run on an iPhone 3G), the app would terminate.

2. **Create a GLKView.** This creates a new instance of GLKView, passes in the context that was created, and makes it the full size of the window.

3. **Set the GLKView's delegate.** This sets the current class (AppDelegate) as the GLKView's delegate. This means whenever the view needs to be redrawn, it will call a method named glkView:drawInRect: on whatever classes you specify here. You will implement this shortly to contain some basic OpenGL ES commands to paint the screen green.

4. **Add the GLKView as a subview.** This line adds the GLKView as a subview of the main window so you can see it.

Since you marked the AppDelegate as the GLKView's delegate, you need to mark it as implementing the GLKViewDelegate protocol. So switch to AppDelegate.m and add a class extension as follows:

```
@interface AppDelegate () <GLKViewDelegate>
@end
```

If you're wondering why you added the protocol declaration to the class extension rather than the header file, check out Chapter 2, "Programming in Modern Objective-C" in *iOS 6 by Tutorials*.

One step left. Add the following method to the file:

```
#pragma mark - GLKViewDelegate

- (void)glkView:(GLKView *)view drawInRect:(CGRect)rect {
    glClearColor(0.0, 0.41, 0.22, 1.0);
    glClear(GL_COLOR_BUFFER_BIT);
}
```

The first line calls glClearColor, which is an OpenGL ES function that lets you specify the RGB and alpha (transparency) values to use when clearing the screen. You set it to a particular shade of green here – does it remind you of anything? ☺

The second line calls glClear, another OpenGL ES function that actually clears the screen. This function allows you to clear different things which you'll learn about when you get more advanced, but for now you just need to know that you pass it GL_COLOR_BUFFER_BIT here, which means it should clear the current render/color buffer that displays on the screen.

Build and run, and with just 6 lines of code you have OpenGL rendering to the screen!

Those of you who are completely new to OpenGL ES might not be very impressed, but those of you used to the old painful way of doing things probably look like this guy right about now:

GLKView properties and methods

So far you've only set two properties on GLKView (delegate directly, and context indirectly), but I wanted to mention the other properties and methods on GLKView that might be useful to you in the future.

> Note: This is an optional section and does not contain any code – it is mostly for the curious and for future reference. If you are a beginner or want to continue coding the sample project, I recommend that you skip to the next section and refer back here when necessary.

Let's go through the properties and methods one group at a time:

context and delegate properties

```
@property (nonatomic, assign) IBOutlet id <GLKViewDelegate>
delegate;
@property (nonatomic, retain) EAGLContext *context;
```

You already learned about these in the previous section, so I won't repeat here.

drawableColorFormat property

```
@property (nonatomic) GLKViewDrawableColorFormat
drawableColorFormat;
```

Your OpenGL ES context has a buffer it uses to store the colors that will be displayed on the screen. You can use this property to set the color format for each pixel in the buffer.

The default value is GLKViewDrawableColorFormatRGBA8888, which means 8 bits are used for each pixel in the buffer (so 4 bytes per pixel). This is nice because it gives you the widest possible range of colors to work with, which often makes your app look nicer.

But if your app can get away with a lower range of colors, you might want to switch this to GLKViewDrawableColorFormatRGB565, which makes your app consume less resources (memory and processing time).

drawableDepthFormat property

```
@property (nonatomic) GLKViewDrawableDepthFormat
drawableDepthFormat;
```

Your OpenGL ES context can also optionally have another buffer associated with it called the depth buffer. This helps make sure that objects closer to the viewer show up in front of objects farther away.

The way it works by default is OpenGL ES keeps a buffer similar to a render/color buffer, but instead of storing color values at each pixel, it stores the closest object to the viewer at each pixel. When it goes to draw a pixel, it checks the depth buffer to see if it's already drawn something closer to the viewer, and if so discards it. Otherwise, it adds the pixel to the depth buffer and the color buffer.

You can set this property to choose the format of the depth buffer. The default value is GLKViewDrawableDepthFormatNone, which means that no depth buffer is enabled.

But if you want this feature (which you usually do to increase performance for 3D games), you should choose GLKViewDrawableDepthFormat16 or GLKViewDrawableDepthFormat24.

The tradeoff between these two options is that with GLKDrawableDepthFormat16 your app will use less resources, but you might have rendering issues when objects are very close to each other.

drawableStencilFormat property

```
@property (nonatomic) GLKViewDrawableStencilFormat
drawableStencilFormat;
```

Another optional buffer your OpenGL ES context can have is the stencil buffer. This helps you restrict drawing to a particular portion of the screen. It's often useful for things like shadows. For example you might use the stencil buffer to make sure the shadows are cast on the floor.

The default value for this property is GLKViewDrawableStencilFormatNone, which means there is no stencil buffer. However, you can enable it by setting it to the only alternative – GLKViewDrawableStencilFormat8.

drawableMultisample property

```
@property (nonatomic) GLKViewDrawableMultisample
drawableMultisample;
```

The last optional buffer you can set up through a GLKView property is the multisampling buffer. If you ever try drawing lines with OpenGL and notice "jagged lines", multisampling can help with this issue.

Basically what it does is instead of calling the fragment shader one time per pixel, it divides up the pixel into smaller units and calls the fragment shader multiple times at smaller levels of detail. It then merges the colors returned, which often results in a much smoother look around the edges of geometry.

Be careful about setting this value because it requires more processing time and memory for your app. The default value is GLKViewDrawableMultisampleNone, but you can enable it by setting it to the only alternative – GLKViewDrawableMultisample4X.

drawableWidth and drawableHeight properties

```
@property (nonatomic, readonly) NSInteger drawableWidth;
@property (nonatomic, readonly) NSInteger drawableHeight;
```

These are read-only properties that indicate the integer height and width of your various buffers. These are based on the bounds and contentSize of the view – the buffers are automatically resized when these change.

snapshot method

```
- (UIImage *)snapshot;
```

This is a handy way to get a UIImage of what the GLKView is currently showing.

bindDrawable method

```
- (void)bindDrawable;
```

OpenGL ES has yet another buffer called a frame buffer, which is basically a collection of all the other buffers we talked about (color buffer, depth buffer, stencil buffer, etc).

Before your glkView:drawInRect is called, GLKit will bind to the frame buffer it set up for you behind the scenes. But if your game needs to change to a different frame buffer to perfrom some other kind of rendering (for example, if you're rendering to another texture), you can use the bindDrawable method to tell GLKit to re-bind back to the frame buffer it set up for you.

deleteDrawable method

```
- (void)deleteDrawable;
```

GLKView and OpenGL ES take a substantial amount of memory for all of these buffers. If your GLKView isn't visible, you might find it useful to deallocate this memory temporarily until it becomes visible again. If you want to do this, use this method.

Next time the view is drawn, GLKView will automatically re-allocate the memory behind the scenes. Quite handy, eh?

enableSetNeedsDisplay property and display method

```
@property (nonatomic) BOOL enableSetNeedsDisplay;
- (void)display;
```

I don't want to spoil the surprise – I'll explain these in the next section.

Updating the GLKView

Let's try to update what shows up in the GLKView periodically, like you would in a game. How about you make the screen pulse from red to black, kind of like a "Red Alert" effect.

Go to the top of AppDelegate.m and modify the @implementation line to add two private variable as follows:

```
@implementation AppDelegate {
    float _curRed;
    BOOL _increasing;
}
```

And initialize these in application:didFinishLaunchingWithOptions: before the return statement:

```
_increasing = YES;
_curRed = 0.0;
```

Then go to the glkView:drawInRect: method and update it to the following:

```
- (void)glkView:(GLKView *)view drawInRect:(CGRect)rect {
    if (_increasing) {
        _curRed += 0.01;
    } else {
        _curRed -= 0.01;
    }
    if (_curRed >= 1.0) {
        _curRed = 1.0;
        _increasing = NO;
    }
    if (_curRed <= 0.0) {
        _curRed = 0.0;
        _increasing = YES;
    }
    glClearColor(_curRed, 0.0, 0.0, 1.0);
    glClear(GL_COLOR_BUFFER_BIT);
}
```

Every time glkView:drawInRect: is called, it updates the _curRed value a little bit based on whether it's increasing or decreasing.

Note: This code isn't perfect, because it doesn't take into effect how long it takes between calls to glkView:drawInRect:. This means that the animation might be faster or slower based on how quickly glkView:drawInRect: is called. You'll learn about a way to fix this later on in the tutorial.

Build and run and… wait a minute, nothing's happens. It's just a black screen.

This happens because by default, GLKView only updates itself on an as-needed basis – i.e. when views are first shown when the view's size changes, and the like. However, most of the time in game programming you need to redraw the screen multiple times per second.

So right now, GLKView will only redraw itself when you explicitly call its setNeedsDisplay: method – and even then, it's not synchronized with anything (such as when the screen refreshes), it's just whenever the next draw cycle happens to occur.

You can disable this behavior setting enableSetNeedsDisplay to false. Then, you can control when the redrawing occurs by calling the display: method at the point you want the screen to be refreshed.

Ideally, you would like to synchronize the time you render with OpenGL to the rate at which the screen refreshes.

Luckily, Apple provides an easy way for you to do this with the CADisplayLink class. This class is really easy to use, so let's just dive in and try it out. First add this import to the top of AppDelegate.m:

```
#import <QuartzCore/QuartzCore.h>
```

Then add these lines to application:didFinishLaunchingWithOptions: before the return statement:

```
view.enableSetNeedsDisplay = NO;
CADisplayLink* displayLink = [CADisplayLink
  displayLinkWithTarget:self selector:@selector(render:)];
[displayLink addToRunLoop:[NSRunLoop currentRunLoop]
  forMode:NSDefaultRunLoopMode];
```

This creates a CADisplayLink and configures it to call a method called render: every time the screen refreshes. Implement the render: method as follows:

```
- (void)render:(CADisplayLink*)displayLink {
    GLKView * view = [self.window.subviews objectAtIndex:0];
    [view display];
}
```

Build and run, and you should now see a cool pulsating "red alert" effect.

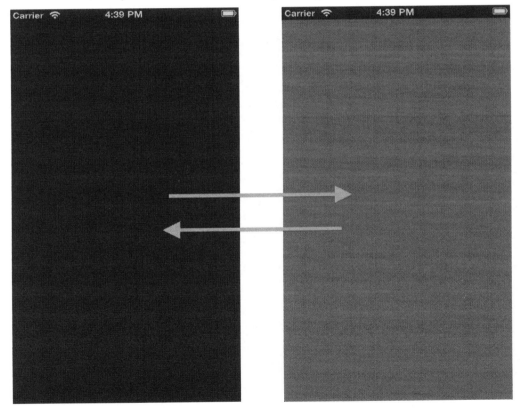

Introducing GLKViewController

You know that code you just wrote in the last section to call `display:` on the `GLKView` every frame? Well you can just forget about it, because there's a much easier way to do so by using `GLKViewController`.

The reason I showed you how to do it with a plain `GLKView` first was so you understand the point behind using `GLKViewController` – it saves you from having to write that code, plus adds some extra neat features that you would have had to code yourself.

So let's try out `GLKViewController`. Modify your `application:didFinishLaunchingWithOptions:` to look like this:

```objc
- (BOOL)application:(UIApplication *)application
  didFinishLaunchingWithOptions:(NSDictionary *)launchOptions
{
    self.window = [[UIWindow alloc] initWithFrame:
      [[UIScreen mainScreen] bounds]];

    EAGLContext * context = [[EAGLContext alloc]
      initWithAPI:kEAGLRenderingAPIOpenGLES2];
    GLKView * view = [[GLKView alloc] initWithFrame:
      [[UIScreen mainScreen] bounds] context:context];
    view.delegate = self;
    // [self.window addSubview:view];

    _increasing = YES;
    _curRed = 0.0;

    //view.enableSetNeedsDisplay = NO;
    //CADisplayLink* displayLink = [CADisplayLink
displayLinkWithTarget:self selector:@selector(render:)];
    //[displayLink addToRunLoop:[NSRunLoop currentRunLoop]
forMode:NSDefaultRunLoopMode];

    GLKViewController * viewController =
      [[GLKViewController alloc]
        initWithNibName:nil bundle:nil]; // 1
    viewController.view = view; // 2
    viewController.delegate = self; // 3
    viewController.preferredFramesPerSecond = 60; // 4
    self.window.rootViewController = viewController; // 5

    self.window.backgroundColor = [UIColor whiteColor];
    [self.window makeKeyAndVisible];
    return YES;
}
```

Feel free to delete the commented lines – I just commented them out so you could easily see what is no longer needed. There are also four new lines (marked with comments):

1. **Create a GLKViewController.** This creates a new instance of GLKViewController programmatically. In this case, it has no XIB associated.

2. **Set the GLKViewController's view.** The root view of a GLKViewController should be a GLKView, so you set it to the one you just created.

3. **Set the GLKViewController's delegate.** Here you set the current class (AppDelegate) as the delegate of GLKViewController. This means that the GLKViewController will call a method on the AppDelegate each frame where you can add game logic, and another method when the game pauses (a nice built-in feature of GLKViewController which you'll learn about later).

4. **Set the preferred FPS.** GLKViewController will call your draw method a certain number of times per second. This number gives a hint to the GLKViewController how often you'd like to be called. Of course, if your game takes a longer time to render frames, the actual number may be lower than this.

   The default value is 30 FPS. Apple's guidelines are to set this to whatever your app can reliably support so that the frame rate is consistent and doesn't seem to stutter. This app is very simple and can easily run at 60 FPS, so set it to that.

   Also, as an FYI, if you want to see the actual number of times the OS will attempt to call your update/draw methods, check the read-only property framesPerSecond.

5. **Set the rootViewController.** You want the GLKViewController to be the first thing that shows up, so here you add it as the rootViewController of the window. Note that you no longer need to add the view as a subview of the window explicitly, because you've set it as the root view of the GLKViewController.

At this point, you no longer need the code to run the render loop and tell the GLKView to refresh each frame – GLKViewController automatically does that for you in the background. So go ahead and delete the render: method now.

Also, remember you set the GLKViewController's delegate to the current class (AppDelegate), so you should mark the class as implementing the GLKViewControllerDelegate. Modify the class extension at the top of AppDelegate.m to the following:

```
@interface AppDelegate () <GLKViewDelegate,
GLKViewControllerDelegate>
@end
```

As a final step, update glkView:drawInRect: and add the new glkViewControllerUpdate: method as follows:

```
#pragma mark - GLKViewDelegate

- (void)glkView:(GLKView *)view drawInRect:(CGRect)rect {
    glClearColor(_curRed, 0.0, 0.0, 1.0);
    glClear(GL_COLOR_BUFFER_BIT);
}

#pragma mark - GLKViewControllerDelegate

- (void)glkViewControllerUpdate:(GLKViewController *)controller
{
    if (_increasing) {
        _curRed += 1.0 * controller.timeSinceLastUpdate;
    } else {
        _curRed -= 1.0 * controller.timeSinceLastUpdate;
    }
    if (_curRed >= 1.0) {
        _curRed = 1.0;
        _increasing = NO;
    }
    if (_curRed <= 0.0) {
        _curRed = 0.0;
        _increasing = YES;
    }
}
```

Note that you moved the code that changes the current color from the old glkView:drawInRect: method (intended for code to draw the current state only) to the new glkViewControllerUpdate: method (intended to update game/app logic).

Also notice you changed the amount the red color increments from a hardcoded value to a calculated value, based on the amount of time since the last update. This is nice because it guarantees the animation will always proceed at the same speed, regardless of the frame rate.

Storing the time since the last update is another of those convenient things that GLKViewController does for you. You didn't have to write any special code to keep track of that – it was done automatically. There are some other time-based properties you might find useful as well that you'll learn about later in this chapter.

GLKViewController and storyboards

So far, you've created a GLKViewController and a GLKView manually because it was a simple way to introduce you to how they work. But you probably wouldn't want to do things this way in a real app – it's much better to leverage the power of Storyboards, so you can include this view controller anywhere you want in your app's flow.

For example, you might have a game where you make the main menu with standard UIKit controls, and the game itself is an OpenGL ES game in a GLKViewController/GLKView.

So let's do a little refactoring to work with this more typical workflow. Let's start by creating a subclass of GLKViewController that you can use to contain your app's logic.

Create a new file with the iOS\Cocoa Touch\Objective-C class template, set the class to HelloGLKitViewController, and make it a subclass of GLKViewController. Make sure both Targeted for iPad and With XIB for user interface are both unselected, and finish creating the file.

Open up HelloGLKitViewController.m, and add a few private instance variables:

```
@implementation HelloGLKitViewController {
    float _curRed;
    BOOL _increasing;
    EAGLContext * _context;
}
```

Then implement viewDidLoad, dealloc, and didReceiveMemoryWarning as the following:

```
- (void)viewDidLoad
{
    [super viewDidLoad];
    _context = [[EAGLContext alloc]
      initWithAPI:kEAGLRenderingAPIOpenGLES2];
    if (!_context) {
        NSLog(@"Failed to create ES context");
    }
    GLKView *view = (GLKView *)self.view;
    view.context = _context;
}

- (void)cleanup {
    if ([EAGLContext currentContext] == _context) {
        [EAGLContext setCurrentContext:nil];
    }
    _context = nil;
```

```
}

- (void)dealloc {
    [self cleanup];
}

- (void)didReceiveMemoryWarning
{
    [super didReceiveMemoryWarning];
    if ([self isViewLoaded] && self.view.window == nil) {
        self.view = nil;
        [self cleanup];
    }
}
```

In viewDidLoad, you create an OpenGL ES 2.0 context (the same as you did last time in AppDelegate) and squirrel it away. Your root view is a GLKView (you know this because you will set it up this way in the Storyboard editor), so you cast it as one. You then set its context to the OpenGL ES context you just created.

Note that you don't have to set the view controller as the view's delegate – GLKViewController does this automatically behind the scenes.

When the view controller is deallocated, you have to handle the case where OpenGL ES's current context is the context you've created for this view controller. You do this in the cleanup method - if they are the same, you need to set OpenGL ES's current context to nil.

You should also perform cleanup upon a memory warning and the view isn't currently visible, since it's important to free as much memory as possible upon a memory warning.

> Note: In the old days, iOS would automatically unload your view controller's view for you upon a memory warning and call viewDidUnload when this occurs. This no longer happens in iOS 6 – check out Chapter 20, "What's New with Cocoa Touch" in *iOS 6 by Tutorials* for more information.

Next, add the implementations for the glkView:drawInRect: and update callbacks, similar to before:

```
#pragma mark - GLKViewDelegate

- (void)glkView:(GLKView *)view drawInRect:(CGRect)rect {
    glClearColor(_curRed, 0.0, 0.0, 1.0);
    glClear(GL_COLOR_BUFFER_BIT);
}
```

```
#pragma mark - GLKViewControllerDelegate

- (void)update {
    if (_increasing) {
        _curRed += 1.0 * self.timeSinceLastUpdate;
    } else {
        _curRed -= 1.0 * self.timeSinceLastUpdate;
    }
    if (_curRed >= 1.0) {
        _curRed = 1.0;
        _increasing = NO;
    }
    if (_curRed <= 0.0) {
        _curRed = 0.0;
        _increasing = YES;
    }
}
```

Note that the update method is called plain update (instead of
glkViewControllerUpdate), because now that you're subclassing
GLKViewController you can just override one of its methods instead of having to set a
delegate. Also, the timeSinceLastUpdate property is accessed via self, not passed in
view controller.

Now that your GLKViewController subclass is in place, let's create the Storyboard.
Create a new file with the iOS\User Interface\Storyboard template, choose
iPhone for the device family, and save it as MainStoryboard.storyboard.

Open MainStoryboard.storyboard, and from the Objects panel drag a GLKit
View Controller into the grid area. Select the GLKit View Controller in the left
sidebar, and in the Identity Inspector set the class to HelloGLKitViewController:

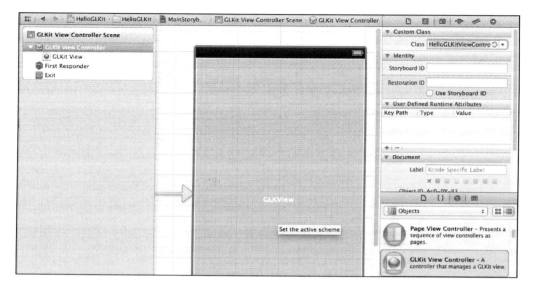

To make this Storyboard run on startup, select HelloGLKit in the Project Navigator and select the Summary tab. Under the iPhone / iPod Deployment Info section, set the Main Storyboard to MainStoryboard.

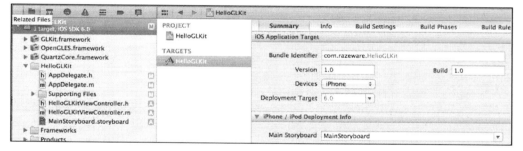

That pretty much completes everything you need, but you still have some old code in AppDelegate that needs to be cleaned up. Luckily this is incredibly simple. Just delete everything in AppDelegate.m and replace it with the following:

```
#import "AppDelegate.h"

@implementation AppDelegate

- (BOOL)application:(UIApplication *)application
  didFinishLaunchingWithOptions:(NSDictionary *)launchOptions
{
    return YES;
}
```

```
@end
```

That's it! Build and run your app, and you'll see the "red alert" effect working as usual.

At this point, you're getting pretty close to the setup you get when you choose the OpenGL Game template with the Storyboard option set. The difference is that template has a bunch of other code in there, which you can delete if you don't need it to get back to this "fresh and simple" starting point.

Feel free to use the OpenGL game template in the future to save a little time – but now you know how GLKView and GLKViewController works from the ground up.

GLKViewController and pausing

Before we move on to rendering geometry with OpenGL ES, let's discuss one last feature of GLKViewController: pausing.

To see how it works, add the following to HelloGLKitViewController.m:

```
- (void)touchesBegan:(NSSet *)touches withEvent:(UIEvent *)event
{
    self.paused = !self.paused;
}
```

Build and run the app, and now whenever you tap, the animation stops or resumes.Behind the scenes, GLKViewController stops calling your update method and your draw method. This is a handy way to implement a pause button in your game.

In addition to that, GLKViewController has a pauseOnResignActive property that is set to YES by default. This means when the user hits the home button or receives an interruption such as a phone call, your app will automatically pause. Similarly, it has a resumeOnDidBecomeActive property that is also set to YES by default, which means that when the user comes back to your app, it will automatically unpause. Handy, that!

You've learned about almost every property on GLKViewController by now, except for the extra time info properties I mentioned earlier:

• timeSinceLastDraw gives you the elapsed time since the last call to the draw method. Note that this might be different than timeSinceLastUpdate, since your update method takes time.

• timeSinceFirstResume gives you the elapsed time since the first time GLKViewController resumed sending updates. This often means the time since your app launched, if your GLKViewController is the first thing that shows up.

- timeSinceLastResume gives you the elapsed time since the last time GLKViewController resumed sending updates. This often means the time since your game was unpaused.

Let's add some code to try these out. Add the following code to the top of touchesBegan:withEvent::

```
NSLog(@"timeSinceLastUpdate: %f", self.timeSinceLastUpdate);
NSLog(@"timeSinceLastDraw: %f", self.timeSinceLastDraw);
NSLog(@"timeSinceFirstResume: %f", self.timeSinceFirstResume);
NSLog(@"timeSinceLastResume: %f", self.timeSinceLastResume);
```

Build and run, and check the console as you play around with the app so you can get familiar with how these work. Then it's time for more fun stuff – rendering a square to the screen.

Creating vertex data for a simple square

> Note: If you skipped to this section from the beginning of this tutorial, you can pick up with the HelloGLKitPart1 starter project, which contains all of the code developed up to this point. It is basically a stripped-down version of the Hello GLKit project template that comes with Xcode.

Now that you have a good understanding of how GLKView and GLKViewController work, you'll do something more interesting than a flashing screen – you'll render a simple square to the screen.

To do this, you need to know the points for the four corners of the square. It's common to call a point in OpenGL ES space a vertex, and a set of points vertices.

The square will be set up like the following:

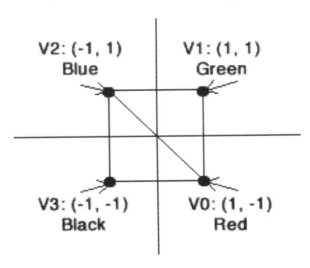

OpenGL ES can't render squares – it can only render triangles. However, you can create a square with two triangles, as you can see in the picture above: one triangle with vertices (0, 1, 2) and one triangle with vertices (2, 3, 0).

One of the nice things about OpenGL ES 2.0 is you can keep your vertex data organized in whatever manner you like, rather than having predefined structures like in OpenGL ES 1.0. Open up HelloGLKitViewController.m and create a plain old C-structure and a few arrays to keep track of the information, as shown below:

```
typedef struct {
    float Position[3];
    float Color[4];
} Vertex;

const Vertex Vertices[] = {
    {{1, -1, 0}, {1, 0, 0, 1}},
    {{1, 1, 0}, {0, 1, 0, 1}},
    {{-1, 1, 0}, {0, 0, 1, 1}},
    {{-1, -1, 0}, {0, 0, 0, 1}}
};

const GLubyte Indices[] = {
    0, 1, 2,
    2, 3, 0
};
```

The above code creates:

- a structure to keep track of your per-vertex information (currently just color and position). This structure defines a structure (think of this as a class with no methods) with an array of 3 floats for the position of the vertex, and an array of 4 floats for the color of the vertex.

- an array with all the info for each vertex. This defines and initializes an array of 4 Vertex structures. The first element in the array has a position of {1, -1, 0} (x=1, y=-1, z=0) and a color of {1, 0, 0, 1} (red=1, green=0, blue=0, alpha=1). The four entries in this array represent the four corners in the square, as shown in the diagram earlier.
- an array that gives a list of triangles to create, by specifying the indices of the 3 vertices that make up each triangle.

Now you have to pass the information to OpenGL.

Creating vertex buffer objects

The best way to send data to OpenGL is through something called vertex buffer objects.

Basically these are OpenGL objects that store buffers of vertex data. You use a few function calls to send your data over to OpenGL-land.

There are two types of vertex buffer objects: one to keep track of the per-vertex data (like you have in the Vertices array), and one to keep track of the indices that make up triangles (like you have in the Indices array).

So first add the following private instance variables to your class:

```
GLuint _vertexBuffer;
GLuint _indexBuffer;
```

Then add a method to create these:

```
- (void)setupGL {
    [EAGLContext setCurrentContext:_context];

    glGenBuffers(1, &_vertexBuffer);
    glBindBuffer(GL_ARRAY_BUFFER, _vertexBuffer);
    glBufferData(GL_ARRAY_BUFFER, sizeof(Vertices),
      Vertices, GL_STATIC_DRAW);

    glGenBuffers(1, &_indexBuffer);
    glBindBuffer(GL_ELEMENT_ARRAY_BUFFER, _indexBuffer);
    glBufferData(GL_ELEMENT_ARRAY_BUFFER, sizeof(Indices),
      Indices, GL_STATIC_DRAW);
```

```
}
```

The first thing this does is set the current OpenGL ES context to the current context. This is important in case some other code has changed the global context.

It then calls glGenBuffers to create a new vertex buffer object. Remember that you need a vertex buffer to store all of the vertices for the square so OpenGL can draw the square for you.

> Note: If you are unfamiliar with C, this syntax might look different to you. To explain the syntax, this is calling a C function called `glGenBuffers` with the first parameter set to 1, and the second parameter set to a pointer to the vertex buffer variable. The ampersand converts a regular variable to a pointer to that variable.
>
> In summary, this line of code is saying "create a new buffer, and store the result in the vertex buffer variable."

Next it calls glBindBuffer to make `vertexBuffer` the active buffer to use for future commands using the `GL_ARRAY_BUFFER` parameter. You need to do this because you're about to tell OpenGL to do something with the vertex buffer you created.

Finally, it calls glBufferData to send the data over to OpenGL-land. Although you have defined your vertices earlier in your own array, this data is on the CPU, not in the graphics card. So you need to call this function to move the data to the graphics card.

Call this method at the bottom of `viewDidLoad`:

```
[self setupGL];
```

And add this to the beginning of your `cleanup` method:

```
[EAGLContext setCurrentContext:_context];
glDeleteBuffers(1, &_vertexBuffer);
glDeleteBuffers(1, &_indexBuffer);
```

This makes sure that you free the memory for the buffers you created when necessary.

You're almost done – you just need to add the code to render the geometry to the screen with `GLKBaseEffect`.

Introducing GLKBaseEffect

In OpenGL ES 2.0, to render any geometry to the scene, you have to create two tiny little programs called shaders.

Shaders are written in a C-like language called GLSL. Don't worry too much about studying up on the reference at this point – you don't even need to know GLSL for this book, for reasons you'll see shortly.

There are two types of shaders:

- **Vertex shaders** are programs that get called once per vertex in your scene. So if you are rendering a simple scene with a single square, with one vertex at each corner, this would be called four times. Its job is to perform some calculations such as lighting, geometry transforms, etc., figure out the final position of the vertex, and pass on some data to the fragment shader.
- **Fragment shaders** are programs that get called once per pixel (sort of) in your scene. So if you're rendering that same simple scene with a single square, it will be called once for each pixel that the square covers. Fragment shaders can also perform lighting calculations, etc, but their most important job is to set the final color for each pixel.

GLKBaseEffect is a helper class that implements some common shaders for you. The goal of GLKBaseEffect is to provide most of the functionality available in OpenGL ES 1.0, to make porting apps from OpenGL ES 1.0 to OpenGL ES 2.0 easier.

To use a GLKBaseEffect, you do the following:

1. Create a GLKBaseEffect. Usually you create one of these when you create your OpenGL ES context. You can (and should) re-use the same GLKBaseEffect for different geometry, and just reset the properties. Behind the scenes, GLKBaseEffect will only propogate the properties that have changed to its shaders.

2. Set GLKBaseEffect properties. Here you can configure the lighting, transform, and other properties that the GLKBaseEffect's shaders will use to render the geometry.

3. Call prepareToDraw on the GLKBaseEffect. Any time you change a property on the GLKBaseEffect, you need to call prepareToDraw prior to drawing to get the shaders set up properly. This also enables the GLKBaseEffect's shaders as the current shader program.

4. **Enable pre-defined attributes.** When you make your own shaders, you set them up to take parameters called attributes, and you have to write code to get IDs that correspond to each attribute so you can set them in code. For GLKBaseEffect's built in shaders, there are predefined constants for their attribute IDs such as GLKVertexAttribPosition or GLKVertexAttribColor. Your job is to enable any parameters that you want to pass in to the shaders, and then pass pointers to your data for each parameter.

5. **Draw your geometry.** Once you have everything set up, you can use normal OpenGL ES draw commands such as glDrawArrays or glDrawElements, and the figure will be rendered using the effect you've set up.

The nice thing about GLKBaseEffect is that if you use it, you don't necessarily have to write any shaders at all. Of course you're welcome to if you'd like – and you can mix and match, rendering some things with GLKBaseEffect, and some with your own shaders. If you look at the OpenGL Game template project, you'll see an example of exactly that.

In this book, you're going to focus on just using GLKBaseEffect, since the entire point is to get you up to speed with the new GLKit functionality – plus it's plain easier.

So let's walk through the steps one at a time in code.

1. **Create a GLKBaseEffect.**

The first step is to simply create a GLKBaseEffect. In HelloGLKitViewController.m, add a private instance variable for a GLKBaseEffect:

```
GLKBaseEffect * _effect;
```

Then in setupGL, initialize it at the end of the method:

```
_effect = [[GLKBaseEffect alloc] init];
```

And set it to nil at the end of cleanup:

```
_effect = nil;
```

Now that you've created the effect, you'll use it in conjunction with your vertex and index buffers to render the square. The first step is to use your effect's projection matrix.

2. **Set GLKBaseEffect properties.**

The first property you need to set is the projection matrix. A projection matrix is how you tell the CPU to render 3D geometry onto a 2D plane. Think of it as drawing a bunch of lines out from your eye through each pixel in your screen. Whatever the frontmost 3D object each line hits determines the pixel that is drawn to the screen.

GLKit provides you with some handy functions to set up a projection matrix. The one you're going to use allows you to specify the field of view along the y-axis, the aspect ratio, and the near and far planes:

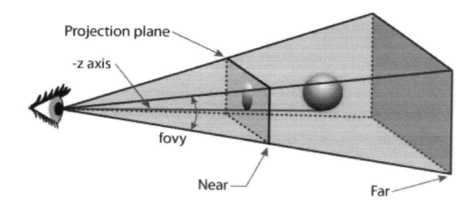

The field of view is similar to what a camera lens perceives. A small field of view (for example 10) is like a telephoto lens – it magnifies images by "pulling" them closer to you. A large field of view (for example 100) is like a wide angle lens – it makes everything seem farther away. A typical value to use for this is around 65-75.

The aspect ratio is the aspect ratio you want to render to (in this case, the aspect ratio of the view). It uses this in combination with the field of view (which is for the y-axis) to determine the field of view along the x-axis.

The near and far planes are the bounding boxes for the "viewable" volume in the scene. So if something is closer to the eye than the near plane or further away from the far plane, it won't be rendered. This is a common problem– you try and render something and it doesn't show up. One thing to check is that it's actually between the near and far planes.

Let's try this out. Add the following code to the bottom of `update`:

```
float aspect =
  fabsf(self.view.bounds.size.width /
    self.view.bounds.size.height);

GLKMatrix4 projectionMatrix = GLKMatrix4MakePerspective(
  GLKMathDegreesToRadians(65.0f), aspect, 4.0f, 10.0f);

_effect.transform.projectionMatrix = projectionMatrix;
```

In the first line, you get the aspect ratio of the GLKView.

In the second line, you use a built-in helper function in the GLKit math library to easily create a perspective matrix. All you have to do is pass in the parameters discussed above. You set the near plane to 4 units away from the eye, and the far plane to 10 units away.

In the third line, you simply set the GLKEffect's projection matrix to the result.

You need to set one more property now – the modelViewMatrix. The modelViewMatrix is the transform that is applied to any geometry that the effect renders.

The GLKit math library again comes to the rescue with some handy functions that make performing translations, rotations, and scales easy – even if you don't know much about matrix math. To see what I mean, add the following lines to the bottom of update:

```
GLKMatrix4 modelViewMatrix =
  GLKMatrix4MakeTranslation(0.0f, 0.0f, -6.0f);
_rotation += 90 * self.timeSinceLastUpdate;
modelViewMatrix = GLKMatrix4Rotate(modelViewMatrix,

GLKMathDegreesToRadians(_rotation), 0, 0, 1);
_effect.transform.modelviewMatrix = modelViewMatrix;
```

If you remember setting up the vertices for the square, recall that the z-coordinate for each vertex was 0. If you tried to render it with this perspective matrix, it wouldn't show up because it's closer to the eye than the near plane!

So the first thing you need to do is move the square backwards. So in this first line, you use the GLKMatrix4MakeTranslation function to create a matrix you'll use to translate the square 6 units backwards.

Next, you'll make the square rotate, for fun. You increment an instance variable that keeps track of the current rotation (which you'll add in a second), and use the GLKMatrix4Rotate method to modify the current transformation by rotating it as well. It takes radians, so you use the GLKMathDegreesToRadians method to perform the conversion. Yes, this math library has just about every matrix and vector math routine you'll need.

Finally, you set the GLKEffect's transform property to the result.

Before you forget, add the rotation private instance variable:

```
float _rotation;
```

You'll play around with more of the GLKBaseEffect properties in the next chapter, since there's a lot of cool stuff and you've barely scratched the surface here. But let's continue on for now, so you can finally get something rendering.

3. Call prepareToDraw on the GLKBaseEffect.

For this step, add the following line to the bottom of glkView:drawInRect::

```
[_effect prepareToDraw];
```

That was easy! Just remember that you need to call this after any time you change properties on a GLKBaseEffect, before you draw with it, or the changes in the properties won't take effect.

4. Enable pre-defined attributes.

Next add this code to the bottom of glkView:drawInRect::

```
glBindBuffer(GL_ARRAY_BUFFER, _vertexBuffer);
glBindBuffer(GL_ELEMENT_ARRAY_BUFFER, _indexBuffer);
glEnableVertexAttribArray(GLKVertexAttribPosition);
glVertexAttribPointer(GLKVertexAttribPosition, 3, GL_FLOAT,
  GL_FALSE, sizeof(Vertex),
  (const GLvoid *) offsetof(Vertex, Position));
glEnableVertexAttribArray(GLKVertexAttribColor);
glVertexAttribPointer(GLKVertexAttribColor, 4, GL_FLOAT,
  GL_FALSE, sizeof(Vertex),
  (const GLvoid *) offsetof(Vertex, Color));
```

If you haven't programmed in OpenGL ES 2.0 before, this code might look pretty confusing to you, so let me explain.

Every time before you draw, you have to tell OpenGL which vertex buffer objects you should use. So here you bind (in other words, select) the vertex and index buffers you created earlier. Strictly, you don't have to do this for this app (because they're already still bound from before), but usually you have to do this because in most games and apps you use many different vertex buffer objects.

Next, you have to enable the pre-defined vertex attributes you want the GLKBaseEffect to use. You use the glkEnableVertexAttribArray function to enable two attributes here – one for the vertex position, and one for the vertex color. GLKit has predefined constants you need to use for these – GLKVertexAttribPosition and GLKVertexAttribColor.

Next, you call glVertexAttribPointer to feed the correct values to these two input variables for the vertex shader.

This is a particularly important function so let's go over how it works carefully.

- The first parameter specifies the attribute name to set. You just use the predefined constants GLKit set up.

- The second parameter specifies how many values are present for each vertex. If you look back up at the Vertex struct, you'll see that for the position there are three floats (x,y,z) and for the color there are four floats (r,g,b,a).

- The third parameter specifies the type of each value – which is float for both Position and Color.

- The fourth parameter is always set to false.

- The fifth parameter is the size of the stride, which is a fancy way of saying "the size of the data structure containing the per-vertex data." So you can simply pass in sizeof(Vertex) here to get the compiler to compute it for you.

- The final parameter is the offset within the structure to find this data. You can use the handy offsetof operator to find the offset of a particular field within a structure.

So now that you're passing in the position and color data to the GLKBaseEffect, there's only one step left…

5. Draw your geometry.

To draw the geometry, add this to the bottom of glkView:drawInRect::

```
glDrawElements(GL_TRIANGLES, sizeof(Indices)/sizeof(Indices[0]),
    GL_UNSIGNED_BYTE, 0);
```

This is also an important function so let's discuss each parameter here as well.

- The first parameter specifies the manner of drawing the vertices. You specify GL_TRIANGLES here, which means the index buffer lists triangles one at a time, with three vertices per triangle.

  There are different options you may come across in other tutorials like GL_LINE_STRIP or GL_TRIANGLE_FAN, but GL_TRIANGLES is the most generically useful (especially when combined with vertex buffer objects), so it's what we cover here.

- The second parameter is the count of vertices to render. You use a C trick to compute the number of elements in an array here by dividing the sizeof(Indices) (which gives you the size of the array in bytes) by sizeof(Indices[0]) (which gives you the size of the first element in the array).

- The third parameter is the data type of each individual index in the Indices array. You're using an unsigned byte for that, so you specify that here.

- From the documentation, it appears that the final buffer should be a pointer to the indices. But since you're using vertex buffer objects it's a special case – it will use the indices array you already passed to OpenGL-land in the GL_ELEMENT_ARRAY_BUFFER.

Guess what? You're done! Compile and run the app and you should see a pretty rotating square on the screen.

Where To Go From Here?

At this point, you have hands-on experience making a simple GLKit based app with OpenGL ES 2.0 – completely from scratch.

If you're new to OpenGL ES 2.0, you've also gotten a great grounding on some of the most important techniques, such as vertex buffers, index buffers, and vertex attributes.

However, there's more cool stuff in store for you with GLKit. Keep reading for the next chapter, where you'll move to full 3D, and demonstrate some of the cool effects you can get with GLKBaseEffect, such as lighting and fog.

Chapter 9: Intermediate OpenGL ES 2.0 with GLKit

By Ray Wenderlich

In the previous chapter, you learned the basics of using OpenGL ES 2.0 with GLKit and created a simple app with a rotating square onto the screen.

In the process, you learned a great deal about `GLKView` and `GLKViewController` and the basics of using `GLKEffect`.

In this chapter, you're going to take things to full 3D and convert your square into a rotating 3D cube. In addition, you'll learn a lot more about the cool things you can do with `GLKBaseEffect`, such as lighting effects, multitexturing, and fog effects.

By the time you're done, you'll have hands-on experience with the four main areas of GLKit and be ready to continue your studies of OpenGL ES 2.0.

Gratuitous vertex array objects

Note: When I first wrote this chapter, I included this section on vertex array objects because Apple was really pushing using these, and I thought it would improve performance of your app by using them. However, after some testing I found that they don't actually improve performance in practice.

After some investigation, I found this great blog post by Daniel Pasco that explains the subject in more detail: http://blackpixel.com/blog/399/iphone-vertex-buffer-object-performance/

> In this updated version of the book, I decided to keep this section anyway since they are still a useful way to keep your code nice and clean, and you might see them in other people's code even if you aren't personally using them. But do note that it might not increase your performance much by using them.

In the last chapter, you rendered your square with vertex buffer objects and index buffer objects, and bound to these objects each time you wanted to draw. This works, but isn't ideal.

If you were drawing a lot of different geometry to the scene, your code would get quite tedious. Every time you want to draw something, you'd have to bind the correct vertex and index buffers, enable the attributes you want for the shader, and specify where their data is located.

In theory, continually making all these calls each time is slow - however this doesn't actually turn out to be the case on iOS devices, as explained in the note above.

Apple's recommendation to solve these issues is to use a technique called vertex array objects. Vertex array objects let you configure all this stuff once, and load back your settings when you're about to draw. They're pretty easy to use too, so let's try them out.

First add an new private instance variable to HelloGLKitViewController.m:

```
GLuint _vertexArray;
```

Then modify your setupGL method as follows:

```
- (void)setupGL {

    // Old stuff
    [EAGLContext setCurrentContext:_context];

    // New lines
    glGenVertexArraysOES(1, &_vertexArray);
    glBindVertexArrayOES(_vertexArray);

    // Old stuff
    glGenBuffers(1, &_vertexBuffer);
    glBindBuffer(GL_ARRAY_BUFFER, _vertexBuffer);
    glBufferData(GL_ARRAY_BUFFER, sizeof(Vertices),
      Vertices, GL_STATIC_DRAW);

    glGenBuffers(1, &_indexBuffer);
    glBindBuffer(GL_ELEMENT_ARRAY_BUFFER, _indexBuffer);
    glBufferData(GL_ELEMENT_ARRAY_BUFFER, sizeof(Indices),
      Indices, GL_STATIC_DRAW);
```

```
// New lines (were previously in glkView:drawInRect:
glEnableVertexAttribArray(GLKVertexAttribPosition);
glVertexAttribPointer(GLKVertexAttribPosition, 3, GL_FLOAT,
  GL_FALSE, sizeof(Vertex),
  (const GLvoid *) offsetof(Vertex, Position));
glEnableVertexAttribArray(GLKVertexAttribColor);
glVertexAttribPointer(GLKVertexAttribColor, 4, GL_FLOAT,
  GL_FALSE, sizeof(Vertex),
  (const GLvoid *) offsetof(Vertex, Color));

// New line
glBindVertexArrayOES(0);

// Old stuff
_effect = [[GLKBaseEffect alloc] init];

}
```

The first group of new lines creates a new vertex array object and binds to it. After doing that, the rest of the setup calls you make will be associated with the new vertex array object.

After setting up the vertex and index buffer, you add the lines of code to set up the vertex attributes that were previously in draw. This configuration will also be associated with the new vertex array object.

Finally, you bind the current vertex array object to 0 since you're done with it.

Next, replace your `glkView:drawInRect:` method with this:

```
- (void)glkView:(GLKView *)view drawInRect:(CGRect)rect {
   glClearColor(_curRed, 0.0, 0.0, 1.0);
   glClear(GL_COLOR_BUFFER_BIT);

   [_effect prepareToDraw];

   glBindVertexArrayOES(_vertexArray);
   glDrawElements(GL_TRIANGLES,
     sizeof(Indices)/sizeof(Indices[0]), GL_UNSIGNED_BYTE, 0);
}
```

Notice how much simpler it is! Now your code is much easier to understand, especially if you had lots of different sets of vertices/indices/attributes you are rendering, so you should get into the habit of using these.

Build and run your app, and it should work as usual!

Gratuitous textures

There's one big aspect of GLKit that you haven't played around with yet – texture loading.

This was one of the new features in iOS 5 that I was most excited about, because the code to do this used to be horrendous, especially when you wanted to support a wide variety of image formats.

But now it's a lot easier! Let's dive right in and try it out.

In the resources for this chapter, you'll find an image called tile_floor.png. Drag it into your project.

Then add the following lines to the end of setupGL:

```
NSDictionary * options =
  @{ GLKTextureLoaderOriginBottomLeft: @YES };
NSError * error;
NSString * path = [[NSBundle mainBundle]
  pathForResource:@"tile_floor" ofType:@"png"];
GLKTextureInfo * info = [GLKTextureLoader
  textureWithContentsOfFile:path options:options error:&error];
if (info == nil) {
    NSLog(@"Error loading file: %@",
      error.localizedDescription);
}
_effect.texture2d0.name = info.name;
_effect.texture2d0.enabled = true;
```

This code loads the tile_floor.png image and sends it to OpenGL ES as a texture that you can use to render with. All you have to do is use the textureWithContentsOfFile:options:error: method on the GLKTextureLoader singleton and pass in a path, and you get back a class with information about the texture, including the OpenGL ES "name" (in other words, "ID") that you can use for rendering.

Note that you pass a dictionary of options into the GLKTextureLoader. By default the origin of a texture you load is the upper left of the texture, but that's annoying because in OpenGL ES the origin is the lower left. So here you set a flag to make the texture coordinates match up to the OpenGL coordinates.

> Note: If you're confused about the syntax for creating a dictionary here, check out Chapter 2 in *iOS 6 by Tutorials*, "Programming in Modern Objective-C."

Also notice that after you load the texture, you set a few more properties on the effect to set up the texture for use. You set the texture's name, and mark it as enabled.

Now to actually render a texture, you need to pass the texture coordinates of each pixel to the GLKBaseEffect's shader. Modify your Vertex structure and array to include the texture coordinates as follows:

```
typedef struct {
    float Position[3];
    float Color[4];
    float TexCoord[2];
} Vertex;

const Vertex Vertices[] = {
    {{1, -1, 0}, {1, 0, 0, 1}, {1, 0}},
    {{1, 1, 0}, {0, 1, 0, 1}, {1, 1}},
    {{-1, 1, 0}, {0, 0, 1, 1}, {0, 1}},
    {{-1, -1, 0}, {0, 0, 0, 1}, {0, 0}}
};
```

Also add these lines to the bottom of setupGL, before calling glBindVertexArrayOES(0):

```
glEnableVertexAttribArray(GLKVertexAttribTexCoord0);
glVertexAttribPointer(GLKVertexAttribTexCoord0, 2, GL_FLOAT,
    GL_FALSE, sizeof(Vertex),
    (const GLvoid *) offsetof(Vertex, TexCoord));
```

These lines should be a good review of what you've already learned in the previous chapter. Try to walk through each of the parameters here and make sure you understand how it works. If you aren't sure, review step 4 in the *Introducing GLKBaseEffect* section in the previous chapter.

Build and run, and now your rotating square has a nice texture applied to it.

Gratuitous multisampling

In this section, I just wanted to show you another reason why GLKit is awesome. Run the app and watch the square rotate, and see if you notice jagged lines.

Then add the following line of code in viewDidLoad, right before the call to [self setupGL]:

```
view.drawableMultisample = GLKViewDrawableMultisample4X;
```

This single line enables multisampling (as you already know if you have read the optional *GLKit properties* section in the previous chapter). This renders your pixels at finer levels of granularity and merges the results to get an anti-aliased look, as you can see below:

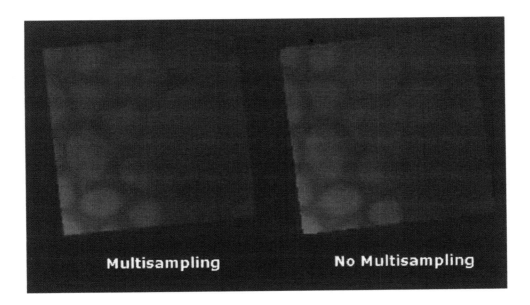

Run the app and see if you notice the difference. Not bad for one line of code, eh? You'll be especially happy if you ever had to write the code the old long way. ☺

Moving to 3D

It's the moment you've been waiting for – now you're going to move into full 3D by converting this square into a cube.

The vertex array for a 3-D object now contains data for each surface. The array specifies each surface in turn, vertex by vertex. After the coordinate of the vertex comes the color followed by the texture data.

In our 2-D version, each coordinate of the square appeared once. In the 3-D version, we're talking surfaces. Each surface is defined by four points, so you now have twenty four sets of vertex coordinates. Another way of looking at it is that three surfaces meet at each vertex of the cube, so each of the eight corners appears three times in the listing.

Replace the Vertices and Indices arrays with the following:

```
const Vertex Vertices[] = {
    // Front
    {{1, -1, 1}, {1, 0, 0, 1}, {1, 0}},
    {{1, 1, 1}, {0, 1, 0, 1}, {1, 1}},
```

```
    {{-1, 1, 1}, {0, 0, 1, 1}, {0, 1}},
    {{-1, -1, 1}, {0, 0, 0, 1}, {0, 0}},
    // Back
    {{1, 1, -1}, {1, 0, 0, 1}, {0, 1}},
    {{-1, -1, -1}, {0, 1, 0, 1}, {1, 0}},
    {{1, -1, -1}, {0, 0, 1, 1}, {0, 0}},
    {{-1, 1, -1}, {0, 0, 0, 1}, {1, 1}},
    // Left
    {{-1, -1, 1}, {1, 0, 0, 1}, {1, 0}},
    {{-1, 1, 1}, {0, 1, 0, 1}, {1, 1}},
    {{-1, 1, -1}, {0, 0, 1, 1}, {0, 1}},
    {{-1, -1, -1}, {0, 0, 0, 1}, {0, 0}},
    // Right
    {{1, -1, -1}, {1, 0, 0, 1}, {1, 0}},
    {{1, 1, -1}, {0, 1, 0, 1}, {1, 1}},
    {{1, 1, 1}, {0, 0, 1, 1}, {0, 1}},
    {{1, -1, 1}, {0, 0, 0, 1}, {0, 0}},
    // Top
    {{1, 1, 1}, {1, 0, 0, 1}, {1, 0}},
    {{1, 1, -1}, {0, 1, 0, 1}, {1, 1}},
    {{-1, 1, -1}, {0, 0, 1, 1}, {0, 1}},
    {{-1, 1, 1}, {0, 0, 0, 1}, {0, 0}},
    // Bottom
    {{1, -1, -1}, {1, 0, 0, 1}, {1, 0}},
    {{1, -1, 1}, {0, 1, 0, 1}, {1, 1}},
    {{-1, -1, 1}, {0, 0, 1, 1}, {0, 1}},
    {{-1, -1, -1}, {0, 0, 0, 1}, {0, 0}}
};

const GLubyte Indices[] = {
    // Front
    0, 1, 2,
    2, 3, 0,
    // Back
    4, 6, 5,
    4, 5, 7,
    // Left
    8, 9, 10,
    10, 11, 8,
    // Right
    12, 13, 14,
    14, 15, 12,
    // Top
    16, 17, 18,
    18, 19, 16,
    // Bottom
    20, 21, 22,
    22, 23, 20
};
```

I got these by simply sketching them out on a piece of paper – it's a good exercise if you want to do the same. However, there is one tricky bit – you need to make sure you specify the indices in counter-clockwise order (from the perspective of looking at the box from the outside), for reasons I'll get into shortly.

Next, make some minor changes to the model view matrix setup at the end of `update`, to switch the rotation axis to the y-axis and rotate it slightly along the x-axis:

```
GLKMatrix4 modelViewMatrix =
  GLKMatrix4MakeTranslation(0.0f, 0.0f, -6.0f);
_rotation += 90 * self.timeSinceLastUpdate;
modelViewMatrix = GLKMatrix4Rotate(modelViewMatrix,
  GLKMathDegreesToRadians(25), 1, 0, 0);
modelViewMatrix = GLKMatrix4Rotate(modelViewMatrix,
  GLKMathDegreesToRadians(_rotation), 0, 1, 0);
_effect.transform.modelviewMatrix = modelViewMatrix;
```

Build and run and it sort of works… but there are some strange oddities. First of all, it looks like the cube is partially transparent sometimes:

That is because you haven't given OpenGL any criteria for how to tell when a surface of the cube is facing the front, or when a surface of the cube is facing the back. Because of this, sometimes it is drawing the back face on top of where the front face should be, or similarly the side faces in front of the front face.

Luckily that is an easy fix. Since you were careful to define the vertices in counter-clockwise order, you can enable an OpenGL flag called GL_CULL_FACE. This makes OpenGL skip drawing any frame that is backwards facing (i.e. not visible, since you have a cube.)

To do this, simply add the following line of code to setupGL after setting the context:

```
glEnable(GL_CULL_FACE);
```

Note: You could have solved this drawing issue by enabling depth testing and the GLKView depth buffer. However, using backface culling like this is much more efficient since it doesn't have to draw the back facing triangles at all. This can be a big performance improvement for more complicated games.

However, depth testing is still necessary when you have geometry that may cover other objects.

Build and run – and it works, you now have a rotating 3D cube with OpenGL ES 2.0 and GLKit!

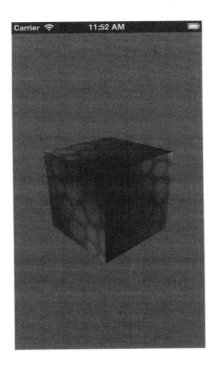

Enabling lighting

Let's start with a bang (or should I say flash?) and try out some of the cool lighting effects you can get rather easily with GLKBaseEffect.

So far you have just set three properties on GLKBaseEffect – the transform.projectionMatrix, the transform.modelViewMatrix, and texture2d0. There are many other properties you can configure as well – including properties to set up lighting.

You can set up to three different lights on a GLKBaseEffect – the properties you use to configure them are named light0, light1, and light2. Each of these are instances of GLKEffectPropertyLight, which is a class that has many properties you can set to configure how the light works.

Let's get a simple light working, then you'll dive deeper into all the various ways you can configure it.

Add the following lines of code to the end of setupGL:

```
_effect.light0.enabled = GL_TRUE;
```

```
_effect.light0.diffuseColor = GLKVector4Make(1, 1, 1, 1.0);
_effect.light0.position = GLKVector4Make(1, 1, 0, 1);
```

Here you set three properties on the light:

• **enabled**: Turns the light on (default is off).

• **diffuseColor**: You'll learn more about this later, but for now just think of this as the color of the light.

• **position**: This vector indicates the position or direction of the light in 3D space. The last component of the vector indicates whether it is positional (1) or directional (0). Here you've set the light to be positional at (1, 1, 0) in 3D space.

w00t you're done, right? Compile and run, and you'll see this:

Sadly, it appears that you have no light at all. What gives?

The answer comes in the next section – vertex normals.!

Vertex normals

In order for the shader to know how to calculate lighting, it needs to know how the light should bounce off a particular surface. The way you handle this is you give OpenGL ES something called a vertex normal, which is a fancy way of saying a unit vector that is perpendicular to the surface at that point.

To see what I mean, here's a diagram of your cube with the normals for each surface:

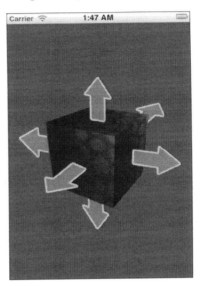

You specify the normals at each vertex rather than each surface, which allows you to get some neat effects such as bump mapping and more realistic looking surfaces. But for your simple cube, the vertex normals will be the same as the surface normals for each vertex on that face.

Note how the vertex array now contains a 3-D vector after each of the vertices that define a face. There is some redundancy here, as each of the vectors points in the same direction. You might think of it as the normal to the surface near the vertex just inside the area enclosed by the vertices. And, of course, a cube's surface is flat, so the normal to the face is the same all across that surface of the cube.

To add vertex normals for each vertex, you need to update your `Vertex` structure and array. So update it to the following:

```
typedef struct {
    float Position[3];
```

```
    float Color[4];
    float TexCoord[2];
    float Normal[3];
} Vertex;

const Vertex Vertices[] = {
    // Front
    {{1, -1, 1}, {1, 0, 0, 1}, {1, 0}, {0, 0, 1}},
    {{1, 1, 1}, {0, 1, 0, 1}, {1, 1}, {0, 0, 1}},
    {{-1, 1, 1}, {0, 0, 1, 1}, {0, 1}, {0, 0, 1}},
    {{-1, -1, 1}, {0, 0, 0, 1}, {0, 0}, {0, 0, 1}},
    // Back
    {{1, 1, -1}, {1, 0, 0, 1}, {0, 1}, {0, 0, -1}},
    {{-1, -1, -1}, {0, 1, 0, 1}, {1, 0}, {0, 0, -1}},
    {{1, -1, -1}, {0, 0, 1, 1}, {0, 0}, {0, 0, -1}},
    {{-1, 1, -1}, {0, 0, 0, 1}, {1, 1}, {0, 0, -1}},
    // Left
    {{-1, -1, 1}, {1, 0, 0, 1}, {1, 0}, {-1, 0, 0}},
    {{-1, 1, 1}, {0, 1, 0, 1}, {1, 1}, {-1, 0, 0}},
    {{-1, 1, -1}, {0, 0, 1, 1}, {0, 1}, {-1, 0, 0}},
    {{-1, -1, -1}, {0, 0, 0, 1}, {0, 0}, {-1, 0, 0}},
    // Right
    {{1, -1, -1}, {1, 0, 0, 1}, {1, 0}, {1, 0, 0}},
    {{1, 1, -1}, {0, 1, 0, 1}, {1, 1}, {1, 0, 0}},
    {{1, 1, 1}, {0, 0, 1, 1}, {0, 1}, {1, 0, 0}},
    {{1, -1, 1}, {0, 0, 0, 1}, {0, 0}, {1, 0, 0}},
    // Top
    {{1, 1, 1}, {1, 0, 0, 1}, {1, 0}, {0, 1, 0}},
    {{1, 1, -1}, {0, 1, 0, 1}, {1, 1}, {0, 1, 0}},
    {{-1, 1, -1}, {0, 0, 1, 1}, {0, 1}, {0, 1, 0}},
    {{-1, 1, 1}, {0, 0, 0, 1}, {0, 0}, {0, 1, 0}},
    // Bottom
    {{1, -1, -1}, {1, 0, 0, 1}, {1, 0}, {0, -1, 0}},
    {{1, -1, 1}, {0, 1, 0, 1}, {1, 1}, {0, -1, 0}},
    {{-1, -1, 1}, {0, 0, 1, 1}, {0, 1}, {0, -1, 0}},
    {{-1, -1, -1}, {0, 0, 0, 1}, {0, 0}, {0, -1, 0}}
};
```

You should sketch out the normals for each surface on a piece of paper, and make sure you understand why the normal is set the way it is.

Now that you have this new information in your Vertex structure, you need to enable the built-in GLKEffect vertex attribute for normals and pass along the pointer to the data. So add the following to setupGL, right before the call to glBindVertexArrayOES(0):

```
glEnableVertexAttribArray(GLKVertexAttribNormal);
glVertexAttribPointer(GLKVertexAttribNormal, 3, GL_FLOAT,
    GL_FALSE, sizeof(Vertex),
```

```
(const GLvoid *) offsetof(Vertex, Normal));
```

This should be familiar to you from the last chapter. If you don't recall, refer back to the last chapter for a full explanation.

One more thing. As you're playing around with lighting the pulsating effect is going to be confusing. So delete the code in update that modifies the _curRed value to disable that.

Build and run, and guess what – you've got lighting, all without writing a single line of shader code!

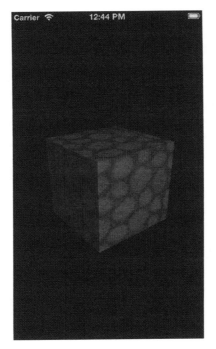

Note: You may notice that the cube appears gray (the color of the tile_floor texture) rather than the neat rainbow-colored cube as before. It turns out that when you enable lighting, by default the GLKBaseEffect shader will ignore any color properties you pass in. Instead, it uses a property on the light called the surface material, which you'll learn about later.

If this is not what you want (and you want the color values you pass in used instead), you can set the GLKEffect's colorMaterialEnabled property to YES.

> If you do this, make sure you don't have any properties set on the material, such as `specularColor`.

Light colors and materials

As I alluded to earlier, there are different types of light that influence the final color of a pixel:

- **Diffuse light**: This is the light that is emitted from a particular point, and the light is stronger the more the surface faces toward the light. This type of light really helps make objects appear 3D.
- **Ambient light**: This is the light that is applied equally to the geometry, no matter what direction it is facing. It simulates the natural light that is just bouncing everywhere around a room, light that might even hit underneath surfaces. Generally, you want to set this to a much smaller intensity than your diffuse color.
- **Specular light**: This is the light that is reflected almost like a mirror off a surface. It provides "shiny spots" on objects (think of a shiny spot on a marble).

When you set up a light on a `GLKEffect`, you can specify the colors for the diffuse, ambient and specular types independently. To make things even more configurable, you can also set the diffuse, ambient, and specular types on the "material" of the geometry itself. The colors of the light and material are combined in order to get the final color.

The easiest way to understand this is to try it out. Replace the code where you set up the light with the following:

```
_effect.light0.enabled = GL_TRUE;
_effect.light0.diffuseColor = GLKVector4Make(0, 1, 1, 1);
_effect.light0.ambientColor = GLKVector4Make(0, 0, 0, 1);
_effect.light0.specularColor = GLKVector4Make(0, 0, 0, 1);

_effect.lightModelAmbientColor = GLKVector4Make(0, 0, 0, 1);
_effect.material.specularColor = GLKVector4Make(1, 1, 1, 1);

_effect.light0.position = GLKVector4Make(0, 1.5, -6, 1);
_effect.lightingType = GLKLightingTypePerPixel;
```

In the first section you set up three types of colors on the light. You set the diffuse color to a teal color, and set the ambient and specular colors to black (which is the equivalent of "no light").

You then set the lightModelAmbientColor, which defines the global ambient light in the scene. For demontration purposes, you want to make sure that no light is affecting your cube except what you specifically set up on light 0, so you turn this off by setting it to black/"no light". The default value is {0.2, 0.2, 0.2, 1.0} by the way.

You then set the specular color of the material to white/"full light". It is important to set this, because the default value is {0, 0, 0, 1}, which means there would be no specular highlight at all, even if you set the light's specularColor.

You move the position of the light to be right above where the box is (remember the box is 1 unit tall, and you translated the box 6 units back so it is visible).

Finally, you set a flag on the effect to make the lighting type "per pixel." The default value is "per vertex", which means that lighting is calculated once per vertex and then interpolated across the surfaces. For some lighting effects this works OK, but sometimes you get strange effects with it set to this (especially when your polygons span across many pixels, like they do here). You get better lighting behavior if you set it to "per pixel", but if course the tradeoff is increased processing time.

Build and run your code, and now you should see a cool teal light shining down on top of the box.

Since you disabled the global ambient component and since the light is right above the top face of the box, the light isn't reaching any of the other faces. Hence they aren't getting any light.

Let's experiment with these color values a bit more so you can get a better feel of how they work. Rather than having to continuously tweak these and recompile, let's add some sliders to the view controller so you can dynamically modify them in real time.

Open up MainStoryboard.storyboard, and drag some labels and sliders into your view controller and make the following arrangement:

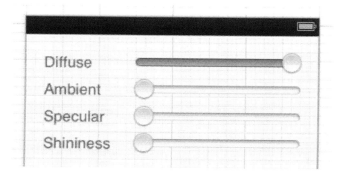

Here are some notes on the setup:

- For the first three sliders, set the min value to 0 and the max value to 1. But for the last slider, set the min value to 0 and the max value to 250.

- For the diffuse slider, set the current value to 1. For the rest, set the current value to 0.

Then bring up your assistant editor, make sure HelloGLKitViewController.m is visible, and control-drag from the diffuse slider down below the @interface on the class extension. Set the connection type to Action and connect it to diffuseChanged.

Repeat this for the other sliders, connecting them to ambientChanged, specularChanged, and shininessChanged, respectively.

Then open HelloGLKitViewController.m and implement these methods as follows:

```
- (IBAction)diffuseChanged:(id)sender {
    UISlider * slider = (UISlider *)sender;
    _effect.light0.diffuseColor =
        GLKVector4Make(0, slider.value, slider.value, 1);
}

- (IBAction)ambientChanged:(id)sender {
    UISlider * slider = (UISlider *)sender;
    _effect.light0.ambientColor =
        GLKVector4Make(0, slider.value, slider.value, 1);
}

- (IBAction)specularChanged:(id)sender {
    UISlider * slider = (UISlider *)sender;
    _effect.light0.specularColor =
        GLKVector4Make(0, slider.value, slider.value, 1);
}

- (IBAction)shininessChanged:(id)sender {
    UISlider * slider = (UISlider *)sender;
    _effect.material.shininess = slider.value;
}
```

The callbacks simply update the various properties on the material. You've seen the first three before, but you haven't seen shininess yet. The higher the shininess value, the more "focused and reflective" the specular component appears.

To see what I mean, you can play around. Build and run, and you'll see the following:

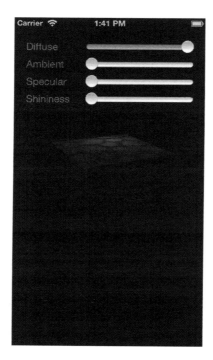

Start experimenting. You should get a good feel of how the various color components work. Be sure to try the following:

- Drag the ambient slider up to see everything light up on the screen – even surfaces not facing the light.

- Drag the specular component and you'll see the top appear to lighten up. This doesn't look very useful until you drag the shininess value up – then you'll see what appears to be a reflection of the light, making the surface appear nice and shiny! The higher you drag the shininess, the more focused the reflection is.

While you're here, feel free to go back to the code and tweak the colors of the light or material if you'd like to play around with those too.

When you're ready, come back here and we'll continue to cover some more cool properties you can set on lights.

Spotlights and attenuation

You can easily configure a light to work as a spotlight by setting the following properties:

- **position**: To make a spotlight, when you set the light's position the last component has to be 1, indicating the light is positional rather than directional. You've already done this.

- **spotDirection**: Once you have a position for the light, you have to specify the direction the spotlight is shining by setting this property to a vector.

- **cutoff**: This defaults to 180 degrees, which means the light spreads all the way across the field of view. If you want a spotlight instead, just set it to less than 180 degrees, and it will indicate the range at which no light is emitted.

- **exponent**: By making this value larger, you make the light brighter toward the center of the spotlight, and darker the further out you get from the center.

You've already set the `position`, and you'll add some sliders later to set the `cutoff` and `exponent`, but you do need to set the `spotDirection`. So add the following to the bottom of `setupGL`:

```
_effect.light0.spotDirection = GLKVector3Make(0, -1, 0);
```

This sets the light to point straight down onto the cube.

You can also specify the light's attenuation properties. These allow you to make the light get darker the further away from the light the geometry is. There are three different values you can set here – `constantAttenuation`, `linearAttenuation`, and `quadraticAttenuation`.

The best way to understand these is through experimentation, so you will add some sliders so you can play around with them and see how they work. But if you're curious and want to see the equation that is used behind the scenes, see the GLKEffectPropertyLight Class Reference.

OK, let's try these out. Open up `MainStoryboard.storyboard`, and add some more sliders and labels into the bottom of the view, like the following:

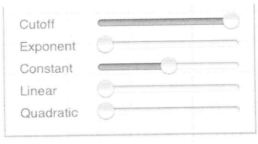

After you add the sliders, connect them to action methods like you did before. Here are some notes on setting everything up:

- The cutoff slider should have min 0, max 180, current 180. Connect it to cutoffValueChanged.

- The exponent slider should have min 0, max 100, current 0. Connect it to exponentValueChanged.

- The constant slider should have min 0, max 2, current 1. Connect it to constantValueChanged.

- The linear slider should have min 0, max 2, current 0. Connect it to linearValueChanged.

- The quadratic slider should have min 0, max 2, and current 0. Connect it to quadraticValueChanged.

Then switch to HelloGLKitViewController.m and implement the methods like the following:

```objc
- (IBAction)cutoffValueChanged:(id)sender {
    UISlider * slider = (UISlider *)sender;
    _effect.light0.spotCutoff = slider.value;
}

- (IBAction)exponentValueChanged:(id)sender {
    UISlider * slider = (UISlider *)sender;
    _effect.light0.spotExponent = slider.value;
}

- (IBAction)constantValueChanged:(id)sender {
    UISlider * slider = (UISlider *)sender;
    _effect.light0.constantAttenuation = slider.value;
}

- (IBAction)linearValueChanged:(id)sender {
    UISlider * slider = (UISlider *)sender;
    _effect.light0.linearAttenuation = slider.value;
}

- (IBAction)quadraticValueChanged:(id)sender {
    UISlider * slider = (UISlider *)sender;
    _effect.light0.quadraticAttenuation = slider.value;
}
```

Here you simply set each of these values so you can experiment with them. That's it — build and run the app, and play around! Be sure to try the following:

- Drag the cutoff slider down until you see a circular spotlight area.
- With a large cutoff, drag the exponent down to see the center area focused with light even though the cutoff is large.
- Play around with the constant, linear, and quadratic attenuation to see the effects of influencing how far the light shines before it fades away (and how quickly it does!)

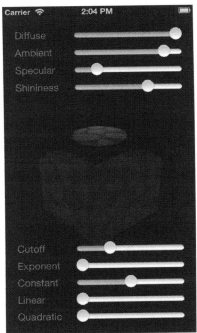

A moving light

I'd like to show you one more thing about lights, and then we're done covering those for now.

Let's add one more light to your scene, that revolves around your cube, just for fun!

First add a private instance variable for the light rotation:

```
float _lightRotation;
```

Then initialize a new light at the end of setupGL with the following properties:

```
_effect.light1.enabled = GL_TRUE;
_effect.light1.diffuseColor = GLKVector4Make(1.0, 1.0, 0.8,
1.0);
_effect.light1.position = GLKVector4Make(0, 0, 1.5, 1);
```

Here you make the light yellowish, and set the initial position to be 1.5 along the z-axis.

Next add the following code inside update, right after setting the projection matrix:

```
GLKMatrix4 lightModelViewMatrix =
GLKMatrix4MakeTranslation(0.0f, 0.0f, -6.0f);
_lightRotation += -90 * self.timeSinceLastUpdate;
lightModelViewMatrix = GLKMatrix4Rotate(lightModelViewMatrix,
  GLKMathDegreesToRadians(25), 1, 0, 0);
lightModelViewMatrix = GLKMatrix4Rotate(lightModelViewMatrix,
  GLKMathDegreesToRadians(_lightRotation), 0, 1, 0);
_effect.transform.modelviewMatrix = lightModelViewMatrix;
_effect.light1.position = GLKVector4Make(0, 0, 1.5, 1);
```

The first thing you do is construct a model view matrix to transform the light's position each frame. You start by moving the light backwards so it stays near the box. Then you rotate it each frame – but the opposite direction of how the cube is rotating.

You set the transform model view matrix with the new transform. When you set the position of the light, it uses whatever the current transform is in the modelViewMatrix to arrive at its final position.

Build and run, and you should see a sweet rotating light around the cube!

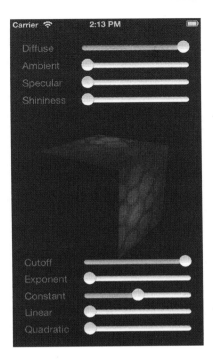

Congratulations, you now have hands-on experience with every property that you can set on GLKBaseEffect related to lighting.

> **Note:** Actually there is just one more — lightModelTwoSided. By default, the lighting algorithms only apply light to the side of the surface that is toward the light (with respect to the surface normal). If you want the light to be applied to both sides, you can set this to YES. But note the tradeoff is decreased performance.

Multi-Texturing

The multi-texturing support in GLKBaseEffect is quite limited, but let's see what it can do.

From the resources for this chapter, drag the item_powerup_fish.png image into your project. Then add the following code at the end of setupGL:

```
path = [[NSBundle mainBundle]
  pathForResource:@"item_powerup_fish" ofType:@"png"];
info = [GLKTextureLoader textureWithContentsOfFile:path
  options:options error:&error];
if (info == nil) {
    NSLog(@"Error loading file: %@",
error.localizedDescription);
}
_effect.texture2d1.name = info.name;
_effect.texture2d1.enabled = true;
_effect.texture2d1.envMode = GLKTextureEnvModeDecal;
```

Here you're loading a texture with GLKTextureLoader just like you did before, except this time you are setting it into the texture2d1 property (the only othe rtexture slot available in GLKBaseEffect).

The other difference is you set the envMode to GLKTextureEnvModeDecal. This tells the GLKBaseEffect to blend the first and second textures, based on the second texture's alpha values.

Still in setupGL, add these lines of code right before the call to glBindArrayOES(0):

```
glEnableVertexAttribArray(GLKVertexAttribTexCoord1);
glVertexAttribPointer(GLKVertexAttribTexCoord1, 2, GL_FLOAT,
  GL_FALSE, sizeof(Vertex),
  (const GLvoid *) offsetof(Vertex, TexCoord));
```

Here you pass in the texture coordinates for the second texture. Note you used the same texture coordinates as the first texture to make things easy, but you could pass in different coordinates if you need to.

Compile and run, and you'll see the glowing fish on top of your textures:

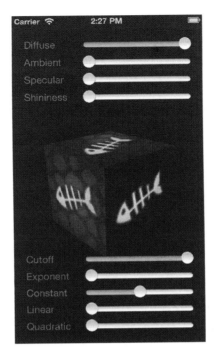

One thing to notice about this technique is the light does not affect the decal texture – it always shows in full color. This may or may not be something you desire in your games.

For more complicated or different effects, you can always write your own custom shaders.

Fog

GLKBaseEffect also supports a fog effect, which can be useful to put where your far clipping plane is to make the transition of far away objects more smooth (instead of having them randomly disappear!) It can also be fun just for a neat fog effect. ☺

Using it is simple. Add the following code at the end of setupGL:

```
_effect.fog.color = GLKVector4Make(0, 0, 0, 1.0);
_effect.fog.enabled = YES;
_effect.fog.end = 5.5;
_effect.fog.start = 5.0;
_effect.fog.mode = GLKFogModeLinear;
```

Here you set the color of the fog black (since your background is black in this app). You also set the fog as enabled, and mark where the wall of fog begins and ends (in amount of units from the eye) and make the mode of the fog linear.

That's it. Compile and run, and you should see a cool fog effect!

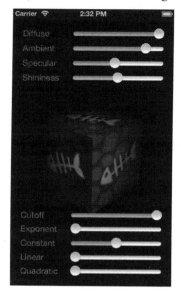

Where to go from here?

Sadly this is a book on the new APIs that came out in iOS 5, not a book on OpenGL ES 2.0, so we're going to have to call it quits from here.

However, at this point you should have a good grounding of the most important aspects of GLKit. You should be ready to use it in your own apps, and continue your studies of OpenGL ES 2.0.

The best books I know of at the moment about OpenGL ES 2.0 is Learning OpenGL ES for iOS by Erik Buck and iPhone 3D Programming by Philip Rideout.

Also, we have several other free tutorials on OpenGL ES on raywenderlich.com, such as a tutorial which shows you how to make a simple 2D game with OpenGL ES 2.0 and GLKit: http://www.raywenderlich.com/9743/how-to-create-a-simple-2d-iphone-game-with-opengl-es-2-0-and-glkit-part-1

Best of luck with your future adventures with OpenGL ES 2.0 and GLKit, and I hope these chapters have helped you get started on your journey!

To be successful on the App Store, your app needs to stand out. The vanilla user-interface "look and feel" provided by Apple just doesn't cut it any more in a crowded market.

Many of the most popular apps on the App Store present standard iOS UI elements in a non-standard fashion:

- Twitter employs a custom `UITabBar`
- Instagram uses both a custom `UITabBar` and a custom `UINavigationBar`
- Epicurious for iPad customizes elements of the standard split-view interface

Prior to iOS 5, many developers had to take somewhat unconventional approaches to achieve these results. Although subclassing and overriding `drawRect:` was the recommended approach, many resorted to the dreaded "method swizzling".

But with iOS 5 and above, those dark days are over! iOS 5 added a bunch of new APIs you can use to easily customize the appearance of various UIKit controls, and iOS 6 added even more.

To illustrate some of these new APIs, in this chapter you're going to take a "plain vanilla" app about surfing trips and customize the UI to get a more "beach-themed" look-and-feel.

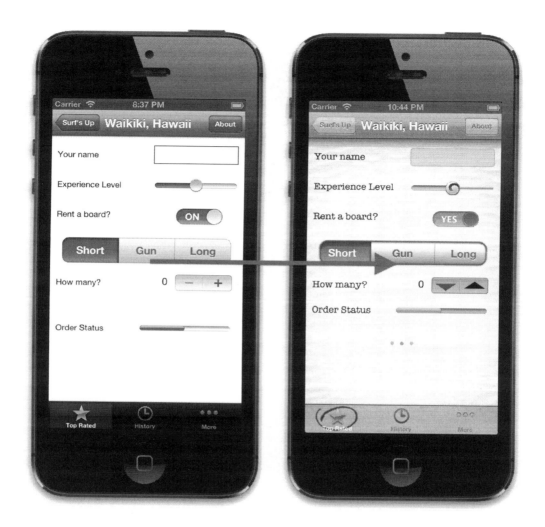

Getting Started

I've created a simple app for you to start with so you can focus on the meat of this chapter that is included in the resources for this chapter.

Go ahead and open the project - it's called Surf's Up. Then take a look around the code and Storyboard. You'll see that the primary view presents a list of the surfing trips, and the detail view allows us to capture more information about each trip individually. With that context, Build & Run the app (Cmd-R) to see what you have to start with.

Huh. Yes, this app is functional, but it's hardly representative of the fun one would expect to have on a surfing trip. Let's survey the scene in more detail.

Let's start with the detail page. Things look pretty standard there, eh?

A plain `UIBarButtonItem` on the `UINavigationBar` at the top, stock `UITabBar` elements at the bottom, and the following "standard" data entry components including the following:

- `UILabels` with "System" Helvetica fonts
- `UITextField`
- `UISlider`
- `UISwitch`
- `UISegmentedControl`
- `UINavigationBarShadow`
- `UIStepper`
- `UIProgressView`
- `UIPageControl`

In this chapter, you'll completely customize the detail screen to give it some style, using the new APIs available in iOS 5 and 6. So with an idea of what's in store, let's convert this app from "zero" to "hero".

Adding a Background Image

If you open up the Images folder in your project, you'll see that you already have some images you can use to customize the UI included in the project – you just need to modify the code to make use of them.

Inside the images folder is a file called **bg_sand.png**. You're going to start your UI customization by making this the background image in the detail view.

Open **DetailViewController.m** and create a **viewDidLoad** method like this:

```
- (void)viewDidLoad {
    [super viewDidLoad];

    self.view.backgroundColor = [UIColor
        colorWithPatternImage:[UIImage imageNamed:@"bg_sand"]];
}
```

If you aren't familiar with this technique, you can actually make a "color" based on an image like you see here. This is an easy way to set the background of a view, because there's no "backgroundImage" property, but there is a "backgroundColor" property!

Compile and run to verify that it worked:

I don't know about you but I can feel the sand between my toes already!

Customizing UINavigationBar

If you look inside the images folder, you'll see two images that you want to use to customize the navigation bar: surf_gradient_textured_32.png and surf_gradient_textured_44.png.

You want to repeat these from left to right across the navigation bar. There are two different heights because the height of the navigation bar shrinks when the phone goes into landscape.

iOS 5 offers two new APIs that can help us with this:

- UINavigationBar has a new backgroundImage property you can use to set a custom background image like this.

- UIImage has a new `resizableImageWithCapInsets` method you can use to create a resizable image. The cap insets allow you to specify the portions of the image that should not be repeated, such as if you have rounded corners for a button on the edges that shouldn't be repeated.

You could go into the detail view and use these new APIs to set the navigation bar's background image directly. But then you'd have to go and do the same thing inside the list view, and any other views you might have in your app!

Obviously this would get old quick. Recognizing this, iOS 5 offers a cool new feature that allows us to customize user interface elements once, allowing it to "stand in" for other elements within the same level in the containment hierarchy.

So starting with the navigation bar, you're going to use this concept of the "appearance proxy" to customize some elements that will be repeated throughout the app.

Let's see how it looks. Inside SurfsUpAppDelegate.m, create a new method right above application:didFinishLaunchingWithOptions:

```objc
- (void)customizeAppearance
{
    // Create resizable images
    UIImage *gradientImage44 =
        [[UIImage imageNamed:@"surf_gradient_textured_44"]
        resizableImageWithCapInsets:
        UIEdgeInsetsMake(0, 0, 0, 0)];
    UIImage *gradientImage32 =
        [[UIImage imageNamed:@"surf_gradient_textured_32"]
        resizableImageWithCapInsets:
        UIEdgeInsetsMake(0, 0, 0, 0)];

    // Set the background image for *all* UINavigationBars
    [[UINavigationBar appearance]
        setBackgroundImage:gradientImage44
        forBarMetrics:UIBarMetricsDefault];
    [[UINavigationBar appearance]
        setBackgroundImage:gradientImage32
        forBarMetrics:UIBarMetricsLandscapePhone];

    // Customize the title text for *all* UINavigationBars
    [[UINavigationBar appearance] setTitleTextAttributes:
    [NSDictionary dictionaryWithObjectsAndKeys:
     [UIColor colorWithRed:255.0/255.0
                     green:255.0/255.0
                      blue:255.0/255.0
                     alpha:1.0],
     UITextAttributeTextColor,
```

```
[UIColor colorWithRed:0.0
                 green:0.0
                  blue:0.0
                 alpha:0.8],
    UITextAttributeTextShadowColor,
    [NSValue valueWithUIOffset:UIOffsetMake(0, -1)],
    UITextAttributeTextShadowOffset,
    [UIFont fontWithName:@"Arial-Bold" size:0.0],
    UITextAttributeFont,
    nil]];
}
```

The first two lines create stretchable images using the
`resizableImageWithCapInsets:` method discussed earlier. Note that this method
replaces `stretchableImageWithLeftCapWidth:topCapHeight:`, which is now
deprecated.

For the cap insets, you basically specify the fixed region of a given image in top, left,
bottom, right. What's left is stretched over the remainder of the region to which the
image is applied. In this particular image you want the whole thing stretched, so you
pass 0 for all of the fixed caps.

The next two lines invoke the appearance proxy, designating these stretchable images as
background images, for the bar metrics specified.

The last line stylizes the title that appears in your detail view. To do so, you pass a
dictionary of title text attributes. The available keys include the following:

- `UITextAttributeFont`
- `UITextAttributeTextColor`
- `UITextAttributeTextShadowColor`
- `UITextAttributeTextShadowOffset`

Almost done – just add the line to call this method at the top of
`application:didFinishLaunchingWithOptions:`

```
[self customizeAppearance];
```

Compile and run, and now you should see the navigation bar has the teal background
image applied in both orientations, with stylized title text as well!

Changing the UINavigationBar Shadow

One of the new things that were added in iOS 6 was a small shadow underneath the navigation bar that adds a nice little transition from the navigation bar to the content. You also have the ability to customize that shadow to something else. Let see how easy that is to do now.

You already have the image navBarShadow.png and navBarShadow@2x.png added to the project so just add the following line to the bottom of your customizeAppearance method:

```
[[UINavigationBar appearance] setShadowImage:[UIImage
                             imageNamed:@"navBarShadow"]];
```

Build and run, and you will see the following:

Viola! Easy, huh? Kinda like a nice cool wave flowing up the sand.

Customizing UIBarButtonItem

Open up the Images directory and look at button_textured_24.png and button_textured_30.png. You want to use these to customize the look and feel of the buttons that appear in the UINavigationBar.

Notice that you're going to set up these button images as resizable images. It's important to make them resizable because the button widths will vary depending on what text is inside.

For these buttons, you don't want the 5 leftmost pixels to stretch, nor the 5 rightmost pixels, so you'll set the left and right cap insets to 5. The pixels in between will repeat as much as is needed for the width of the button.

Let's try this out! You'll use the appearance proxy to customize all the UIBarButtonItems at once, like you did last time. Add the following code to the end of customizeAppearance:

```
UIImage *button30 = [[UIImage imageNamed:@"button_textured_30"]
    resizableImageWithCapInsets:UIEdgeInsetsMake(0, 5, 0, 5)];
UIImage *button24 = [[UIImage imageNamed:@"button_textured_24"]
    resizableImageWithCapInsets:UIEdgeInsetsMake(0, 5, 0, 5)];
[[UIBarButtonItem appearance] setBackgroundImage:button30
                    forState:UIControlStateNormal
                  barMetrics:UIBarMetricsDefault];
[[UIBarButtonItem appearance] setBackgroundImage:button24
                    forState:UIControlStateNormal
                  barMetrics:UIBarMetricsLandscapePhone];

[[UIBarButtonItem appearance] setTitleTextAttributes:
    [NSDictionary dictionaryWithObjectsAndKeys:
        [UIColor colorWithRed:220.0/255.0
                        green:104.0/255.0
                         blue:1.0/255.0
                        alpha:1.0],
        UITextAttributeTextColor,
        [UIColor colorWithRed:1.0 green:1.0 blue:1.0 alpha:1.0],
        UITextAttributeTextShadowColor,
        [NSValue valueWithUIOffset:UIOffsetMake(0, 1)],
        UITextAttributeTextShadowOffset,
        [UIFont fontWithName:@"AmericanTypewriter" size:0.0],
        UITextAttributeFont,
        nil]
    forState:UIControlStateNormal];
```

This looks familiar. You create the stretchable images for the buttons and set them as the background for both display in both portrait & landscape orientation. You then format the text to match the typewriter-style font you saw at the outset of the chapter.

Note you can set different images for different types of buttons such as the "Done" type.

The "back" bar button item needs special customization, because it should look different – like it's pointing backwards. Take a look at the images you're going to use to see what I mean: Images\button_back_textured_24.png and Images\button_back_textured_30.png.

Add the following code at the bottom of customizeAppearance to take care of the back bar button item:

```
UIImage *buttonBack30 = [[UIImage
                imageNamed:@"button_back_textured_30"]
    resizableImageWithCapInsets:UIEdgeInsetsMake(0, 13, 0, 5)];
UIImage *buttonBack24 = [[UIImage
                imageNamed:@"button_back_textured_24"]
    resizableImageWithCapInsets:UIEdgeInsetsMake(0, 12, 0, 5)];
[[UIBarButtonItem appearance]
                setBackButtonBackgroundImage:buttonBack30
                forState:UIControlStateNormal
                barMetrics:UIBarMetricsDefault];
[[UIBarButtonItem appearance]
                setBackButtonBackgroundImage:buttonBack24
                    forState:UIControlStateNormal
                barMetrics:UIBarMetricsLandscapePhone];
```

Note that you use different cap inset values because the back image has a wider left hand side that shouldn't stretch. Also note that there is a separate property on UIBarButtonItem for backButtonBackgroundImage that you use here.

Compile and run, and you should now see some cool customized UIBarButtonItems in your UINavigationBar!

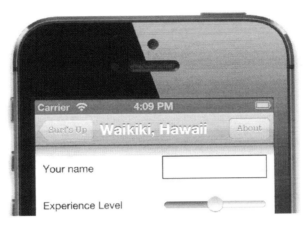

Customizing UITabBar

To customize a UITabBar, iOS 5 offers an API to let you change the background image of the toolbar, and the image to indicate the selected item. Take a look at Images\tab_bg.png and Images\tab_select_indicator.png to see the images you'll use for these.

Although your mockups only depict one UITabBar, these will in all likelihood have the same appearance if others appear, so you'll use the appearance proxy to customize this as well.

Add the following code to the bottom of customizeAppearance:

```
UIImage *tabBackground = [[UIImage imageNamed:@"tab_bg"]
    resizableImageWithCapInsets:UIEdgeInsetsMake(0, 0, 0, 0)];
[[UITabBar appearance] setBackgroundImage:tabBackground];
[[UITabBar appearance] setSelectionIndicatorImage:
        [UIImage imageNamed:@"tab_select_indicator"]];
```

Compile and run again... nice! The background and selected image are nice touches.

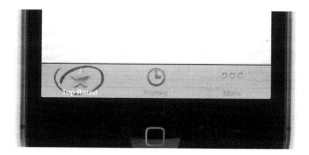

Note you can also specify "finished" and "unfinished" images if you wish to modify the manner in which the selected & unselected images appear.

Customizing UISlider

Open up Images\slider_minimum.png, Images\slider_maximum.png, and Images\thumb.png to see the images that you're going to use to customize the UISlider.

iOS 5 makes it ridiculously easy to customize the UISlider by just setting the maximumTrackImage, minimumTrackImage, and thumbImage properties of a UISlider.

Let's try it out. Add the following code to the bottom of customizeAppearance:

```
UIImage *minImage = [[UIImage imageNamed:@"slider_minimum.png"]
    resizableImageWithCapInsets:UIEdgeInsetsMake(0, 5, 0, 0)];
UIImage *maxImage = [[UIImage imageNamed:@"slider_maximum.png"]
    resizableImageWithCapInsets:UIEdgeInsetsMake(0, 5, 0, 0)];
UIImage *thumbImage = [UIImage imageNamed:@"thumb.png"];

[[UISlider appearance] setMaximumTrackImage:maxImage
    forState:UIControlStateNormal];
[[UISlider appearance] setMinimumTrackImage:minImage
    forState:UIControlStateNormal];
[[UISlider appearance] setThumbImage:thumbImage
    forState:UIControlStateNormal];
```

Compile and run, and check out your cool and stylish UISlider!

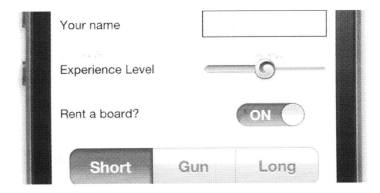

Customizing UISegmentedControl

Now you'll customize your segmented control. This component is a little bit more complicated; you have both selected & unselected backgrounds, as well as varying states for the adjacent regions (e.g., selected on left, unselected on right; unselected on the left & selected on the right; unselected on both sides).

Take a look at the images you'll use for this to see what I mean:
Images\segcontrol_sel.png, Images\segcontrol_uns.png,
Images\segcontrol_sel-uns.png, and Images\segcontrol_uns-uns.png.

Then add the code to make use of these to the bottom of customizeAppearance:

```
UIImage *segmentSelected =
    [[UIImage imageNamed:@"segcontrol_sel.png"]
    resizableImageWithCapInsets:UIEdgeInsetsMake(0, 15, 0, 15)];
UIImage *segmentUnselected =
    [[UIImage imageNamed:@"segcontrol_uns.png"]
    resizableImageWithCapInsets:UIEdgeInsetsMake(0, 15, 0, 15)];
UIImage *segmentSelectedUnselected =
    [UIImage imageNamed:@"segcontrol_sel-uns.png"];
UIImage *segUnselectedSelected =
    [UIImage imageNamed:@"segcontrol_uns-sel.png"];
UIImage *segmentUnselectedUnselected =
    [UIImage imageNamed:@"segcontrol_uns-uns.png"];

[[UISegmentedControl appearance]
             setBackgroundImage:segmentUnselected
                       forState:UIControlStateNormal
                     barMetrics:UIBarMetricsDefault];
[[UISegmentedControl appearance]
             setBackgroundImage:segmentSelected
                       forState:UIControlStateSelected
```

```
                                    barMetrics:UIBarMetricsDefault];

[[UISegmentedControl appearance]
              setDividerImage:segmentUnselectedUnselected
         forLeftSegmentState:UIControlStateNormal
            rightSegmentState:UIControlStateNormal
                   barMetrics:UIBarMetricsDefault];
[[UISegmentedControl appearance]
              setDividerImage:segmentSelectedUnselected
         forLeftSegmentState:UIControlStateSelected
          rightSegmentState:UIControlStateNormal
                   barMetrics:UIBarMetricsDefault];
[[UISegmentedControl appearance]
             setDividerImage:segUnselectedSelected
        forLeftSegmentState:UIControlStateNormal
         rightSegmentState:UIControlStateSelected
                   barMetrics:UIBarMetricsDefault];
```

Compile and run, and now your `UISegmentedControl` has a completely different look!

Customizing UISwitch

In iOS 5 you only had the ability to customize the tint of the On side of the switch (which was kinda a weird decision if you ask me). But luckily in iOS 6 you now have access to the Off side and the thumb (middle) part.

So, add the following code to set the tint colors `customizeAppearance` method:

```
[[UISwitch appearance] setOnTintColor:
                        [UIColor colorWithRed:0
                                        green:175.0/255.0
                                         blue:176.0/255.0
                                        alpha:1.0]];
[[UISwitch appearance] setTintColor:
                        [UIColor colorWithRed:1.000
                                        green:0.989
                                         blue:0.753
                                        alpha:1.000]];
[[UISwitch appearance] setThumbTintColor:[UIColor cyanColor]];
```

Compile and run, and check out your newly colored switch!

The switch fits the look now but "ON" and "OFF" don't really make sense. I mean if someone asked you if you'd like a glass of water and you said "ON", they'd probably look at you kinda weird!

Well, it just so happens that in iOS 6 you gained the ability to customize the images inside of the switch as well. It's not text, but if you make an image that is text, it works just as well. Add the following lines at the end of the `customizeAppearance` method:

```
[[UISwitch appearance] setOnImage:[UIImage
                        imageNamed:@"yesSwitch"]];
[[UISwitch appearance] setOffImage:[UIImage
                        imageNamed:@"noSwitch"]];
```

Now the switch says "Yes/No" instead of "On/Off"! You could change this to an icon if you'd like too.

Things are looking pretty good, but you still have a couple of items outstanding. You need to update the labels and set the background of your custom `UITextField`.

Customizing UILabel

The labels are one part of the detail view you won't customize via the appearance proxy. Open the storyboard and navigate to the `DetailViewController`. Start by selecting the first label (i.e., "Your name") in the main view, the in the Utilities view (i.e., the right pane), select the Attributes Inspector and set the following:

- **Font**: Custom
- **Family**: American Typewriter
- **Style**: Regular
- **Size**: 16

Repeat this for the four remaining labels: "Experience Level", "Rent a board?", "How many?", and "Order Status".

Compile and run, and now your labels have a neat typewriter feel!

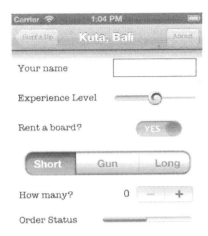

Customizing UITextField

Our UITextField has already been set to use UITextBorderStyleLine. Since you're still in Interface Builder, let's set the font to American Typewriter, Size 12, Regular. Now if you look at the Identity Inspector, you'll see that the Custom Class has been defined as something other than UITextField – CustomTextField. If you look in the Navigator pane on the left, there is a group called Custom Views. Expand that, and you will see that you have a type called exactly that.

Right now the drawRect: method of your UITextField delegates to the superclass implementation. But in order to paint the teal background, you are going to override drawRect: as another customization technique.

Replace the implementation of drawRect in CustomTextField.m with the following code:

```
- (void)drawRect:(CGRect)rect
{
    UIImage *textFieldBackground =
            [[UIImage imageNamed:@"text_field_teal.png"]
        resizableImageWithCapInsets:UIEdgeInsetsMake(15.0, 5.0,
                                                     15.0, 5.0)];
    [textFieldBackground drawInRect:[self bounds]];
}
```

Here you create yet another stretchable image with appropriate insets, and draw it in the rectangle defined by the bounds of this view (i.e., your UITextField). Build and Run, and you'll see the following:

Customizing UIStepper

With iOS 5 you gained the ability to change the tint color of the stepper and now in iOS 6 you can change the individual icons in the sides and middle of the control. Let's see how you can do this now. Add the following code to the end of your customizeAppearance method in SurfsUpAppDelegate.m:

```
[[UIStepper appearance] setTintColor:
                        [UIColor colorWithRed:0
                                        green:175.0/255.0
                                         blue:176.0/255.0
                                        alpha:1.0]];
[[UIStepper appearance] setIncrementImage:
                        [UIImage imageNamed:@"up"]
                        forState:UIControlStateNormal];
[[UIStepper appearance] setDecrementImage:
                        [UIImage imageNamed:@"down"]
                        forState:UIControlStateNormal];
```

Build and run, and enjoy your stylish stepper!

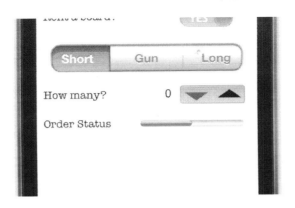

Customizing UIProgressView

The UIProgressView is a pretty simple control to customize, just a track tint and a completed tint. Add the following code to the end of your customizeAppearance method:

```
[[UIProgressView appearance] setProgressTintColor:
                        [UIColor colorWithRed:0
                                        green:175.0/255.0
                                         blue:176.0/255.0
                                        alpha:1.0]];
[[UIProgressView appearance] setTrackTintColor:
                        [UIColor colorWithRed:0.996
                                        green:0.788
                                         blue:0.180
                                        alpha:1.000]];
```

Give it another build and run and see your lovely progress bar!

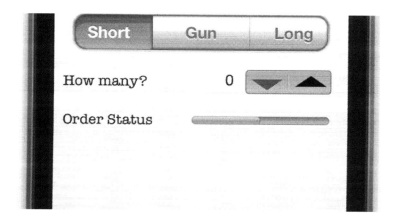

Customizing UIPageControl

UIPageControl is the last control you're going to customize. You can customize the page indicators as well as a separate color for the current page, both properties are new to iOS 6. Add the following code to the end of your customizeAppearance method:

```
[[UIPageControl appearance] setCurrentPageIndicatorTintColor:
                            [UIColor colorWithRed:0
                                           green:175.0/255.0
                                            blue:176.0/255.0
                                           alpha:1.0]];
[[UIPageControl appearance] setPageIndicatorTintColor:
                            [UIColor colorWithRed:0.996
                                           green:0.788
                                            blue:0.180
                                           alpha:1.000]];
```

Build and run... ahh, how beautiful!

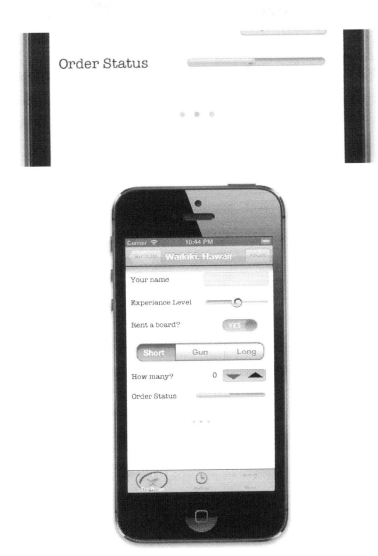

Congratulations – the detail view is complete, and you've learned a ton about customizing the looks of your apps!

Where To Go From Here?

Congratulations - you now have experience customizing the most common controls in UIKit with the new `UIAppearance` APIs! You'll never have to make a plain vanilla UIKit app again :]

If you want to learn more about customizing `UIKit` controls, keep reading the next chapter, where you'll learn how to customize the table view, port the app to the iPad, and much more!

Chapter 11: Intermediate UIKit Customization

By Steve Baranski and Adam Burkepile

In the previous chapter, you took a "plain vanilla" app with the default UIKit controls, and customized the look-and-feel to add some style and flair. You customized the background image, `UINavigationBar`, `UIBarButtonItems`, `UITabBar`, `UISlider`, `UISegmentedControl`, `UISwitch`, `UILabel`, `UITextField`, `UISwitch`, `UIProgressView`, `UIStepper`, and `UIPageControl`.

Wow, you were busy!

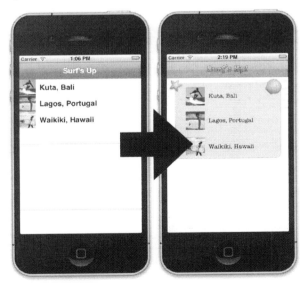

In this chapter, you're going to learn how to customize the remaining elements: the `UITableView` and the `UINavigationBar` title image. Most of this tutorial is focused around customizing the `UITableView` by adding custom cells, layout, and artwork.

Even if you're already familiar with customizing `UITableViews`, you might want to read this chapter, because it covers some new APIs introduced in iOS 5 and 6 that you may not have seen.

Later in the chapter you're going to customize a popover controller. In order to do this, you have to convert Surf's Up to a Universal Binary. To keep the focus purely on UIKit Customization, I've done that work for you already.

In the resources for this chapter, you'll find a folder named Surf's Up Starter. Open up the Xcode project, and build and run the app in the iPhone Simulator. You'll see a similar project to the one you had before:

The code and supporting file structure, however, is quite different.

You'll notice that you have some additional groups, and in each of those groups, there are now files with "_iPad "& "_iPhone" suffixes to reflect subclasses and storyboards specific to the target device. This is now a universal app, capable of running on the iPhone and iPad.

Without further ado, let's surf the iOS customization wave and dive into finishing this app.

Customizing the UINavigationBar Title

In the previous chapter, you customized parts of the navigation bar via the appearance proxy, but you still need to add the title graphic. Let's do that first, then you'll proceed to customize the UITableView.

The title graphic can actually be placed in a UIImageView and set as the titleView of your primary view controller's navigation item. This sounds more complicated than it actually is, so let's see what the code looks like.

Open up SurfsUpAppDelegate_iPhone.m and find the application:didFinishLaunchingWithOptions: method. You give it a title, which is currently displayed in the center navigation bar, and in the back button in your detail view. Right after the line of code that sets the title, add the following code:

```
UINavigationController* navController =
    (UINavigationController*)[[UIApplication
        sharedApplication].windows[0] rootViewController];
UIViewController* rootVC = navController.viewControllers[0];
[[rootVC navigationItem] setTitleView:
    [[UIImageView alloc] initWithImage:
        [UIImage imageNamed:@"title.png"]]];
```

Repeat this for SurfsUpAppDelegate_iPad.m:

```
UISplitViewController* splitVC = (UISplitViewController*)
    [[UIApplication sharedApplication].windows[0]
                                    rootViewController];
UINavigationController* navController =
                        splitVC.viewControllers[0];
UIViewController* rootVC = navController.viewControllers[0];
[[rootVC navigationItem] setTitleView:
    [[UIImageView alloc] initWithImage:
        [UIImage imageNamed:@"title.png"]]];
```

Build and run, and check out how it looks:

Customizing UITableView: Overview

To finish the customization of the primary view, turn your attention to SurfsUpViewController, a subclass of UITableViewController. Even though you're going to use the "plain" style for the UITableView, the artwork you're going to use to customize it will make it more closely resemble the "grouped" style. Here's a screenshot of the look we're trying to get for this table:

There are four possible cases to consider.

1. **A single row** in a one-row table.
2. **The top row** in a table with more than one row.
3. **A middle row** in a table with more than one row.
4. **A bottom row** in a table with more than one row.

Although each of these cases has its own background images, there are several characteristics that each of the cells have in common:

- **Inset surfing photo** associated with each individual trip
- **Font** used for the name of each surfing trip

You can take advantage of this shared scenario. You'll create one subclass of UITableViewCell in code and then associate four distinct cell types with that class. Finally, you'll employ automatic cell loading – a new feature in iOS 5 – to streamline the use of these custom cells in the table view controller.

Creating a Custom UITableViewCell

Let's start by creating a new group in Xcode. Right-click on the root "Surf's Up" folder, and select New Group. Name it Custom Cells. Then create a new file in this group with the Objective-C class template, named CustomCell, and a subclass of UITableViewCell.

Now select CustomCell.h. You're going to add two properties that each of the custom cells will rely on. Specify the following properties in your header:

```
@property (nonatomic, strong) IBOutlet UIImageView *tripPhoto;
@property (nonatomic, strong) IBOutlet UILabel *tripName;
```

These outlets will allow you to "wire in" the image view and label for the cell that you'll create in Interface Builder to this subclass of UITableViewCell. This will come in handy later when you want to refer to the image view and label in code.

Creating a UITableViewCell in Interface Builder

Next, you're going to create the `UITableViewCell` for the topmost row in the storyboard. This is something new in iOS 5 and makes it much easier to create custom cells. Instead of having to create a custom cell programmatically (the worst) or create a cell in a separate xib and load it into the table through the controller (better), you can create prototype cells directly in the UITableview.

To get started, open the Utility Pane (i.e., the rightmost tab in the View toolbar) and drag a Table View Cell into the middle of the screen:

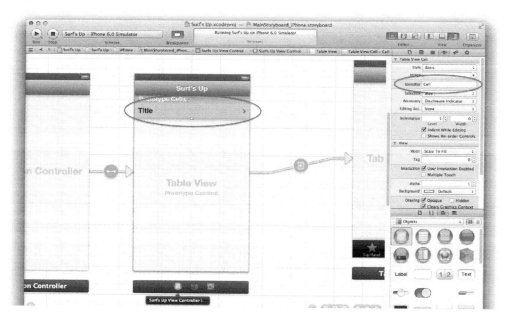

Open the `MainStoryboard_iPhone.storyboard` and find the Details View Controller. Here you can see the plain old normal tableview cell. Note that the identifier is simply "Cell". You only have one type of cell right now but you are going to add some new ones and this **Identifier** field is how you will create a new cell of the correct type.

Select the cell, then select the third option on the right – the Identity Inspector. In the Custom Class input field, enter the name of class you created earlier, **CustomCell**.

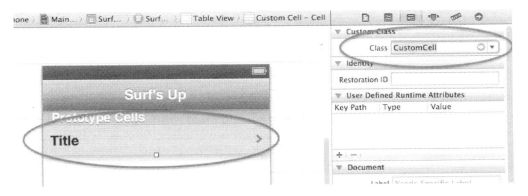

Now select the Attributes Inspector (the fourth tab). Change the Style to "Custom" and enter "TopRow" in the Identifier input field. This is the identifier your table view will use to manage cells of this type in the reuse queue.

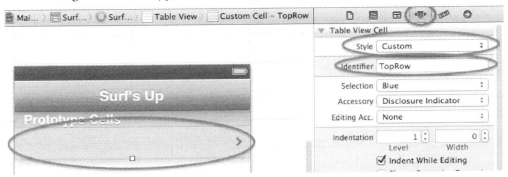

Now select the Size Inspector (fifth tab) and enter 83 as the height in pixels of the cell. This corresponds to the height of the custom images used to create the top row.

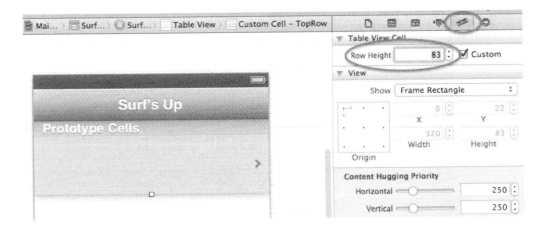

Next, drag an Image View from the library into the cell. You'll use this to display the surf trip photos. Select the image view in the left IB region and select the Size Inspector. Enter X = 50, Y = 25, W = 50, and H = 50. This may look a bit off-center vertically, but recall that the top row has a starfish and a seashell that require a vertical offset.

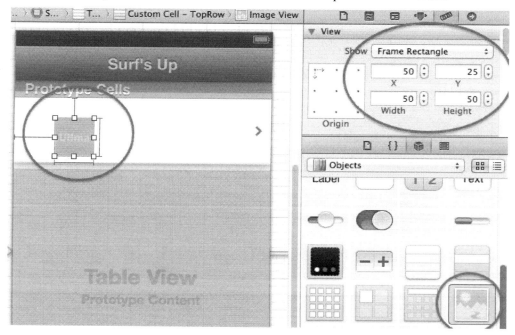

Next add your UILabel in a similar fashion. Drag it from the Library into the cell, and set its position/size to X = 110, Y = 39, W = 200, H = 21.

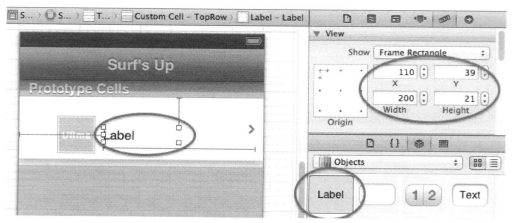

With the UILabel still selected, select the Attributes Inspector. Set the Font to Custom, Family to American Typewriter, Style to Regular, and Size to 16.

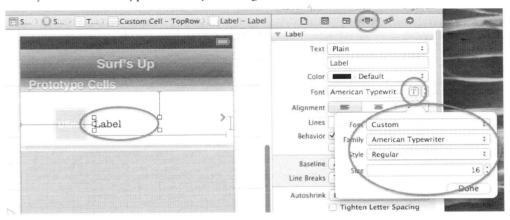

Finally, you need to connect the IBOutlets defined in your custom cell class to the corresponding elements in your cell. To do so, select the entire custom cell in the left pane and the Connections Inspector in the right. Drag the circle next to tripName to the label to connect it, then drag the circle next to tripPhoto to the image to connect it too.

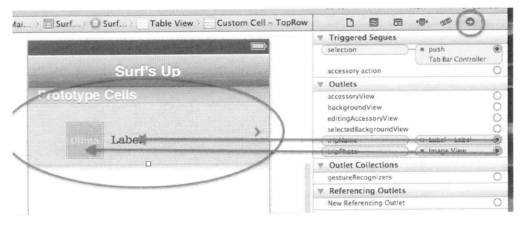

Other Cells

After completing these steps for the top tableview cell, most of the work for the remaining cells amounts to "rinse & repeat" from the steps used to create the cell for the top row.

To create the different cell types, select the tableview, then increment Prototype Cells count to 4.

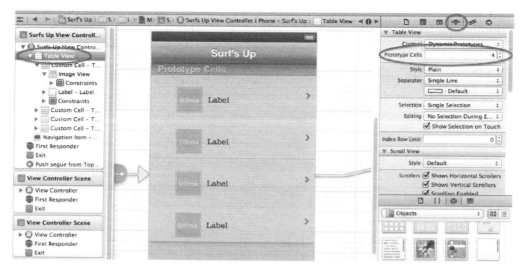

Look at that! It was even intelligent enough to copy the style from the last cell. So you just have to change the Identifier property and make the size adjustments.

The following table summarizes each of the unique parameters from the three remaining cell types:

Cell	Name/Reuse ID	Height	Image Frame (x, y, w, h)	Label Frame (x, y, w, h)
Middle	MiddleRow	67	50, 8, 50, 50	110, 22, 200, 21
Bottom	BottomRow	70	50, 11, 50, 50	110, 26, 200, 21
Single	SingleRow	92	50, 21, 50, 50	110, 35, 200, 21

When you're all done, your table filled with the prototype cells should look something like this:

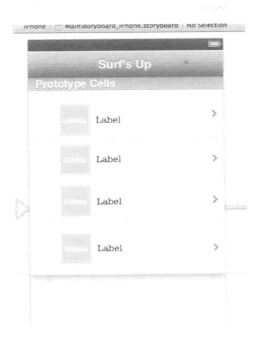

The last thing you need to do is connect the cells to the next view controller (the tabbar controller). So control-drag from a cell to the tabbar controller and select the push segue. Repeat for the other three cell types.

Because you are using different storyboards for the iPhone and iPad versions, you need to create these in the iPad storyboard as well. Luckily you can just copy and paste the cells instead of creating them again. Select one of the cells then hold down shift and click the other three to select them all. Copy them and switch to the iPad storyboard. Delete the regular old "Cell" tableview cell and then select the tableview and paste. Viola!

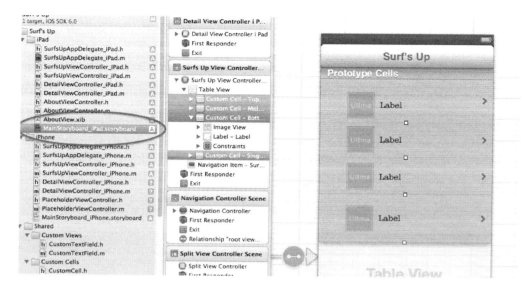

One thing that you do have to do is recreate the segue so that the app actually does something when you tap on one of the cells. Control-drag from a cell to the navigation controller (just to the right) and select the Replace segue.

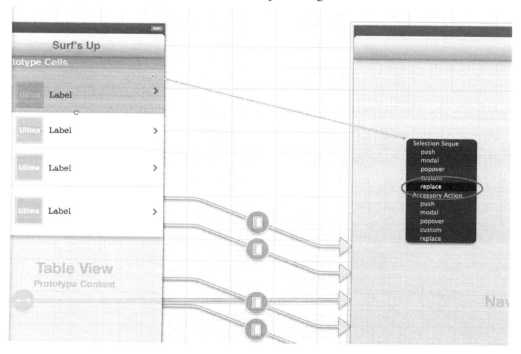

Then select the segue (arrow part connecting the two View Controllers) and change the Identifier to locationDetailsSegue. The other defaults should be fine.

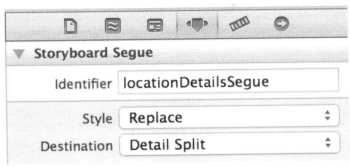

Repeat these steps for the other three cell types.

Using the Custom UITableViewCells in the UITableViewController

You've created four custom cells and one custom class. Now it's time to integrate it with your table view controller. Open up SurfsUpViewController.m and make the following modifications:

```objc
// Add to top of file
#import "CustomCell.h"

// Add constants for each of our reuse identifiers, right after
// the imports (these are the cell identifiers)
NSString * const REUSE_ID_TOP = @"TopRow";
NSString * const REUSE_ID_MIDDLE = @"MiddleRow";
NSString * const REUSE_ID_BOTTOM = @"BottomRow";
NSString * const REUSE_ID_SINGLE = @"SingleRow";
```

Now you'll turn your attention to the logic required to identify which custom cell to use. In SurfsUpViewController.m, add the following method:

```objc
- (NSString *)reuseIdentifierForRowAtIndexPath:
(NSIndexPath *)indexPath
{
    NSInteger rowCount = [self tableView: [self tableView]
                                  numberOfRowsInSection:0];

    NSInteger rowIndex = indexPath.row;
```

```
    if (rowCount == 1)
    {
        return REUSE_ID_SINGLE;
    }

    if (rowIndex == 0)
    {
        return REUSE_ID_TOP;
    }

    if (rowIndex == (rowCount - 1))
    {
        return REUSE_ID_BOTTOM;
    }

    return REUSE_ID_MIDDLE;
}
```

And replace `tableView:cellForRowAtIndexPath:` with this:

```
- (UITableViewCell *)tableView:(UITableView *)tableView
        cellForRowAtIndexPath:(NSIndexPath *)indexPath
{
    NSString *reuseID =
        [self reuseIdentifierForRowAtIndexPath:indexPath];
    UITableViewCell *cell = [[self tableView]
        dequeueReusableCellWithIdentifier:reuseID];
    return cell;
}
```

This code just checks the current row in the table view and compares it to the total number of elements. Based on this information, you know whether you should display the top, middle, bottom, or "single row" case. You haven't evaluated your progress in a while, so compile and run to see where you're at:

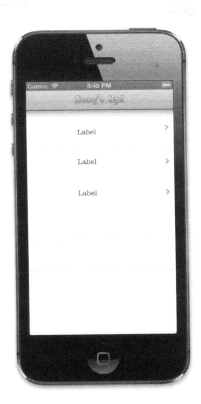

Wow – it appears that you've actually regressed! You don't have your photos & titles, nor do you have the custom background images. If it's any consolation, each of the first three rows does appear to have a different cell height. This is encouraging, as it suggests that you are returning the proper reuse identifiers for each cell.

So, what's wrong? Well, when you replaced the old code, you actually removed your cell configuration logic. You lost your specification of the trip photo and the naming of the trip. Moreover, IB doesn't appear to let you set the `backgroundView` and `selectedBackgroundView` properties, so you need to create `UIImageViews` that use your custom cell background images.

Let's work on that now. Create a new method `configureCell:forRowAtIndexPath:` and begin by adapting your existing methods for determining the appropriate trip photo and name to use for a given row. Add the following method to the file:

```
- (void)configureCell:(CustomCell *)cell
forRowAtIndexPath:(NSIndexPath *)indexPath
{
    [[cell tripPhoto] setImage:
        [self tripPhotoForRowAtIndexPath:indexPath]];
```

```
    [[cell tripName] setText:
        [self tripNameForRowAtIndexPath:indexPath]];
}
```

Now you need to call that method from `tableView:cellForRowAtIndexPath:`. Add the following line immediately after you've dequeued a cell for use / reuse:

```
[self configureCell:(CustomCell *)cell
    forRowAtIndexPath:indexPath];
```

Compile and run, and you'll see that you're back to where you were originally:

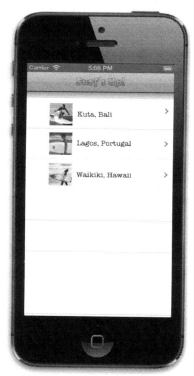

You're using custom cells, but they aren't very good looking yet! So let's take care of that next.

Beautifying UITableViewCells

To make the cells good looking, you need to incorporate the background images for each of the respective cells.

To do that, you're going to create two new methods: one will return the background image for the normal state and one will return the background image for the selected state. These methods will accept an index path as input, then instantiate a UIImage stretched to properly fit the size of the table view cells.

Add the code for this right above configureCell:

```objc
- (UIImage *)backgroundImageForRowAtIndexPath:(NSIndexPath *)indexPath
{
    NSString *reuseID = [self reuseIdentifierForRowAtIndexPath:indexPath];
    if ([REUSE_ID_SINGLE isEqualToString:reuseID] == YES)
    {
        UIImage *background = [UIImage imageNamed:@"table_cell_single.png"];
        return [background resizableImageWithCapInsets:UIEdgeInsetsMake(0.0, 43.0, 0.0, 64.0)];
    }
    else if ([REUSE_ID_TOP isEqualToString:reuseID] == YES)
    {
        UIImage *background = [UIImage imageNamed:@"table_cell_top.png"];
        return [background resizableImageWithCapInsets:UIEdgeInsetsMake(0.0, 43.0, 0.0, 64.0)];
    }
    else if ([REUSE_ID_BOTTOM isEqualToString:reuseID] == YES)
    {
        UIImage *background = [UIImage imageNamed:@"table_cell_bottom.png"];
        return [background resizableImageWithCapInsets:UIEdgeInsetsMake(0.0, 34.0, 0.0, 35.0)];
    }
    else    // REUSE_ID_MIDDLE
    {
        UIImage *background = [UIImage imageNamed:@"table_cell_mid.png"];
        return [background resizableImageWithCapInsets:UIEdgeInsetsMake(0.0, 30.0, 0.0, 30.0)];
```

```objc
        }
    }

    - (UIImage
    *)selectedBackgroundImageForRowAtIndexPath:(NSIndexPath
    *)indexPath
    {
        NSString *reuseID = [self
    reuseIdentifierForRowAtIndexPath:indexPath];
        if ([REUSE_ID_SINGLE isEqualToString:reuseID] == YES)
        {
            UIImage *background = [UIImage
    imageNamed:@"table_cell_single_sel.png"];
            return [background
    resizableImageWithCapInsets:UIEdgeInsetsMake(0.0, 43.0, 0.0,
    64.0)];
        }
        else if ([REUSE_ID_TOP isEqualToString:reuseID] == YES)
        {
            UIImage *background = [UIImage
    imageNamed:@"table_cell_top_sel.png"];
            return [background
    resizableImageWithCapInsets:UIEdgeInsetsMake(0.0, 43.0, 0.0,
    64.0)];
        }
        else if ([REUSE_ID_BOTTOM isEqualToString:reuseID] == YES)
        {
            UIImage *background = [UIImage
    imageNamed:@"table_cell_bottom_sel.png"];
            return [background
    resizableImageWithCapInsets:UIEdgeInsetsMake(0.0, 34.0, 0.0,
    35.0)];
        }
        else     // REUSE_ID_MIDDLE
        {
            UIImage *background = [UIImage
    imageNamed:@"table_cell_mid_sel.png"];
            return [background
    resizableImageWithCapInsets:UIEdgeInsetsMake(0.0, 30.0, 0.0,
    30.0)];
        }
    }
```

Because you've applied your table logic to determine the reuse identifier, you rely on it to load the appropriate image for the corresponding cell. If you look at the images, however, each of them is narrower than the full width of the screen. Once you've loaded your image, you resize your image by specifying UIEdgeInsets – these essentially define the portion of the image that is not stretched. Because the height of your cells matches that of your images, you simply set your top & bottom insets to 0.

With these methods implemented, add the code to incorporate them at the bottom of `configureCell:forIndexPath:` method like so:

```
CGRect cellRect = [cell frame];
UIImageView *backgroundView = [[UIImageView alloc]
                                 initWithFrame:cellRect];
[backgroundView setImage:[self
              backgroundImageForRowAtIndexPath:indexPath]];
[cell setBackgroundView:backgroundView];

UIImageView *selectedBackgroundView =
        [[UIImageView alloc] initWithFrame:cellRect];
[selectedBackgroundView setImage:[self
        selectedBackgroundImageForRowAtIndexPath:indexPath]];
[cell setSelectedBackgroundView:selectedBackgroundView];
```

Compile and run again, and you should see the following:

Success! Well, sort of. Your cells now include the custom graphics, and subsequently mimic the "grouped" style. Unfortunately, however, you have some residual artifacts from creating the controller in the "plain" style.

Customizing the Table View Background

The last of your customizations address the remnants of creating the table with "plain" look & feel. You'll tidy this up in viewDidLoad. Add the following lines to your method:

```
[[self tableView] setSeparatorStyle:
        UITableViewCellSeparatorStyleNone];
[[self tableView] setBackgroundView:
        [[UIImageView alloc] initWithImage:
                [UIImage imageNamed:@"bg_sand.png"]]];
```

The first line removes the separator lines that separate your individual table view cells.
The second line introduces the sandy background. As with the navigation bar before,
you're simply creating a UIImageView with your background graphic, and then
designating it as the background view for the table.

Compile and run one more time, and you'll see the following:

Order has been restored! You've taken advantage of a number of iOS 5 features so far:
you've customized the navigation bar, created four unique table view cells, and used
automatic cell loading to render the table view.

Customizing a Popover

In earlier stages of this chapter, you used the new features of iOS 5 and 6 to create an iPhone app with a custom look & feel. You may recall that your detail screen from Part 1 possessed an About button. Admittedly, it's a bit contrived to have an About button on the detail screen, but that aside, it's less excusable for your button to serve as a "road to nowhere".

So in this part of the chapter, you'll use the About button to present a custom popover. If you've used iBooks on the iPad you've seen how nice a customized appearance can be. Popovers were one of the most significant new UI elements introduced with the iPad. The color of their borders, however, were like Model T cars.

"Any customer can have a car painted any color that he wants so long as it is black."

-- Henry Ford

While it was certainly possible to create a popover that mimicked the look of the iOS standard popovers, it was difficult to match the *feel* of the popovers. Fortunately, Apple has heard our pleas for customization, and answered them in iOS 5.

Unfortunately, however, popovers are still limited to iPads. If you attempt to present a popover on the iPhone, it may appear to "work" at compile-time, but at run time you will be presented with the following message:

```
-[UIPopoverController initWithContentViewController:] called
when not running under UIUserInterfaceIdiomPad.'
```

In portrait, the detail view takes advantage of the iPad's increased screen real estate, "flattened" from three tabs to a single screen. You'll also note that the UINavigationBar adopts the look & feel you customized earlier in the tutorial – isn't the appearance proxy wonderful?

Build and run the app in the iPad Simulator. As you know, you'll need to select the iPad Simulator from the Scheme (see below), and then click Run.

You should see something like the following:

Fortunately, your custom table view still looks pretty good as the master view. The "model" layer is admittedly shallow for in this example – selecting a trip in the master view changes the title of the detail view controller rather than pushing a new view controller onto the navigation controller's stack.

If you look in the project, there are additional files for your newly introduced popover:

• **AboutViewController.h** & **AboutViewController.m** – the view controller used to present your popover

• **AboutView.xib** – the view your popover will present

• A resizable image named **popover_stretchable.png**

Unfortunately, however, you have the same black border around your popover. This throws off the surfing vibe you worked so hard to create previously. So let's tidy that up.

Customizing the Popover

There are two facets of customizing your popovers. First, you must create an object to render that view, a subclass of type `UIPopoverBackgroundView` that's new to iOS 5. Second, you must set a value for the `popoverBackgroundViewClass`, a new property of `UIPopoverController`.

Start by making a subclass of `UIPopoverBackgroundView` to serve as the background for your About view. Create a new file with the Objective-C class template, named AboutBackgroundView, and a subclass of UIPopoverBackgroundView.

Add the following import statement to AboutBackgroundView.h to successfully build the project after creation:

```
#import <UIKit/UIPopoverBackgroundView.h>
```

If you've done any kind of customization before, you may think that this is where you proceed to override `drawRect:`. `UIPopoverBackgroundView`, however, requires a bit more consideration. As with all framework code, you are encouraged to consult Apple's documentation by clicking Help\Documentation and API Reference.

To sum up the API reference, there are few takeaways to be mindful of:

"The background contents of your view should be based on stretchable images.

The images you use for your popover background view should not contain any shadow effects. The popover controller adds a shadow to the popover for you."

You must override two methods – `arrowOffset` and `arrowHeight` – to describe the geometry of the popover arrow. The fact that these are static methods implies that these values should not change.

You must describe the geometry of the content view in relation to its container, the popover. This is also a static method, `contentViewInsets`.

Finally, you must override properties describing the `arrowOffset` and `arrowDirection`. The mutability of these properties implies that they can be changed, but given the fixed position of your "anchoring" About button, these will be fixed for your purposes.

The backing image for your popover, `popover_stretchable.png`, looks like this.

Once you're finished, you'll have a nice teal border with a lighter turquoise background. To accommodate that, you must change the opaque background of the content view (initialized to white in **AboutView.xib**). You must add this implementation to **AboutBackgroundView.m**:

```
- (id)initWithFrame:(CGRect)frame
{
    self = [super initWithFrame:frame];
    if (self)
    {
        [self setBackgroundColor:[UIColor clearColor]];
    }
    return self;
}
```

Now you must override **drawRect:** to create a resizable image and present it:

```
- (void)drawRect:(CGRect)rect
{
    UIEdgeInsets popoverInsets =
            UIEdgeInsetsMake(68.0f, 16.0f, 16.0f, 34.0f);
    UIImage *popover =
            [[UIImage imageNamed:@"popover_stretchable.png"]
                    resizableImageWithCapInsets:popoverInsets];
    [popover drawInRect:rect];
}
```

This approach is similar to your earlier use of resizable images with the appearance proxy. Again, the stretching relies on insets. In this case, the insets are as follows:

- **Top**: 68 pixels
- **Left**: 16 pixels
- **Bottom**: 16 pixels
- **Right**: 34 pixels

Your static methods should be implemented as follows:

```
+ (CGFloat)arrowBase
{    return 26.0f;
```

```
}
+ (CGFloat)arrowHeight
{
    return 16.0f;
}
+ (UIEdgeInsets)contentViewInsets{
    return UIEdgeInsetsMake(40.0f, 6.0f, 8.0f, 7.0f);
}
```

Finally, you must override properties as follows:

```
- (void)setArrowDirection:(UIPopoverArrowDirection)direction {
  // no-op
}
-  (UIPopoverArrowDirection)arrowDirection {
    return UIPopoverArrowDirectionUp;
}
-  (void)setArrowOffset:(CGFloat)offset { // no-op }
-  (CGFloat)arrowOffset {return 0.0f; }
```

Now that you've created your custom background view, you need to instruct your popover to use that view when it is presented. To do so, first import AboutBackgroundView.h at the top of DetailViewController_iPad.m:

```
#import "AboutBackgroundView.h"
```

Then add the following line to viewDidLoad:

```
[[self aboutPopover] setPopoverBackgroundViewClass:
    [AboutBackgroundView class]];
```

Build and run – and voila!

Where To Go From Here?

It's been quite a ride! You've customized UI elements on both iPhone & iPad interfaces, and you've used a number of different iOS 5 and 6 techniques to do so:

- Customization via Interface Builder

- Customization of UIView instances

- Customization by subclassing UIView

- Customization via the appearance proxy (UIAppearance protocol), and overriding the appearance proxy when necessary.

- Customization by subclassing UIPopoverBackgroundView

In these chapters you learned about many of the new user interface customization capabilities in iOS 6, but if you're curious to learn even more, check out Chapter 22 in *iOS 6 by Tutorials*, "What's New with User Interface Customization."

Hopefully you've had as much fun as I've had, and I look forward to seeing your customized UIKit apps in the future!

Conclusion

Congratulations, you have made it through Volume 1 of *iOS 5 by Tutorials*!

At this point, you have hands-on experience with some of the most important new APIs in iOS 5. Now might be a good time to try out some of these in your own apps!

If you're still eager to learn more, you might want to check out Volume 2 of *iOS 5 by Tutorials*, where you will learn about some other cool new APIs from Turn-Based Gaming to Core Image and more.

If you have any questions or comments as you go along, please stop by our book forums at http://www.raywenderlich.com/forums.

Thank you again for purchasing this book. Your continued support is what makes everything we do on raywenderlich.com possible, so we truly appreciate it!

Best of luck with your iOS adventures,

- Steve, Adam, Jacob, Matthijs, Felipe, Cesare, Marin and Ray from the Tutorial Team

Made in the USA
Charleston, SC
14 April 2013